Change and Continuity in Indian Sūfīsm

Islamic Heritage in Cross-Cultural Perspectives

1. Gandhi's Responses to Islam; by Sheila McDonough (ISBN 81-246-0035-X)

2. Fawā'id al-Fu'ād — Spiritual and Literary Discourses of Shaikh Nizāmuddīn Awliyā; Originally Compiled by Amīr Ḥasan 'Alā' Sijzī Dehlawī; English Translation with Introduction and Historical Annotation by Ziya-ul-Hasan Faruqi (ISBN 81-246-0042-2)

Islamic Heritage in Cross-Cultural Perspectives, no. 3

Change and Continuity in Indian Sūfīsm

A Naqshbandi-Mujaddidī Branch in the Hindu Environment

Thomas Dahnhardt

D.K. Printworld (P) Ltd.
New Delhi

Cataloging in Publication Data — DK
Courtesy: D.K. Agencies (P) Ltd. <docinfo@dkagencies.com>

Dahnhardt, Thomas, 1964 –
Change and continuity in Indian sūfism.
(Islamic heritage in cross-cultural perspective, no. 3).
xv, 447 p., 23 cm.
Includes bibliographical references (p.)
Includes Index.
ISBN 8124601704

1. Sufism — India. 2. Naqshbandīyah — India. 3. Islam — Relations — Hinduism. 4. Hinduism — Relations — Islam. I. Title. II. Islamic heritage in cross-cultural perpectives, no. 3.

ISBN 81-246-0170-4 (Hardbound)
ISBN 81-246-0405-3 (Paperback)
First Published in India in 2002
Second impression in 2007

Published and printed by:
D.K. Printworld (P) Ltd.
Regd. office : *'Sri Kunj'*, F-52, Bali Nagar
Ramesh Nagar Metro Station
New Delhi - 110 015
Phones : (011) 2545-3975; 2546-6019; *Fax* : (011) 2546-5926
E-mail: dkprintworld@vsnl.net
Web: www.dkprintworld.com

Foreword

IN the 1970s, as a young Indologist, I dedicated myself to the comparative study of some aspects of Hindu *bhakti* and Sufism. For five years I spent the months of the monsoon along the banks of the Yamunā, going to visit *āśrama*s of the *sant* tradition, especially in Braj, and *khānaqāh*s of *Ciśtī* and *Naqshbandī* derivation. I had the privilege of knowing and be close to the *pīr* of the *Naqshbandīyya*, Shah Abul Hasan Zaid Faruqi, a fine intellectual with also a surprising wealth of knowledge in yogic and Vedāntic Hindu spirituality. During my stays in Delhi, I used to visit the old sufi at dawn, and I still treasure a few notebooks in which I wrote down the profound and wise teachings he offered me during our conversations. He often told me that some Hindu *yogin*s, hailing from Uttar Pradesh and Bengal (?), used to come in pilgrimage to the tomb of his predecessor Maẓhar Jān-ī-Jānān, situated right in the courtyard of the *khānaqāh* where he lived, honouring it with the chanting of hymns and sprinkling it with petals and water. Despite the profound tie which united me to Shah Abul Hasan and which lasted till his death, I never had the chance of meeting a Hindu devotee of the great Maẓhar within the *khānaqāh*. The *pīr* himself, who remembered with prodigious memory the *Mazhariyya* interpretation of Śaṅkara's Vedāntic doctrine, exhibited a curious amnesia regarding the precise whereabouts of the Bengali and U.P. *yogin*s. None the less, destiny would subsequently bring me in contact with this peculiar *sant paramparā* quite a number of times. Around the end of the 1980s, my dearest Indian friend, Hazari Mull Banthia, an old Jain gentleman from Kanpur, confided to me quite casually of the existence in his town of a Hindu *sampradāya* following a sufi spiritual method. Few years later, I was drawn to a study of some stanzas in the *Mahābhārata*, a research which led me to embark on an archaeological campaign of excavation in the Farrukhabad District. I thus discovered that I was treading along the pilgrimage paths leading to the funeral monuments of Maulana Fadl Ahmad Khan and Sri Ramchandrji Fatehgarhi. But I had the most welcome surprise when Dr. Thomas Dahnhardt — now my colleague but in those days one among my most brilliant students — came to visit me informing me that during one of his sojourns in India he had met with Shah Abul Hasan Sahab. With him he had discussed at length about those *yogin*s who followed the *Naqshbandī* method. Having gone to Kanpur, he was then able to identify their milieu and to become quite close with them. In fact, the young researcher had come to see me precisely to propose this topic as the subject of his research. It looked as if an invisible hand had been guiding his steps: indeed he was in no way aware of the antecedents, since on the matter I had been as discreet as Shah Abul Hasan. The research of Dr. Dahnhardt continued in India as well as in Europe, especially in Venice, London, and Oxford, through meetings with the living protagonists and via the analysis of the fundamental texts of both traditions, i.e., the sufī and the yogic. In this way, an important spiritual patrimony of India has been salvaged, which illustrates the intimate identity of vision on ultimate truths between a Ḥindu environment and a Muslim one. And this ultimately proves how love and knowledge lead to union, whereas, on the contrary, separation leads humans to reciprocal hate and ignorance. In the *āśrama*s of Purī, Kanpur, and Mathurā as well as in the *khānaqāh*s of Delhi, Sirhind, and Quetta that synthesis which in vain Mogul emperors sought has truly been achieved.

This book and his author have the merit of unearthing for the benefit of scholars an important component of Indian culture, which uptil now has remained practically unknown. This book and his author have also the merit of opening up a spiritual treasure which chronicles, politics, and ideology utterly ignore.

Venice, 20 March 2002 **Gian Giuseppe Filippi**

Preface

THE present study consists of an attempt to delineate the meeting of two different esoteric currents in a cross-cultural encounter between Islam and Hinduism on the Indian subcontinent from the second half of the last century down to the present. Against the background of the millenary co-habitation of these two major world-religions in that part of the world, it describes the particular outer and inner circumstances that made such an encounter possible, trying, moreover, to focus on the spiritual history of the traditions involved. Based largely on the data collected during an eight-month field research conducted in 1995-6 among the Muslim and Hindu representatives of the Indian lineage of the Naqshbandiyya generally known as the Mujaddidiyya, the book seeks to highlight through a concrete example the possibility of an intense spiritual symbiosis between India's two main communities that contrasts sharply with the widespread idea of prevalent social and religious tension.

After ascertaining the social and historical background of the cultural components involved, viz. a lineage of the Naqshbandiyya Mujaddidiyya on one side and the contemporary heritage of the *sant*-tradition on the other, and furnishing a biology of single members of this peculiar initiatory chain, the research concentrates on the theoretical elaborations which, from a doctrinal point of view, stand at the base of the synthesis operated by the figures directly taking part in this process. Special attention is given to the possible parallels traceable in the symbols and metaphors traditionally employed by the respective perspectives of Sufism and Yoga in formulating their cosmogonical and metaphysical theories. This predominantly gnostic point of view is then integrated by a description of the methodological aspects arising from this theoretical back-ground. The concluding part of the study is concerned with a brief description of different sub-branches within the Hindu environment which began to develop from the mainstream lineage over the last fifty years and sharing the gradual process of cultural absorption and progressive Indianisation of a corpus of teachings originally pertaining to an orthodox Sunni environment.

Contents

Acknowledgements

THE present research owes much to the numerous persons who have contributed through their suggestions, assistance, hospi-tality and financial support to the final completion of this thesis. I want to express my gratitude above all to Shah Anas Abul Nasr Faruqi Mujaddidī, the nephew of the late Shah Abul-Hasan Zaid and present head of the Naqshbandi *khānaqāh* at Old Delhi, for offering me his hospitality over a period of several months, assisting me in the research of written sources and patiently answering my numerous questions, to Shah Umar Abu Hafs Faruqi, head of the Mujaddidī *khānaqāh* at Quetta for his ready provision of written material; to Dr. Sayyid Ausaf Ali, retired director of the Jamiya Hamdard University (New Delhi), for his precious suggestions and hospitality; to Dr. Masud Anwar Kakorwi (Aligarh Muslim University) for his help and hospitality; to Bashir Faruqi Sahib, caretaker at the tomb of Shah Murad Allah at Lucknow, to Sayyid Jamil Ahmad (Bahraich), to Sri Omkar Nath Saksena, the present head of the Hindu Naqshbandīs at Kanpur, to Ravindra Nath Saksena (Kanpur), to B.K. Khare (Varanasi), to Muhammad Toha (Etawah), to D.K. Saksena (Bareilly), to Dr. H.N. Saksena (Jaipur) and to B.K. Singhania (New Delhi), who all agreed to be repeatedly interviewed and who provided me with rich material and precious information, and to Prof. G.G. Filippi (Venice University) who encouraged me to undertake this research and who assisted me throughout the period of compilation of the thesis.

Many thanks go also to the Central Research Fund of the University of London for providing me with the financial resources to undertake my field research in India during the period 1995-6, and to the Spalding Trust (Suffolk) whose generous scholarship allowed me to compile the final version of my thesis in London.

Most of all, I wish to thank my supervisor, Prof. C. Shackle, for assisting me throughout the last four years with his constant advice and expert quidance, and to Mr. Simon Weightman who kept a close eye on the progress of my work while in London. Special thanks go also to my parents who never lost their confidence in the successful outcome of my research, to Miss Michela Macchiavello for her precious technical and moral assistance, and to my numerous friends who helped me in many ways to overcome the endless obstacles encountered during the prolonged period of lonely work.

Abbreviations

AIB	*A'īn-i 'Ilm al-Bāṭin*
*AIO**	*Annali dell'Istituto Orientale di Napoli*
AY	*Ānanda-Yoga*
EI	*Encyclopedia of Islam*
HdT	*Hidayāt al-Ṭālibīn*
*IC**	*Islamic Culture*
*JAOS**	*Journal of the American Oriental Society*
JC	*Jīvan-Caritra*
KmI	*Kamāl-i Insānī*
MnS	*Manāḥij al-Sair wa Madārij al-Khair*
MqM	*Maqāmāt al-Maẓhariyya*
MuM	*Ma'mūlāt-i Maẓhariyya*
*MW**	*Muslim World*
*RSO**	*Rivista degli Studi Orientali* (Rome)
SD	*Santmat Darśana*
SkA	*Sādhanā ke Anubhav*
SkR	*Sākṣātkār kā Rahasya*
*SI**	*Studia Islamica*
*StI**	*Studies in Islam*
TP	*Tattva Prabodhanī*
VS	*Vedānta Sāgara*

* = Periodicals

Introduction

Much has been written about the relationship and the reciprocal influence Hinduism and Islam have exercised on each other over the ten centuries of their cohabitation in South Asia. The innumerable works revolving around this topic include a wide range of studies dealing with one or the other aspect of this encounter which has so decisively contributed to the formation of the present-day cultural environment of the Indian subcontinent.

Especially in the wake of recent developments such as the destruction of the Bābrī Masjid at Ayodhyā in December 1992 and the constant political tension between the two newly emerged nuclear powers India and Pakistan over the Kashmir issue, the present situation of that area and the division of its societies along communal lines have attracted the world's attention. Major stress is thereby laid on the dividing factors which have led to an increasing distance between Hindus and Muslims over the last century. If these certainly represent a continuous feature in the twentieth-century history of the subcontinent, it is nevertheless equally true that this situation does not reflect the whole reality and relegates many fertile contacts between these two communities to the margin of attention.

In the wave of enthusiasm for the secular policy pursued by the Republic of India after Independence in 1947, many indigenous scholars had begun to exalt the glorious past of the India's middle ages during which an intense symbiosis involving many charismatic personalities on both sides stimulated and produced some of the finest cultural achievements in Indian history. These ranged from the development of an Indo-Islamic architectural style and the distinctive tradition of north-Indian classical music to widely acclaimed poetic currents and a richly blended cuisine, all of which survive in various forms till the present day and contribute much to the attractive picture of India's exotic culture.

Less attention has been given outside academic circles to the often intense spiritual contacts between the elite representatives of both traditions, operating from the top and reaching down to the level of popular understanding, where they have largely contributed to the creation of a common basis for a peaceful cohabitation of the members of both religious groups. It was in this field too that India's extraordinary capacity of assimilation has given rise to some extremely stimulating examples of collaboration and synthesis transcending the numeorus divisions that characterise the religious, social and ethnic peculiarities of each tradition.

From the thirteenth century AD onwards, the devotionally oriented *bhakti* movement provides us with a series of outstanding saints, both Hindus and Muslims, who were drawn by their sincere love arising from the depths of their longing hearts to experience the immutable Divine truth and were able to bridge the gap between their respective communities by stressing that common aim all sacred traditions have described since time immemorial. Culminating in the fifteenth and sixteenth centuries with Kabīr and Gurū Nānak, both pertaining to the *nirguṇa* current that emphasises the unqualified, transcendent aspect of the Divine while openly mocking the rigid ritualism of priestly orthodoxy as narrow-minded and hypocritical, many of these *sant*s, although hailing from the lower sections of society, were able to maintain a truly synthetic vision that goes beyond the formal barriers of institutionalised religion. Basing their teachings on the assertion of an underlying common human ground, irrespective of the religious and social background and any erudite expertise in the holy scriptures, which if cultivated in its purest aspect of love for God and the world would allow every earnest seeker to experience the presence of his Lord and thereby render meaningless any religious discrimination. Their nearness to the people was expressed in their poetry using the simple and straightforward style of the north-Indian vernaculars used in their poetry. They there by contributed decisively to the formation of a multi-cultural and multi-religious society long before modern secular ideas began to penetrate into the subcontinent from the Western world.

As a matter of fact, for centuries religious hatred, intolerance and communal divisions were phenomena largely unknown to Indian society. If ever, they remained mostly confined to the sporadic initiatives of zealous rulers or governors eager to promote their image as firmly orthodox Islamic potentates. It was with the beginning of the modern age introduced to India during the colonial period that many indigenous intellectuals grew up in the imported educational system of their foreign rulers started to reinterpret the teachings of many religious and spiritual leaders of the past in a key that contrasted with the traditional perspective and which was prone to promote a growing division between the two communities. Although initially this did not reach down to the hundreds of thousands of Indian villages where Hindus and Muslims had since long shared the anxieties and needs of common life, they nevertheless began to gain ground in the circles of the nascent Indian bourgeoisie. Later, during the years of struggle for political freedom and assisted by the increasingly efficient means of propaganda, these ideas gradually penetrated further down to the masses. This process of growing division led eventually to the partition of the subcontinent into two separate nations: an almost entirely Muslim Pakistan oriented along lines of religious cohesion, and a secular India whose Western styled Constitution reflects the concern of its founders to guarantee freedom of expression to its innumerable religious groups.

The rise of a nationalistic ideology with both communal and secular dimensions which accompanied India's passage during the later nineteenth century from a feudal society for hundreds of years governed largely by Muslim dynasties to a colonial system concerned with imposing a modern European mentality, is an impressive example of the impact of this process. It demonstrates at the same time impressively the loss of influence of traditional authorities on policy and society. This applies in particular to the Muslims most hardly hit by the disastrous consequences of the 1856-7 War. The dwindling influence of Sufi leaders on all social classes appears particularly striking in the case of the Mujaddidiyya, the dominant Indian branch of the Naqshbandiyya based on the teachings of Shaikh Aḥmad Sirhindī (1564-1624), the 'renewer of the second millennium of Islam' (hence the title *Mujaddid*), whose leaders had tried hard to exercise their influence on the ruling class during the Mogul period.[1] The frequent letters addressed by Shaikh Aḥmad and his successors to the emperor and members of the Court nobility inviting them to adjust their lifestyle and policies according to Islamic norms show their concern and involvement in worldly affairs beyond their immediate responsibilities in the field of spiritual education. In tune with the particular vision held by this order which desired to encourage reforms from within the tradition based mainly on the Sunna of the prophet Muḥammad, its authorities were looked at with the utmost suspicion by the British rulers as potential reactionaries against their own concept of a new order.[2]

As a result and reaction of the impact left by the latter, at the turn of the present century and on the wave of Muslim protest after World War I began to gain weight the interpretation among Muslim intellectuals of the image of Shaikh Aḥmad Sirhindī and his successors as religious, social and political reformers. In a successive stage, this led to Sirhindī's depiction, in either negative or in positive terms according to their authors being Pakistani or Indian, as the defender of the

1. For Naqshbandī influence on Muslim rulers, see Yohanan Friedmann: *Shaikh Aḥmad Sirhindī: An Outline of His Thought and a Study of His Image in the Eyes of Posterity* (1971), pp. 77-87, and his article: 'The Naqshbandis and Aurangzeb: a reconsideration', in Varia Turcica: *Naqshbandis* (1990), pp. 209-20. See also K.A. Nizami: 'Naqshbandi influence on Mughal rulers and politics', in *IC* 38 (1965), pp. 41-53.

2. In fact, some revivalist factions of the Mujaddidī branch around Shaikh Isma'īl 'Shahīd' (1779-1831) and Sayyid Ahmad Barelawī (d. 1831) promoted violent action against all infidels including the Sikhs in the Punjab, the Marāṭhās in northern India and the British, organising armed volunteers to fight in the North-East of the subcontinent and in the Anglo-Afghan wars. For details, see S.A.A. Rizvi: Shāh 'Abd al'Azīz: *Puritanism, Sectarian Polemics and Jihad* (1982).

Muslims against the majoritarian community and thereby an indirect forerunner of the Muslim nationalism which finally resulted in the creation of Pakistan. But notwithstanding the often highly exalted political role played by the 'renewer of the second millennium of Islam', it has been correctly pointed out in accordance with his image in the seventeenth and eighteenth centuries, that Sirhindī 'was primarily a Sufī and must be assessed as such'.[3]

Particularly disturbing in the image drawn of Shaikh Aḥmad and his successors by some modern Indian scholars is the often repeated assumption that his behaviour was guided by an uncompromising and radical Islamic position 'trying to disrupt the peaceful co-existence of Hindus and Muslims'.[4] Such a stand is hardly tenable in view of the existing sources and appears to be itself politically motivated. It fails to take into due account the change of mentality that has occurred during the last four centuries even if it is undeniable that in more recent times some leaders affiliated to the Naqshbandiyya have been adopting what are nowadays defined as 'fundamentalist positions'. This contrasts with the attitude assumed by those authorities of the order who consider themselves as the spiritual heirs of Sirhindī, as I have experienced during my field research. These generally refuse to pronounce themselves in public about political problems and apparently do not nourish any particular aversion or hatred towards Hindus. In keeping with the traditional attitude mentioned by Friedmann, they remain rather indifferent to both questions and prefer to concern themselves with instructing the ever-decreasing number of disciples in the spiritual sciences and keeping the Naqshbandī tradition alive.

In view of the prevailing idea of the Mujaddidīs as intolerant and rigid Sunni purists unwilling to compromise, it may therefore be surprising that it was from the descendants of

3. Friedmann (1971), p. 330.

4. S.A.A. Rizvi, *Muslim Revivalist Movements in northern India in the Sixteenth and Seventeenth Centuries*, 1965, p. 330. Cf. also M. Mujeeb, *The Indian Muslims*, 1967.

Shaikh Aḥmad Sirhindī and his renowned heir at Delhi, Mīrzā Maẓhar Jān-i Jānān (*d.* 1780), that contacts were established with non-Muslims which eventually led to an intense spiritual collaboration and the transmission of the *ṭarīqa*'s teachings and methods into a Hindu environment. This occurred during the second half of the last century, i.e., at a time when the relations between the two communities began to be increasingly strained, and, therefore, furnishes a concrete example of behaviour that openly contradicts the above-mentioned assertions about the Mujaddidiyya. The successors of these shaikhs and *guru*s used to teach their particular elaboration of a joint spiritual discipline to a mixed audience of Hindus and Muslims, unperturbed by the growing unrest and turmoil that has gripped the north-Indian society over the last decades. They, thus, insert themselves in the mediaeval *sant* context set out by their illustrious predecessor Kabīr to whom they claim affiliation, thereby giving proof of the perpetuation of this tradition over the centuries until today.

During the eight months of field research I carried out in India from October 1995 to May 1996. I was welcomed by the members of both religious groups affiliated to the Mujaddidiyya at different places in Uttar Pradesh, Punjab, Rajasthan and Delhi. Thanks to their generous hospitality, it was possible for me to take part at their meetings and *satsaṅg*s, listening to their oral teachings and participating at the performance of the techniques used in their daily practice. The natural and spontaneous openness and tolerance I witnessed among these masters, who pay regular homage in their prayers to the ancestors of the *ṭarīqa* Naqshbandiyya Mujaddidiyya include Shaikh Aḥmad Sirhindī, the alleged scorner of Hindus, at whose tomb they perform annually prayers and meditations, thus, convinced me of the liveliness of India's spiritual culture and its continual ability to contradict the common stereotypes of rigidly erected mental categories.

Attentive reading of the textual sources of these Hindu Naqshbandīs revealed that their teachings consist of a curious blend of elements originally pertaining to both the Islamic background of their Mujaddidī ancestors and that of the *nirguṇa sants*, especially Kabīr and his successors in the *panth* bearing his name. It, thus, became clear that even a tendentially conservative environment like that of the Mujaddidīs reacted in different ways to the challenge of modernity, and that at least some of its leaders did not perceive any contradiction with the teachings of the *Mujaddid* in enlarging their spiritual wealth to members from outside the Sunni community.

The present study was encouraged by one of the great spiritual authorities of the *silsila* at Delhi, the late Shāh Abūl Ḥasan Zaid Fārūqī Mujaddidī (*d*.1993), who first informed me of the existence of a Hindu branch and who directed me to Kanpur to search for those people who use to come from time to time to the tomb of their revered spiritual ancestor Mīrzā Maẓhar Jān-i Jānān. It attempts to identify the factors that made such a cross-cultural link possible, from a religious, social and historical point of view, thereby trying to outline the perspective held by those who so bluntly disregard the formal divisions between a doctrine so deeply related to the fundamentals of the Islamic *Dīn* and the adherents of India's *Sanātana Dharma*.

1

The Masters of the *Naqshbandiyya Mujaddidiyya Maẓhariyya Na'īmiyya*

Shaikh Mīrzā Jān-i Jānān (1111/1701-1195/1780)

THE account of this particular branch of the *Naqshbandiyya Mujaddidiyya* begins with the figure of Mīrzā Jān-i Jānān. First of all because he played a central role in the eighteenth-century history of the *ṭarīqa* reunifying several lines of descent derived from Shaikh Aḥmad Sirhindī.[1] Mīrzā Jān-i Jānān thereby successfully reverted the trend of gradual fragmentation that regularly occurs in the vacuum left in the spiritual hierarchy after the death of a charismatic leader. Through his vigorous character and intellectual acuteness Mīrzā Jān-i Jānān was capable of revitalising the spiritual and social legacy he had inherited from his illustrious ancestors in the *silsila* at a time when large parts of northern India's Islamic society were facing threats of ruin and disintegration. In recognition to the important role played by him, his line of the order became afterwards known as *Shamsiyya Maẓhariyya*, providing evidence of the particular imprint he left on the history of the lineage.

1. For a graphical illustration of the different lines of descent converging in the figure of Mīrzā Jān-i Jānān, see W.E. Fusfeld's study: *The Shaping of Sūfī Leadership in Delhi: The Naqshbandiyya Mujaddidiyya, 1750 to 1920*, PhD thesis, Dept. of History, University of Pennsylvania, 1981, p. 127. This work provides a detailed analysis of Mīrzā Jān-i Jānān's double role as spiritual leader and social reformer, and provides an account of the subsequent history of his lineage at Delhi.

The second reason is that it was an initiatory chain that developed from Mīrzā Jān-ī Jānān which eventually extended into a Hindu environment splitting from the main branch which from its *khānaqāh* at Shāhjahānābād provided its affiliates with spiritual leadership almost uninterruptedly till the present day. Hence, Mīrzā Jān-i Jānān constitutes the point of departure of the distinctive lineage we are concerned with and is considered by its later authorities as the forefather of their peculiar tradition.

There is a third certainly not less important reason that justifies Mīrzā Jān-i Jānān's prominent role in the biographical frame-work provided by the present chapter. It bears a direct relation with the preceding one and consists of the fact that he was apparently the first among the accredited Mujaddidī authorities to pronounce himself openly about the Hindu tradition from an Islamic legal viewpoint. In one of his epistles,[2] the learned Sunni scholar and authoritative Sūfī leader has provided a fairly detailed account of the basic outlines of the Hindu tradition, leading him to the conclusion that Hindus have had their share in the Divine revelation in the past and that it was delivered to humanity through prophet-like messengers (*bashīr*) including Rāmacandra and Kṛṣṇa.

If the resulting availability to include Hindus among the 'People of the Book' (*ahl-i kitāb*) does not represent a radical innovation in Islamic perceptions of Hinduism, it is Mīrzā Jān-i Jānān's practical attitude towards Hindus that constitutes a surprising aspect of this orthodox Naqshbandī shaikh. Several indications suggest that he admitted a number of Hindus to enrol among his disciples and some hints contained in his letters suggest that he provided spiritual guidance to some of them

2. For the original version of this letter, see *Kalimāt-i Tayyibāt, Matba'-i 'Ulum*, Muradabad, 1891, letter no. 14, pp. 27-9. Its Urdu version, is rendered by Khaliq Anjum in: *Mīrzā Maẓhar Jān-i Jānān ke khuṭūt* (1989), pp. 131-4 and Shāh Abūl Ḥasan Zaid Fārūqī in: *Hindūstānī qadīm madhāhib* (1986), pp. 9-13. An English version of it has been proposed by a number of modern scholars among which S.A.A. Rizvi in *Shāh Walī Allāh and his times* (1980), pp. 332-4.

without insisting on their previous conversion to Islam. Although it is impossible to infer from the few sources at our disposal to what extent those Hindu disciples were allowed access to the esoteric teachings of his *silsila,* their mere presence in his *ḥalqa* indicates that Mīrzā Jān-i Jānān had no basic objection towards granting initiation (*bai'at*) to non-Muslims.[3]

Mīrzā Jān-i Jānān's relevance for the present study, thus, becomes immediately evident, and it is probably more than a casual coincidence that he is held in high esteem and reverence among the order's contemporary Hindu members, many of whom consider his tomb within the precincts of the Delhi *khānaqāh* an important destination on the itinerary of their ritual pilgrimage and a source of blessings and spiritual inspiration.

However, an assessment of the role played by this important eighteenth-century Sūfī leader in the specific context needs to take into account the socio-political circumstances prevailing in northern India and especially in Delhi during his lifetime.[4] The rapid decline of Mogul imperial authority following the death of emperor Aurangzeb in AD 1707 accelerated by the emergence of non-Islamic regional forces and foreign powers (Sikhs, Jāṭs, Marāṭhās and

3. From the sources available, it is not entirely clear whether this affiliation of Hindus was subject to any prior condition since any explicit mention of this topic has been carefully avoided in the texts at our disposal. As I was told by the present head and *sajjāda nashīn* of the Delhi *khānaqāh*, Ḥaḍrat Anas Abūl Naṣr Fārūqī Mujaddidī, a preliminary condition which most probably was incumbent on Mīrzā Jān-i Jānān's Hindu disciples consisted in the pronouncement of the *kālima-i tawḥīd*, thus, proclaiming the unicity of the metaphysical Principle and Its projection as Creator. This does not automatically imply a conversion to Islam as a whole and would probably not have caused any embarassment for any spiritually inclined Hindu.

4. For a detailed account of the socio-historical circumstances of the eighteenth century with special regard to Muslim society in the Mogul capital Delhi, see the first chapters of S.A.A. Rizvi (1980), pp. 3-203. For an appreciation of the intellectual movements within Muslim society, see also Muhammad Umar: *Islam in Northern India during the eighteenth century* (1993), and William Irvine: *The Later Mugals* (1972).

European colonialists) compelled India's Muslims to confront an unprecedented situation in which a temporal authority guided by Islamic principles and endorsing its traditional values for the maintenance of an Islamic world-order could no longer be taken for granted. Consequently, a number of Muslim intellectuals who recognised the danger of a possible loss of Muslim identity and who witnessed the disintegration of large segments of this social structure around them struggled to provide an answer on different levels to this deep crisis, especially in the old Mogul capital Delhi where these tendencies were most strongly perceived. Renowned names like Shāh Walī Allāh Dihlawī (1114/1703-1176/1762)[5] and his son Shāh 'Abd al-'Azīz (1159/1746-1239/1824),[6] Khwāja Muḥammad Naṣīr 'Andalīb' (1105/1694-1172/1759), and his son Khwāja Mīr 'Dard' (1133/1721-1199/1785),[7] Shaikh Kalīm Allāh Shāhjahānābādī (1060/1650-1142/1729) and his disciple Maulānā Fakhr al-Dīn Dihlawī (1126/1714-1199/1785)[8] to name only a few, furnish ample proof of the intellectual vitality that characterised the capital's Muslim society during that time.

The flourishing of a refined Persian and Urdu literary culture around the Mogul Court and its aristocracy promoted and promulgated during the frequent *mushā'ira* meetings ranges among the most excellent expressions of this era of incumbing decadence, which witnessed the presence of such outstanding poets as Mīrzā 'Abd al-Qādir 'Bedil' (1054/1644-1133/1721), Mīrzā Muḥammad Rafī' 'Saudā' (*d.* 1195/1781), Mīr Taqī 'Mīr' (1137/1724-1225/1810) and many others.[9] The

5. For him and his works, see G.N. Jalbani: *Life of Shāh Walyullah* (1980), J.M.S. Baljon: *Religion and Thought of Shāh Walī Allāh Dihlawī (1703-1762)* (1986), and A. Bausani's article: 'Note su Shāh Walī Allāh di Delhi', in *AIO* X (1961), pp. 93-147.

6. For him, see S.A.A. Rizvi: *Shāh 'Abd ul-'Azīz: Puritanism, Sectarian Polemics and Jihād* (1982).

7. For these two, see Annemarie Schimmel: *As through a Veil*, and *Pain and Grace* (1976).

8. For these two, see Muhammad Umar (1993).

9. For the last two, see Ralph Russell and Khurshidu'l-Islam: *Three Mughal Poets* (1991), pp. 37-69 (Saudā) and pp. 95-271 (Mīr Taqī Mīr).

steady decline of political authority was, therefore, not immediately accompanied by a sudden interruption in Delhi's cultural life. Rather, it provided the stimulus for a period of flourishing activity among Muslim intellectuals that led to a series of unique achievements in numerous cultural fields.

However, the invasions of Nādir Shāh in 1739 followed by that of Shāh Aḥmad Durrānī in 1761 gave a decisive blow to the city's status. The simultaneous dispersal of material wealth compelled many Muslim intellectuals to migrate towards the emerging provincial centres in the periphery of the former empire, such as Awadh in the Northern Gangetic plain and Golkonda/Hyderabad in the Deccan.

The growing feeling of insecurity which began to pervade large sections of Delhi's population led to social unrest that manifested itself in the outbreak of open factional conflicts, mainly between rival Shi'a and Sunni groups, and was further fuelled by the inconsistent religious policies of the emperors and their influential supporters at court.[10]Even if these conflicts were only part of the wider context of a struggle for political power between the two predominant factions of Shi'a Iranis and Sunni Turanis of Afghan origin, the sharpness of their ideological undertone indicates the fragility of the inner equilibrium that by than characterised the local Muslim society throughout.

In such a climate many people sought refuge in the presence of spiritual and religious leaders who, from the

---

10. The son and successor of emperor Aurangzeb, known under his title Shāh-i 'Ālam Bahādur Shāh (*r.* AD 1707-12) reportedly shifted from the orthodox Sunni religious policy of his father towards a more or less open support of the Shi'a faction altering the traditional *khuṭba* read out in Delhi's Jama Masjid. This strongly offended the feelings of the Sunni scholars estranging great parts of them from their idea of the emperor as grant of orthodoxy. On a popular level, the growing popularity of the *Muḥarram* celebrations to commemorate the martyrdom of the prophet's grandsons Ḥasan and Ḥusain, introduced to northern India from the Deccan, constitute an important example of the new self-confidence shown by the Shi'a population patronised by the newly emerging regional dynasty of Awadh.

secluded surroundings of their *khānaqāh*s and *madrasa*s, continued to represent an element of stability and continuity of the old order.[11] Many Sūfī leaders attentively observed the deepening crisis afflicting the outside world and perceived the urgency to counteract its centrifugal tendencies. Hence, they began to assume a broader role of leadership by expanding their earlier position of exclusively spiritual preceptors to a more contingent kind of moral and social tutorship with aimed at providing a safehaven for people in all sectors of society. This newly emerging pattern of behaviour accounts for the large following many of these shaikhs are reported to have attracted into their fold. They began to enrol an increasing number of affiliates into the rank of their *ṭarīqa*, appointing innumerable deputies, delegates and spiritual successors (*khulafā'*) who were despatched to the remotest corners of the country in order to provide maximum guidance per outreach through a dense coverage of the territory. Reflecting the specific Naqshbandī tendency to exercise a corrective influence on worldly leaders, it is not difficult to understand how a prominent Sūfī leader like Mīrzā Jān-i Jānān perceived it as his stringent duty to follow in the steps of his predecessors trying to prevent the process of degradation he witnessed all around.

Mīrzā 'Maẓhar' Jān-ī Jānān: Life and thought

Like most prominent figures in Indian Muslim culture, Mīrzā Jān-i Jānān claimed descendance from a noble ancestry (*ashrafī*) originally hailing from outside the subcontinent. According to the shaikh's own statements, he descended in the 28th generation from a family whose genealogy goes back through Imām Abū Ḥanīfa (*d.* 150/767) to 'Alī ibn Abū Ṭālib,

11. For a more elaborated description of the changing socio-political situation and shifting of leadership from the worldly to the spiritual authorities during the eighteenth and early nineteenth centuries until the final breakdown of the old Muslim society after 1857/8, see W.A. Fusfeld (1981), Introduction and chapter 1, pp. 1-52.

the fourth caliph of Islam.[12] More traceable in historical sources, his paternal forefathers were members of the Afghan Qāqshāl tribe who accompanied the Mogul emperor Humāyūn on his way from Kabul to Delhi to reconquer the lost throne of Hindustan.

After Humāyūn regained power at Delhi in 1555, the two Qāqshāl brothers Amīr Majnūn Khān and Amīr Bābā Khān were awarded posts as *jāgīrdār* at Narnaul (about 25 miles south-west of Delhi). Later in the reign of Akbar (*r.* AD 1556-1605) some of their descendants were assigned a *jāgīr* at Ghoraghat in Bengal in reward for their loyalty during a series of military campaigns. But this loyal relationship ended abruptly in 1580-1 when the Turānī nobility in those eastern regions engaged in a revolt against the imperial authority and in which Amīr Jabbārī Khān, son of Majnūn Khān, and other Qāqshāls were found to have taken active part. Once the rebellion was crushed, its leaders were disgraced.[13]

Nothing is known about the following generations of the clan after the loss of its privileged status. The family chronicle becomes traceable again with the figure of Mīrzā Jān, the father of ours who reportedly held a *mansab* in the army of Aurangzeb (*r.* 1658-1707), which led him to accompany the emperor on his extensive military expeditions to the Deccan. There, Mīrzā Jān apparently distinguished himself in quelling a rebellion through diplomatic ability.[14] However, soon afterwards he decided to resign from his post and to leave the imperial camp for his native town of Akbarābād

12. Thanā al-Ḥaqq Amīn dedicates one chapter of his book *Mīr wa Saudā kā daur* to Mīrzā Jān-i Jānān (pp. 185-211) providing an extensive account of the latter's ancestry.

13. *Akbar-Nāmā*, vol. III, pp. 469-70 and 567.

14. This event refers probably to the rebellion of a Marāṭhā faction guided by a certain Rājā Rām inside the fortress of Jinjī (dist. Arcot, Tamil Nadu) which, from a chronological and geographical point of view, corresponds to the account given by Maulawī Na'īm Allāh Bahrāichī in his biographical work on Mīrzā Jān-i Jānān, *Bashārāt-i Maẓhariyya*, folio 118. Cf. 'Abd al-Razzaq Quraishi: *Mīrzā Maẓhar Jān-i Jānān aur unkā kalām* (1979), pp. 27-30.

(modern Agra). On his way to the north, his wife[15]gave birth to their only son who was for this reason named after his father Mīrzā Jān-i Jān.[16]Gradually, this name evolved into Mīrzā Jān-i Jānān and was eventually adopted by himself, as the signature on his letters indicates. His pen-name (*takhalluṣ*) 'Maẓhar', used to sign the verses he composed in both Persian and Urdu, became an integral part of his name. Adding the title conferred upon him as leader of Delhi's Naqshbandī Mujaddidī *khānaqāh*, and the honorific title of *shahīd* attributed to him by many Sunni Muslims after his death, his full name emerges as Shams al-Dīn Ḥabīb Allāh Mīrzā Jān-i Jānān Maẓhar 'Alwī Shahīd.[17]

Mīrzā Jān-i Jānān spent his early childhood in his father's hometown Agra receiving an education consistent with his social status. Encouraged by his father, he underwent an intensive training in the traditional, religious, literary, martial and artistic sciences typical of his times, Mīrzā Jān himself providing great part of the instructions until his death in 1130/1717, when the age of his son was sixteen.[18]

It is not clear when and in what circumstances Mīrzā Jān-i Jānān moved from Agra to Delhi, but most likely it

---

15. According to the author of the *Ma'mūlāt-i Maẓhariyya*, Mīrzā Jān's wife and mother of Mīrzā Jān-i Jānān descended from the ruling family of the Bahmanikingdom of Bijapur in the Deccan; if this is the case, their marriage occurred probably during Mīrzā Jān's stay in the following of the Mogul emperor in that area. Cf. *MuM*, p. 19.

16. While the place of this event is mentioned in most authoritative sources as Kalabagh, a small *qaṣba* in the Malwa region, there are differences regarding the exact date of birth: according to his two main diciples and biographers, Shāh Na'īm Allāh Bahrāichī, author of the *Ma'mūlāt-i Maẓhariyya* and the *Bashārāt-i Maẓhariyya*, and Shāh Ghulām 'Alī Dihlawī, author of the *Maqāmāt-i Maẓharī*, his birth-date has been mentioned as 11 Ramaḍān 1111/February 1700. Mīrzā Jān-i Jānān's own statements in this context slightly contradict each other and range from AH 1110 (cf. Ghulām 'Alī Āzād Bilgrāmī in Sarw-i Āzād) to AH 1113 (see Khaliq Anjum (1989), letter no. 1, p. 96-7). Cf. also 'Abd al-Razzaq Quraishi (1989), pp. 31-2 and Maulānā Muḥmmad Ḥusain Āzād's *Āb-i Ḥayāt*, pp. 137-8.

17. Cf. *Hindūstānī qadīm madhāhib*, p. 4, *MuM*, p. 12.

18. *MqM*, p. 260.

took place during the last years of his father's life or shortly after his death. There, he continued his religious education under the guidance of Qārī 'Abd al-Rasūl Dihlawī who taught him Qur'ānic exegesis (*tafsīr*) and instructed him in Qur'ānic recitation (*qirā'at*). He further studied *ḥadīth* and jurisprudence (*fiqh*) with Ḥājī Muḥammad Afḍal Siyālkoṭī (*d.* 1146/1733), a grandson of Shaikh Aḥmad Sirhindī and well-known authority in the traditional religious sciences,[19] to whom he remained attached long after the beginning of his own spiritual career when he himself started instructing his disciples in the science of *ḥadīth*.

Most sources report that Mīrzā Jān-i Jānān's inclination towards the Sūfī way of *darweshī o faqr* emerged at the age of eighteen following an unsuccessful attempt to obtain the restoration of his father's *mansab* at the Court of the emperor Farrukhsiyar (*r.* AD 1712-19).[20] The emperor was reportedly unable to attend the Court audience compelling Mīrzā Maẓhar to leave empty-handed. The following night, the latter had a dream in which the Chishti saint Quṭb al-Dīn Bakhtiyār Kākī (*d.* 654/1256) called him towards a life dedicated to spiritual pursuits.[21] Deeply impressed by the powerful vision, Mīrzā renounced any further thought of a worldly career and eventually became the disciple of Sayyid Nūr Muḥammad Badāyūnī (*d.* 1135/1722), a descendant of Shaikh Sa'īf al-Dīn in the line of Shaikh Aḥmad Sirhindī, who initiated him into the *Naqshbandiyya Mujaddidiyya*.[22]

Mīrzā Jān-i Jānān remained with his spiritual preceptor for four years until the latter's death in 1722. During that

---

19. For a detailed biographical account of this great scholar, see among others *MqM*, pp. 244-6, and Muhammad Umar (1993), p. 140 (notes to chapter II).
20. *MuM*, p. 20.
21. *MqM*, p. 282.
22. For biographical details of this saint whose grave is located within the precincts of the cemetery at the outskirts of the *dargāh* of Niẓām al-Dīn Awliyā' at New Delhi, see *MqM*, pp. 280-5. For his position in the spiritual genealogy of the order, see Appendix I of the quoted work.

period he reportedly made rapid progress on the spiritual path qualifying for full investiture (*khilāfat*) and the licence of initiating new disciples into the order (*ijāzat*).[23]After his master's death he remained for nearly six years immersed in deep meditation next to his shaikh's tomb until reaching the degree of 'supreme sainthood' (*wilāyat-i 'uliyā*), apparently through hidden guidance by his shaikh.[24] Then, one night his preceptor appeared to him in a vision (*rū'ya*) directing him to persist in his quest for Truth and to look for a new living master.

Mīrzā Jān-i Jānān next enrolled as the disciple of Shāh Ḥāfiẓ Sa'd Allāh (*d.*1152/1739),[25]a renowned authority of the Mujaddidī lineage at Delhi at that time, and of Shāh Muḥammad Zubair (*d.* 1152/1739)[26]a grandson of Shāh Ḥujjat Allāh Naqshbandī and preceptor of numerous noblemen at the imperial Court. But the master who brought to completion Mīrzā's spiritual education was Shaikh Muḥammad 'Ābid Sunāmī 'Gulshan' (*d.* 1160/

23. *MuM*, p. 20.

24. *MuM.*, p. 20.

25. For biographical details of him, see *MqM*, pp. 293-7. According to this biography, Mīrzā Maẓhar was assisted by the spirit of his defunct master, a method often described by and characteristic for this order since the its earlier days headed by the Khwājagān during the eleventh to fourteenth centuries, which include Khwāja 'Abd al-Khāliq al-Gujdawānī, Khwāja 'Ārif Riwgārī and Khwāja Yūsuf al-Ḥamadānī. For this pattern of spiritual transmission typical among Naqshbandī leaders, see: Hamid Algar's article 'A Brief History of The Naqshbandi Order' in *Varia Turcica: Naqshbandis* (1990), pp. 6-12, and Stéphane Ruspoli's 'Réflexions sur la voie spirituelle des Naqshbandis', in *supra*, pp. 95-109.

    Another example of this way of spiritual transmission outside the Naqshbandī context is that of the Algerian Sūfī Amīr 'Abd-al Qādir al-Djizāīrī (*d.*1867) who claimed to have been connected with his spiritual instructor Shaikh al-Akbar Ibn al-'Arabī through 'hidden initiation'. For a general acknowledgement of this spiritual relationship with a defunct master, see A.S. Husaini's article 'Uways al-Qaranī and the Uwaysi Sūfīs' in *MW* 57 (1967), pp. 103-14.

26. For biographical details, see *MuM*, pp. 21-2.

1747),[27] another prominent Naqshbandī authority with a large following who had reached Delhi from Sirhind following that town's destruction by the Sikhs.[28] The shaikh initiated his disciple into the Qādirī, Chishtī and Suhrawardī *silsilas*, thus, bringing to perfection his spiritual career and preparing him for his role as an independent authority.

By the time of the shaikh's death, Mīrzā Jān-i Jānān had spent a period of about thirty years under the guidance of several prominent Naqshbandī authorities, thus, bringing together the main lines of descent that had developed from Shaikh Aḥmad Sirhindī through his two sons and chief successors, Muḥammad Ma'ṣūm (*d.* 1079/1668) and Muḥammad Sa'īd (*d.* 1070/1659).[29] Having acquired full maturity as a shaikh and endowed with a solid knowledge in both religious and spiritual matters Mīrzā Jān-i Jānān was ready to fulfil the mission of propagating the *ṭarīqa*'s message reassumed in the principle of 'solitude among the crowd' (*khilwat dar anjuman*).[30]

By the mid-eighteenth century, the order's centre of activity had already moved from Sirhind, the hometown of Shaikh Aḥmad the *Mujaddid*. Its core areas comprehended now the capital Delhi, the provincial centres of the

---

27. For biographical details, see *MqM*, pp. 293-7.

28. This former centre of the Mujaddidiyya in Punjab that developed around the tomb of Shaikh Aḥmad was raided by the Sikh armies in 1710 and again in 1758 leading to an exodus of the order's authorities to Delhi, Rampur and other places. See also Arthur F. Buehler: *Sufi Heirs of the Prophet: The Indian Naqshbandiyya and the Rise of the Mediating Sufi Shaikh* (1997), pp. 170-1.

29. For an assessment of the life, works and role of these two prominent sons of Shaikh Aḥmad Sirhindī, see Yohanan Friedmann's article 'The Naqshbandis and Aurangzeb: a reconsideration' in Varia Turcica: *Naqshbandis* (1990), pp. 209-20.

30. For a further explanation of this fundamental principle which in a sense sums up the attitude of the Naqshbandī shaikhs, see Shāh Abūl Ḥasan's treatise *Manāhij al-Sair*. . . . (Urdu version), pp. 42-4. See also Qāḍī Thanā Allāh Pānīpatī's *Kitāb al-najatī 'an ṭarīqī al-ghairatī*, a gist of which regarding the eleven fundamental principles of the order is given in *MuM*, pp. 70-6.

Rohilkhand including Rampur, Muradabad and Badayun, and the Punjab.[31] It was from Delhi that Mīrzā Jān-i Jānān began to exercise an influence that eventually reached far beyond the city's boundaries. His importance as an all-India leader, in a way comparable to that of the Chishtī shaikhs in the early period of the Delhi Sultanate, is evidenced by the presence of his *khulafā'* and disciples all over the country, from the Punjab and Gujarat to the Deccan, although he concentrated his efforts largely on the Afghan Rohilās who had settled in the ancient land of Katehar in the north-western Ganges plain.[32] His spiritual influence radiated from Delhi to the various secondary centres in the periphery maintaining an intense correspondence with the deputies despatched in those places and was further enhanced by the transmission of spiritual attention (*tawajjuh*).[33] This concept of action through presence notwithstanding, it appears from several of Mīrzā Maẓhar's letters that anxious about the worsening social and political circumstances in the capital he occasionally left Delhi to pay personal visits to his chief deputies and trusted friends in places with a notable presence of followers, like Sambhal, Amroha, Panipat, etc.[34] Such a behaviour reflects the extent to which the impact of the dramatic historical events that led to an exodus of Delhi's population towards the newly emerging provincial capitals did not spare even this charismatic leader.

---

31. See, for instance, the description of various lineages from Shaikh Aḥmad mentioned in Badr al-Dīn Sirhindī's *Ḥaḍrāt al-Quds* and Muḥammad Hāshim Kishmī's *Zubdat al-maqāmāt*, both of which furnish a detailed account of the developments of the order from Shaikh Aḥmad onwards to the next three generations.

32. For a detailed account of the Rohila Afghans and their rise to power in the eighteenth century, see Jos J.L. Gommans: *The Rise of the Indo-Afghan Empire, c. 1710-1780*, E.J.Brill, Leiden, 1995.

33. For more details regarding this technique, see chapters 3 and 4 of the present study. For Mīrzā Jān-i Jānān's own references regarding the transmission of *tawajjuh*, see letters no. 30 and no. 42 of his letter collection in Khaliq Anjum (1989), pp. 172 and 191.

34. See letters no. 40 (p. 189), no. 52 (p. 202), no. 74 (p. 235) of Khaliq Anjum's Urdu rendering of Mīrzā Jān-i Jānān's letter collection.

In spite of the large number of disciples,[35] Mīrzā Jān-i Jānān reportedly remained very careful in selecting those admitted into his inner circle. In view of the responsibility involved for both master and disciple in establishing such a link,[36]he is described as extremely reluctant in granting initiation (*bai'at*). Aware of the risks of degeneration implied in enlarging indiscriminately the number of adherents to the *ḥalqa*, he initially tried to discourage all potential novices in order to test the firmness of their determination. Once this was ascertained, he carefullly tested each candidate's suitability before proceeding to grant full spiritual assistance to the neophyte.[37]

On the other side, it was, considered equally important for the aspirant novice to recognise a perfect master (*shaikh-i kāmil*) and to distinguish him from other people with apparently attractive features. Qāḍī Thanā Allāh Pānipatī, one of Mīrzā Jān-i Jānān's main disciples and successors, very much in line with the Mujaddidī perspective, writes at this regard:

> . . . the criterion while searching for a perfect spiritual guide should not remain confined to the abilities of producing extraordinary things (*kharq-i 'ādat*), being aware of the dangers and distractions afflicting the heart or the obtainment of spiritual states and emotional rapture (*ḥāl, wajd*), because many of these things can be attained also from Yogis and Brahmins; therefore, these matters alone constitute no guarantee for prosperity (*dalīl-i sa'ādat*). The real proof and the distinctive sign by which a perfect master can be

---

35. Mīrzā Jān-i Jānān himself occasionally refers in his letters to the growing number of disciples present at the *khānaqāh* to whom he had to impart spiritual assistance and *tawajjuh*. Cf. Khaliq Anjum (1989), letters no. 27 and 57.

36. For the conventional procedure of Mīrzā Jān-i Jānān's spiritual guide, Sayyid Nūr Muḥammad Badāyūnī, in enrolling new disciples, see *MuM*, p. 21.

37. Cf. *MuM*, pp. 38-41.

> recognised is his uprightly following of the revealed Law (*shar*ʿ) and his acting in perfect accordance with the Holy Scripture (*al-Kitāb*) and the Tradition of the prophet (*sunnat*). . . .[38]

This passage reproposes the everlasting problem faced by many earlier shaikhs, including Shaikh Aḥmad Sirhindī, of safe-guarding the esoteric tradition from degenerating into a sort of cheap witchcraft popular among the masses. In fact, the criterion for recognition of a genuine shaikh, which the author explains in minute detail in this text, reconfirms Mīrzā Jān-i Jānān as deeply rooted in the Mujaddidī tradition, for whom a shaikh of uppermost spiritual perfection (*shaikh-i kāmil wa mukammal*) acts outwardly as a perfect follower of the Law as represented by the prophet Muḥammad (*ittibā' al-sunnat*). All sources agree upon Mīrzā Jān-i Jānān's insistence on a minute adherence to the prescriptions of the *sharīʿat*. He reportedly requested his disciples to point out to him any shortcoming in his own behaviour which could contradict the principles of orthodox Sunni Islam.[39]

Yet another aspect emerging from the above-quoted statement which puts Mīrzā Jān-i Jānān in line with his famous predecessor from Sirhind is his attempt to purify Islam by expelling the numerous indigenous customs, popular beliefs and superstitions that had crept into many Muslim's daily routine during the centuries of cohabitation with India's other traditions. Although certainly more sympathetic towards the spiritual achievements of the Hindus, he

38. Cf. *MuM*, p. 35.
39. Shāh Ghulām ʿAlī, reports that one day when Mīrzā Jān-i Jānān took his son to his shaikh, a Qādirī master, he (Shāh ʿAbd al-Raḥman Qādirī) happened to be so absorbed by his love for *samā*ʿ that he neglected the punctual performance of the afternoon and evening prayers. The young Mīrzā Jān-i Jānān was reportedly so impressed by this evident negligence of a Muslim's duties that he later told his father that he would never agree to become a disciple of a master of such sinful inclinations. See *MqM*, p. 262, and *MuM*, p. 12. For other anecdotes exemplifying Mīrzā Jān-i Jānān's strict adherence to the *sharīʿat* and the *sunnat*, see ʿAbd al-Razzaq Quraishi (1989), pp. 114-25.

perceived the pure Sunni way represented by the attitudes and practices of the Mujaddidī family (*khāndān*) as the safest way for the members of his own community. Strictly adhering to the examples set by the archetypes of perfect behaviour, Muḥammad, his companions (*ṣaḥāba*) and early followers (*tābi'īn*), he extended his missionary effort to the whole of society, including women, to whom he occasionally even granted initiation into the order.[40]

But in spite of the documented evidence that Mīrzā Jān-i Jānān considered himself in many ways as heir and propagator of the pre-existing Mujaddidī tradition, one can detect in him a somewhat less austere position than that held by Shaikh Ahmad Sirhindī.[41] Given the scarcity of available material, it is extremely difficult to draw any exhaustive conclusion about whether the reasons for this lie more in the changed historical circumstances or rather in a difference of individual attitude and character of the two leaders, or a combination of both.[42] Certainly, it is possible to recognise Mīrzā Jān-i Jānān's role as more cautious and, therefore, less prone to advocate radical changes, both from a spiritual

---

40. See *MuM*, pp. 41-50, S.A.A. Rizvi (1980), pp. 321-3 and Muhammad Umar: 'Mirza Mazhar Jan-i Janan: a religious reformer of the eighteenth century', in *StI* 6 (1969), p. 130.

41. In contrast to many contemporary Sūfī leaders, Mīrzā Jān-i Jānān did not leave any systematic written testimony of his thoughts and teachings regarding specific problems, with the exception of his letters which, as compared those of Shaikh Aḥmad Sirhindī, are, however, very few in number and extremely concise in their content.

42. It would be extremely interesting to compare these two characters while trying to establish whether the nature of Shaikh Aḥmad Sirhindī was a primarily intellectual one inclined towards analytical enquiries as expressed in his numerous treatises and in his newly formulated doctrines, and the more emotional nature of Mīrzā Jān-i Jānān who produced comparatively little theoretical elaborations but who was renowned for his tireless efforts in instructing disciples, a reportedly powerful *tawajjuh* and an emotionally charged poetry reflecting the strength of his spiritual rapture (*jadhba*). Interpreted in this way, these two personalities incorporate the two complementary aspects of *sulūk* and *jadhba* that characterise the Naqshbandī way.

or simply from a social point of view. The way he perceived the distribution of roles in the *pīr-murīdī* relationship, although not his exclusive, and articulates itself in the emphasis on bestowing spiritual attention on the subtle organs (*laṭā'if*, pl. of *laṭīfa*) of his disciples from the very beginning of their spiritual curriculum.[43] And the focus on the subtle heart-organ (*laṭīfa-i qalb*) as the central essence of Man's unperishable suprahuman component reveals an adaption of spiritual guidance restoring it to essentials. The moving away from the highly intellectual speculations of Shaikh Aḥmad Sirhindī towards a more practical oriented approach that stresses a more active participation of the spiritual perceptor towards an increasingly passive though receptive disciple, probably constitutes one of Mīrzā Jān-i Jānān's main contributions towards the revivification and popularity of the order perpetuated among his successors as the *Naqshbandiyya Mujaddidiyya Maẓhariyya* and puts him in tune with the new era the dawn of which he witnessed so clearly around himself.[44]

However, most attention has been given by scholars to the Sūfī Mīrzā Jān-i Jānān for his supposed tolerant and sympathetic attitude towards Hindus and Hinduism in contrast to the alleged hostility of Shaikh Aḥmad Sirhindī. Here again, caution is needed to avoid both overenthusiastic interpretations that favour the promotion of the modern ideal of communal harmony dear to many contemporaries,[45] and

---

43. This is clearly expressed in *MuM*, pp. 40-1, where the author describes his masters' peculiar way of granting initiation.

44. This new definition of the master-disciple relationship assumes an increasing importance in all branches derived from Mīrzā Jān-i Jānān, be it in the Hindu one described in this study, be it in the strictly orthodox Muslim branches in modern India or Pakistan. (Cf. more recent doctrinal treatises like Maulānā Shāh Abūl Ḥasan Zaid Fārūqī's *Manāhij al-Sair wa Madārij al-Khair* or Maulānā Abū Sa'īd's *Hidāyat al-Ṭālibīn*.)

45. See Murshir al-Haqq's article 'Muslim Understanding of Hindu Religion', in *Islam and the Modern Age* 4 (1973), pp. 71-7, and Muhammad Mujeeb's *The Indian Muslims*, p. 281.

the dismissal of any relevant conciliatory element in the thought of this saint towards the problem.[46]

As a matter of fact, one of Mīrzā Jān-i Jānān's few open statements at this regard consists of the already mentioned letter in which the author comments on different aspects of the Hindu tradition.[47] The content of the epistle which replies to an enquiry by an anonymous petitioner regarding the legal status of Hindus from an Islamic point of view, constitutes, technically speaking, a juridic opinion (*istiftā*) and reflects the author's acquaintance with the fundaments of the Hindu *dharma*. As implied in the question, the subtle difference between infidels (*kuffār*) and polytheists (*mushrikīn*) represents an important point in the context of the letter since it refers to two different categories of non-Muslims each being accorded a different legal status. Accordingly, the author, acknowledging the celestial origin of the Veda and the direct derivation of the six fundamental doctrines (*darśana*, lit. 'points of view') which constitute the universal Hindu doctrine from it, reaches to the conclusion that

> . . . all classes of Hindus unanimously agree upon the Unity (*tawḥīd*) of the Most Exalted God (*khudāwand-i ta'ālā*), consider the world to be ephemeral (*ḥādith*) and created (*makhlūq*), contemplate its ultimate dissolution (*fanā*) and believe in the physical resurrection (*ḥashr-i jismānī*) of the body and the reward for good actions as well as punishment for their bad actions. Their custom of worshipping idols

46. Yohanan Friedmann, for instance, after a careful examination of Mīrzā Jān-i Jānān's position in his article 'Muslim Views of Indian Religions' in *JAOS* 95 (1975), pp. 117-26, comes to the conclusion that 'the views of Jān-i Jānān . . . really constitute, . . . , a relapse into conventional mediaeval attitudes if compared with the thought of such thinkers as al-Birūnī and Dārā Shūkoh.' (p. 121).

47. *Kalimāt-i Ṭayyibāt*, letter no. 14, pp. 25-37, quoted in Khaliq Anjum (1989), pp. 131-4.

> (*but-parastī*) is not based on the attribution of a Divine rank on these, but its truth is somewhat different. . . .[48]

Through this unequivocal statement, Mīrzā Jān-i Jānān attributes a fundamentally different position to Hindus as compared to the polytheists of ancient Arabia and, thus, discharges the former from the commonly pronounced accusation of polytheism. If this statement represents, in a sense, the reiteration of a concept already anticipated by al-Bīrūnī in the eleventh century AD, the Naqshbandī shaikh seven centuries later assumes a more radical point of view. Recognising the Divine origin of the Veda and the direct relationship the orthodox Hindu doctrines bear with it he goes a step further than his illustrious ideological ancestor by affirming that essentially all Hindus keep in view the fundamental unity and unicity of the transcendant Principle that underlies all apparent diversity and in front of which all earthly creatures are ultimately relative and contingent.

Though Mīrzā Jān-i Jānān carefully refrains from any possibly compromising statement regarding the position of Hindus from a spiritual point of view, he further elaborates on his concept of truth behind their alleged idol-worship in a subsequent passage of the same letter:

---

48. Cf. letter no. 14 in Khaliq Anjum (1989), p. 132. There are numerous English versions of this letter. I have, however, preferred to propose my own translation of that letter in view of its importance in the context of Mīrzā Jān-i Jānān's thought regarding the topic. Moreover, the last sentence quoted is missing in the original version given in the *Maqāmāt-i Maẓharī*, and consequently all those authors who have based their translations exclusively on that version (Abdul Wali (1923) and S.A.A. Rizvi (1980)) have equally left out that part. The version cited in the *Bashārāt-i Maẓhariyya* found in the India Office Library in London (Or. 220) includes this sentence and is reported by Friedmann (p. 218) in his above-mentioned article as well as in the Urdu translation presented by Khaliq Anjum (p. 132) who based himself on a manuscript of these letters in possession of the Maulana Azad Library of the AMU, a supposed part of an older manuscript version of the *Maqāmāt-i Maẓharī*.

> . . . the inherent truth (*ḥaqīqat*) of their idol-worship is [their belief] that there are certain angelic beings (*malā'ika*) who, following the Divine decree, can divert their powers towards this created and corrupt world (*'ālam-i kawn wa farad*). These include the spirits of perfect beings (*arwāḥ-i kāmilān*) who, after the relinquishment of the relation with their physical frame, continue to exercise their influence in this contingent universe (*kā'ināt*). There are other living beings who, in [the Hindus'] opinion, are endowed with eternal life (*zinda-yi jāvīd*) similar to *Ḥaḍrat Khiḍr* — peace be upon him! —. Having carved idol-statues of these, they focus their spiritual intention on them, through which, after a while, they develop an intimate relationship (*rābiṭa*) with the inherent power of that outer representation (*ṣāḥib-i ān ṣūrat*); on the base of this special relationship they are able to satisfy their needs related to this world and the hereafter (*ḥawā'ij-i ma'āshī wa ma'ādī*).[49]

In this passage, the author's acquaintance with the intellectual perceptions at the base of the Hindu way of worshipping becomes sufficiently clear and confirms his universalistic vision of the world which goes far beyond that of most Hindus and Muslims who fall short of penetrating the outer appearances. It betrays Mīrzā Jān-i Jānān's metaphysical perspective that comprehends the essential aspects underlying the Hindu doctrines and indicates his capacity to reconcile the inner values of both traditions behind their sharply contrasting religious, ritual and social attitudes. He, thus continues his letter:

> This practice resembles closely to the technique of *rābiṭa*, a method commonly used by the Sufis, which consists of concentrating interiorly on the figure of the shaikh thus obtaining the effluence of spiritual

49. Cf. *Kalimāt-i Tayyibāt*, letter no. 14, and also Maulavī Abdul Wali: 'Hinduism according to Muslim Sufis', in *Journal of the Royal Asiatic Society* 19 (1923), p. 248.

> grace irradiating (*faiḍ*) from him. The only difference [between this method and the way of worship common among Hindus] being that [the Sufis] do not build any exterior image of their shaikh. . . .[50]

Thus, from the esoteric perspective the difference between exoteric Islam and Hinduism results further reduced and narrows the distance between the two great traditions to little more than a formal divergency.[51] Not even the act of prostration (*sijda, ḍanḍavat*) in front of these 'exterior representations' of suprahuman powers practised by Hindus induces Mīrzā Jān-i Jānān to label them as polytheists since, he underlines,

> . . . this custom must be interpreted as a kind of respectful salutation rather than as an act of worship, identical to that made to elders in the place of greeting.[52]

But however contingent the difference in Mīrzā Jān-i Jānān's explanation may appear from an esoteric point of view, there remains a fundamental issue in the Islamic dogma that cannot be ignored by an authority of the *Naqshbandiyya Mujaddidiyya*. After reiterating in similar if smoother terms Shaikh Aḥmad Sirhindī's idea which admits for the fact that in accordance to some Qur'ānic verses (9:48, 11:78, 35:24) great and perfect prophets were sent also to such countries

50. Abdul Wali (1923), p. 248.

51. The method of *taṣawwur-i shaikh* or inner visualisation of the spiritual preceptor which has assumed a particular importance in the history of the *ṭarīqa*, has provoked some harsh criticism from the exoteric milieu which considers it irreconcilable with the orthodox perceptions of the Islamic law.

52. If this reflects Mīrzā Jān-i Jānān's real position towards the question of respectful prostration, its legitimacy remains, however, confined to Hindus alone while it is still considered unlawful for Muslims. In fact, a well-known anecdote in the Mujaddidī hagiography tells us that Shaikh Aḥmad Sirhindī refused to prostrate himself in front of the emperor Jahāngīr and protested vehemently against this un-Islamic custom at the Mogul Court. For an interesting controversy regarding this topic, see *MnS*, pp. 47-9.

as India whose mention can be found in the Vedas, Mīrzā Jān-i Jānān concludes:

> . . . after the advent of our messenger (*ẓuhūr-i paighambar-i mā*) who was the final seal of all legislators (*khātim al-mursalīn*), whose Law has abolished the laws of all easts and wests until the end of this world, he is now to be obeyed and followed by everyone. Therefore, from the advent of the prophet till the present day (1180/1766), whosoever does not follow the tenets of the true faith delivered by him (*mu'taqid*) is an unbeliever (*kāfir*).[53]

This passage sets the limit that separates the rightful believer from the infidel in the conventional terms crossing which would be equivalent to depriving Islam of one of its most fundamental pillars. Hence, notwithstanding some surprising concessions to a non-Islamic tradition, Mīrzā Jān-i Jānān remains faithful to the orthodox line adopted by his famous predecessor at least in dialectic terms. On the other hand, Mīrzā Jān-i Jānān's position must be considered the closest an orthodox Muslim can come towards the recognition of another religious tradition without causing irritation among the orthodox exoterists. The difference with Shaikh Aḥmad Sirhindī lies hence, less in a new position *vis-à-vis* Hindus than in a more explicit elaboration of some particular doctrinal points which testify Mīrzā Jān-i Jānān's partial interest in some aspects pertaining to their holy scriptures. A great number of them had been translated into either Arabic or Persian by that time and were easily available. It is also possible that Mīrzā Jān-i Jānān received additional oral information from his Hindu followers or other authorities.

Maulawī Na'īm Allāh Bahrāichī reports another interesting anecdote providing further evidence for Mīrzā Jān-i Jānān's acquaintance with some aspects of the Hindu doctrine. In the course of a discussion held in the presence of Ḥājī Muḥammad Afḍal, Mīrzā Jān-i Jānān's teacher,

53. *MnS*, p. 133.

someone present in the *ḥalqa* told about a dream he had of a desert engulfed by an immense fire. Inside the fire appeared Kṛṣṇa while at the edge of it stood Rāmacandra. Those present interpreted this dream as symbolising the fire of hell but Mīrzā Jān-i Jānān argued for a different, more sophisticated interpretation. In his opinion, it would be illicit to refer to the ancient sages of India as infidels in the absence of any concrete scriptural basis; indeed, the Qur'ānic verse that sanctions that to every country there has been sent a warner, makes it likely that also the country of the Hindu and had witnessed the dispatch of a Divine messenger (*bashīrī*) or prophet (*nazīrī*) holding the rank of a *walī* or *nabī*. Rāmacandra, who was born at the beginning of the creation of subtle beings (*jinn*), at a time when people were endowed with longevity (*'umrhā-yi darāz*) and extraordinary powers (*quwwathā-yi bisyār*),[54] was able to lead the people of his time on the 'way of *sulūk*' ' (*nisbat-i sulūk*). However, Kṛṣṇa, who in the Hindu holy texts is mentioned among the last in the series of these outstanding personalities, appeared at a time when the life-span and the inherent spiritual powers of humanity had notably diminished. Consequently, argues Mīrzā Jān-i Jānān, Kṛṣṇa instructed his contemporaries in the 'way of Divine attraction' (*nisbat-i jadhbī*), in tune with their nature and temper. The frequent indulgence of this prophet in both vocal and instrumental music (*ghinā wa samā'*) must be considered as a proof for Kṛṣṇa's adherence to the way of Divine attraction.

In the context of the dream, Mīrzā Jān-i Jānān interprets the fire in the desert as an allegory for the heat of passionate love (*'ishq-o muḥabbat*). Hence, Kṛṣṇa, associated with love from which the state of spiritual rapture arises, appeared inside the fire while Rāmacandra, associated with the cool tempered way characterised by inner perception and austerity, appeared at the margin of the fire. According to Mīrzā Jān-i Jānān's biographers, Ḥājī Muhammad Afḍal was

54. *MnS*, p.133.

extremely pleased with the interpretation (*ta'bīr*) of his favourite disciple.[55]

Although this story has frequently been quoted by scholars concerned with the figure of Mīrzā Jān-i Jānān, the importance attributed to it has remained restricted to the implicit recognition of Rāma and Kṛṣṇa as prototypes of Indian prophets prior to the advent of the prophet of Islam. Even if Mīrzā Jān-i Jānān repeatedly insists upon the necessity of silence in this regard, the idea of his quiet approval appears plausible in consideration of the above-mentioned interpretation. However, the signifi-cance it contains shows other important elements, especially in view of the subsequent developments in the *ṭarīqa* that developed from him. The most striking element consists perhaps in Mīrzā Jān-i Jānān's assimilation of Rāma and Kṛṣṇa to different moments in the history of humanity. Such a statement requires some awareness of the place these two Divine messengers hold in Hindu mythology. It presupposes moreover a certain familiarity with the closely connected theory of the *avataraṇa*, that contemplates the ten terrestial descents (*daśāvatāra*) of the Hindu god Viṣṇu sent to mankind in order to re-establish the cosmic equilibrium put in danger by the rise of power of the *asuras* that represent the power of darkness and ignorance. This is then closely related to the traditional cyclical conception of time within the present *manvantara* or human cycle, complemented by the theory of *caturyuga*, the four major cosmic eras that sanction the history of the Universe, at which Mīrzā Jān-i Jānān briefly hints in his letter.[56]

---

55. Cf. Shāh Na'īm Allāh Bahrāichī: *Bashārāt-i Maẓhariyya dar faḍā'il-i Ḥaḍrāt-i ṭarīqa-i Mujaddidiyya*, OICL, Ms. Bm. Or. 220, folio 43a-43 b, and also Abdul Wali (1923), Appendix B, pp. 248-9.

56. There is general if not unanimous agreement that Rāmacandra, the semi-historical son of king Daśaratha of Ayodhyā and hero of the Hindu epic *Rāmāyaṇa* by Vālmikī, is considered as the seventh descent of Viṣṇu. He accomplished his mission in a period corresponding to the third of the four cosmic ages or *yugas*, while Kṛṣṇa, eighth in the series of ten *avatāras*, is supposed to have sanctioned the beginning of the actual *kali-yuga* which marks the final and most unstable of the four periods. It would be extremely →

In addition to this, Mīrzā Jān-i Jānān's interpretation of the dream associates Rāmacandra with the 'way of *sulūk*' and Kṛṣṇa with the 'way of *jadhba*'. Both conceptions are closely interconnected elements of the Naqshbandī methodology and related to the idea that occasionally the *ṭarīqa* needs to be adapted to the particular requirements of each period in order to facilitate the access to the Divine mysteries to a larger number of contemporary individuals. According to the orders authorities, this is achieved by anticipating at the very beginning of the spiritual journey what in other initiatic orders can be reached only at the end of it.[57]

The Naqshbandī tradition claims that it was through the intervention of *al-Khiḍr*, the anonymous guide of Moses mentioned in the *Qur'ān*,[58] that many of the order's leading authorities have received spiritual guidance and inspiration for the introduction of new methods. Among these, the gradual shift towards the *jadhbī* element becomes

→ interesting at this regard to analyse the content of the *Yoga-Vāśiṣṭha*, included as part of the *Rāmāyaṇa*, with that of the *Bhagavad Gītā*, part of the second of the great epics of Hinduism, the *Mahābhārata*.

57. These two complementary stages correspond to the active and passive aspects assumed by the disciple during his inner journey (*sair al-bāṭinī*), in this case either considered as *sālik* (he who crosses the spiritual path, *sulūk*, gradually as a traveller, from *maqām* to *maqām*, through his own efforts or *mujāhadat*) or as *majdhūb*, a term which in the technical context of the Naqshbandī doctrine assumes the meaning of 'he who is attracted by the grace of God or of his shaikh towards the Goal'.

58. Cf. *Qur.* 18:60-82. This enigmatic figure is often included among the four immortal prophets, along with Enoch (Idrīs), Elias (Ilyās) and Jesus ('Isā). For these, see A. Schimmel: *Mystical Dimensions of Islam* (1976), p. 202.

Al-Khiḍr is said to have quenched his thirst at the 'spring of eternal life' (*chashma-i āb-i ḥayāt*) and possesses particular prophetic qualities related to a special kind of knowledge. For him, see Irfan Omar: 'Khidr in the Islamic Tradition', in *MW* 83 (1993), pp. 279-91.

increasingly important with the progression of time.[59] Mīrzā Jān-i Jānān's letter associates *al-Khiḍr* with the subtle power coagulated in the Hindu idol-statues.

Although these are little more than veiled hints (*ishārā*) and as such must command caution in interpreting them, they betray the degree of Mīrzā Jān-i Jānān's insight into some peculiar aspects of the Hindu doctrine suggesting not only his interest in these subjects but perhaps also the perception or his side of a subtle link established between the two esoteric traditions involved. Since the episode is said to have taken place during the lifetime of Mīrzā Jān-i Jānān's spiritual director Ḥājī Muḥammad Afḍal (*d.* 1146/1733), it results that Mīrzā Jān-i Jānān's acquaintance with these Hindu matters predates his completion of the Naqshbandī path, and it is possible that he had by that time already come into contact with some members pertaining to the *sant*-environment living in and around Delhi. He may have indeed acquired most of these notions during or shortly after the death of his first shaikh, Sayyid Nūr Muḥammad Badāyūnī, a period for which very little information is available. While the absence of concrete evidence must dictate caution, it is indicative that among Mīrzā Jān-i Jānān's Hindu descendants at Kanpur, most of whom pertain to a Vaiṣṇava devotional tradition, Rāmacandra and Kr̥ṣṇa occupy the rank of highly revered divinities, placing them in line with the *sant* tradition.

Interestingly, such a concilatory position is not seen as implying a radical departure from previous Mujaddidī positions in the eyes of later authorities in the order. This appears clearly from a comment made by the contemporary head of Delhi main Naqshbandī *khānaqāh*, Shāh Abūl Ḥasan

---

59. The best known of these is probably Khwāja 'Abd al-Khāliq al-Gujdawānī (*d.* 606/1220) who is said to have been revealed the method of silent recollection (*dhikr-i khafī*) by *al-Khiḍr*. For details, see 'Abd al-Rahman Jāmī's *Nafaḥāt al-Uns*, Marijan Molé's article 'Autour du Daré Mansour: l'apperentissage mystique de Baha' al-Din Naqshband', in *Révue des études islamiques* 27 (1959), pp. 35-66, and Stéphane Ruspoli (1990), pp. 98-107.

Zaid Fārūqī Mujaddidī (1324/1906-1412/1993). In one of his numerous writings, he mentions his meeting with a group of Hindus who had come to visit the tomb of Mīrzā Jān-i Jānān seeking to derive spiritual benefit from it through contemplation (*murāqaba*). Recalling Shaikh Aḥmad Sirhindī's alleged hostility towards Hindus, this venerable Sūfī saint and orthodox heir of his spiritual line observes:

> If the revered *Mujaddid* had felt an absolute aversion (*nafrat*) towards all Hindus, he would have certainly left instructions to his successors and descendants at this regard, who in their turn would have acted accordingly. Neither has he left such instructions nor did those respected ones act in such a way. . . .[60]

The author then describes in some detail the encounter with those Hindus and concludes with two sentences from Shaikh Aḥmad Sirhindī's *Maktūbāt* which read:

> The second group has to be concerned with love, and for some reason they are loved. . . .[61]

And further:

> . . . it is possible that the inner truths of the infidels might in a certain way have partaken of the beloved-ness which may be the cause of the attain ment of Divine attraction of theirs. . . .[62]

In the eyes of this contemporary Naqshbandī saint, Mīrzā Jān-i

---

60. Cf. Shāh Abūl Ḥasan Zaid Fārūqī: *Ḥaḍrat Mujaddid aur unke nāqadīn* (1977), p. 223. See also Marc Gaborieau's article covering a detailed recension of this book: 'Les protéstations d'un soufi indien contemporain. . . .', in Varia Turcica: *Naqshbandis*, pp. 237-67. It is noteworthy that the Pakistani translator of the book by Shāh Abūl Ḥasan, Miyan Mir, has left out the entire passage in his English version. Hence, the quoted opinion acquires even more importance in this context, since it is by no means possible to attribute any secular tendencies to our Sūfī author who, at the contrary, does not hide his critical position towards these modern interpretations.
61. *Mak.* III:100.
62. *Mak.* III:121, quoted by Shāh Abūl Ḥasan, *op. cit.*, p. 223.

Jānān's attitude is therefore perceived from a perspective of continuity. Concluding in this line of thought, he finally asks:

> . . . and why than should have those who go back to [his teachings] (*mutawassilīn*) have conferred spiritual initiation on Hindus?[63]

The author thus makes the point that if the authorities in Mīrzā Jān-i Jānān's line themselves did and do not perceive any contra-diction in this tolerant attitude towards Hindus with the traditional principles of the *ṭarīqa*, why should it be a inferred by others from outside?

On the other hand, there are numerous examples of seventeenth and eighteenth century Chishtī shaikhs, including Shāh 'Abd al-Raḥman Chishtī (*d.* 1095/1683),[64] Shāh Kalīm Allāh Shāhjahānābādī (1060/1650-1142/1729)[65] and Shāh Fakhr al-Dīn Dihlawī (1126/1714-1200/1784),[66] who have shown a certain readiness for similar kinds of inter-communal consi-derations. But while the *Chishtiyya* is generally credited with a 'tolerant, open-minded and deep-rooted' attitude of tolerance advocating a peaceful co-existence with Hindus,[67] and prone to promote communal harmony without incurring into strong criticism from the orthodox, the Naqshbandiyya is generally associated with a rigidly orthodox Sunni interpretation of Islam that does not allow for any concessions towards other communities, let alone with Hindus.

According to Yohanan Friedmann, who echoes in modern

---

63. *Ibidem*, p. 223.

64. For details on this figure, see Roderic Vassie: " 'Abd al-Rahman Chishti and the *Bhagavad Gītā*: 'unity of religion' theory in practice" in *The Legacy of Mediaeval Persian Sūfism* (1992), pp. 367-77.

65. For him, see S.A.A. Rizvi (1980), pp. 358-70, and Muhammad Umar (1993), pp. 54-66.

66. For him, see Muhammad Umar (1993), pp. 66-70.

67. See S.A.A. Rizvi (1980), p. 358, K.A. Nizami's *Some Aspects of Religion and Politics during the thirteenth century* (1961), and also Muhammad Habib: 'Shaikh Naṣīr al-Dīn Chirāgh Dehlawī' (1950).

scholarly terms the opinion of the traditional shaikh at Delhi, this image became dominant only in more recent times and culminated with the appropriation and projection Shaikh Aḥmad Sirhindī and his teachings as the ideological forerunner of the two nation/seperate Muslim homeland theory in the first decades of the present century. As such, it remains the prevailing tenet among many contemporary scholars who variously interpret this alleged position according to their own point of view.

That tolerance towards non-Muslims from above did not necessarily imply a departure from orthodox Sunni positions is amply demonstrated by Mīrzā Jān-i Jānān and many of his contemporary Sūfī authorities, who in other occasions took a decisively unfavourable stand towards Muslim adoption of Hindu rituals and customs.[68] It is a rather interesting characteristic of the eighteenth century that if from an esoteric perspective we find a number of outstanding figures ready to narrow the gap between Muslims and non-Muslims, on the other side the exoteric antagonism between Sunnis and Shī'as kept growing and was fomented by those same authorities that pronounced themselves in favour of more elasticity towards Hindus. The declared aversion of Shaikh Aḥmad Sirhindī towards Shī'as impressively documented in his small but influential treatise titled *Radd-i Rawāfiḍ*,[69] anticipates the views of his heir and successor Mīrzā Jān-i Jānān, but also of the Chishtī shaikh Shāh Kalīm Allāh Shāhjahānābādī, himself the author of a treatise bearing the same title, who pronounced himself openly against granting initiation to Shī'as.[70] Most plausibly, this

68. Cf., for instance, the *waṣiyatnāma* of Shāh Walī Allāh, and also *MuM*, pp. 41-4.

69. The term *rawāfiḍ*, lit. 'deserters', was applied to the Shi'as because of their alleged desertation of the son of 'Alī ibn Ḥusain, Zaid, when he reproached them for their speaking against the Companions of the Prophet (*ṣaḥāba*). The use of this term by the shaikh, thus, reflects the ongoing dispute between the two largest factions in Islam. The Urdu version of this treatise has been published under the title *Risāla dar kawā'if-i Shī'a*, ed. by Ghulam Mustafa Khan, Rampur, 1388/1965.

attitude can be explained by rapidly growing influence of Shī'a culture in India under the successors of Aurangzeb. Originally dating back to the times of Akbar and Jehāngīr,[71] it received a further boost from the openly declared inclination of those Moguls like Muḥammad Shāh (*r*. 1718-44) and Aḥmad Shāh (*r*. 1748-54) towards Shī'a doctrines and customs and led to the emergence of an influential Shī'a political class headed by leaders like Safdar Jang and Mīrzā Najaf Khān, who notably reduced the power of the Sunni Turrānī party both at the centre and in the provinces. The Rohillā war in 1748 which opposed many influential Sunni nobles like Intizām al-Daulat and 'Imād al-Mulk[72] who supporting the Rohillā faction, to the alliance of Safdar Jang and the Marāṭhā leader Sūraj Mal,[73] certainly contributed to create an atmosphere of tension between the members of these two religious groups which reached all the way down to the popular level.

It is against this socio-political background that the position of many of Delhi's Sūfī leaders must be understood, even more so as the established Sūfī orders, though far from

---

70. See S.A.A. Rizvi (1980), pp. 369-70, who quotes the *Maktūbāt-i Kalīmī*, Delhi, 1315/1897-8, compiled by Maulawī Muḥammad Kalīmī, pp. 13 and 76.

71. While the former began to encourage the recruitment of great a number of Irani officials for imperial service, it was the latter who, through his marriage with the daughter of his Iranian treasurer Ghiyāth Begh, Miḥr al-Nisā in AD 1611, sanctioned the beginning of a period of increasing influence of Iranian Shī'as at the Mogul Court and on its politics.

72. Significantly, both officials at the Mogul Court were devoted disciples of Mīrzā Jān-i Jānān, as emerges from a number of letters the latter had written to them urging them to remain faithful to the respect towards *darwishes* and *faqīrs*. See, Mīrzā Jān-i Jānān's letters no. 60-5.

73. Cf. Richard B. Barnett: *North India between empires: Awadh, The Mughals and the British 1720-1801* (1980).

denying a honorific rank to 'Alī ibn Abū Ṭālib[74] and his two sons Ḥasan and Ḥusain, attributed a supreme importance and veneration to the prophet of Islam and his Companions.[75] Significantly, in one of his letters, Mīrzā Jān-i Jānān, in line with his conciliatory attitude regarding many fundamental issues, while answering the question about what to think regarding the controversies between Shī'as and Sunnis pertaining to the Companions (*ṣaḥāba*) and members of the Prophet's family (*ahl-i bait*), carefully avoids open controversy and limits himself to affirming that this does not figure among the essentials of orthodox Islam. Although he later confirms the fault of the Shī'as (referred to as *nufus-i khabthiya*, lit. the 'corrupted souls') in denying the outstanding role of the Companions and family members in the prophetic mission, his attempt to maintain moderation indicates the delicacy of the topic in an environment loaded with social tension and of prevailing anarchy.[76] Nevertheless, the caution of Mīrzā Jān-i Jānān cannot obscure the fact that his personal convictions were determined by a strong anti-Shī'a feeling arising out of his strict adherence to the Sunna and hostility to the infiltration Shī'a customs imported from Iran.

In later years, Mīrzā Jān-i Jānān repeatedly hints in his letters at his worsening health and the growing difficulties encountered in pursuing his activities in Delhi. In 1183/1769 he, decides to migrate to Rohilkhanḍ, traditional stronghold of the *Mujaddidiyya* and its Afghan allies. But disappointed by the lack of response encountered to his efforts, he remained

74. It is sufficient to remember that in most Sūfī genealogies 'Alī is considered as the immediately successive link after Muḥammad. This testifies the enormous importance attributed to him in the spiritual hierarchy and in the spiritual genealogies of the Sūfī orders. Mīrzā Jān-i Jānān himself traces his ancestry back to the fourth caliph of Islam.

75. Cf. Khaliq Anjum (1989), letter no. 20, pp. 149-51 for Mīrzā Jān-i Jānān's stress on the necessity to follow the example of the Companions of the Prophet.

76. Khaliq Anjum (1989), letter no. 18, pp. 145-6.

attached to the city where he had spent most of his life and to which he remained emotionally related through the presence of his family and intimate friends (*'azīzān wa aqārib*).[77] He spent the last years of his life in seclusion in his *khānaqāh* at Delhi, focusing his attention on the instruction of a restricted number of disciples.

His health steadily deteriorated, as results from a letter addressed to Mīr Muḥammad Mu'īn Khān, one of his disciples at Panipat, in which he remarks:

> . . . my weakness has become such that I am constrained to impart my teachings while lying down; though no pleasure is left in my life, the life of a Sūfī is a God-sent blessing (*ghanīmat*), both for myself and for others. . . .[78]

Elsewhere he asks his disciples not to expect any more replies to their letters being too weak to write and even to reach the nearby Jama Masjid for the Friday prayer.[79]

During the month of Muḥarram 1195/1780, a group of Shī'a mourners carrying some *ta'ziya* icons in procession through the streets of Delhi, happened to pass by Mīrzā Jān-i Jānān's *khānaqāh*.[80] Consistent with his temper, Mīrzā reportedly made some sarcastic remarks to his followers criticising this Shī'a custom as a 'vain action of heresy and unlawful innovation'. These words reached the ears of some members of the procession and soon a wave of outrage swept through their *imāmbārā*s and *maḥfil*s.[81]

In the night of 7 Muḥarram 1195/January 1781, three men appeared at Mīrzā Jān-i Jānān's residence pretending

---

77. Letter no. 54, p. 204.
78. Letter no. 56, p. 207.
79. Letters no. 31 (p. 175), no. 35 (p. 181) and no. 51 (p. 201).
80. For a description of other Sūfī authorities regarding the growing popularity of *ta'ziya* processions during Muḥarram, see Shāh 'Abd al-'Azīz's *Sirr Al-shahādatain* and his *Tuḥfat-i ithnā'-i 'Ashariyya*.
81. *MuM*, Part II, pp. 37-8.

to have come to pay homage to the renowned shaikh. When they came before him, one took out a pistol and shot him in his breast. All three managed to escape without being recognised, and though none of them was ever arrested, there is little doubt that the men belonged to an extremist Shī'a faction which had vowed to revenge the shaikh's offensive remarks.[82]

Although seriously wounded, Mīrzā Jān-i Jānān remained alive for another three days during which he reportedly declined any medical treatment from a European (*firangī*) doctor offered to him by the emperor Shāh-i 'Ālam II (*r*. 1759-1802) and asked for his aggressors not to be prosecuted since he himself had forgiven them.

On the evening of the 10 Muḥarram1195/6 January 1781, Mīrzā Jān-i Jānān eventually succumbed to his injuries and was buried a few days later in the precincts of a mansion situated in the Chitli Qabar Bazar acquired shortly before by his wife.[83]That site was to become the place where his disciples under the guide of Mīrzā's official successor, Shāh Ghulām 'Alī Dihlawī (1156/1749-1240/1824), established the new *khānaqāh* of the *Naqshbandiyya Mujaddidiyya*

---

82. The only reliable source that seriously questions the religious identity of the attackers is Muḥammad Ḥusain Āzād's *Āb-i Ḥayāt* (pp. 144-5), but apart from his *tadhkira* styled biography written about one century after the actual event had taken place, it seems too obvious that his intention as a Shī'a is to discharge the blame for this action from the Shī'a community. Moreover, as Quraishi has shown, Āzād's version is mainly based on a distorted interpretation of a passage from Qudrat Allāh Qāsim's *Majmū-i Naghz* (*op. cit*., p. 75). Even Rizvi, himself a Shī'a and certainly not suspectable of great sympathies for the leaders of the Naqshbandiyya, admits: '. . . he was certainly a Shī'a fanatic from Iran', in *op. cit*. (1980), p. 341.

83. In his *waṣiyatnāma* Mīrzā Jān-i Jānān expressed the desire that his burial should be accomplished according to the Sunna of the Prophet in every smallest detail. He also showed himself disgusted for the *hawelī* acquired by his wife vividly requesting his family members not to be buried there. This testament was handed over to his *khalīfa* Shāh Na'īm Allāh Bahrāichī who took over the responsibility of supervising the construction of his master's *maqbara*. For further details, see *MqM*, pp. 157-9.

Maẓhariyya which exists until the present day at the same location under the name of *Dargāh-i Shāh Abūl Khair*.

Shāh Na'īm Allāh Bahrāichī (1153/1740-1218/1803)

The death of Mīrzā Maẓhar Jān-i Jānān left a void in the leader-ship of the *Naqshbandiyya* in Delhi at a time of increasing crisis and instability in the city's political and cultural environments. Although he had been largely successful in building up a network of deputies elsewhere,[84] the staunch Sunni Mīrzā Jān-i Jānān apparently had made no arrangement for his succession at his headquarter in Delhi.[85]

Apart from Mīrzā Jān-i Jānān's biographers Shāh Ghulām 'Alī Dihlawī and Shāh Na'īm Allāh Bahrāichī, two other disciples are noteworthy among his main successors: Qāḍī Thanā Allāh Pānīpatī (1138/1725-1225/1810), a prominent scholar of *fiqh* and *ḥadīth* who had studied with Shāh Walī Allāh Muḥadīth Dihlawī before undertaking the spiritual path first under guidance of Sayyid Muḥammad 'Ābid Sunāmī and later with Mīrzā Jān-i Jānān. After completing his spiritual education at the age of 18, he returned to his native town of Panipat while maintaining close contacts with his spiritual perceptor. Qāḍī Thanā Allāh Pānipatī was among Mīrzā Jān-i Jānān's most intimate and estimated disciples and was appreciated for his virtuous character and extensive knowledge. Mīrzā Jān-i Jānān himself repeatedly went to stay with him at Panipat and

84. Shāh Ghulām 'Alī reports that the number of Mīrzā Jān-i Jānān's *khulafā'* was uncountable, impossible to mention all of them. *MqM* p. 388.

    Nevertheless the author gives an extensive account of 45 *khulafā*, introducing each of them with a short biographical note (*op. cit.*, p. 394-473). Muhammad Umar lists 76 *khulafā'* cf. (1993), pp. 81-3.

85. This uncharacteristic negligence might be attributed to his ideal of following the ways and customs of the Prophet in every detail, as Sunnis believe that the Prophet did not clearly appoint any of the members of his community as his successor.

later entrusted him the care for his wife and insane son after his death.[86]

Another of Mīrzā Jān-i Jānān's eminent *khulafā'* was Maulawī Ghulām Yāḥyā 'Aẓīmābādī (*d.* 1186/1772), native of a small place close to modern Patna who spent most of his time at Lucknow. Initially admitted into the Qādiriyya by a descendant of Shāh Pīr Muḥammad Lakhnawī (*d.* 1085/1674), he started his discipleship in the *Naqshbandiyya* through Mīrzā Maẓhar, and after obtaining *khilāfat* and *ijāzat* returned to Lucknow to propagate his master's teachings.[87]

Apparently, a dispute arose in the aftermath of Mīrzā Jān-i Jānān's death between two of his other main successors, Shāh Ghulām 'Alī Batālwī and Shāh Na'īm Allāh Bahrāichī, which eventually saw the former prevailing.[88] Shāh Ghulām 'Alī, the author of the *Maqāmāt-i Maẓharī*, was born in 1158/1745 in the Punjabi town of Batala. He arrived at Delhi as a child accompanied by his father who sought an adequate education for his eldest son. After studying *ḥadīth* with Shāh 'Abd al-'Azīz, in 1180/1767 he enrolled as a disciple of Mīrzā Jān-i Jānān with whom he remained for the remaining period of latter's life. According to the sources, the Shāh Ghulām Alī contributed notably to the establishment and widely diffused the reputation of the Delhi *khānaqāh* attracting scholars from all over the country his fame reaching far beyond India. After his death in 1240/1824 he was buried

86. *MqM*, pp. 390-3, S.A.A. Rizvi (1980), pp. 558-73, 'Abd al-Razzaq Quraishi (1989), pp. 87-9.

87. A prolific author of religious works, his most famous treatise is the *Risālat-i Kalimāt-i Ḥaqq*, apparently written at the instance of Mīrzā Jān-i Jānān, which deals extensively with the problem of the *waḥdat al-wujūd* vs. *waḥdat al-shuhūd*, in which he strongly defends the doctrine of Shaikh Aḥmad Sirhindī.

88. Fusfeld mentions the existence of a manuscript written by Na'īm Allāh Bahrāichī and commented upon by Shāh Ghulām' Alī whose content reflects the uneasy feelings between these two leaders. This manuscript is in possession of Prof. Nizami, ex-professor in the History Department of the AMU. See Fusfeld (1981), p. 153.

next to his shaikh in the very *khānaqāh* over which he had presided for almost half a century and which under his leadership had become centre of esoteric teaching known throughout the Islamic world.[89] While Shāh Ghulām 'Alī took upon himself the task of establishing a permanent basis for the *silsila* at Delhi, it was the concern of Maulawī Shāh Na'īm Allāh Bahrāichī to guarantee for the continuity and diffusion of the *ṭarīqa* in Awadh.[90]

Sayyid Maulawī Shāh Na'īm Allāh Bahrāichī was born in 1153/1740 in the small provincial headquarter of Bahraich[91] in a family that claims descent from the caliph 'Alī through Ghāzī Salār Ma'sūd that gained them the title

89. One of his prominent disciples and deputies was the Kurdish shaikh Maulānā Khālid al-Kurdī (1193/1776-1242/1827) who introduced the *Mujaddidiyya* in the regions of the Ottoman empire where it gained wide acceptance and importance under the name of *Khālidiyya*. He spent a year from 1810-11 at the Delhi *khānaqāh* headed by Shāh Ghulām 'Alī before returning to his native town of Sulaymaniya and later proceeding to Baghdad and Damascus where he lies buried. For his role as spiritual guide and his influence on the rise of Kurdish nationalism, see Joyce Blari's, Butrus Abu Maneh's and Martin van Bruinessen's articles in Varia Turcica: *Naqshbandis*, pp. 289-370.

90. It is important to point out that notwithstanding the presence at Delhi of other outstanding personalities linked to the *Mujaddidiyya*, like Shāh Walī Allāh and his sons Shāh 'Abd al-'Azīz (1721-1823) and Shāh Rafi' al Din (*b.* 1749) as well as Khwāja Muḥammad Naṣīr and his son Khwāja Mīr Dard (1721-85), the founders of the *ṭarīqa-i muḥammadiyya*, it was the genealogic line Mīrzā Maẓhar inherited through Shāh Nūr Muḥammad Badāyūnī which was considered the *silsila*'s most authentic line of descent. This link was further enhanced by Mīrzā's relation with other Naqshbandī shaikhs, all of whom descended directly from one of the Mujaddid's sons.

91. This small centre close to the Nepali border is mainly known for the tomb and *dargāh* of Ghāzī Sālār Ma'sūd (*b.* 405/1015), nephew and commander-in-chief of Maḥmūd Ghaznawī's army who is locally venerated for his miraculous deeds by both Hindus and Muslims. His *dargāh* is the centre of a big annual fair when thousands of devotees of both communities gather around his tomb. For more details, see Christian Troll: *Muslim shrines in India: their character, history and significance* (1989), pp. 24-33.

of *mulk* from later Islamic rulers. His father, Ghulām Quṭb al-Dīn 'Ārif Kāke reportedly was a locally renowned *zamīndār* of high rank (*ra'īs*).[92] For his traditional education, Na'īm Allāh was at first entrusted to Muḥammad Roshan Bahrāichī with whom he remained until 1171/1757. During that year his father took him to Lucknow, the capital of Awadh and emerging centre of learning during the time of the Nawābs between the eighteenth and nineteenth centuries, where he received training from various religious authorities such as Maulawī Khalīl.[93]

In 1186/1772, shortly after completing his religious curriculum, he met Muḥammad Jamīl, one of Mīrzā Jān-i Jānān's *khulafā'* at Lucknow. On the insistence of Na'īm Allāh, he initiated him into the *ṭarīqa* providing him with the first elements of spiritual guidance.[94]The desire to meet Mīrzā Jān-i Jānān induced him in 1189/1775 to seek his master's permission to reach Delhi presenting himself at the service of the prominent shaikh.

The biographies tell us that when he first introduced himself to Mīrzā Jān-i Jānān with the request for spiritual initiation, the latter enquired about his name to which he replied: 'People call me Maulawī Na'īm Allāh'. Hearing this, Mīrzā Jān-i Jānān's temper roused by the pride in the young man's tone, and he ordered him to get out of his way, since there was no need of any Maulawī in his *khānaqāh*. Na'īm Allāh though humiliated by the harsh treatment remained steadfast and decided to stay on. Some days later, Mīrzā Jān-i Jānān's eyes again fell on the young scholar from Bahraich and in the same angry tone he asked him why he was still there. Na'īm Allāh Bahrāichī humbly inclined his head in repentance and apologised for his misbehaviour begging for the master's pardon. As a result' he was eventually forgiven and officially admitted into the order.[95]

92. *MqM*, p. 420.

93. *Ibid.*; cf. *Tadhkira-i 'ulamā'-i Hind*, pp. 528-9.

94. *Ibid.*, p. 421; cf. also *Nuzhat al-Khawāṭir*, vol. 7, pp. 507-8.

95. *Dibācha-i Ma'mūlāt-i Maẓhariyya* by Shāh Abūl Ḥasan Naṣīrābādī, pp. 10-11.

Shāh Na'īm Allāh Bahrāichī remained with his spiritual preceptor for about four years during which he wholeheartedly dedicated himself to the spiritual discipline. His devotional rapture (*jadhba*) is said to have reached such a degree that he not even read the letters from home in order to avoid distractions. Under the expert guidance of Mīrzā Jān-i Jānān he finally reached the highest degree of spiritual realisation (*maqām-i 'aliyā*), attaining to the reception of *khilāfat* and *ijāzat*.[96] On advice of his master, he than chose to return to his native land to provide guidance to the seekers of Truth over there. It is said that the very day he took leave, Mīrzā Jān-i Jānān blessed him with the words: 'Today, you are returning to your country as Maulānā Na'īm Allāh! May God bless you and enable you to enlighten the world (*munawwar-i'ālam*)'.[97] He than presented his newly appointed *khalīfa* with the three volumes of the *Maktūbāt-i Rabbānī*, underlining the special favour this gift implied and asking him to read out these letters for the guidance of his future disciples after the afternoon-prayer (*namāz-i 'aṣr*).[98]

Back at Bahrāich, his father assigned him some land for the establishment of a small spiritual retreat (*zāwiya*). However, the Na'īm Allāh soon decided to move to Lucknow where he started his missionary activity in an area called Bangālī Ṭolā providing the funds for the erection of a mosque and a small attached shelter for himself and his disciples.[99]

Praised by his followers for his patience and trust in God, Shāh Na'īm Allāh Bahrāichī began to exercise his role as

---

96. Shāh Ghulām 'Alī reports in *Maqāmāt-i Maẓharī* (p. 420) that Mīrzā Jān-i Jānān was so impressed by his application that he told him the progress made by him in four years was equivalent to that made by others in twelve.

97. *MuM*, p. 88.

98. *Ibid.*, p. 87.

99. *MqM*, p. 421. In letter no. 33, Mīrzā Jān-i Jānān expresses his satisfaction about this transfer and encourages his *khalīfa* to remain confident of the success of granting profit to as many people as possible. Once more he insists on the necessity of following the *sunnat* for an eventual reward in this world and the next (pp. 177-8).

spiritual preceptor while maintaining contact with the *khānaqāh* at Delhi. After the death of Mīrzā Jān-i Jānān, he together with Shāh Ghulām 'Alī and Qāḍī Thanā Allāh Pānīpatī took over the responsibility for the legal and administrative transactions leading to the institution of the Delhi *khānaqāh*.[100] He died in his native Bahraich in 1218/ 1803 where he lies buried in a small tomb (*maqbara*) situated at the outskirts of the modern town.

His literary heritage includes two biographies (*tadhkira*) of his spiritual guide Mīrzā Jān-i Jānān, the *Ma'mūlāt-i Maẓhariyya* and the less known *Bashārāt-i Maẓhariyya*.[101] A hand-written copy of the *Qur'ān* by Shāh Na'īm Allāh is preserved by a spiritual descendant in his line, Shāh Manẓūr Aḥmad Khān, at the latter's residence in Bhopal. The present *sajjāda-nishīn* at the family's residence at Bahraich, that includes a nearby mosque and the former *khānaqāh*, Maulānā Aghrāẓ al-Ḥusn, still preserves part of the private library and belongings of his ancestor which include two precious relics attributed to Mīrzā Jān-i Jānān: the plain robe worn at the time of his assassination, sprinkled with his blood, and the bed-stead (*cārpāī*) on which he is said to have taken rest. Although it is difficult to asscss the authenticity of these objects, I have been assured of their genuineness by the head of the Naqshbandī convent in Old Delhi, who continues the

100. *MqM*, p. 157.

101. The first one furnishes, together with Shāh Ghulām 'Alī's *Maqāmāt-i Maẓharī*, the most systematic, detailed and renowned biographical account of Mīrzā Jān-i Jānān and its original Persian version, apart from a number of manuscripts some of which are kept in the old library in Bahraich, was first published at Kanpur in 1275/1859 under the title *Ma'mūlāt-i Maẓhariyya-Maḥbūb al-'Ārifīn*, Nizami Press, Patkapur (Kanpur). Other editions followed at the turn of the century from the same town and editor.

The second text is a kind of supplementary biography-cum-*malfūẓāt* of the founder of the *Shamsiyya Maẓhariyya* branch of the *Naqshbandiyya* and exists, according to my knowledge, in three ascertained manuscript at Bahraich, Aligarh Muslim University and London (OIOC/IOL, Ms. Bm. Or. 220.

long going tradition paying regular visits to Bahraich in occasion of the *'urs* of Shāh Na'īm Allāh which is celebrated in a simple way by the order's local affiliates.

Shāh Murād Allāh Thānesarī Fārūqī Mujaddidī (1166/1752-1248/1833)

Considered in most genealogies as the principal *khalīfa* of Shāh Na'īm Allāh Bahrāichī,[102] Shāh Murād Allāh descended from a noble family of the small Punjābī town of Thanesar (now in Haryana about 120 miles north of Delhi).[103] Claiming descent from the caliph 'Umar Fārūq, the family bears the title *Fārūqī* (*Fārūqī al-nasb*).[104] His father, Maulānā Qalandar Bakhsh, reportedly a person of high rank in his hometown, was a devoted disciple of Mīrzā Jān-i Jānān who paid regular visits to his *khānaqāh* in the Mogul capital. He was later appointed *khalīfa* by the illustrious master[105] and despatched to his native place to act as deputy of the *ṭarīqa* there.

From his childhood, Shāh Murād Allāh occasionally accompanied his father on his visits to Delhi. There, he was allowed to attend the *ḥalqa* of Mīrzā Jān-i Jānān's intimate disciples and honoured with the latter's spiritual attention (*tawajjuh*). At the time of the Sikh wars against the Afghan Shāh Aḥmad Durrānī and his Rohillā allies (AD 1762-8), Thanesar like many other centres of Muslim culture in the region suffered attacks from the invading sikh armies led by

---

102. Apart from the genealogies produced in the various hagiographies compiled by later disciples of that particular *silsila*, it is noteworthy that also the later edition of the *Ma'mūlāt-i Maẓhariyya* in Persian edited from Kanpur presents a list of the masters who constitute the initiatic chain down from Mīrzā Jān-i Jānān for the following three generations, including the members mentioned in the present study. See *MuM*, pp. 158-9.

103. For details on him, see also *Tadhkira-i 'ulamā'-i Hind,* pp.490-1.

104. *MuM*, p. 90.

105. Cf. Muhammad Umar (1993), p. 82.

the Budha Dal, during one of which Maulānā Qalandar Bakhsh was killed.[106]

Left as an orphan, the young Murād Allāh was forced to abandon Thanesar and to migrate to Lucknow[107] where he continued to receive his religious education from a number of local authorities while living with the family of his maternal grandfather.[108] Some sources inform us that it had been the desire of Murād Allāh's late father that his son should receive training in the traditional medical sciences (*al-tibb*) that would enable him to carry out a respected profession. The boy was, thus apprenticed to a series of local doctors, but lacking the required enthusiasm he was eventually sent back home with the recommendation to his grandfather to look out for a spiritual preceptor.[109]

But when Murād Allāh's own desire to undertake the spiritual path grew stronger, Mīrzā Jān-i Jānān had already passed away. Hence, he decided to make his way from Lucknow to Bahraich to meet Shāh Na'īm Allāh with the quest of being initiated into the *ṭarīqa*. The shaikh, however,

---

106. For a detailed account of the tumultuous events in the Punjab during that time, see among others Qāḍī Nūr Muḥammad's eyewitness report, the *Jang-Nāma* (English translation by Ganda Singh, Amritsar, 1939) and Nūr al-Dīn Ḥusain's *Life of Najīb al-Dawla*. An outline of the events in the second half of the eighteenth century is also provided by S.A.A. Rizvi (1982), pp. 9-74.

107. The available sources do not furnish any information about the fate of the other family members, nor do they mention any date for the Shāh's transfer from the Punjab to Awadh. Since we know, however, from the same sources that Shāh Murād Allāh died in 1248/1833 at the age of 82 according to the Islamic lunar calendar, his date of birth most likely falls in the year 1166-7/1752-3, so that his age at the time of migration to Lucknow cannot have been more than 12 years. This would agree with the reports of his hagiographers who state that Murād Allāh was still a student at that time.

108. See the excerpts of a discourse held by Oṁkār Nāth on Sunday, 6 July 1975 at Kanpur, typed and edited along with a series of other discourses by his disciple B.K. Singhania at Delhi (p. 270).

109. *Ibidem*, pp. 270-1.

at that time already lived at Lucknow forcing Murād Allāh to return there accompanied by a group of local devotees and was finally successful in enrolling as the Shāh's disciple.[110]

After a total period of twelve years with his master, he was appointed as his *khalīfa* in Lucknow and entrusted with the correction (*islāḥ*) and guidance (*hidāyat*) of a number of his master's disciples. At the time of his death in 1218/1803, Maulānā Shāh Na'īm Allāh is said to have transferred the 'crown of full successorship' (*tāj-i khilāfat-i khāṣṣ*) to his favoured deputy advising him further to concentrate his spiritual attention on the most perfect among the sublime stations of the *sulūk*.[111]

After the death of his shaikh, Shāh Murād Allāh stayed for some years in Bahraich in order to supervise his preceptor's disciples there. Later, however, he entrusted these to Shāh Bashārat Allāh Bahrāichī, a *khalīfa* and son-in-law of Shāh Ghulām 'Alī Dihlawī who had spent several years with his master at Delhi. Although it was reportedly painful for him to leave his master's tomb, Shāh Murād Allāh finally decided to return to Lucknow for the sake of the local spiritual community of which he reportedly took care for a period of about 40 years.[112]

According to Maulānā Muḥammad Ḥasan, the author of the *Ḥālāt-i Māshaikh-i Naqshbandiyya Mujaddidiyya*, Shāh Murād Allāh was married to a girl from Ronahi (dist. Faizabad) whose nephew, a certain Shāh Walī Allāh, became a favourite of the Shāh. Although too young to be introduced as his disciple, the *pīr* had him taken care of by his chief deputy, Shāh Abūl Ḥasan Naṣīrābādī, who appointed him

110. *Gulzār-i Murād, tadhkira* of Shāh Murād Allāh Thānesarī by Bashīr Fārūqī (1988), p. 8, and *Ḍamīma-i Māshaikh-i Naqshbandiyya Mujaddidiyya*, a later appendix to the biographical work by Maulānā Muḥammad Ḥasan, written by Maulānā Shaikh Faḍl Aḥmad Khān (1943), p. 3.

111. *Ibidem*, p. 9.

112. *Nuzhat al-Khawāṭir*, vol. 7, p. 469.

his official successor and caretaker at Bahraich and Lucknow before retiring himself to a life of seclusion in his hometown Nasirabad.[113]Some sources inform us that Shāh Murād Allāh spent also some time in the former capital of Awadh, Faizabad, to which he was linked by parental ties. There he took shelter in the cell of the local patron-saint Ṭāṭ Shāh situated in the eponymous mosque in the centre of town.[114]

According to the later, revised editions of the *Ma'mūlāt-i Maẓhariyya* which the Hindu sources along with the author of the *Ḍamīma* seem to follow, the shaikh's death occurred on Saturday, 21 Dhī'l-Qa'da 1248/14 April 1833 in his *khānaqāh* in Lucknow's Qandahari Bazar at the age of 82.[115] His body was buried within the precincts of what was later to become the mausoleum of his successor Karīm Allāh Shāh in a popular neighbourhood in what is now a densely populated area in the centre of Lucknow. An annual festival on the occasion of his death anniversary is organised by the present *sajjāda-nishīn* when a number of influent Naqshbandī authorities of different local sub-branches derived from the shaikh use to meet for a two or three day *maḥfil*.

113. The present *sajjāda-nishīn* at the modest tomb of Shāh Murād Allāh in Lucknow, Bashīr Fārūqī, claims to be a direct descendant of Shāh Walī Allāh in the sixth generation. The short biography of Shāh Murād Allāh, a booklet titled *Gulzār-i Murād*, shows that one of the author's main aims is to establish a link between himself and the Shāh through Shāh Walī Allāh. The genealogy he produces seems authentic, but apparently the successors of Walī Allāh played no significant role in the spiritual history of the order although parts of the tradition are still preserved with the present caretaker. Significantly, Bashīr Fārūqī has received his initiation from Shāh Abūl Ḥasan Zaid Fārūqī, the head of the Delhi *khānaqāh* until 1993, a fact that indicates the survival of the ancient links to the present.

114. Along with the mausoleum of Nawāb Shuja al-Dawla (*r.* 1754-75), son and successor of Safdar Jang, and that of his wive Bahū Begum Shāh, this mosque with its peculiar architectural features and extremely colourful painting represents one of the most noteworthy building of that town.

115. *MuM*, p. 90; *Gulzār-i Murād*, p. 16.

Among the unspecified number of Shāh Murād Allāh's successors, two are mentioned unanimously in all sources: Shāh Ghulām Rasūlnumā Kānpurī (*d.* 1318/1900) popularly known as Dādā Miyān whose tomb and *dargāh*-cum-mosque complex still contains a functioning small *madrasa* in the Begumpur neighbourhood of central Kanpur,[116]and Maulānā Shāh Abul Ḥasan Naṣīrābādī, the chief *khalīfa* of Shāh Murād Allāh and next link in the mainstream *silsila* in Awadh.[117]

Sayyid Maulānā Shāh Abūl Ḥasan Naṣīrābādī (1198/1784-1272/1856)

With this prominent shaikh, the spiritual centre of this lineage shifted to yet another place of emerging importance at the times of the later Nawābs. It provides evidence for the *ṭarīqa*'s peculiar characteristic to be active not only in those places where its presence was supported by a favourable socio-religious climate (as in Rohilkhaṇḍ during the late eighteenth and early nineteenth centuries under the rule of Najīb al-Dawla[118])' but also in those centres of Muslim power which

---

116. The present *khādim* at the *dargāh*, Abūl Barakāt informed me that the spiritual line of his ancestor was extinguished and passed over to other branches of the *Mujaddidiyya* in Awadh, mainly through disciples of Shāh Abūl Ḥasan Naṣīrābādī. He himself, as well as his brothers and forefathers, were mainly concerned with running the *madrasa* established by the Shāh and meant to provide basic education for children from indigent families of the area, and with the upkeeping of the *dargāh*. Interview on 24 January 1996.

117. *MuM*, p. 90 (Urdu version) and p. 159, *Ḍamīma* . . . , p. 4., *Sūfī Santmat kā Naqshbandiyya silsila* (1984), vol 2, p. 169. The *Gulzār-i Murād*, most probably in order to stress the legitimacy of the present line leading to the present caretaker of the *maqbāra* and author of the biography, mentions also the name of his ancestor Shaikh Ilāhī Bakhsh Ṣiddiqī among his *khulafā'*. The author of the *tadhkira* of Shāh Murād Allāh points out that in 1305/1887-8, Shāh Ilāhī Bakhsh appointed the author's paternal grandfather, Shāh Ḥakīm Karīm Allāh, as his *khalīfa* providing also a *khalīfatnāma* at this regard (*Gulzār-i Murād*, p. 17). The latter lies buried next to Shāh Murād Allāh.

118. For a detailed account of this Afghan leader, see Nūr al-Dīn Ḥusain: *A detailed history of Najīb al-Dawla, OIOC*, Add. 24, 410.

did not provide such a favouable environment. The task of the order's leading authorities there was to guarantee the integrity of Sunni orthodoxy representing a point of reference for the common local population (*al-'awāmm*) while providing spiritual guidance to those qualified for entering the initiatic path (*al-khawāṣṣ*).

In our specific case, the developments in Awadh which saw the rise to power of the Shī'a dynasty of the Nawābs in the first half of the eighteenth century constituted yet another symptom of the growing influence of the Iranian nobility in different parts of the subcontinent.[119] The spread and growth of Safavid-style Shī'ism challenging the long established Sunni hegemony over most parts of Muslim India was perceived as a concrete danger by the Naqshbandī leaders from as soon as the times late sixteenth century with Khwāja Bāqī Billāh (*d.* 1012/1603), and was further pursued by his renowned disciple Shaikh Aḥmad Sirhindī. It gained renewed actuality during the reigns of the later Mogul emperors Bahādur Shāh and Shāh-i 'Ālam II, and reached its apex with the rise to power of Mīrzā Najaf Khān AD 1708-82 at the Mogul Court in Delhi who was a fervent Shī'a and a staunch enemy of the Afghan Rohillās.[120]

It is in this context that the despatch of one of Mīrzā Jān-i Jānān's closest *khulafā'* to Lucknow must be interpreted as part of a conscious attempt to create an influential outpost of the order in an area where the Sunni establishment was under threat from the growing influx of Iranian Shī'as. The frequent shifting of Shāh Murād Allāh between Lucknow, Faizabad and Bahraich, all major centres of Awadhī culture at that time, also seems to have been

119. For a detailed analysis of the various factors leading to the rise of Shī'a power in Awadh, see J.R.I. Cole: *Roots of North Indian Shi'ism in Iran and Iraq* (1988) and Muhammad Umar (1993), pp. 177.

120. His alleged involvement in the assasination of Mīrzā Jān-i Jānān, although never definitively established, has since formed an essential part reported by all Naqshbandī hagiographers.

motivated by the desire to maintain a foothold in these places of emerging Shī'a intellectual culture.[121]

It appears, therefore, more than a coincidence that the main heir of this tradition in that area and *khalīfa* of Shāh Murād Allāh Thānesarī hailed from the small but important *qaṣba* of Nasīrābād (dist. Rae Bareli), about 50 miles to the east of Lucknow, which flourished under the patronage of the Nawābs, in particular Aṣaf al-Dawla (*r.* AD 1775-97).[122] The tolerant and generous policy of this ruler encouraged a great number of influent local Sayyids to adopt Imami Shī'ism, developing Nasīrābād into a renowned centre of Shī'a clerics, such as Sayyid Dildar 'Alī (AD 1753-1820) and his son Sayyid Muḥammad Naṣīrābādī (AD 1785-1867), the chief *mujtahid* of Lucknow from 1820 to 1867 and staunch adversary of the Sunni community.[123]

Maulānā Sayyid Abūl Ḥasan Naṣīrābādī bin Maulawī Nūr al-Ḥasan bin Maulawī Muḥammad Mahdī Ḥusain came from an influential family claiming a genealogy that goes back to Ḥusain son of 'Alī.[124]Notwithstanding its ancestry,

---

121. Faizabad, the first capital of the Nawābs, became shortly again centre of political power in 1756 during the reign of Shuja al-Dawla (*r.* 1754-75), under whose rule it developed into an important intellectual centre, renowned for the scholarship of tradition physicians. Cf. Cole (1988), pp. 55-8.

122. Like many other places in the area, Nasīrābād along with the neighbouring town of Jais rose to prominence through the settlement of the Sayyid class of 'Ashrafī Muslims made wealthy by generous land endowments received from earlier Islamic rulers and influent *zamīndārs* in many parts of the Gangetic plain. The Nasīrābādī Sayyids who trace their ancestry back to the line of Sayyid Najm al-Dīn al-Sabzawārī, an alleged companion of Ghāzī Sālār Ma'sūd of Bahrāich, began to convert to Shī'ism under the Mogul emperor Bahādur Shāh, and under the patronage of the Nishapuri house of Awadh. Cf. Cole (1988), p. 77.

123. Cole gives an extensive account of the role these two scholars played in the formation of a well organised Shī'a clerical class in Awadh and also mentions the sometimes rather aggressive stand the latter took towards Sunnis and Sūfis. (*op. cit.*, pp. 146-59).

124. See *Nuzhat al-Khawāṭir*, vol. 7, p. 12; *Tadhkira-i 'ulamā-i Hind*, pp. 74-5.

his family did not follow the example of many local Sayyid clans of adopting the Shī'a creed and remained faithful to their native Sunni tradition. Born in 1198/1783-4, Sayyid Abūl Ḥasan was sent by his father to study with a series of learned authorities in Nasīrābād, Salon, Rae Bareli and finally Lucknow where he completed his studies in *ḥadīth*, jurisprudence and theology at the age of 18 with the highest attainments (*dastār-i faḍīlat*) from the Firangī Maḥal, the one important Sunni oriented institution left in the Awadhī capital at that time. It was during those years that the young Sayyid came into contact with a group of Shāh Murād Allāh's disciples who awakened his interest for the path of spiritual realisation. Notwithstanding his direct links with the family of Shāh Na'īm Allāh Bahrāichī — his father Maulawī Nūr al-Ḥasan had married one of the latter's daughters[125] — he was not in time to enrol as his disciple since the Shāh passed away shortly afterwards in 1218/1803, not, however, without recommending his nephew to his *khalīfa* Murād Allāh.

As a result, the young Sayyid made the vow of allegiance (*bai'at*) to him and spent the following sixteen years at the feet of his shaikh in the Lucknow *khānaqāh*.[126] The young disciple's extraordinary qualification allowed him to progress so rapidly under the guidance of Shāh Murād Allāh that his master urged him to confer his spiritual attention (*tawajjuh*) on his own disciples, the power of which was apparently of unusual intensity. Abūl Ḥasan soon gained the highest degree of spiritual licence (*ijāzat-i muṭlaq*) taking over many of his master's disciples and leading them to the stages of *fanā wa baqā*.[127] All sources agree, moreover, on his capability to lead

125. B.B. Basuk: *Lakṣya vedhī vaṁśāvalī ke santon kā sāṁskṛtik jīvan paricaya* (1992), p. 113.

126. *Ḍamīma* . . . , p. 4.

127. These two complementary stages of the spiritual journey are fundamental to the doctrines of all Sūfī orders and correspond to closely related degrees of inner realisation. Their meaning will be analysed in the next chapter including the concept of *tawajjuh*, which assumes a key importance in the doctrines of the later *Naqshbandiyya* and is an essential pillar in the master-disciple relationship.

all those who looked at him with right determination (*irādat*) and firm persuasion (*'aqīdat*) to their goal.[128]

In keeping with the Naqshbandī tradition and on the basis of his authority as an *'ālim*, and *maulawī*, Shāh Abūl Ḥasan's disciple and *khalīfa*, Ḥājī Aḥmad 'Alī Khān, confirms his master's rigorous orthodoxy and adherence to the Sunna when he metaphorically refers to him as 'holding the *Qur'ān* in one hand and the *ahādīth* in the other,...'.[129] His biographers invariably stress his endeavour to act in strict accordance with the precepts of the revealed Law (*al-Dīn*) and the Traditions, expecting his disciples and followers to conform to these principles. In the initial stages of a disciple's apprenticeship, regular morning sessions dedicated to the study of the exoteric sciences (*'ulūm al-ẓāhir*) were as much part of his daily routine as the punctual leadership of the five canonical prayers in the mosque, each followed by a prolonged meditation session during which he used to grant his *tawajjuh* to a restricted number of disciples residing in his *khānaqāh*s at Lucknow and Nasīrābād.

The importance Shāh Abūl Ḥasan attributed to his role as authoritative leader of a Sūfī-Sunni faction is reflected in his spending most of his time in company of his numerous disciples or simple followers, including his meals and afternoon rest. He thereby enabled a great number of people to benefit passively from his presence. It can be interpreted as part of an attempt to exercise his influence on large sections of Awadh's increasingly insecure Sunni Muslims. It is exactly in this combination of powerful spiritual authority for his *ḥalqa* with that of a learned scholar for the pious ones and a

---

128. It is important to notice that the shaikh's spiritual attention reaches the disciple through the contact established by the means of the eyesight. Obviously this sort of contact occurs on a subtle level beyond the modalities that regulate the gross reality to which the common senses apply.

129. It might be worth to recall that also in the sources consulted for the present study, the traditional title of *'ālim* is gradually replaced by the more recent term *maulawī*.

centre of charitable refuge for the needy that we recognise a typical Mujaddidī attitude ever since Mīrzā Jān-i Jānān. Since very little is known about the doctrinal elaborations of the Sayyid from Nasīrābād, it is rather the increasingly extroverted attitude turned towards all sections of the surrounding world (*al-khalq*) which characterises the shaikhs during the early modern period and which becomes particularly evident in the earlier period of Shāh Abūl Ḥasan's life that is most striking.[130] The use of *tawajjuh* as an important means both of propagating reorming efforts and of raising members of the *ṭarīqa* to a higher degree in their spiritual quest constitutes an unequivocal sign of this tendency and will assume even greater importance with subsequent shaikhs.[131]

This public democratisation of the order goes along with Shāh Abūl Ḥasan's biographer's picture of a contemplative, amicable and mild character (*jamālī*) that stands in contrast to the impulsive, hot-tempered and often awe-inspiring characters (*jalālī*) of many of his predecessors. Confident of his subtle power of persuasion, the Shāh reportedly never reprimanded openly any of his intimate disciples but preferred to take a paternal attitude by saying:

---

130. That this attitude represents a gradual adaption of the role played by the shaikh rather than a radical departure from the positions held by traditional Naqshbandī authorities is, thus, noted by one of the lineages's later Hindu masters: 'None of the Naqshbandi masters has changed the *ṭarīqa* till the present day, nay it is by the means of this ancient order that, having captivated the people's hearts through their affectionate love, they continue to exercise their duty without any tie, bestowing the essential thing to the heart of all. This task involves multiple risks and dangers, this is why great care has been taken by them, and Khwāja al-Naqshband has put the entire responsibility for it on the shoulders of the pir, so that he may do most of the work for the *murīd* . . . ', in *Discourses* . . . , p. 288.

131. For the first time, we find numerous hints pointing towards the assumption that a single glance can bring the *murīd* to the highest station of the path, an element that from now on will accompany the descriptions of most later authorities, especially in the Hindu context.

> If my company (*ṣuḥbat*) does not leave its effect on them, what can a mere verbal reproval (*naṣīḥat*) do. The real *faqīr* is the one who infuses his colour into the disciple's heart rendering him similar to oneself.[132]

In fact, the greatest munificence (*karāmat*) attributed to the Shāh was that whosoever took part of his company repented within a few days for all transgressions commited in the past (*'amāl khilāf-i shar'*) complying instead with the example set by the master.[133] Although this sounds like an stereotyped attempt by his hagiographers to exalt their shaikh's virtues, in line with the Mujaddidī vision, it fits well into the general picture and reflects the prevailing anxieties of his times.

The high rank Sayyid Abūl Ḥasan occupied in the Mujaddidī hierarchy is confirmed by the statements attributed to his shaikh, Shāh Murād Allāh, who did not hesitate to recognise the superiority of his talented disciple.[134] He used to send many of his own followers to the Sayyid accompanied by the words:

> Maulawī Abūl Ḥasan is pre-eminent to us in several ways: first of all, he descends from an authentic Ḥusainī Sayyid family; secondly, he excels us in the knowledge of the exoteric sciences, thirdly, he equals us in the esoteric sciences and fourthly, he never committed any major offence (*gunāh-i kabīra*).[135]

As a sign of reverence, Shāh Murād Allāh handed over the affairs of his *khānaqāh* at Lucknow to his successor and transmitted to him in the most intimate way (*rū ba rū*) the

---

132. *Ḍamīma . . .*, p. 6.

133. *Ibidem*, p. 3.

134. Due to this central importance in the history of the Na'īmiyya (the Awadhī branch of the *Mujaddidiyya*), he bears the title of *quṭb al-Zamān*, denoting a very elevated position within the Sūfī hierarchy. For the different degrees in the Sūfī hierarchy, see M.E. Blochet: *Études sur l'ésoterisme musulman* (1979).

135. *Gulzār-i Murād*, p. 17.

whole spiritual wealth of the *silsila* and the responsibility of its affairs.[136]

During the following years, Sayyid Abūl Ḥasan Naṣīrābādī remained the *silsila*'s undisputed leader in Awadh. Refraining from any involvement in the political activities promoted by his fellow-citizen Sayyid Aḥmad Barelwī (AD 1786-1832),[137]he dedicated himself entirely to the strengthening of the spiritual network in Awadh travelling to many places (Faizabad, Ghazipur, Sultanpur, etc.) in order to supervise the activities of his deputies. During the last year of his life, together with a number of selected disciples he retired to his native Nasīrābād where he immersed himself in prolonged contemplation in almost total seclusion. In those turbulent years preceding the British annexion of Awadh, he handed over the responsibility for the *khānaqāh* at Lucknow to the nephew of his spiritual guide, Shāh Walī Allāh, to whom he entrusted also the esoteric education of his son Miyān Hādī Ḥasan.[138]

---

136. This particular ritual usually takes place shortly before the death of the old *pīr* and marks the passage of authority to his chosen successor. During the rite, the *pīr* orders his *khalīfa* to sit in front of him while reciting the names of the authorities included in the order's chain (*khatm-i khwājagān*), accompanied by that of different Qur'ānic verses and other devotional formulas. Finally, the master puts his breast in front of that of the disciple taking his right hand and embracing him intimately.

    Interestingly, some sources add that while accepting the spiritual leadership from his shaikh, Shāh Abūl Ḥasan passed on all material donations (*futūḥāt*) involved to his disciple Shāh Walī Allāh, a relative of Shāh Murād Allāh. *MuM*, p. 92.

137. For details regarding this eccentric disciple of Shāh 'Abd al-'Azīz as well as his famous contemporary, Shāh Isma'īl Shahīd, regarding their political interpretation of the Naqshbandī doctrine and the derived inglorious *jihād*-movement fought mainly against the Sikhs, see S.A.A. Rizvi (1982), pp. 471-541, and Aziz Ahmad: *Studies in Islamic Culture in the Indian Environment* (1964). For a traditional Naqshbandī position in their regard, see also Shāh Abūl Ḥasan Zaid Fārūqī Mujaddidī: *Maulānā Isma'īl Dihlawī* (1983).

138. *Ḍamīma* . . . , p. 7. Nothing precise can be gathered from the sources regarding the successive history of the *khānaqāh* at →

The last great regional leader of the *Mujaddidiyya* in Awadh, though having been at the head of a tight network of deputies resched as far as Gorakhpur and extended even into Bengal, died retired from the world on Monday, 1 Sha'bān 1272/May 1856 in Nasīrābād where he is buried in a simple tomb in the ancient graveyard of this now forgotten village.[139]

While the geographical distribution of most of his deputies tend to indicate a movement towards the eastern periphery of Awadh, Ḥājī Aḥmad 'Alī Khān, apparently was one of the leading successors of Sayyid Abūl Ḥasan in western Awadh after the dissolution of the *khānaqāh* at Lucknow. He constitutes the next link in the spiritual chain examined in the present study. Remembered by his biographies as a passionate poet, to him are attributed the following verses in honour of his deceased *pīr*, engraved on the latter's tombstone at Nasīrābād:

> Oh Abūl Ḥasan, chief of the Naqshbandi order
> to whom none of the *ṭarīqa's* other authorities could reach
> when he passed away the angels of the hidden world recited:
> One of the sworn ones of God, a man of Truth, has met This Lord.
>
> Maulawī Sayyid Abūl Ḥasan, shaikh of his time,
> when, by the favour of God, he took his place in the abode of heaven
> I did not count him as dead, he exchanged this world for paradise

---

→ Lucknow, but it appears likely that it was destroyed during or shortly after the 1857-8 War and its inmates either dispersed or killed. Only very vague information was available to me at this regard from the present *sajjāda-nishīn* who resides close to the tomb of Shāh Murād Allāh, Bashīr Fārūqī.

139. The date of death given by Cole in the footnote on p. 234 of his work as 1768, apparently based on Rahman 'Ali's *Tadhkira-i 'ulamā'-i Hind*, is incorrect.

where his ultimate desire was to reside;
when the end of his days came closer, the repenting angels requested him:
He who has changed his mansion, come home, from earth to Heaven.[140]

Maulānā Khalīfat al-Rahman Aḥmad 'Alī Khān Māū Rashīdābādī (*d.* 1307/1889)

Unlike his predecessors, Shāh Aḥmad 'Alī Khān hailed from a humble social background in a small village close to the *qaṣba* of Kāimgañj in Farrukhabad district. The political turmoil during the 1856-8 War had considerably diminished the position of the *Mujaddidiyya* in Awadh and was further aggravated by the disappearance of its most authoritative figure, Sayyid Abūl Ḥasan Naṣīrābādī, leading eventually to the order's split into several minor branches of merely local importance in the region's periphery.

The figure of Aḥmad 'Alī Khān exemplifies in a way the order's dispersal from Awadh's major urban centres, now under direct British colonial rule, and its survival on a reduced scale in the rural areas away from the centres of political power. Interestingly, these centrifugal tendencies that took the *ṭarīqa* from the cosmopolitan centres of cultural and intellectual life to small towns and villages coincide with a shift of the authori-tarian leadership held by members of upper class *'ashrafī* Muslims claiming noble descent to those from a more humble, indigenous social background. Consequently, for the first time, the hagiographical sources concerned with this shaikh lack the customary eulogising accounts of the master's ancestry.

Aḥmad 'Alī Khān's father Shāhāmat Khān, himself affiliated to a local Chishtī *pīr* claiming descent from Shāh Mīna Lakhnāwī (*d.* 874/1470), reportedly led an austere and

---

140. *Ḍamīma . . .* , p. 8. Reportedly, A favourite couplet often recited by Shāh Abūl Ḥasan was the following : *Dil-i man dānad o dānam-o dānad dil-i man*.

detached life earning his livelihood through occasional employment. The limited resources of his family notwithstanding, Shāhāmat Khān took great care in providing an adequate education for his son. Apparently well versed in both Arabic and Persian, the young boy is said to have acquired considerable skills in the art of reciting the *Qur'ān* and the investigation of subtle theological problems. A passionate poet throughout his life, Aḥmad 'Alī claims authorship of two poetry-collections and of a small volume titled *Muḥāsaba-i Kābul* containing a series of *inshā* passages in praise of the Afghan fighters against the infidels during the first Anglo-Afghan War (1839-42).[141]

Like most Naqshbandī biographies and hagiographies, the sources underline the great importance Aḥmad 'Alī Khān attributed to meticulous adherence to the tenets of the Islamic Law and the Sunna of the Prophet fuelled by an aversion for all illiterate Sūfīs (*fuqarā-i jāhil*).[142]

An interesting anecdote informs us about the encounter that allegedly inclined him towards the spiritual path. While at Lucknow as a student, Aḥmad 'Alī Khān frequently came through a place called Ku'a Khaira which was attended by a *faqīr* who used to keep a number of dogs with him. Moved by his orthodox zeal, one day Aḥmad 'Alī Khān approached the *faqīr* objecting to his habit of allowing those impure animals near him. The *faqīr* remained outwardly unimpressed. All of a sudden, the young Aḥmad 'Alī Khān began to feel ashamed for his disrespectful behaviour and apologised to the saint

---

141. Only fragments of these manuscripts have survived, some of which are preserved with Shāh Manẓūr Aḥmad Khān, a descendant of Shāh Aḥmad 'Alī Khān's *khalīfa*, Shāh Faḍl Aḥmad Khān, at his residence in Bhopal. Moreover, a small treatise entitled *Fatwā-i Aḥmadī* dealing with some aspects of the importance attributed to the adherence to the Sunna from a Naqshbandī point of view have been attributed to him.

142. *Ḍamīma* . . . , p. 9. Although this sounds as the usual stereotyped statement, it nevertheless acquires some importance in the socio-historical context of pre-1857 Lucknow. It also provides some clues as to the future development of the *silsila*.

who replied: 'It was not for you to pronounce those words'. The effect of this answer on the young student was apparently devastating. Overcome by a wave of forgetfulness of himself (*be-khudī*), he experienced according to the notes of his disciple Faḍl Aḥmad Khān a state of delight and inner happiness (*lazzat wa masarrat*) and his breath kept flowing with the rythm of the words *Allāh hū*. When he recovered from this state of spontaneous spiritual rapture (*wajd*), the young scholar apologised once again to the unknown saint only to receive the same reply that again plunged him into the previous state, now even more intense than before. The *faqīr* finally embraced him whispered into his ears: 'Let your breath not flow in vain', and left the scene.[143]

After staying for some time with a Chishtī shaikh from the Gorakhpur region a certain Amīr 'Alī Khān Chilaulī, Aḥmad 'Alī Khān came into contact with Sayyid Miyān Afḍal Rā'īpurī, a contemporary *khalīfa* of Sayyid Abūl Ḥassan Naṣīrābādī at Lucknow, who was impressed by the fervour of the young student and kept him at his service. He later recommended him to his *pīr*, but not yet feeling prepared for the task, the young Aḥmad 'Alī Khān refused the offer.

Annoyed by this reluctance, Miyān Afḍal sent him away with the warning that all pleasant states he had so far experienced would soon vanish. It happened exactly as predicted, and once again repenting his mistake. Aḥmad 'Alī Khan sought refuge in the *dargāh* of Shāh Mīna Lakhnawī. During that same night he had a dream in which Shāh

---

143. *Ibidem*, pp. 10-11. It is noteworthy that this key event in the life of Aḥmad 'Alī Khān is related by his biographer using the traditional Sūfī terminology we know from the previous descriptions. Yet another much later Hindu source, clearly based on the former, employs an entirely Hindu terminology to describe the same event. These substitutions, from now on a regular pattern encountered in the Hindu sources, provide an extremely useful means for further doctrinal considerations and constitute an important key for the understanding of the gradual shifting to a new cultural environment. See *LVV*, p. 119.

Mīna[144] directed him to a place where an initially unknown person kept waiting for him with the promise to restore his lost wealth. After that very dream repeated itself for three consecutive night he eventually decided to meet Sayyid Abūl Ḥasan at Nasīrābād and ask him for discipleship.[145]

While at Lucknow, Aḥmad 'Alī Khān began to earn his live as a teacher of Arabic and Persian in different local *madrasas* while remaining attached to the *ḥalqa* of Sayyid Miyān Afḍal Rā'īpurī who had been entrusted with the supervision of his master's *khānaqāh* following his retreat to Nasīrābād.[146]

According to his biographer Faḍl Aḥmad Khān, Shāh Aḥmad 'Alī Khān spent a period of altogeher four times forty days of isolation (*cilla*)[147] with his spiritual perceptor at Naṣīrābād during which he received intense spiritual training. Finally, his shaikh honoured him with full spiritual authority (*ijāzat-i muṭlaq*) outwardly marked by the handing over of the traditional headwear (*dastār*), dress (*kurta*) and rosary (*tasbīḥ*).[148] He was than ordered to return to his native place to start teaching and spreading the message of the *ṭarīqa* on his own authority.

Aḥmad 'Alī Khān spent the remaining thirty-five years of his life at his native village of Mau Rashidabad leading a simple life as a teacher in the local *madrasa* and as a private

---

144. According to other sources, it was Shāh Abūl Ḥasan himself who appeared in this nocturnal vision to his future disciple.

145. *Discourses* . . . , p. 293.

146. After the death of Miyān Afḍal, the *khānaqāh*'s trust passed to Shāh Walī Allāh Lakhnawī, the nephew of Shāh Murād Allāh Thānesarī and *khalīfa* of Sayyid Abūl Ḥasan who nevertheless kept a close eye on its affairs while passing prolonged periods at the place.

147. Rather unusual in a Naqshbandī context, this may indicate an initiation to the methods of the *Chishtiyya* as part of the spiritual discipline imparted to Aḥmad 'Alī Khān which were since long part of the patronage of the Mujaddidī shaikhs.

148. *Ḍamīma* . . . , p. 11.

tutor for the offspring of the leading local families. In 1303/1886, he set out for Arabia to perform the *ḥajj* during which he met, among others, Shāh 'Abd Allāh Abūl Khair Fārūqī Mujaddidī[149] who was reportedly very impressed with his spiritual achieve-ments.[150] On his way back from the Hijaz in Ṣafar 1304/December 1886-January 1887, Aḥmad 'Alī Khān visited Sirhind where he spent a period of forty days at the tomb of Shaikh Aḥmad Sirhindī. During those days, he reportedly dedicated himself to contemplation at the grave of the *ṭarīqa's* illustrious ancestor and is said to have received blessings from the 'lord of the tomb' (*ṣāḥib-i mazār*) and other renowned authorities of the *silsila*.[151]

Two years later, on 9 Rabī' al-Awwal 1307/4 November 1889, Shāh Aḥmad 'Alī Khān died at an advanced age in his hometown Mau Rashidābād. There, his grave is found inside the cemetry of the locality today called Kuberpur, just outside the ruins of the old congregational mosque.

The written sources still extant tell us very little about the activities of the Maulawī during the years after his

---

149. Shāh Abūl Khair Fārūqī Mujaddidī (1272/1856-1341/1923) was a descendant in the ninth generation of Shaikh Aḥmad Sirhindī through his nephew Sa'īf al-Dīn and the latter's lineage perpetuated at Rampur. His father, Shāh Aḥmad Sa'īd (1217/1802-1277/1860) following a period at Lucknow and Rampur, was appointed head of the Delhi *khānaqāh* in 1834, shortly before his father left India for the *ḥajj*, until 1858 when he was forced to migrate to the Hijaz in the aftermath of the violent events that followed the 1857 War. Along with his father Muḥammad Umar (*d.* 1298/1880), he grew up in the *ḥaramain* before taking over again, in April 1889, the leadership of the Mujaddidī *khānaqāh* at Delhi until his death in 1923. He was the father of the renowned late Shāh Abūl Ḥasan Zaid Fārūqī Mujaddidī, until recently the head of the Delhi seat of the *Mujaddidiyya* and biographer of his father Shāh Abūl Khair, *Maqāmāt al-Khair* (1409/1989 reprint).

150. The reverential attitude that shines through the mention of Shāh Abūl Khair in these sources and the weight attributed to his judgement meant to increase Maulawī Aḥmad 'Alī Khān's reputation suggest the recognition of the Fārūqī lineage at Delhi as the ultimate spiritual authority at that time after the extinction of the Na'īmiyya line at Lucknow.

appointment by Sayyid Abūl Ḥasan Naṣīrābādī, nor do we learn much about his disciples, with the exception of Shāh Faḍl Aḥmad Khān through whom the *silsila* was to continue. The few written sources left by him, while confirming his scholarship, do not contribute any valuable information about his role as spiritual guide. A limited number of biographical ancedotes handed down by his successor Shāh Faḍl Aḥmad Khān are too strongly hagiographical in their contents hardly containing any useful material, and also the later Hindu sources do not reveal anything substantial about the later stages of his life.[152]

From the few reported events, it emerges nevertheless that with the generational passage from Sayyid Abūl Ḥasan Naṣīrābādī to Shāh Aḥmad 'Alī Khān, the lineage was reduced from a position of regional importance well connected with the overall Mujaddidī network to a rural offshoot of limited importance in the oerall history of the *ṭarīqa*.[153]

This contraction reflects the devastating effects the 1857-8 War had left not only on Awadh but on the entire north of the subcontinent marking the formal end of almost seven centuries of uninterrupted Muslim rule over these areas. This turning point which sanctioned the penetration of modernity into north-Indian society considerably weakened the position

151. The spiritual experiences the Maulawī went through during that time along with a collection of biographical and esoteric notes regarding Shaikh Aḥmad Sirhindī have been described by him in a small treatise bearing the title *Tuḥfat al-Mujaddidain*, preserved with Shāh Manẓūr Aḥmad Khān at Bhopal.

152. Most of the described events, from the conversion of a money-lender (*sūd-khor*) who allegedly repented for his bashful behaviour of taking interests to his rescue of a local Shī'a Imām whose ship happened to run into heavy waters during the pilgrimage-journey, are of quite ordinary nature and draw a picture of a locally respected authority typical for India's rural environment. The Shāh entertained, however, contacts with other Naqshbandī authorities and with many local saints affiliated to other orders. See *Ḍamīma* . . . , pp. 13-14.

153. The district of Farrukhabad, despite its strong Afghan presence, never constituted a significant centre of Naqshbandī activities.

of all traditional Islamic institutions. Significantly, the Naqshbandī headquarters at Delhi and Lucknow, always looked at with suspicion by the British authorities, suffered badly from the repressions that followed the rebellion and both were abandoned, that in Lucknow permanently and that in Delhi until AD 1889, forcing their leaders into a prolonged exile.[154]

But notwithstanding a certain presence of authoritative leaders, Awadh unlike Delhi, Rohilkhaṇḍ and parts of the Punjab, could at no time be considered a stronghold of the *Mujaddidiyya*. The introduction of *ṭarīqa* in these areas goes mainly back to a number of deputies of Mīrzā Jān-i Jānān, such as Ḥājī Muḥammad Yār,[155] Mīr Ghulām Yāḥyā,[156] Ghulām Ḥasan,[157] Muḥammad Jamāl[158] and Shāh Na'īm Allāh Bahrāichī. Only the latter held the rank of a central authority whose influence radiated over a large surrounding area. His successors, Shāh Murād Allāh and Shāh Abūl Ḥasan, both charismatic personalities endowed with the required qualities for authoritative leadership were able to expand the order's presence even in increasingly difficult circumstances. But after the death of the last recognised *quṭb al-zamān* in AD 1856, none of his successors was able to fill the void at the top of the regional Mujaddidī leadership. This eventually led the split into a number of isolated sub-branches in different parts of the region which began to develop in dependently on a local scale where they often survive until the present day.[159]

---

154. For a description of the events in and around the Delhi *khānaqāh* during that period and the reaction of its leaders to it, see *MqK*, pp. 32-85.

155. For him, see *Kalimāt-i Tayyibāt*, letter no. 50.

156. For him, see Muhammad Umar (1993), p. 82, *MqM*, pp. 416-19.

157. *MqM*, pp. 402-3.

158. *Bashārāt-i Maẓhariyya*, folio 1a. It was he who first introduced Shāh Na'īm Allīh into the *ṭarīqa*.

159. Apart from the *silsila* examined in the present study, I traced three more surviving spiritual descendants of the order who claim legitimacy through different *khulafā'* of Shāh Abūl Ḥasan →

The *khānaqāh* at Lucknow that had served as the principal base of the *Mujaddidiyya Maẓhariyya* in the region for the past three generations was entrusted to the *quṭb*'s closest disciples and successors, at first to Sayyid Afḍal Miyān Rā'īpurī and later to Shāh Walī Allāh Lakhnāwī. The latter fell victim to historical circumstances, his fate remaining hidden in the darkness of the following years. Deprived of that vital point of reference, the leaders of the numerous secondary branches had to rely on their own inherent authority in their respective zones of influence, although it appears that later renewed contacts with the re-activated headquarters in Delhi provided some opportunities for re-establishing the old links.[160]

In this context, the relation between Sayyid Abūl Ḥasan Naṣīrābādī and his *khalīfa* Shāh Aḥmad 'Alī Khān acquires particular importance since it contains an essential element for the further development of the lineage. This is testified through a number of letters the former has written between 1270/1853-4 and 1272/1856 to his deputy at Kāimgañj containing specific spiritual instructions. Along with more general pieces of advice on doctrinal issues, these include hints at a special task entrusted to the Maulawī which certainly constitutes a so far unparalleled depature from the principles of the *ṭarīqa*. In one of his letters, Sayyid Abūl Ḥasan writes:

> By the grace of God, through your most intimate essence a new world will be illuminated. Some from among the Hindus (*ahl-i hunūd*) will come to enjoy your company . . . and since they possess the qualities [required for this task], do not refuse them this uncomparable treasure [of our spiritual heritage]. . . .[161]

→ Naṣīrābādī, none of them, however, bearing any relation with a non-Muslim environment; two of them are found in Tanda and Jalālpur in Faizābād district, descending of Shāh Bakhsh Allāh Nāgpurī (*d.* 1298/1881) and Chand Shāh Ṭanḍawī, and one at Madarpur (dist. Azamgarh) through Ḥaḍrat Naṣīr Allāh Ghāzīpurī.

160. See *MqK*, pp. 188-200.

161. *Makātib-i Sayyid Shāh Abūl-Ḥasan*, letter no. 1. Cf. also *Ḍamīma* . . . , p. 11.

In another letter, he adds referring to the same point:

> . . . this matter will constitute the proof of your being a pole of divine instruction (*quṭb al-irshād*); . . . if your particular spiritual attention (*tawajjuh-i khāṣṣ*) will reach the infidels and the transgressors of the right path (*kuffar wa fāsiq-i rāh-i mustaqīm*), they will attain to the perfection of true faith (*kāmil al-īmān*). . . .[162]

It thus emerges that it was the 'Pole of Awadh' Sayyid Abūl Ḥasan Naṣīrābādī who shortly before his death decided to assign a singular role to one of his successors that was to go far beyond the cautious approach initiated by Mīrzā Jān-i Jānān. This assignment was meant not only to allow non-Muslims, and specifically Hindus, significantly still defined as 'infidels' (*kuffār*), to enrol as disciples into the order and therefore to benefit passively from the spiritual influence of its masters, but included the rather explicit invitation to hand over the spiritual authority inherent in one of its legal representatives to members of another community thus enabling them to perpetuate it independently among themselves.

Though the reasons for such a decision, purportedly based on a supra-human intuition (*kashf*) granted to Sayyid Abūl Ḥasan, remain within the realms of speculation in the absence of any further explicit evidence by the author of these letters,[163] it is noteworthy that some of the order's contemporary Hindu leaders affirm that the Sayyid accompanied his instructions with the claim that to confer spiritual blessings (*waẓīfa*) on Hindus would mean to return

162. *Ibidem*, letter no. 3. Cf. *Ḍamīma* . . . , p. 11.

163. Significantly, not only I found the order's contemporary authorities extremely reluctant to grant me access to the sources related to this delicate topic, but they were also unwilling to give any clear and direct answer to my questions trying to play down the significance of the event and seeking refuge in vague statements about the universal values of spiritual truths.

a lost treasure to its original source and should therefore be considered as a natural development in the *ṭarīqa*'s history.[164]

Notwithstanding the implications such a statement could have if corroborated by further evidence, it is important to bear in mind that these instructions were directed to one among the secondary successors of the Mujaddidī tradition in Awadh and represent a so far unique example of its kind among the numerous other sub-branches that developed in that area and elsewhere at the time. For a correct assessment of this phenomenon, it is thus essential to attribute its importance not so much to any alleged general degeneration or radical overall change in the order's established principles as such, but to the fact that one of the *silsilā*'s eminent authorities in the line of Mīrzā Jān-i Jānān, in spite of his undisputed orthodoxy in religious matters, felt no contradiction in assigning to one of his deputies the task of introducing 'infidels and trasgressors of the right path' into the order, going so far as to authorise their promotion to the rank of directing authorities. It should moreover be noted that in order to reduce the risk of a possible failure of what we prefer to define as a bold experiment that could seriously jeopardise the continuity of a regular chain of initiatic transmission, the main line of descent was guaranteed through the deputyships of the Sayyid's many *khulafā*' at Lucknow and elsewhere. This clearly counters the possible objection that would deny the validity of this affair by playing down the whole event, judging it as a sign of degeneration of a minor branch at the periphery of the order's mainstream history and therefore void of any real interest. The inherent authority of Sayyid Abūl Ḥasan as the *quṭb* of his time and his conscious choice of one of his intimates (though not only

164. This discussion emerged during an interview held with the present leader of the *silsila* at Kanpur, Oṁkār Nāth Saksenā, in the occasion of the annual *bhaṇḍārā* held in memory of Mahātmā Raghubar Dayāl on Vasant Pāñcamī, 24 January 1996, and was later confirmed also by some Muslim authorities in the same line. See also the textual references in *Discourses . . .*, p. 158.

successor) for this purpose suggest that neither an over-valuation of this issue for the general situation and further prospects of the *Mujaddidiyya Maẓhariyya* nor an underestimation of it aimed at reducing its significance would represent a correct assessment.[165] Our account of later developments will be helpful to further understanding of the curious example of Hindu-Muslim cultural symbiosis that was to develop here from an esoteric point of view.

However, Shāh Aḥmad 'Alī Khān, a reputedly orthodox Sunni scholar, was not able to fulfil the directions received from his master. The *Ḍamīma-i Ḥālāt-i Māshaikh-i Naqshbandiyya Mujaddidiyya Maẓhariyya* informs us in a strongly hagio-graphical tone about the Maulawī's deputyship conferred on his disciple during the last years of his life:

> When my spiritual guide Ḥaḍrat Aḥmad 'Alī Khān bestowed the honour of his licence (*ijāzat*) and deputyship (*khilāfat*) on this humble servant [Shāh Faḍl Aḥmad Khān], he put the first of these letters [written by Sayyid Abūl Ḥasan] in front of me and asking me to read it. Accordingly, this humble one read out the letter. When I had gone through it, he told me: "Faḍl Aḥmad, these directions could not have been fulfilled by me!" I replied: "Now, if the Most Highest God wishes so, they will be manifested". The Ḥaḍrat replied: "The time has come for me to reach the edge of the hereafter, only little time is left and nothing significant is going to happen anymore". When this worthless one listened to these words, he began to weep but was interrupted by the master's

165. It is noteworthy that the last great shaikh of the *Mujaddidiyya Maẓhariyya* at Delhi, Shāh Abūl Ḥasan Zaid Fārūqī who mentions the Hindu Naqshbandīs at Kanpur in one of his books and who was the first to inform me about their existence, takes a rather neutral if not very sympathetic stand towards them; the very fact that they are mentioned is highly indicative in that context of defending Shaikh Aḥmad Sirhindī against the alleged anti-Hindu position of this famous Indian Naqshbandī leader. Cf. *Ḥaḍrat Mujaddid aur unke nā-qadīn*, p. 223.

immediate reply: "This is not the time for weeping". At once, my heart turned cheerful and merry. He went on saying: "These will not remain empty words, now they will manifest themselves through yourself. . . ."

Thereafter, my revered master continued: "Until today, your role has been easy and comfortable, but from now on I will consign you a difficult and burdensome command (*amr-i 'azīm wa fakhīm*), if you will cleave to it you will become famous along with the prophets and saints, otherwise you will drag this very *khirqa* [viz. himself, Shāh Aḥmad 'Alī Khān] into the regions of hell. . . ."

Listening to these words, this humble one began to cry and asked for forebearance, but his master consoled him reminding him that God would make the task easy for him. He than recited some prayers for the sake of his disciple and presented him with the blessed objects (*tabarrukāt*) of the order's ancestors, including some former belongings of Sayyid Abūl Ḥasan Naṣīrābādī and his letters with the words: "Every shaikh offers his *tabarruk* to his *khalīfa*. For your good fortune, you receive also the blessed ones of Sayyid Abūl Ḥasan. . . ."[166]

The responsibility of granting Hindus access to the order's mysteries had, thus, to wait until the next generation without having been accomplished by Shāh Aḥmad 'Alī Khān to whom it had originally been entrusted.

Maulānā Shāh Faḍl Aḥmad Khān Rā'īpurī (AD 1838-1907)

Maulānā Faḍl Aḥmad Khān was born in 1838 in the small village of Rā'īpur Khās, about four miles west of *qaṣba* Kāimgañj on the road to Kāmpilya, the ancient capital of the kingdom of Pāñcāla, in Farrukhābād district. His family

166. *Ḍamīma* . . . , p. 11.

belonged to a clan of Qilzāī Afghans tracing their ancestry back to Sultan Maḥmūd Ghaznawī (*d.* AD 1030).[167] His father, Shāh Ghulām Ḥusain Khān, was affiliated to the *khalīfa* of a Chishtī shaikh called Shāh Walī al-Dīn Kashmīrī. In line with his family's martial traditions, he had been in the service of a high-ranking Mogul military cmmander.[168]His mother was a disciple of Afḍal Miyān Rā'īpurī, the *khalīfa* of Sayyid Abūl Ḥasan Naṣīrābādī at Lucknow who originally belonged to the same village.

While studying at an English medium school at Kāimgañj, Shāh Faḍl Aḥmad Khān acquired his traditional Islamic education partly from his father partly from Maulawī Aḥmad 'Alī Khān. The biographies relate that since those early days, the Maulawī and his wife felt a deep affection for the young pupil, and after the premature death of their only son his wife reportedly was so distressed that her husband advised her to consider Faḍl Aḥmad as her adopted son.[169] While still a toddler, Fazl Aḥmad Khān thus, established an intimate relationship with his teacher and underwent intensive training in the religious sciences under his guidance. Finally, in 1867, at the age of 29, he was initiated into the*ṭarīqa* by the Shāh remaining at his service until the latter's death in 1889.

During that period Shāh Faḍl Aḥmad renounced government employment as a school master and preferred to stay close to his spiritual perceptor while giving occasional lessons and living mostly on unsolicited offerings (*futūḥāt*) received for his services.[170]Only after the death of Shāh Aḥmad 'Alī

167. For the genealogy of the family, see *LVV*, p. 125.

168. *Mahān Sūfī Sant Ḥaẓrat Maulānā Faḍl Aḥmad Khān Rā'īpurī: unkī dhārmik evam sāmpradāyik ekatā*, Sarvoday Sahitya Prakashan (1981), p. 23.

169. *LVV*, p. 124.

170. His financial situation was extremely tense as emerges from an anecdote related by the same Faḍl Aḥmad Khān which describes his great hardship when unemployed and the miraculous intervention of his master's prayers to save him. Though meant to →

Khān he decided to move from his nattive village to the district headquarters of Farrukhabad where he was offered a post as Persian and Urdu teacher at the local Mission School.[171] It was there that he met his future disciple Rāmcandra Saksenā who was to become the first Hindu initiated by Shāh Faḍl Aḥmad and through whom the instructions of Sayyid Abūl Ḥasan Naṣīrābādī were eventually to become true. Gradually, an increasing number of Hindus were attracted into his sphere of influence, attending his company (*suḥbat*) and enrolling as his disciples.

This unconventional behaviour soon saw the Shāh exposed to open criticism by the local Muslim authorities which began to harass him publicly. It is reported that one day he was beaten up by a group of young Muslim scholars. Other sources inform us that a Muslim mob once threw pieces of rotten meat through the window of his habitation.[172]

Probably due to these difficulties, Shāh Faḍl Aḥmad Khān decided at last to leave Farrukhabad and to return to Rā'īpur where he continued to practice as teacher and to receive his numerous disciples for spiritual instruction.[173] Early in 1325/1907, his health began to deteriorate, compelling him to interrupt his daily routine for medical treatment at Kanpur. When all attempts to check an advanced cancer proved futile, he returned home to spend his last days among his dear ones. He died in the early evening of 22 Sha'bān 1325/30 November 1907 in the presence of a number of Muslim

---

→ exalt the Maulawī's miraculous powers, the story throws some light on the economic difficulties of his family in spite of its noble ancestry. See *Ḍamīma* . . . , p. 13.

171. Apart from the governmental employment at the school, Faḍl Aḥmad Khān used to teach Arabic and Persian in the *madrasa* of the Muftī of Farrukhābād. In change, the *mūftī* assigned him a small dwelling (*koṭhī*) adjacent to the *madrasa*, *Mahān Sūfī Sant* . . . , p. 29.

172. *LVV*, p. 125; *JC*, p. 26.

173. From one of the Shāh's letters written to Rāmcandra we know that in Muḥarram 1316/May 1898 he had been at Delhi visiting the *dargāh* of Mīrzā Maẓhar Jān-i Jānān. See *JC*, p. 38.

disciples and was buried at the top of a small mound just outside the village.[174]

Although the present study will remain focused on the Hindu disciples of Shāh Faḍl Aḥmad Khān, it is relevant to mention the considerable number of his Muslim *khulafā'*. The biographies list a total of seventeen officially invested deputies out of which fifteen were members of the Sunni community, most of them living within or in the immediate surroundings of Farrukhabad district.[175] Out of these only three are of any further relevance for the history of the lineage. However, the considerable presence of local Muslims among his deputies leads to the conclusion that in spite of the readiness to disclose the esoteric teachings of the *ṭarīqa* to a limited number of Hindus, Shāh Faḍl Aḥmad Khān was aware of the importance to gurantee the continuity and survival of the order's original socio-cultural setting in the Islamic environment and that his Muslim affiliates were apparently ready to accept his unusual attitude in spite of the opposition from other sides.

A few days before his death, Shāh Faḍl Aḥmad Khān reportedly invested his younger brother Wilāyat Ḥusain Khān as his main successor, thus, ensuring the continuity of the *silsila* in its Islamic context.[176]

---

174. The grandson of Shāh Faḍl Aḥmad Khān and present authority of the Muslim lineage, Maulawī Shāh Manẓūr Aḥmad Khān (*b*.1344/ 1925), has in recent years ordered the construction of a mausoleum for his grandfather and other close relatives, including other attached facilities for the annual *'urs* held during the Easter days in memory of the saint.

175. From the diary of Rāmcandra, in possession of his grandson Dinesh Kumār Saksenā at Bareilly, cf. also *LVV*, p. 126.

176. *LVV*, p. 126. The biographical sources tell us little about Shāh Faḍl Aḥmad's family. He was married to a woman who gave birth to two sons and two daughters before she died at a relatively young age. The eldest son, Niyāz Aḥmad Khān, though too young at the moment of his father's death to receive initiation, is said to have received the Shāh's blessings while praying at his tomb. He later left Rā'īpur for Bhīlwārā (Rajasthan) where he acquired some notoriety as →

Together with Wilāyat Ḥusain Khān,[177] the responsibility of perpetuating the order's tradition than fell to Shāh 'Abd al-Ghanī Khān (1283/1867-1374/1953) who had been granted access to the *silsila* by Shāh Aḥmad 'Alī Khān and was later entrusted to Shāh Faḍl Aḥmad Khan for the perfection of his spiritual curriculum.[178]

→ wandering saint known under the name of Nabban Miyān Jalālī, but nothing is known about his spiritual affiliation. According to other sources, he was cursed by his father to lead a life of continuous unrest after buying some sweets with stolen money. He reportedly died in a forest near Ajmer. The Shāh's younger son, Maḥmūd Aḥmad Khān, born in 1316/1898, was only nine when his father died. Hence, he received his traditional education from his uncle Wilāyat Ḥusain Khān before joining his sister's family at Gwalior where he worked in the local army's hospital. In 1931, he obtained *ijāzat* and *khilāfat* from his father's younger brother, but died unexpectedly three years later at Gwalior. His son, Manẓūr Aḥmad Khān (*b.*1344/1925) received initiation into the order through Shāh 'Abd al-Ghanī Khān following a pilgrimage to the *dargāh* of Ḥaḍrat Mu'īn al-Dīn Chishtī at Ajmer. He is still alive (1996) and holds the rank of one of the *ṭarīqa*'s leading spiritual authorities maintaining intimate contacts with the order's contemporary Hindu leaders.

177. Wilāyat Ḥusain Khān received instruction in Arabic and Persian first from his mother and later from Shāh Ahmad' Alī Khān who issued him with a diploma and certificate of authority with distinction (*dastār-i faẓīlat*) in this subject. In 1892, he passed the teacher's training exam for Arabic, Persian and Urdu from the Punjab University at Lahore but continued to study the traditional sciences, especially *fiqh*, from different authorities while posted at Kanpur and Bijnor. In 1894 he was appointed teacher at the High School of Muzaffarnagar and two years later moved to Bijnor where he kept teaching until his retirement. After his investiture by his elder brother, he started propagating the *ṭarīqa* in that area where he is said to have had more than 500 disciples. Reportedly an authority in both exoteric and esoteric domains, he is described as a rather ascetic character with a great passion for fasting and praying. During the last years of his life he returned to Rāī'pur where he died on 28 Muḥarram 1356/7 April 1937. His only son and successor, Ghaffar Ḥusain Khān, lives at present in Malerkotla (Punjab) as a retired teacher, cf. *Dhārmik evam sāmpradāyik ekatā* ...., pp. 77-9, *LVV*, pp. 129-31.

178. 'Abd al-Ghanī Khān was the only son of Ḥajī Muḥammad Ḥasan Khān, a Paṭhān *teḥsīldār* at Kāimgañj. Since his early childhood, →

Through these two authorities, the leadership of the *ṭarīqa* remained, therefore, in accordance with the traditional custom, with those who were linked either through direct blood relation or through an intimate tie that provided the required conditions for a reliable guarantee for the survival of the tradition. After the death of Shāh Faḍl Aḥmad Khān, all his Hindu disciples including Rāmcandra Saksenā significantly continued to pay their respect to these two Muslim deputies.[179] Moreover, we learn from the Hindu sources that just as Rāmcandra and his younger brother Raghubar Dayāl were admitted into the *ṭarīqa* through the intervention of Shāh Faḍl Aḥmad Khān, so did their younger sons turn to Shāh 'Abd al-Ghanī Khān for their vow of spiritual allegiance receiving periodical guidance from him.

The figure of Shāh Faḍl Aḥmad Khān emerges thus as representing another exceptional stage in the special development of this Mujaddidī branch after Mīrzā Maẓhar Jān-i Jānān and Sayyid Abūl Ḥasan Naṣīrābādī. His initiative led to a new type of development in the history of the *ṭarīqa*, for it was his unheard interpretation of the conventional attitudes of many of his predecessors that paved the way for a close association of Hindus with this allegedly conservative and puritanical Sunni order. It comes therefore as no surprise that the all Hindu hagiographies praise him as their *Ḥuḍūr Mahārāj*, and their leaders pay regular homage to his tomb in occasion of the *'urs* held every year to commemorate the anniversary of his departure from this world.

The way many Hindus connected with the

→ his father sent him to Aḥmad 'Alī Khān for his religious education, but in 1883 he became his spiritual disciple as well. Though described as highly intelligent, he could not reach perfection during the six years spent with his first master and was, therefore, entrusted to Shāh Faḍl Aḥmad Khān from whom he received in 1897 full deputyship of the *ṭarīqa* and entrusted to his Hindu disciples to his guidance. See *Mahān Sūfī Sant* . . . , pp. 70-1.

179. *Dhārmik evam sāmpradāyik* . . . , p. 85.

Naqshbandiyya through this sub-branch conceive his attitude is character-istically resumed in the following paragraph by one of the more sober biographers, Bāl Kumār Khare:

> . . . possibly *Ḥuḍūr Mahārāj* [Shāh Faḍl Aḥmad Khān] was the first Sūfī saint of the Naqshbandī *silsila* who has divulged the secret spiritual science (*gupta ādhyātmik vidyā*) pertaining to the Muslim saints without any religious discrimination. Though he himself adhered to the Islamic faith he was completely free from any religious bias. He never indulged in any kind of controversy regarding different religions nor did he ever reprimand anybody for his religious affiliation. Whenever he came across any sort of criticism of any religion, he felt extremely displeased and tried to avoid the company of such persons. He used to say that the spiritual component (*ṭarz-i rūḥāniyat, ādhyātmikatā kī paddhatī*) is every human being is only one, while the manners of social life (*ṭarz-i mu'āsharat*) can be numerous. He paid equal respect to all sacred traditions and used to repeat that spiritual life is free from all institutional boundaries pronoucing himself against any exterior noise and battle. . . .[180]

Such an attitude of religious tolerance, although not altogether unprecedented among other Sūfī authorities in the past, goes beyond the *ṭarīqa*'s proposed aim of preserving the Islamic *'umma* through emphasis on the prophetic principle. This becomes clear from the concluding part of the paragraph quoted above:

> . . . one of his Hindu disciples had adapted the Islamic manners and way of life. . . . When this disciple reached [Shāh Faḍl Aḥmad Khān] in that habit, the Shāh reprimanded him: "Now you do not comply with my work. I will not allow any blame on my role of

180. *Ibidem*, p. 33.

> religious devotee. Remain as you have been before! One should lead exterior life in accordance with the tradition inherited through birth. . . ." He did not like any religious conversion. Asserting the distinction between exterior social life and interior spiritual life, Ḥuḍūr Mahārāj often recited the following verses [of Kabīr]:
>
> *jāti na pūchai sādhu kī, pūch lījiye jñān*।
> *kām karo talvār se, parī rahan do miyān*॥
>
> Do not ask about the caste of a *sādhu*, ask for his knowledge
> accomplish your task with the sword, leave the sheath where it is.[181]

From other sources we learn that Shāh Faḍl Aḥmad Khān's first foremost Hindu disciple, Rāmcandra, at some stage felt ready to convert to Islam, but was strongly discouraged by his shaikh from doing so. Khare relates this anecdote in the following way:

> . . . Once a fellow Muslim disciple of *Lālājī Ṣāḥib* [Rāmcandra] told [Shāh Faḍl Aḥmad Khān] that no spiritual progress could be achieved on the Naqshbandī *sulūk* without adhering to the tenets of the Islamic law. While in the presence of *Ḥuḍūr Mahārāj*, the *Mahātmājī* replied that in this case he was ready to embrace Islam. Hearing this, the eyes of *Ḥuḍūr Mahārāj* turned red out of anger and he left that place immediately. After sometime, he returned and asked *Lālājī Ṣāḥib*: What sort of reprobate told you this? Having calmed himself, he explained to *Lālājī* that spiritual knowledge does not depend on any particular religious observance (*madhhab*), since pure spirituality lies far beyond the religious sphere.[182]

---

181 *Ibidem*, p. 33.

182 *Ibidem*, p. 33.

Such a stand clearly reflects the shift from previous positions like those held by Shaikh Aḥmad Sirhindī and Mīrzā Jān-i Jānān towards Hindus or non-Muslims in general inasmuch as it makes a net distinction between the exoteric and esoteric aspects of the Islamic tradition. Such a view would be less surprising in exponents of the *wujūdī* point of view, like many Chishtī or Qādirī shaikhs than in a spiritual authority of the *Naqshbandiyya Mujaddidiyya* whose entire doctrinal edifice had been built since Shaikh Aḥmad Sirhindī on a *shuhūdī* position that contemplates the integration of the tenets of the Islamic Law with the inner truths (*ḥaqā'iq al-bāṭinī*) of the initiatic path. The implications of such a radical change of perspective in the order's doctrinal perceptions as handed over to the Hindu disciples will require a thorough investigation in the light of the teachings handed down by the contemporary Islamic authorities as well as those transmitted by the Hindu offspring of the *ṭarīqa*.

Whatever these may finally turn out to be, Shāh Faḍl Aḥmad Khān in his way accomplished the instructions received by Shāh Aḥmad 'Alī Khān and began to share the initiatory secrets safeguarded by the masters of the *Naqshbandiyya* with members of the Hindu community. From that day onwards, the relations between the Muslims and Hindus of this small branch of the *ṭarīqa* were to remain intimately linked.

Mahātmā Rāmcandrajī Mahārāj (AD 1873-1931)

With Rāmcandra Saksenā, the history of this lineage shifts decisively into a new cultural context, from its original religious embedding in the Islamic tradition to the larger framework represented by the Hindu *dharma*. Though lacking the intellect-ual characteristics of Brāhmaṇical orthodoxy, this environment brought about a series of interesting doctrinal and social adaptions. From that moment onwards, this extra-Islamic offshoot, though maintaining intimate contacts with the parallel Sūfī leadership, began to develop on its own lines and transmitted the secrets of Divine knowledge (*brahma-vidyā*) to an increasing number of Hindu disciples whose religious and social background called for cautious doctrinal adaptions and reformulations while leaving its original integrity intact.

This tendency becomes evident in the course of the following generations when the degree of the *ṭarīqa*'s success and survival as a living exoteric tradition was to depend largely on the intellectual capacities and the authoritative charisma of every single member admitted into the spiritual chain to grasp its underlying esoteric truths and to transmit them through adequate verbal formulations without losing sight of the natural differences of perspective involved in the two different traditions received.

First, though, a brief biographical introduction to the foremost masters in the order's Hindu genealogy, selected from the enormous amount of hagiographical material produced by their followers, will be useful in providing the outer frame of the picture.

Rāmcandra Saksenā was a member of a wealthy and influent Kāyasth family whose ancestors originally belonged to the small town of Adhaul near Delhi.[183] During the reign of the Mogul emperor Akbar (*r.* AD 1556-1605), four brothers of this clan were reportedly endowed with a number of *jāgīr*s in areas today situated in the Mainpurī and Farrukhābād

---

183. According to some traditions, the Kāyasths (the term is derived from the Sanskrit *kāya* and *sthā*, literally bearing the meaning of 'situated in the body', 'incorporate', referred to the *paramātmā*) originally descend from a common ancestor sprung from the union of a kṣatriya father and śūdra mother. His name was Citragupta, the legendary scribe at the service of the god of death, Yama, incharged of writing down the good and bad deeds of every single human being and presented to the judgement of his Lord at the moment of death.

Hence, derives the Kāyasths' traditional occupation of scribes and clerks in government service, especially during the times of the Mogul empire, an occupation that made the acquaintance with the languages of the ruling class, Arabic and Persian in a first moment and Urdu at a later stage, as well as many of their customs necessary leading to their close affinity with different aspects of Islamic culture.

districts of the fertile *Doāb* between the rivers Ganges and Yamunā, and settled down in and around the town of Bhūgrām, the modern Bhogaon. The eldest of these four, known by the name of Sambharīdās, apparently was granted a *jāgīr* of 555 villages, along with a golden sword, a dress (*khil'at*) and the conferment of the title of 'Caudharī' inheritable by the future generations of his clan.[184] One of his descendants in the twelfth generation, Caudharī Bṛndāvan Bābū, left his hometown Bhogāon after it suffered widespread devastation in the 1857 upheaval and settled with his wife and two sons Haribakhsh Rāy and Ulfatī Rāy in the Nitgañj neighbourhood of Farrukhābād.[185]

Rāmcandra's father Haribakhsh Rāy, although described as an upright character that allowed him to rise to the rank of local customs superintendent (*cuṅgī*), dissipated much of the family's fortune he had inherited on his pleasures. The debts left after his death compelled his sons to sell their ancestor's land and possessions at a forced auction at Mainpuri, reducing them to a life of relative poverty.[186]

According to the hagiographies, the births of Rāmcandra on Vasant Pāñcamī, the 4 February 1873, and of his younger brother Raghubar Dayāl two years later were propitiated miraculously through the blessings of an unknown Muslim saint confered after living offered a dish of cooked fish by Rāmcandra's mother, whose pious character induced her to offer charity in the form of 'hidden gift' (*gupta dāna*). In

---

184. This honorific title (from the Sanskrit *cakra+dhārin*, literally the 'discus-bearer') denotes usually a chief of a village, of a caste or of a particular profession and as such bears a distinctive kṣatriya connotation as a minor reflection of the *cakravartin*, the universal monarch in traditional Hindu conceptions. As such, the ancestry of Rāmcandra Saksenā bears some evident elements pertaining to the kṣatriya environment, although probably due to some ritual offences, this caste is nowadays considered in a social context closer to the vaiśya environment.

185. Prem Bahadur Sharma: *Bhogāv: atīt se vartamān* (1989), p. 77.

186. *Ibidem*, p. 78.

sharp contrast with the worldly inclinations of her husband, she is described as deeply imbued with a spirit of devotion that led her to spend much of her time in domestic worship and the recital of Tulsidās' *Rāmacaritmānasa*.[187] Reportedly, she felt great veneration for Kabīr whose verses (*sākhī*) she used to sing to her sons in the cradle.[188]

Rāmcandra and his younger brother thus spent the first years of their life in relative comfort in the devotional atmosphere of this strictly Vaiṣṇava household. Following the sudden death of their mother in 1880, the care of the two brothers was entrusted to an old Muslim servant living with the family. After the *vidyārambha* ritual that marks the beginning of apprentice-ship for young Hindu upper caste males, Rāmcandra received his basic education in Urdu and Persian from an old Maulawī who also instructed him in the skills of poetry, a passion he would preserve for the rest of his life. Later on, at the age of ten, he entered the Mission School at Farrukhābād where he obtained his English medium degree in 1891.[189]

A few months before his death in the same year, Haribakhsh Rāy arranged the marriage of his two sons. Due to the severe financial constraints missing fom the adverse judgement in a lawsuit over his father's debts Rāmcandra was compelled to give away almost all the family's belongings and accept a minor post as clerk in the Collector's Office at nearby Fatehgarh.[190] As the family's eldest male member, the responsibility for the maintenance of his younger brother and his cousin Kṛṣṇasvarūp fell on him, their life abruptly plummeting from its former comfort to a struggle for mere survival.[191]

---

187. *JC*, pp. 2-3.
188. *JC*, p. 5.
189. *JC*, pp. 16-17.
190. *LVV*, p. 143.
191. Kṛṣṇasvarūp was the younger of the two sons of Haribakhsh Rāy's brother Caudharī Ulfatī Rāy who was the administrator of the family's possessions. He was born in 1879 and along with his elder →

From his student years, Rāmcandra reportedly spent much time in the company of a certain Svāmī Brahmānanda, an old Hindu sage affiliated to the Kabīr-panth who lived by the Ganges near Fatehgarh. From him Rāmcandra not only received some general notions regarding the Hindu *dharma* but was also granted formal initiation into the Kabīr-panth, a fact of great importance for his future role as spiritual authority. Interestingly, the sources inform us, moreover, that the Svāmī used to meet regularly Shāh Faḍl Aḥmad Khān to whom he reverentially referred as the '*quṭb* of Farrukhābād'. The latter was then living near the local *madrasa*.[192]

In the same period, Rāmcandra compelled to look for his own accomodation, happened to rent a small room near the same *madrasa*. The episode of his first encounter with his future shaikh has been described at great length by his hagiographers, for it constitutes the point of departure of the Hindu *paramparā* that was to develop from him:

> One day [in 1891], Mahātmā Rāmcandrajī Mahārāj was late on his way home from the office when suddenly a violent thunderstorm broke out accompanied by heavy rain. It was winter and his clothes were completely soaked. When the *Mahātmājī*, according to his daily habit, passed in front of the Maulawī's residence, he respectfully conveyed his greetings trembling all over his body. The Maulawī asked him with great affection: "Where are you coming from in this storm and under this rain? Come

---

→ brother Rāmsvarūp adopted by Haribakhsh Rāy after their father's death in 1884. Since that time, the family used to live jointly at Farrukhabad. After five years as medical officer at Ratlām (M.P.) from 1915 to 1920, he became a doctor at Ajmer and Jaipur where he settled down with his family. After receiving *bai'at* from Shāh Faḍl Aḥmad Khān and *khilāfat* from his cousin Rāmcandra in 1931, he began to spread the teachings of the order in Rajasthan where he died at Jaipur in 1958. For notices on him, see *LVV* pp. 164-9.

192. *JC*, p. 18; *JC*, p. 14; *LVV*, p. 143.

> on, change your clothes and sit with me. Meanwhile I will prepare the brazier". Soon afterwards, the *Mahātmājī* returned to the Maulawī who covered him with a warm quilt. Then the *Mahātmā* all of a sudden lost his senses, and without any hesi-tation the Maulawī disclosed his entire [spiritual] wealth through a flight of subtle energy (*śakti pat*) to the heart of Rāmcandrajī, thus fulfilling the wishes of his venerable spiritual master Ḥājī Aḥmad 'Ali Khan according to whom one day a Hindu boy would come to meet the Shāh who was to bestow this Divine knowledge on him, since this science originally belonged to the Hindus.[193]

The meeting radically changed the life of Rāmcandra who from that day remained strongly attracted by the Naqshbandī saint. Quite remarkably, his hagiographers describe the nocturnal vision he experienced immediately after this first encounter in terms very similar to those that charactrise the premonitory visions experienced commonly by Muslim novices prior to their affiliation to a spiritual master: the young initiate appears in an assembly of saints, all in luminous shape, in the midst of whom a radiant throne descends from above and on which is seated the shaikh immediately concerned with the initiation into the order, in this particular case Shāh Faḍl Aḥmad Khān. The future spiritual guide gets up from the throne and introduces the new disciple to the other members present in the assembly who are in fact the order's prominent leaders.[194]

The sense implied in this kind of premonitory night vision (*rū'ya*) points to the establishment of a spiritual link (*nisbat*) between the master and the novice and is traditionally valued as the unfolding of the 'spiritual seed' implanted by the shaikh into the disciple's heart proving that it has fallen on a fertile soil.

---

193. *Bhogāv — atīt se vartamān*, p. 79. For details, see *JC*, pp. 20-2.
194. *JC*, p. 22.

From that day on, Shāh Faḍl Aḥmad began to direct his spiritual energy (*tawajjuh*) on Rāmcandra during the latter's regular visits. It was, however, not until four years later, on 23 January 1886, that the young Hindu received his formal initiation (*bai'at*) into the *Mujaddidiyya*.[195] Such a gap of time between first contact and formal enrolment is uncommon in this order. It must be attributed to the exceptional circumstances of the inter-religious passage involved in the relationship between master and disciple, particularly in view of the continuous spiritual attention (*tawajjuh*) Rāmcandra received from his Muslim preceptor during the span of time prior to his initiation clearly meant to prepare the inner ground of his future successor.

In his diary, Rāmcandra describes the change that occurred in his life following the encounter with the Naqsbandhī shaikh:

> The very first light of spiritual guidance (*hidāyat*) has been infused into my heart while I was still in the womb of my mother. The heat of this luminosity nourished me for seven years [until her death]. O Merciful One! Your mercy did not leave me for long without assistance, nay on one blessed day of my nineteenth year, my whole being has been delivered to Your embodied mercy, the spiritual guide of the order (*hādī-i ṭarīqat*) and sun of knowledge (*shams-i ma'rifat*) [Shāh Faḍl Aḥmad Khān]. . . .[196]

It is noteworthy that apart from his religious education in accordance with the customs of his castle, Rāmcandra mentions no education in the sacred science of the kind expected from a twice-born Hindu. On the other hand, the eloquent Urdu style and the choice of vocabulary used in his writings betray the typical familiarity of a Kāyasth Hindu not only with the language but also with the religious

---

195. *JC.*, p. 30.

196. Quoted from the diaries of Rāmcandra, in possession of his nephew Dinesh Kumār Saksenā. See also *JC*, p. 24.

background of his Islamic masters. His doctrinal authority and knowledge appear to have been largely derived from his spiritual affiliation to the Kabīr-panth and the *Naqshbandiyya*. Important for an analysis of his later doctrinal elaboration, this association should be understood in the context of his social background as a member of the north-Indian Kāyasth community that for centuries had entertained close contacts with the ruling Islamic class and the connected Muslim culture much more favourable for such a link.[197]

Shāh Faḍl Aḥmad Khān had clearly kept observing the young Hindu for some time before choosing the moment to establish the contact that would fulfil the desire of his master. In his diary, Rāmcandra writes:

> The very first day, [of our encounter] my [spiritual] director whispered into my ear: "Your life has been inclined towards the way of Truth since long before, for this reason It shall be revealed to you. And you yourself shall relate the Truth to others. Relate the Truth, relate the secrets of the [Divine] principle in such a way as to make its transmission and the refuge your sword. Take the help of the shade to create your own display and do not rely on anything but the Pure Essence (*dhāt-i muṭlaq*)".
>
> After giving me such a hint, my director did not leave me on my own, but he himself acting like a shadow provided me for a period of sixteen years with his inner and outer attention. He ordered me to keep always apart from the outer tenets of the *ṭarīqat*, and finally entrusted me with the task of spreading his mission to the people. . . .[198]

197. In fact, the social decline of Rāmcandra's family whose fortunes were closely related to those of their Muslim chiefs, coincided with the formal end of Islamic temporal power during the late nineteenth century and the contemporary loss of many acquired privileges under European colonial rule.

198. *JC*, p. 24.

Rāmcandra Saksenā, thus, became the first Hindu disciple of Shāh Faḍl Aḥmad Khān, who thereby accomplished the task Sayyid Abūl Ḥasan Naṣīrābādī had entrusted to his *khalīfa* half a century earlier. He thereby opened the gate for the establishment, within the context of the *Naqshbandiyya Mujaddidiyya*, of a new tradition of Hindu-Muslim relationship that during the next century was spread over many parts of northern India.

On 11 October 1896, after only ten months of intensive training following his initiation, Shāh Faḍl Aḥmad Khān conferred full licence and deputyship (*kullī ijāzat o khilāfat, pūrṇa adhikārī* or *ācārya padavī*) on his Hindu disciple, thus, laying the foundation for the perpetuation of the *silsila* in Rāmcandra's predominantly Hindu environment.[199]

At the end of 1896 Rāmcandra was transferred from Fatehgarh to Aligarh, a village in Farrukhabad district situated on the northern bank of the Ganges, as deputy inspector (*nā'ib naẓīr*) of the local tax-revenue office where he remained posted until 1903.[200] It was during this period that he began to put in practice the instructions imparted to him by his shaikh providing guidance to a growing number of Hindus in the area and starting to organise his spiritual sessions (*satsang*) as an independent authority. In accordance with the Naqshbandī principle of *khilwat dar anjuman* ('solitude amidst the crowd'),[201] he spent the day at his office

199. *JC.*, p. 30.

200. In spite of the shift in power from the Islamic government of the Moguls to European colonial rule, Rāmcandra and his fellow Hindu disciples, almost entirely hailing from the Kāyasth background, were able to preserve their traditional employment in the local administration, albeit on a reduced scale. The family exemplifies the effects left by these altered social patterns on this community, and the loss of prestige in their forced adaption to the new circumstances implied. For a detailed case study of the north Indian Kāyasths who migrated in search of employment to Hyderābād, see Karen Isaksen Leonard: *Social History of an Indian caste: the Kāyasths of Hyderabad* (1994).

201. A similar principle in the Hindu terminology is *gṛhastha-yogī*, denoting those who exercise their role of spiritual perfectioners →

and dedicated the evening to the instruction of his disciples.[202] During these initial stages of his mission, however, he limited himself to the transmission of his inner spiritual power (*tawajjuh*), a technique peculiar to the Naqshbandīs that consists of the infusion of the shaikh's subtle energy to the inner state of the disciple who has to surrender himself completely to his master in order to derive passive benefit from it. This method had gained increasing importance in the *ṭarīqa* over the last three centuries as a means to facilitate the spiritual progress of the desciple during the initial stages of his initiative itinerary and was to become the dominant feature of imparting their teachings among the Hindu authorities.[203]

One of Rāmcandra's later disciples present at the ritual conferment of *khilāfat* during which the Saksenā master had to give evidence of his capacity as a special instructor describes the effects of his master's *tawajjuh* in the following manner:

> *Ḥuḍūr Mahārāj* [Shāh Faḍl Aḥmad Khān] told the *Mahātmā*: "My son Pattulāl, confer your *tawajjuh* to all these people and answer any of their questions. May God grant you success. . . ." The *Mahātmā* began to bestow his *tawajjuh* upon us. At the beginning, I began to feel a strange sort of happiness (*ānanda*), than gradually my mind was emptied of all thoughts; finally, nothing remained except the remembrance of the Supreme Being (*paramātmā*). Then, all the great masters of the *silsila* appeared in front of me. Slowly, luminosity began to appear until finally nothing but pure light subsisted, everything

---

→ among the people, according to an ideal that comes close to the *bodhisattva* in Mahāyāna Buddhism as superior to the *arhat* of the Hīnayāna doctrines. For an episode meant to illustrate the superiority of the *gr̥hasthī* above the *saṁnyāsin*, see *JC*, p. 233.

202. *LVV*, p. 147.

203. See infra chapter 2.

> around me vanished from my sight, heaven and earth, all disappeared in a unique radiant light that was accompanied by a charming sensation of love and attraction. All of us were in a state of inebriation (*mast*), and the echo of a very alluring sound reached my ear. Our mind became restless. I felt my body's desire to burst and to immerse my innermost self in that source of light. . . . A little later, this condition changed and the light gradually disappeared. Neither any awareness nor any unawareness remained in that state that was beyond any possible description. . . .[204]

This typical description of the impact left by the spiritual power of a Naqshbandī saint on the inner states of a novice is found in similar versions in many treatises by the order's authorities and resembles very closely Rāmcandra's own experience during his first encounter with his master. It constitutes a constant feature of the immediate effect a disciple experiences with his shaikh and follows the established Naqshbandī principle of first inducing a direct spiritual experience (*ḥāl*) brought about by the master's intention before providing any sort of doctrinal preparation and intellectual elaboration of the *sulūk*. It is, however, significant that although Rāmcandra was licensed to transmit his *tawajjuh* to other disciples, it was not until many years later that he began to initiate new disciples on his own initiative. Only in 1914, that is to say seven years after his master's death did he begin deliver instructions regarding the different stages of the spiritual path derived from the Naqshbandī doctrine but integrated with elements pertaining to the Kabīr-panthī background.[205]

This is not the place for an account of Rāmcandra's adaptations of traditional Naqshbandī teachings and methods from an Islamic into a Hindu context. Obviously, however, such a task required fundamental changes in doctrinal

---

204. *LVV*, pp. 146-7.

205. *LVV*, pp. 148-9.

perspective and technical applications. Deprived of the homogeneous frame of the *sharī'at* which provided both a formal code of social and ritual behaviour as well as an essential element in the esoteric vision of the Naqshbandī shaikhs, the process of spreading the *ṭarīqa*'s teachings to a large segment of non-Muslims, without regard to their social origins and intellectual capacities, implied an increasing democratisation or wider divulgation of at least parts of its message. Faithful to his master's recommendation that all new Hindu members should stick outwardly to the religious and social customs they had inherited by birth, the Hindu Sūfī master elaborated a new code of outer discipline (*yama-niyama*) based on elements pertaining to the Vaiṣṇava traditions of his own Kāyasth background,[206] which included such regulations as abstaining from the consumption of wine and meat, avoid gambling and the performance of daily prayers (*sandhyā*) and ritual ablutions (*śauca*).[207]

That this newly established relationship between a Naqshbandī shaikh and a Hindu disciple was unfavourably perceived in some conservative Muslim circles in Farrukhabad has already been mentioned. Similar objections, though not reaching the degree of intimidation faced by Shāh Faḍl Aḥmad Khān, were apparently also raised against the Kāyasth master by some of his Hindu associates, especially by some members of the priestly caste. One of those who reportedly raised strong objections against this cross-cultural relationship was a certain Mātā Prasād, an old friend of the family and active member of the Ārya Samāj who repeatedly

206. Although the Kāyasth community has been noted throughout India as a 'heavily Islamicised one' (K.I. Leonard (1977), p. 14), their domestic religious observances, style of life and relationship with other high caste Hindus (i.e., the Kannaujiyā brāhmaṇas) clearly indicate their integration into Hindu society.

207. *Santmat Praveśikā*, pp. 2-5. Vegetarianism and abstinence from liquor, though typical of orthodox Vaiṣṇavas, were not largely diffused among Kāyasths, who are renowned for their drinking habits and a diet including most kinds of meat.

tried to dissuade Rāmcandra from maintaining contacts with members of the Muslim community.[208]

But the main obstacle Rāmcandra had to face during the initial period of his missionary activity consisted rather in the indifference shown by most people in his entourage towards the message he tried to deliver, as appears from some of the letters written to his shaikh in 1899.[209]

The Shāh's reply indicates his master's attitude towards the problem:

> Nowadays, the *pīr-murīdī* relationship is not left even by name. This is not due to the people's shortcomings, but the result of our own failings. . . . To meet a veracious disciple (*murīd-i ṣādiq*) is as rare as meeting a phoenix, and the very same can be said about a true *pīr*. God forbid, there are only very few devoted and self-sacrificing people left. What shall we do? If the time does not suit you, suit yourself to it! . . . So, if you are able to, do not defame the honour of our respected spiritual ancestors and arise to treat God's creatures with kindness, affability and comprehension. Even if people show aversion to this, pray for them, for the devil has overcome them. They deserve compassion. . . .[210]

---

208. According to an episode, the *paṇḍit* once tried to force Rāmcandra to consume an intoxicating drink (*bhang-tanḍāī*) prepared on the occasion of a Hindu festivity. Later the *paṇḍit* was reportedly converted to Rāmcandra's message and even attended his *satsang*. Cf. *Bhogāv — atīt se vartamān*, p. 80.

209. This attitude betrays Rāmcandra's anxiety to spread the message of the *ṭarīqa* entrusted to him by his master and reflects the radical departure of this particular *silsila* from the traditional pattern followed by previous generations of Naqshbandī masters: The cautiousness in enrolling only those disciples sufficiently qualified for their arduous spiritual task is replaced by the desire to reach out to the greatest number of people. Such an attitude indicates the process of divulgation pursued by the last authorities of the order. This typically modern development is associated with the requirements of survival of the esoteric orders.

210. *JC*, p. 36.

The shaikh, thus, makes clear that in these difficult times the old principles governing the spiritual tradition can no longer be taken for granted, and so it is necessary for the directing authority to adapt to prevailing outer circumstances in order to preserve the tradition and save those who have fallen under the sway of negligence and devilish aberrations (*shaiṭān unko maghlūb kar liya hai*) from going astray.

This may appear to dismiss the basic principle through which in the past the aspirant's spiritual qualification was carefully ascertained by the presiding authority of the order as an essential criterion for an eventual admission into the *ṭarīqa*. It is nevertheless possible to recognise here the practical application of the vision set out by Shaikh Aḥmad Sirhindī and Mīrzā Jān-i Jānān which makes the effort to reform society a pivotal duty of the Mujaddidī shaikh. In this sense, the maxim 'if time does not suit you, suit yourself to it' assumes a central significance in this particular sub-branch and furnishes a key element in the positions assumed by its leaders in the wake of the profound changes brought about by the arrival of modernity and the connected weakening of traditional values in Indian society. The passage from Islam to Hinduism, though smoothened by the acquaintance of the Kāyasths with several cultural values, pertaining to the Islamic tradition left a deep impact on the order's subsequent developments. But the sources justify the assertion that the seeds of such adaptations had been already sown in the original Islamic environment of the order. It may also be assumed that the contacts between Muslims and Kāyasth Hindus through the employment of the latter in the court administration of the Moguls and other local dynasties had permitted earlier contacts between Kāyasths and the Naqshbandī environment, perhaps as early as Shaikh Aḥmad's time.

The developments of this lineage during the next fifty years also need to be considered in the context of the relative closeness of the Kāyasths to the colonial rulers. With the imposition of the colonial ideology perpetrated by the European rulers, the country's entire civil and military administration passed under direct British control and the Indian employees of this huge bureaucratic machine were those most directly exposed to any sort of cultural expression linked with the new mentality.[211] Though explicit reference is not found to support the idea of Rāmcandra's direct involvement in any of the various social and religious reform movements that flourished at the turn of this century in both Hindu and Islamic cultural environments, his strong opinions in favour of the abolition of caste barriers and of the remarriage of Hindu widows (*vidhavā-vedān*) appear to be influenced not only by his relation with a Muslim environment,[212] but also reflect the ideas promoted by the numerous social reform movements and political parties, i.e., the Ārya Samāj and the Indian National Congress.[213]

In 1898, Rāmcandra's wife, Brija Rānī Saksenā, hailing from a pious though impoverished family of Kamalainpur in Shahjahanpur district,[214] gave birth to their eldest son Jag

---

211. K.I. Leonard's work shows an increasing participation of Hyderabad Kāyasths in public activities and organisations which were to a large extent influenced by a Western or at least Westernised mentality though with slightly different aims: Urdu and Persian literary activities and the already mentioned Ārya Samāj and also particular Kāyasth associations such as the All India Kāyasth Conference (AIKC) organised in 1887 by Munshi Kālī Prasād with the purpose of unifying the Citragupta Kayasths of northern India. See K.I. Leonard (1977), pp. 198-9 and pp. 200-2.

212. The only reported relation with a political association I have come across in the sources examined hints at the participation of Rāmcandra and some of his family members at the annual meeting of the All India Congress Session held at Kanpur in December 1925, a political movement to which the order's current authorities and family members still adhere. Cf. *JC*, pp. 103 and 369.

213. For an acount of the Ārya Samāj and other associations with similar purposes and aims, see Kenneth Jones: *Ārya Dharm*, (1976) and the somewhat outdated but still interesting account of J.N. Farquhar in his: *Modern Religious Movements in India* (1918).

214. She died in 1955 at the age of 85. For further information on her and the rest of the family, see *JC*, Appendix II.

Mohan Narāyaṇ.[215] In 1903, Rāmcandra was transferred from Aligarh to Kāimgañj as treasury accountant (*siyāha-navīs*) allowing him to remain close to Shāh Faḍl Aḥmad Khān until the latter's death in 1907.[216]Earlier that year, when the Shāh's physical conditions worsened and he decided to go to Kanpur for medical treatment, Rāmcandra remained close to his master visiting him there every weekend by train.[217] Back at Rāipur, a few days before his death, the shaikh summoned his Hindu disciple and deputy at his death-bed and advised him to regard Shāh 'Abd al-Ghanī Khān, his *khalīfa-i khāṣṣ*, as his future guide and point of reference in spiritual matters.[218] It appears, therefore, that in spite of the authority vested in Rāmcandra after his investiture as *khalīfa*, as a non-Muslim he still relied on the ultimate authority and expertise of a Muslim master of the *ṭarīqa* and could not yet claim total independence.

In 1908, shortly after his *satguru*'s death, Rāmcandra was transferred from Kāimgañj to Fatehgarh where he remained posted until his retirement in 1929 and where he

---

215. Jag Mohan Nārāyaṇ, though his father's only son, never attended any school but received education at home from his father; he was later offered several jobs by members of his father's *satsaṅg*, but contented himself with running a small shop at Fatehgarh. He received his initiation into the order from Shāh 'Abd al-Ghanī Khān, but never assumed a prominent role in its spiritual hierarchy. From his third marriage in 1923, he had two sons, Akhileś Kumār (*d.*1974) and Dineś Kumār. The latter lives at present with his wife and children at Bareilly where he works in the Railway department. See also *LVV*, pp. 208-9, *JC*, Appendix IV.

216. *JC*, pp. 44-5. During that period he reportedly covered the three miles separating Kāimgañj from Rāipur daily on foot to pay homage to his shaikh.

217. *JC*, p. 49.

218. A curious hagiographical anecdote tells the story of a Sūfī master from Farrukhābād who disapproved of the Shāh's unconventional behaviour towards Hindus and is said to have cast the evil eye on Rāmcandra depriving him temporarily of his spiritual powers, but who later repented from his wicked behaviour. This confirms that until the end, Shāh Faḍl Aḥmad Khān had to face a stiff opposition from parts of the local Muslim community. Cf. *JC*, pp. 45-8.

lived until his death in a house spacious enough to hold the growing number of *satsaṅgīs* who used to gather around their master.[219] It is reported that during those first years after his master's death, Rāmcandra paid regular visits to Shāh 'Abd al-Ghanī Khān at Bhogāon or Mainpurī while directing his own aspirant disciples to the Shāh for initiation. But encouraged by the latter's insistence he gained confidence and gradually began to assume the responsibility for doctrinal instruction and technical teaching. With the continuous increase in the number of those who began to consider him as a saint endowed with extraordinary capacities, he finally overcame his reluctance and in 1914, at the age of 41, began acting as an independent spiritual authority.[220]

During the next fifteen years, Rāmcandra's daily routine closely reflected that of his spiritual predecessors, including regular teaching sessions from seven to half past nine in the morning and from six to ten in the evening, interrupted by his working hours in the tax department. Occasionally, he travelled around the United Provinces providing supervision to his disciples.

After his retirement in 1929, most of the day was dedicated to the instruction of his disciples and the compilation of a series of books, treatises and articles in Urdu dealing with different aspects of the spiritual discipline.[221] These provide a precious source of information about the way this first-generation Hindu master conceived the teachings received from his Naqshbandī shaikh and provide evidence for the

---

219. He later bought this mansion which his family's descendants still own. At present (1996), it is inhabited by the widow of Rāmcandra's grandson Akhileś Kumār (*d.* 1974).

220. *JC*, pp. 59-63. It appears from the biographical notes on Rāmcandra that this very slow process of recognition after the initial distrust was accelerated by his positive influence on the bad behaviour of many local boys that aroused the curiosity of their parents and other residents.

221. In 1928, he began to publish a monthly review from Fatehgarh called 'Farrukhsiyar' which until his death in 1931 continued publishing articles and essays on spiritual and social problems.

degree the process of Hinduisation had already assumed during that initial period. It is important to note that since most of these writings date to the final period of Rāmcandra's life, they can be regarded as the sum of his doctrinal elaborations.[222]

After two years of intense activity, in May 1931 Rāmcandra's health began to worsen leaving him considerably weakened. After undergoing Āyurvedic treatment at Lucknow and Kanpur, he returned to Fatehgarh where he expired on 14 August 1931.[223]The next day he received his last rites (*antyeṣṭi*) in accordance with Hindu custom on the banks of the Ganges at Fatehgarh where his ashes were strewn into the river after cremation.

It is difficult to establish the exact number of Rāmcandra's disciples or to assess the diffusion of his teachings calling for moral reform and spiritual emancipation among large sections of Hindu society. The lists contained in his biographies give the names of up to 65 disciples. Most of these lived either in the immediate surroundings of Fatehgarh, Farrukhabad, in the neighbouring districts, such as Etah, Shahjahanpur, Hardoi and Kanpur, or to places bearing some direct relation with his own family's history, like Jaipur and Lucknow.[224] It is significant that in spite of the expressed intention to open up the esoteric teachings to all those who felt naturally attracted to it, independent of social or religious background, his influence remained largely confined to members of his own community. By far the most common names appearing in those lists are Saksenā, Śrīvāstava, Bhaṭnāgar and Kulśreṣṭha, all of them belonging to the twelve sub-castes that constitute the north-Indian Kāyasth community. They show the extent to which the social affinity continued to

222. Chapter 3 of the present study will examine their content trying to assess how far these works reflect an adherence to the original Naqshbandī doctrine he received and how and why it has been modified or adapted.

223. *JC*, pp. 62-3.

224. *LVV*, pp. 155-7.

represent a determining factor in the contacts of Rāmcandra.[225] Those among his intimate disciples who were granted the highest degree of licence as spiritual authorities *ijāzat-i ta'amma* or *pūrṇācārya padavī*) include apart from his younger brother Raghubar Dayāl, his nephew Bṛja Mohan Lāl, Dr. Chaturbhuj Sahāy Kulśreṣṭha of Mathura, Dr. Kṛṣṇa Lāl Bhaṭnāgar of Sikandarabad and Rāmcandra of Shahjahanpur.

Mahātmā Paramsant Bṛja Mohan Lāl Mahārāj (AD 1898- 1955)

According to the hagiographical accounts, the birth of Raghubar Dayāl Saksenā's (*d.*1947) eldest son Bṛj Mohan Lāl occurred on 31 March 1898 following Shāh Faḍl Aḥmad Khān's blessings on his wife Jaya Devī, after the young couple had long been unsuccesful in begetting a child.[226] It appears also that from birth he was chosen by the Naqshbandī shaikh as the designated heir in the Hindu line of spiritual transmission. Due to the family's lack of resources, the child's care was entrusted to Rāmcandra who was responsible not only for his secular education at home and later at school, but who also first introduced him to the esoteric discipline.

---

225. Most non-Kāyasth disciples were brāhmaṇas often influenced by modern ideas, like those promoted by Dayānand Sarasvatī in his Ārya-Samāj, sharing to some extent the ideas against casteism and many Hindu social customs. A number of Rāmcandra's disciples are said to have been former followers of the Ārya *Samāj*.

226. Jayadevī was convinced by her mother to perform a pilgrimage to Rāmeśvaram and pray there for a son. When she and her husband were about to leave, the Shāh allegedly offered her a cup of blessed water to drink. Ten months later, she gave birth to her first son who was to become the heir of the Hindu *paramparā* after his father.

This strongly hagiographical episode illustrates the religious attitude prevalent in the family of these Hindu saints and their Ramaite tradition, and the greater stress they laid on their new personal connection with the saints of the Naqshbandiyya. See, *Bhogāv — atīt se vartamān*, p. 85 and *LVV*, p. 197.

We know that Bṛja Mohan Lāl shared his father's fondness for classical Indian music and that he was a capable singer who accompanied his self-composed religious and devotional hymns on the harmonium; he often was joined by his father playing the *tablā* during the meetings with their disciples.[227] But his main interest reverted around the painting (*citrakalā*), especially of Hindu religious motifs and divinities. He dedicated much time to this skill and worked for some time as a teacher at the Art School of Gwalior state before being offered a permanent post in 1925 as police officer in Kanpur which he was to retain until his retirement in 1951.[228]

When Bṛja Mohan Lāl grew older, Rāmcandra presented him to Shāh 'Abd al-Ghanī Khān who initiated him into the *ṭarīqa* and instructed him for about three years in the teachings and methods of the Naqshbandiyya Mujaddidiyya Maẓhariyya.[229] Shāh 'Abd al-Ghanī Khān then reportedly had a dream in which he was ordered by his master to put his cap on the head of his young Hindu disciple, the conventional metaphorical image among Sūfīs for assigning

227. *Bhogāv — atīt se vartamān*, p. 86 and *Roshan-i Chirāgh*, pp. 7-8.

228. According to the hagiographies, his High school qualifications allowed him to be offered a place as police officer (*thānedār*) at Kanpur, but his uncle Rāmcandra wanted him to start from a more humble position so he renounced this offer but was later promoted due to his honesty and application. This hagiographical report appears doubtful in the light of his high income. See *LVV*, p. 200 and *Roshan-i Chirāgh*, p. 11.

229. No exact date is mentioned in the hagiographies, but his presentation to Shāh Faḍl Aḥmad Khān's main successor suggests that it had certainly taken place after the latter's death in 1907. Interestingly, we are told that during the initiation rite he was given the Islamic name of Muḥammad Sa'īd. This indicates the extent to which the relation of this Kāyasth family with the Naqshbandī shaikhs superseded its preexisting Hindu traditions. In fact, one source points out that it was Shāh Faḍl Aḥmad Khān's main successor who intervened during the preparations for the pilgrimage stressing the futility of such customs, for 'Allāh is present everywhere and unlimited in His wishes to bestow His mercy on anyone He likes at any place and at any time'. See *Roshan-i Cirāgh*, p. 2.

the rank of *khilāfat* to a disciple. This premonitory dream led, in autumn 1928, to the conferment of *ijāzat o khilāfat* by the Naqshbandī shaikh of Bhogaon, followed in January and July 1929 by that of Rāmcandra and his father Raghubar Dayāl respectively.[230] At the age of 31, Bṛja Mohan Lāl had thus inherited and unified in his person the authority and responsibility of the entire Hindu lineage assuming leadership of that *paramparā* while his father was still alive.[231]

An extremely interesting hint relating to the ritual conferment of *khilāfat* by Rāmcandra emerges from the accompanying message to him from the latter:

> By the grace of the Almighty, today I have been relieved from the weight of my responsibilities. This assignment (*amānat*) has now been entrusted to you. From this moment, the *ṭarīqa*'s charge will remain on your head. . . . All the links and licences (*nisbat wa ijāzat*) this sinful servant has attained to in the Kabīr-panth, Nānak-panth and from various Muslim saints along with their respective skills are handed over to you. . . .[232]

This short passage contains the only explicit reference to Rāmcandra's link with non-Naqshbandī spiritual traditions, although their influence is reflected in numerous ideas and

---

230. *LVV*, pp. 198-9 and *JC*, pp. 10-12. The rapid succession with which all three contemporary shaikhs passed their authority to the order's young leader reproduces precisely the established hierarchy from the top downwards in the leadership of this Naqshbandī sub-branch. This is even more important if considering that Bṛja Mohan Lāl was the son of Raghubar Dayāl and, thus, had already supplanted his father during his lifetime.

231. This prominent position exceeding that of his father is outwardly reflected in the assumption of leadership of his father's *satsaṅg* and the annual *bhaṇḍārā* at Fatehgarh established by Rāmcandra in 1923. In his *waṣīyatnāmā*, Rāmcandra also entrusted his son Jag Mohan Nārāyaṇ to the guidance of Bṛj Mohan Lāl for further spiritual instruction.

232. *JC*, p. 11 and *LVV*, p. 199.

references found in his works. We have already mentioned the early contacts Rāmcandra reportedly maintained with Svāmī Brahmānanda, the saint affiliated to the Kabīr-panth who apparently entertained regular contacts Shāh Faḍl Aḥmad Khān. Although the biographers maintain silence about the nature of the relations between the Svāmī and the Naqshbandī shaikh on one side and the Svāmī with Rāmcandra on the other, from the information contained in the passage quoted above it may be inferred that notwithstanding his authority in a branch of the Naqshbandiyya Mujaddidiyya Maẓhariyya, Shāh Faḍl Aḥmad Khān maintained regular relations with an authority pertaining to the rather ecumenical Kabīr-panth, a fact that has certainly contributed to his openness towards Hindus and the connected desire to confer to the Naqshbandī teachings a universalistic, superconfessional dimension. It may also be inferred that Rāmcandra had direct access to the teachings and methods of the Kabīr-panth and Nānak-panth from a living authority of these two spiritual lineages, the only way through which a licence to further transmit the doctrine and methodology annexed to it and a regular spiritual link (*nisbat*) could be accomplished.

Apart from these two initiatory traditions whose adherents shared a tolerant attitude attempting to fill the gap between Hinduism and Islam stressing their common elements, it is no less important to note that the *khilāfat* conferred by the Naqshbandī shaikhs on their Hindu disciples includes the link (*nisbat*) with other Sūfī orders as traditionally held by the leading authorities of the *ṭarīqa*, including the access to some specific methods currently used by the members of these orders. In fact, there are some elements which bear evidence of an influence of Sūfī orders other than the Naqshbandiyya on their teachings.

Bṛj Mohan Lāl's first marriage was arranged while he was still a student with the daughter of a respected Kāyasth family of the town of Tirva (dist. Farrukhābād). After her premature death in 1927 followed by that of his daughter Suṣamā a few month later, on his uncle's advice he married again in 1928. Śakuntalā Devī Saksenā of Farrukhābād remained with him for the rest of his life and later had some say in the affairs of the *satsaṅg* after receiving initiation into the *ṭarīqa* from Shāh 'Abd al-Ghanī Khān besides some spiritual training from Rāmcandra.[233]

After receiving full investiture of the three masters of the *silsila* in 1928-9, Bṛja Mohan Lāl assumed a leading role in the order's spiritual affairs. All newly initiated Hindus were either delegated directly to him or were ultimately sanctioned on his explicit approval.[234] The importance of his role was further enhanced after the death of Rāmcandra two years later when the centre of the Hindu branch of the Naqshbandiyya moved from Fatehgarh to Kanpur and many of his older disciples began to attend the circle of Raghubar Dayāl and his son there.[235] A few months before his death, Rāmcandra summoned his designed successor from Jhansi

233. Bṛj Mohan Lāl attributed great importance to that marriage from a spiritual point of view since Śakuntalā Devī used to assist the female members of her husband's *satsaṅg*. She and her husband had a number of children of whom Oṁkār Nāth and his younger brother Devendra Nāth are still alive. The latter at present holds the rank of the order's foremost spiritual authority. Śakuntalā Devī died in 1974 at Kanpur. See *Roshan-i Chirāgh*, pp. 9-11 and *JC*, pp. 386-7.

234. During the great *satsaṅg* at Kanpur in January-February 1929, when Rāmcandra conferred his *khilāfat* upon him, he officially handed over the responsibility of initiating new members into the *ṭarīqa*, instructing his successor in the correct procedure of this important ritual. On that same occasion, Bṛja Mohan Lāl admitted two new disciples into the order, Bābū Durgā Svarūp and Śrī Gaṅgā Prasād, both from Kanpur. The lengthy description the sources offer us of this event reveal that the method adopted still followed closely the original Naqshbandī ritual. Cf. *Roshan-i Chirāgh*, pp. 13-18.

235. The death of Rāmcandra led to the gradual dissolution of the *satsaṅg* at Fatehgarh. His son Jag Mohan Nārāyaṇ never appeared sufficiently qualified for the task of spiritual leadership, while his numerous disciples began to organise their own circles in other places, in many cases going beyond the authorisation inherent to their degree of inner realisation and often altering considerably the doctrine and methods in base of their own criteria.

to Fatehgarh to stay at his side and transmitted to him privately the last details and subtle points of the spiritual teachings and methods he himself had previously received from his shaikh.[236]

The activities of Bṛj Mohan Lāl during the next years were divided between his family's home at Kanpur, the seat of the order's main *satsaṅg* led by his father, and his various postings at Fatehpur, Jhansi, Etah and Lucknow. The continuous transfers which coincided with his emergence as charismatic propagator of the message inherited from his predecessors, contributed to the *paramparā*'s rapid expansion during the thirties and forties and resulted in an unprecedented increase in the number of adherents. On his occasional visits to Kanpur, Raghubar Dayāl presented his son with those selected disciples who qualified for formal initiation, the official rite then being performed by his son.[237] Among these, Bābū Prasād Dayāl 'Peśakār' of Urai and Prof. Rajendra Kumār Saksenā of Lucknow in 1932 are regarded as Raghubar Dayāl's closest disciples.

In 1938, after the completion of the new mansion at Ārya Nagar acquired after his appointment as police officer at Kanpur, the whole family went to live there jointly. On the insistence of Raghubar Dayāl, Bṛj Mohan Lāl succeeded in being transferred from Fatehpur to Kanpur where he took over the leadership of the spiritual community built-up by

236. He proceeded similarly with Dr. Kṛṣṇa Lāl Bhaṭnāgar of Sikandarābād, one of his oldest and most intimate disciples who throughout his life maintained close contacts with Bṛj Mohan Lāl. These two must be regarded as the main successors of Rāmcandra. See *JC*, pp. 410-14.

237. A significant change between the old Sūfī pattern and its Hindu derivative consists in its reinterpretation of an esoteric order reserved to the intellectual élite into a mass-movement with immediate appeal. This change accounts for the great number of followers able to derive some benefit from their presence in the *satsaṅg* without having been granted *waẓīfa*. Only a far more restricted number of these were later recognised as qualified for effective enrolment, though this was an essential departure from former customs.

his father. However, the family did not stay together for long. A year later Bṛj Mohan Lāl decided to leave with his family for a small flat at Phūlbāgh in the centre of Kanpur where he continued to supervise his *satsaṅg* until 1944,[238] the year in which, in collaboration with Bābū Prasād Dayāl 'Peśakār', he began to publish a collection of his uncle Rāmcandra's letters under the title *Rām Sandeśa* ('The Message of Rām').[239]

Later that year, he was transferred to Bulandshahr for about six months using the proximity of this town to the capital Delhi to organise his *satsaṅg* at there. It was there that the first Muslim disciples began to attend his circle asking Bṛj Mohan Lāl for initiation into the *silsila* which had started its movement eastwards from Delhi two centuries earlier with the disciples of Mīrzā Maẓhar Jān-i Jānān.[240]

Bṛj Mohan Lāl kept being transferred to different places including Hamirpur, Unnao and Fatehpur until he was finally posted at Lucknow where he was to remain posted as Police Head Officer until his retirement in 1951. In all these places, but above all at Fatehpur where he spent a total of eleven years, he attracted a large audience of devoted disciples. Only a few were part of his inner circle receiving effective training in the spiritual discipline while most were simple followers who were attracted by his charming character and

238. The break may have been caused by the jealousy of his younger brother, and is perpetuated in the continuing rivalry between their respective sons. Without any need to go into further details of this querry of which I was a direct witness during my stay at Kanpur in winter 1995-6, it may be noted that these symptoms of apparent decadence do not diminish the spiritual authority of Bṛja Mohan Lāl and his son and successor Oṁkar Nāth, but may throw some light on the Sufi guide of Irina Tweedie, the co-founder of the Golden Sufi centre at London who unfortunately has contributed very negatively to the image of this order in the eyes of both Indian and Western scholar.

239. Its first edition was published in 1944 from the Tandari Press, Kanpur.

240. The first among his Muslim disciples was Dr. Hasan Aḥmad 'Abbāsī, a former principal of Delhi's Tibbiya College. He left India in 1947 and spent the rest of his days in Lahore.

appealing social message, a fact that underlines how the double function inherent to the Naqshbandī shaikhs was perpetuated among its Hindu authorities.[241]

After the death of Raghubar Dayāl in 1947, Bṛj Mohan Lāl to whom his disciples referred respectfully as *Ḥuḍūrwālā*, remained the undisputed authority in the order's Hindu environment being second in the initiatic hierarchy only to Shāh 'Abd al-Ghanī Khān Bhogāonvī who died in 1952 leaving his only son Shāh 'Abd al-Ghaffar Khān (*d.*1957) as his successor.[242] Although the *satsaṅg* at Kanpur was formally kept alive by Jaya Devī, the widow of the deceased *Cācājī*,[243] the number of its attendants gradually diminished in the absence of a central figure there while some of the closer followers began to attend the gatherings organised by Bṛja Mohan Lāl at Fatehpur. In spring 1949, the latter contracted a serious desease but recovered after being sent to the hill station of Nainital in the Kumāun region of the Himālaya.

In 1951, his wife Śakuntalā Devī fell seriously ill and was sent to Lucknow for medical treatment. By the end of that year, Bṛja Mohan Lāl retired from his government post settled down in Lucknow with his family in the house of a local devotee decided to dedicate the remaining years of his life to the instruction of his disciples, the organisation of the *satsaṅg* and of the annual *bhanḍārā*. From late 1951 to early

241. *Roshan-i Chirāgh*, pp. 27-8. A detailed account of his activities at Fatehpur is given in form of a hagiographical diary his close disciple Śiva Pratāp Narāyaṇ, published and edited under the title *Yādon ke ujāle* (1973).

242. The official succession of Raghubar Dayāl by his eldest son was sanctioned officially on the thirteenth day after the former's death, the day on which orthodox Hindus celebrate the rite of *piṇḍadān* for the soul of the deceased, when following the indications received in a dream by his closest disciples, the *dastārbandī* or 'making of the turban' rite was celebrated by a number of chosen people and family members, conferring upon him the rank of fully recognised deputy. This rite is usually celebrated during the life of the predecessor and under his direct supervision. See *JC*, pp. 522-3.

243. She passed away in June 1950 due to injuries incurred after falling from a rickshaw (sic!). Cf. *JC* p. 529.

1955, Lucknow became thus after again a century once after a century the centre of the Mujaddidiyya where people from Uttar Pradesh, Delhi, Madhya Pradesh, Rajasthan and Bihar used to flock to attend the company of the *silsila*'s last prominent saint. These were the years of the order's greatest popularity during which Bṛj Mohan Lāl undertook numerous journeys to the many places where his followers were concentrated, assisting his appointed successors — and instructing his many followers in the basic principles of his method. The strong authority of this last outstanding figure of the Hindu lineage enabled him to check the centrifugal tendencies that had arisen after the death of the two saints of the previous generation, successfully keeping the widespread community of followers united under his authoritative leadership. The great *bhaṇḍārās* held in Lucknow in 1951, 1952 and 1953 held under the patronage of Shāh 'Abd al-Ghanī Khān and his son Shāh 'Abd al-Ghaffar Khān,[244] were probably the greatest meetings ever in the history of this *ṭarīqa*. They saw a large number of devotees, including many Muslims, attending a three-day programme which included public lectures on the Hindu epics by brāhmaṇa priests, and on the *Korān* and on Maulānā Jalāl al-Dīn Rūmī's *Mathnawī* by Muslim scholars.[245]

In early summer 1954, after the annual *bhaṇḍārā* at Fatehgarh, Bṛja Mohan Lāl went with about a hundred disciples to Rishikesh where they remained for nearly two weeks on a spiritual retreat. During those last days, a meeting of three or four hours was held every afternoon in the course of which he delivered to a selected audience detailed

---

244. The old Shāh was at that time no longer able to attend the meeting but gave it his blessings.

245. Although the hagiographies claim that this programme was fixed according to the hidden instructions of Raghubar Dayāl, the authenticity of such claims is highly questionable and the whole thing appears rather as a contribution to the secular constitution of the newly born Republic of India to promote communal harmony among the masses in accordance with the prevailing ideology of the Congress Party in power. In fact, the meetings of 1952 and 1953 were to remain the only ones of such type

instructions about the essential principles, methods and spiritual secrets (*asrār-i rūḥāniyat, ādhyātmika rahasya*) of the order.[246]

This and the following gatherings at Lucknow and Bhogāon were to be his last important public appearances. In early January 1955, Bṛj Mohan Lal set out for what was to be his last journey that took him to Shajahanpur, Bareilly, Muradabad, Delhi[247] and finally Bombay where he died from the conse-quences of protracted tuberculosis in the evening of the 18 January 1955 while being immersed in meditation amidst a group of local devotees. His body was brought back by train to Lucknow where he was offered the last rites (*namāz-i janāza, antyeṣṭi*) by a Muslim divine and than cremated according to Hindu custom.[248]

After his death, the leadership of the *ṭarīqa* passed over to Oṁkār Nāth (*b.* 1933), Bṛja Mohan Lāl's eldest son and *ṣāḥib-i waqt* at his grandfather's residence at Kanpur till the present day. However, this posthumous decision taken by the most intimate disciples shortly after Bṛja Mohan Lāl's death could not prevent the unfolding of the gradual process of dissolution and dispersion of this once numerous circle. The absence of a distinguished successor among the disciples and devotees of *Ḥuḍūrwālā* again left a void which inevitably led to splits further fomented by factional tensions and the individual ambitios of some disciples. A number of minor *satsaṅg* assemblies nevertheless has survived in different parts of the country. In the Ārya Nagar quarter of Kanpur, at Raghubar Bhavan, the former residence of Raghubar Dayāl, many of the original traditions appear to remain very much alive, and are perhaps merely awaiting for a prosperous moment for their outer resurrection.

---

246. *Roshan-i Chirāgh*, pp. 50-1.

247. On that occasion Brij Mohan Lal led a group of devotees to pay homage to the tombs of the Naqshbandī saints and ancestors of the *silsila*, including Khwāja Bāqī Billāh, Shāh Nūr Muḥammad Badāyūnī and Mīrzā Maẓhar Jān-i Jānān. Ibidem, p. 53.

248. Ibidem, pp. 62-4.

2

The Naqshbandiyya Mujaddidiyya Maẓhariyya at Delhi

Continuity in the Tradition

AFTER the death of Mīrzā Maẓhar Jān-i Jānān in 1195/1781, the leadership of the Maẓhariyya branch of the Mujaddidiyya fell on Shāh Ghulām 'Alī Dihlawī (1156/1743-1240/1823)[1] who established the new *khānaqāh* around the sepulchre of his shaikh in the heart of Old Delhi.[2] Except for the period following the 1857-8 War when his later successor Shāh Aḥmad Sa'īd Fārūqī Rāmpurī (1217/1802-1277/1860) along with many other leading Muslim authorities were forced into exile seeking refuge in the holy territories of Arabia, this place has remained for the

---

1. Apparently Mīrzā Jān-i Jānan did not indicate his chief *khalīfa* at Delhi, leaving his disciples to dispute the issue after his death. According to the biographies the position was disputed between Shāh Ghulām 'Alī and Shāh Na'īm Allāh Bahrāichī, with the former finally prevailing over his alleged rival. For biographical details regarding Shāh Ghulām 'Alī, see the *Ḍamīma-i Maqāmāt-i Maẓharī* by Shāh 'Abd al-Ghanī Mujaddidī, an appendix to the famous *Maqāmāt-i Maẓharī*, the *Jawāhir-i 'Alwiyya* by Shāh Rauf Aḥmad Rāmpurī and the *Manāqib-i Aḥmadiyya wa Maqāmāt-i Sa'īdiyya* by Shāh Muḥammad Maẓhar.
2. According to tradition, the foundation of this *khānaqah* rests on the spiritual influence (*baraka*) attributed to the tomb of the head of the lineage posthumously irradiating its blessings to the surrounding environment. This explains the enormous importance attached by the monastery's inmates to reverential greetings of the founder's sepulchre in their daily devotional routine.

last two centuries one of the most important Naqshbandī centres in the Indian subcontinent.[3]

During the six generations from Shāh Ghulām 'Alī to Shāh Abūl Ḥasan Zaid Fārūqī (1324/1906-1414/1993), its spiritual leaders of this *ṭarīqa* have continued to consider themselves as legitimate representatives of the authentic Mujaddidī lineage, perpetuating the spiritual heritage handed down by their illustrious predecessors.[4] Faithful to established Sūfī custom, many of them have compiled treatises whose topics range from the discussion of general theological and juridical questions to the explication of the most subtle points of the esoteric doctrine.[5]

These works, which provide evidence for the author's scholarship and expertise, are usually circulated only within the restricted circle of adherents to the author's spiritual lineage. In view of the subtle issues they deal with such restrictions applied naturally to the interior sciences (*'ulūm al-bāṭin*) of the spiritual path and its numerous stages including its methods and techniques.

Especially from the twelfth century AD onwards, the compilation of works dealing with *taṣawwuf* gained increasing importance, and there is hardly any recognised shaikh who has

---

3. Other centres of Naqshbandī presence are mainly concentrated in the urban areas of Rohilkhaṇḍ, the Punjab and Sind, but most of these nowadays look to Delhi as ultimate point of reference.

4. A summary account of the ancestors of this lineage from Shaikh Aḥmad Sirhindī up to Shāh Abūl Khair Fārūqī Mujaddidī (*d.* 1341/ 1923) is presented in the voluminous *Maqāmāt-i Khair* written by the last great Sūfī leader of the *khānaqāh*, the recently deceased Shāh Abūl Ḥasan Zaid Fārūqī who provides detailed accounts of the lives of his father and of himself (second Urdu edition of the original version in Persian, 1989, pp. 34-150). For a study of the institution of the *khānaqāh* and the role played by its earlier leaders, see W.E. Fusfeld: *The Shaping of Sufi Leadership in Delhi: the Naqshbandiyya Mujaddidiyya, 1750-1920*, Ph.D. thesis, University of Pennsylvania, 1981.

5. The compilation of such range of topics covering the entire sphere of the traditional sciences serves the purpose of reconfirming the double exoteric and esoteric authority inherent in the shaikhs of this *silsila*. For a comprehensive list of these works, see again *MqK*, pp. 22-5.

not left a written testimony to his knowledge in the field of the esoteric science and the related methodology as developed in the various orders.[6] Later on, it become equally a custom among Sūfī leaders to send letters to followers unable to attend the *ḥalqa* of their shaikh. These letters, known as *maktūbāt,* often contain precise instructions on subtle spiritual issues and doctrinal clarifications, and their posthumously assembled editions often constitute our major source of information regarding their teachings, as the cases of Shaikh Aḥmad Sirhindī and his sons as well as that of Mīrzā Jān-i Jānān impressively demonstrate.[7]

These letters, along with the records of oral teachings imparted by the shaikhs to their disciples known as *malfūẓāt* and the more recent *ma'mūlāt* genre containing synthetic abridgements of doctrinal and technical aspects, constitute the main source available to the 'profane' scholar concerned with this field of investigation. Although the presence of a living master leaves open the possibility of gaining direct access to this source of knowledge, these authorities are often quite, understandably reluctant to disclose their treasure to outsiders and even if some of them are ready to reveal a certain amount of information to the academic investigator, a full grasp remains far from easy. Their essential meaning necessarily remains beyond the comprehension of the uninitiated whose

6. Interestingly, the Arabic term *ṭarīqa*, derived from the root *ṭaraqa* implying the meaning of 'to beat', designates in the *taṣawwuf* context both the beaten track followed by the disciple who walks in the footsteps of his spiritual preceptor and the methods used for this purpose. It therefore comes close to the Hindu concept of *yoga* which describes at once the aim to be reached and the tools employed for its achievement.

7. Apart from the famous *Maktūbāt-i Rabbānī* which contain in three volumes the letters of Shaik Aḥmad Sirhindī and the 88 letters written by Mīrzā Jān-i Jānān collected by an anonymous editor under the title *Kalimāt-i Tayyibāt*, other important collections include the *Makātīb-i Ma'ṣūmiyya*, containing the letters of Shaikh Aḥmad's eldest son and chief *khalīfa*, Khwāja Muḥammad Ma'ṣūm (1007/1599-1079/1668). Another collection hitherto less studied includes the *Maktūbāt* of Shāh Ghulām 'Alī Dihlawī, edited by his disciple Shāh Rauf Aḥmad and author of his master's *malfūẓāt*, entitled *Durr al'Ma'ārif*.

understanding remains confined to the realm of what the members of *taṣawwuf* refer to as 'discoursive knowledge' (*'ilm-i ḥuṣūlī*) if the risk of distorting their meaning is to be avoided.

After these preliminary observations, we shall now investigate to which extent the teachings of the spiritual authorities of the Maẓhariyya[8] at Delhi reflect the heritage of their spiritual ancestors, especially that of Shaikh Aḥmad Sirhindī who so largely contributed to crystallising a coherent and substantially unprecedented doctrinal perspective on the 'Divinely inspired science' (*'ilm al-ladunnī*). Since the description of the special features of this *ṭarīqa*, the fundamental principles it rests on and the methods it employs as depicted by earlier authorities of the order (*buzurgān-i ṭarīqat*) along with the many innovative aspects elaborated by Shaikh Aḥmad Sirhindī in his works[9] has already been exhaustively undertaken by a number of scholars,[10] it would be of little interest to reiterate these once

8. The explicit reference to the Maẓhariyya lineage within the mainstream Naqshbandiyya Mujaddidiyya is important in so far as it distinguishes itself from the line of Shāh Walī Allāh Dihlawī (1114/1703-1176/1762), a contemporary of Mīrzā Maẓhar's at Delhi, which was later perpetuated by his two sons Shāh 'Abd al-'Azīz (1159/1746-1239/1824) and Shāh Rafī' al-Dīn (1163/1749-1233/1818) — both contemporaries of Shāh Ghulām 'Alī — who are part of the same spiritual family (*khāndān*) and whose descendants are still present in Delhi.

9. Shaikh Aḥmad Sirhindī's principal work at this regard, apart from the *Maktūbāt* is a treatise entitled *Mabdā o Ma'ād* in which the shaikh describes in great detail the various degrees of the inner path. A similar though extremely concise work is the *Ma'ārif-Ladunīyah*, ('The Divinely Inspired Knowledge') whose title hints at its distinctive esoteric character.

10. Among the numerous works on this topic, we may mention Dr. Burhan Ahmad Faruqi's *The Mujaddid's Conception of Tawḥīd* (1947), a pioneering work which remains, however, limited to the explanation of the assets and implications of the doctrine of *waḥdat al-shuhūd*, Y. Friedmann's *Shaikh Aḥmad Sirhindī: An Outline of His Thought and a Study of His Image in the Eyes of Posterity* (1971) and J.G.J. terHaar's *Shaikh Aḥmad Sirhindī (1564-1624): follower and heir of the Prophet* (1990), along with a series of articles dealing with aspects of Naqshbandī doctrine. See also the recent work by A.F. Buehler *Sufi Heirs of The Prophet: The Indian Naqshbandiyya and the Rise of the Mediating Shaykh* (1997) for an interesting analysis of the changing role of the Shaikh in modern terms.

again in detail in the present context. The following chapter is, therefore, designed as an outline of the doctrine and the methodology of the more recent shaikhs of the Delhi *khānaqāh*, namely Shaikh Abū Sa'īd Fārūqī Mujaddidī (*d.* 1250/1835), successor of Shāh Ghulām 'Alī, and author of the *Hidāyat al-Ṭālibīn wa Marqat al-Sālikīn*,[11] and Shāh Abūl Ḥasan Zaid Fārūqī (*d.* 1414/1993) author of the treatise *Manāhij al-Khair wa Madārij al-Khair*.[12] Both works were compiled with the explicit purpose of providing the order's initiates with a detailed though easily comprehensible account of the doctrinal background, rules and methods of the *ṭarīqa*. While the former consists of a first-hand description of the author's experiences during his apprenticeship at Delhi which was successively corrected and approved of by his shaikh, the second work represents a compendium of the esoteric doctrine of the Mujaddidiyya, based on the author's elaborations and integrated by passages quoted from other great authorities of the order including the instructions he himself had received from his father and spiritual guide Shāh Abūl Khair.[13]

11. According to its author, this work was compiled at Lucknow between 1225/1810, the year of his arrival at the *khānaqāh* of Shāh Ghulām 'Alī, and 1230/1815, on the insistence of some companions of the order. I base myself on the printed bilingual edition (Persian/Urdu) of Dr. Ghulam Mustafa Khan, Karachi, 1377/1958. Some passages of it have been quoted in English translation by Mir Valiuddin in his *Contemplative Disciplines in Sufism* (chapter 7, pp. 109-36), unfortunately without due indication of his source.

12. This work was originally published in Persian in 1376/1957 from Qandahar (Afghanistan); however, to meet the needs of the shaikh's numerous followers in India and Pakistan less acquainted with that language, it has been translated into Urdu by one of his disciples, Muḥammad Na'īm Allāh Khayālī. This Urdu version was approved, edited and published from the Delhi *khānaqāh* under the abbreviated title *Madārij al-Khair* in 1404/1989. References to all passages quoted from that treatise refer to the Persian version followed by the reference to the parallel Urdu translation.

13. The works which the author lists in the preface of his book (pp. 6-7/ 17-18) as authoritative sources on this topic include, apart from the already mentioned works attributed to Shaikh Aḥmad Sirhindī, the *Ma'mūlāt-i Maẓhariyya* by Shāh Na'īm Allāh Bahrāichī, the *Īḍāḥ al-Ṭarīqat*, the *Rasā'il-i sab'a saiyāra* and the epistles of Shāh Ghulām →

The first part of the following chapter is mainly concerned with the description of the spiritual journey (*al-sair*) and the presumptions it is based on, i.e., the constitution of man perceived as a reflection of the Universe and includes a detailed description of the all-comprehensive 'science of the subtle centres' (*'ilm-i laṭā'if*). The second part will then focus on the techniques employed in order to achieve progress on the path from one stage to another. The chapter thus, tries to illustrate how the esoteric tradition of the Mujaddidiyya has been preserved in the orthodox Islamic environment of the Delhi *khānaqāh* after the beginning of the modern age. It is also intended as a preliminary base for the later discussion of the *sādhanā* developed by Rāmcandra Saksenā and his descendants and will therefore help to understand how far these have remained in accordance with parallel developments in the original Islamic setting.

Man and his role in the universe

The authorities of the Mujaddidiyya base the entire edifice of their esoteric doctrine, including their conceptions regarding mankind (*al-insān*), its nature and the position it holds in the realm of creation (*al-kawn*), on the subtle hints contained in the two most authoritative sources of Islam, the *Koran* and the prophetic Traditions (*al-aḥādīth*).

This topic has always occupied a fundamental position among the tenets of the *ahl-i ma'rifat* for it determines the point of departure for all those human beings who, in imitation of the nocturnal ascension (*mi'rāj*) accomplished by the archetype of perfect human behaviour, the prophet Muḥammad, wish to undertake the inner path that leads towards the restoration of the 'perfect Man' (*al-insān al-kāmil*), viz., the perfection of the human condition. For this reason, Shāh Abūl Ḥasan dedicates considerable space in the opening pages of his work to this topic beginning with an extensive quotation from Maulānā Jalāl al-

---

→ 'Alī, the *Hidāyat al-Ṭalibīn* by Shāh Abū Sa'īd, the *Marātib al-wuṣūl* by Shāh Rauf Aḥmad and a work titled *Anhār al'Arba'* by Shāh Aḥmad Sa'īd.

Dīn Rūmī's *Mathnawī*,[14] followed by several Koranic verses and prophetic Traditions, all meant to emphasise the essentially supra-human origin of Man, his intimate participation in the Divine nature and the eminent position he occupies among the creatures (*al-makhlūq*).

The *Ḳoran* affirms:

> Behold, thy Lord said to the angels: I am about to create man from clay: When I have fashioned him and breathed into him of My spirit, fall ye down in prostration unto him. — *Koran*. 38:71-2

This verse, is interpreted in the sense that, descending from its archetype Adam, mankind is endowed with a composite nature consisting of a spiritual or 'heavenly' (*rūḥānī*) and a physical or 'earthen' (*jismānī*), element. Man thereby participates in the formal creation of Allāh (*al-khalq*), represented by the clay,[15] while maintaining a close link with the informal, purely

---

14. Cf. *Mathnawī*, vol. IV. This passage has sometimes been interpreted in a modern fashion, emphasising its apparent agreement with the evolutionary theories of the Darwinian type, but I would rather plead for an interpretation in a key similar to that implied in the 'knowledge of the quintuple fire' (*pāñcāgni-vidyā*) as described in the *Chāndogya Upaniṣad* which plays a role also in the doctrinal elaborations of the Hindu masters of the lineage.

    This masterpiece of the celebrated Persian master Maulānā Jalāl al-Dīn al-Rūmī (604/1207-672/1273), along with the *Futūḥāt al-Makkiyya* of the Shaikh al-Akbar Muḥy al-Dīn Ibn al-'Arabī (560/1165-638/1240) was and still is considered a standard work in Ṣūfī circles, for it combines coverage of an enormous range of topics comprising the whole Ṣūfī doctrine from a gnostic point of view with the elegant beauty of its Persian verses. As we learn, for instance, from the *malfūẓāt* of Shāh Ghulām 'Alī, the *Durr al-Ma'ārif* (cf. note taken on 9 Rajab 1231/1816), it has been a common practice among the masters of this order too to hold regular lectures and lessons on the *Mathnawī*, and even the Hindu descendants of the order frequently cite verses from it.

15. It should be noticed that the reference to Adam's nature in relation to the element earth does not imply his been exclusively creation from this element; rather, as we know from later Ṣūfī doctrines also found in other traditions, the physical component of man is imagined as being constituted of four or five basic gross elements (*'anāṣir-i* →

transcendent dimension of his Creator (*al-Khāliq*) through the infusion of the spirit (*al-rūḥ*) into the physical frame.[16] It is this essential link that confers upon Man the sublime degree of dignity that renders him superior to all other creatures, including the angels (*malā'ika*) who were ordered to bow down before him in token of reverence.[17] God's reviving Spirit is, moreover, described as having come into being instantaneously (*Koran*, 17:85: '. . . the Spirit is from the Command of my Lord.', and also *Koran*, 36:82: 'Verily, when He intends a thing, His Command is, "Be", and it is!'), that is to say without any temporal succession, on a single order of the Lord (*al-amr*), analogous to the manifestation of light (*al-nūr*) and the logos at the beginning of the biblical Genesis.[18] But this cosmological vision needs further specifications. Again the author draws from the primary source of the Islamic tradition that states:

> We did indeed offer the Trust to the Heavens and the Earth and the Mountains; but they refused to undertake it, being afraid thereof. But man undertook it. . . .
>
> — *Koran*, 33:72

This verse further enhances Man's superiority in the world since he is charged by his Cherisher with the responsibility of His deputyship (*al-khilāfat*), that is to say Man is entrusted with the privilege and burden of acting as a governor on behalf of his Lord. If previously Man was described as pre-eminent to all other living creatures including the inhabitants of the celestial

---

→ *arba', pāñcabhūta*), namely earth, water, air and fire (the fifth element included in other traditions is represented by the ether). The explicit mention of only one element, earth, the grossest of the four, must be symbolically intended to include the others, since it indicates the extreme limit of downwards projection and, thus, stands for the expansion of the entire physical world; hence, the image of kneading the clay that is given form by the Divine artisan.

16. It is interesting to notice the resemblance not only in Islam but also in circles of many other esoteric traditions between this second part of the creative act and the transmission of the spiritual influence (*baraka*) from master to disciple in the course of the initiatory rites.

17. Cf. also *Koran*, 32:9 and 15:29.

18. Cf. *Moses* I:3.

regions, this verse summarises Man's position as superior to the two poles of creation, symbolised respectively by Heaven and Earth. The former indicates the superior regions of the Universe populated by various groups of subtle beings, while the latter represents the realm of form down to the grossest level (*al-ākhir al-farsh*). These two are connected by the mountains which, though their lofty elevation, metaphorically represent the vertical axis linking these two dominions.

In order to confer upon man the dignity of bearing the task of deputyship, it is said that when God witnessed the impotence manifested by the single parts of His creation, He moulded him at last from the particles of the entire Universe symbolically represented by the clay as allegorical image of the primordial substance (*al-fiṭrat*), to become the most perfect of all beings containing the possibilities of the entire cosmos and therefore truthfully representing the 'essence of all contingencies' (*khulaṣā-i mumkināt*).[19]

Hence, derives the image of Man conceived as a microcosm (*'ālam-i ṣaghīr*) which on a minor scale reflects everything present in the complementary image of the Universe conceived as a macrocosm (*'ālam-i kabīr*).[20]

All that exists in a distinctive and particularised manner

---

19. This idea is contained in the symbolism of the world-revealing cup (*jām-i jahān-numā*) described as holding the essence of the Universe, an image very popular in Sūfī poetry. Cf. *MnS*, p.12/24:

dar justan jām-i jam-i jahān paimūdan
rūze na nishastam wa shabe na ghanūdam
ustād chū wuf jām-i jam bashunūdam
khūd jām-i jahān-numā-yi jam man būdam.

In the search of the measuring of cup of the world
I could neither find prest during the day
nor could I find sleep during the night
until I realized that my inner self (essence)
was the holder of the cup of the world.

20. Cf. *Koran*, 41:53: 'Soon will We show them Our signs in the furthest regions of the earth and in their own souls . . .'.

> (*mufaṣṣal*) in the world is found in an abridged and compendious way (*mujmal*) in the constitution of Man.[21]

However, in addition to these there are a few qualities which pertain exclusively to the human condition. These comprehend, according to the Mujaddidī shaikh, the faculty of analysing and reasoning (*nazr o istidlāl*), the faculty of discrimination (*tamīz*),[22] the variety of language (*anwā'-i ḥarf*) and the skill of craftmanship (*ṣana'āt*).[23]

The mention of these distinctive specialisations makes it clear that Man must not be conceived as a mere conglomerate of particles bearing a distinctive existence in different parts of the Universe, but that he has been endowed, moreover, with series of specifically human qualities which enable him potentially to carry out the role of God's vicar and to regain his pivotal position lost after the fall from paradise. Hence, man is described as 'adorned with the crown of knowledge' and as 'holding in his hands the keys of the treasure-house of Divine wisdom'.[24]

Other hints further qualify the relationship between God and the world. Again, these are based exclusively on quotations from the *Koran* and from the Traditions. They contain elements which are important in Islamic theology (*kalām*) as well as in

---

21. *MnS*, p. 12/25.
22. This faculty becomes particularly relevant if contemplated from the perspective of man after his fall from paradise following his disobedience to the Divine order, which implied a reduction from a vision of primordial unity to that of duality. It is noteworthy that the Vedānta too attributes to the faculty of discrimination (*viveka*) a very high rank indispensable for those who want to recognise the Reality beyond things.
23. *MnS*, p.13/26.
24. Obviously, this sort of knowledge refers to a dominion beyond the realm of creation and hence participates in a major measure at the Divine knowledge (*al-'ilm*), one of the main attributes of Allāh. This point has given rise to many discussions among the theologians who are restricted to an exclusively exoteric point of view in contrast to the Sūfīs who, hold the keys to the treasury of wisdom (*mafātiḥ-i khazān*).

the elaborations of both Ibn al-'Arabī and Shaikh Aḥmad Sirhindī, such as the affirmation of the absolute independence of God (*kamāl-i istighnā*) on one side and the absolute dependence of His creatures (*fuqarā'*) on their Creator on the other.[25] This dogmatic sanction is of utmost importance since it creates the link with the doctrine according to which everything that exists in the world owes its existence to the theophanies of the names and attributes of God (*tajalliyāt-i asmā' o ṣifāt*). The most elaborate though not the only expression of this concept is found in Ibn al-'Arabī's doctrine of the 'unicity of existence' known as *waḥdat al-wujūd*. It develops around the concept of the quintuple planes of existence (*tanazzulāt*) through which the Necessary Being (*wājib al-wujūd*) reveals Itself in a gradually descending order of degrees of existentialisation in the realms of creation.[26] One of the sources frequently cited by the adherents to this doctrine to support its validity consists in the famous *ḥadīth qudsī*:

> I was a hidden treasure, hence I longed to be known; therefore I created the world so that I should be known.

This passionate desire of the Necessary Being (*wājib al-wujud*) came to be considered as the primordial determination (*ta'ayyun-i awwal*) of the Divine Essence in Its undifferentiated state (*dhāt-i aḥadiyat*), and was hence also referred to as 'determination of passionate longing' (*ta'aiyyun-i ḥubbī*). In accordance with the doctrine expounded by the Shaikh al-Akbar, Shāh Abūl Ḥasan identifies the focal point on which this desire is directed with the 'reality of Muḥammad' (*ḥaqīqat-i muḥammadī*) or 'spirit of Muḥammad' (*rūḥ al-muḥammadī*).[27]

---

25. Cf. *Koran*, 29:6: '. . . For Allāh is free of all needs from all creation.' and *Koran*. 35:15: 'O ye men! It is ye that have need of Allāh . . . '. For a detailed discussion of this topic as exposed by the two renowned shaikhs, see terHaar (1990), ch. IX, pp. 117-36.

26. For an extensive discussion of this theory in base of Shaikh al-Akbar's elucidations, see A.E. Affifi: *The Mystical Philosophy of Muhid Din Ibn ul Arabi* (1964) and the more recent works by the American scholar William Chittick: *The Sufi Path of Knowledge* (1987).

27. *MnS*, p.14/27-8. This focusing on the transcendent principle of creation identified with the essence of the prophet of Islam is further evidenced →

To avoid any possible confusion between this 'Muhammadan principle' and the historical founder of the Islamic faith, one pertaining entirely to the transcendent sphere (*tanzīha*) while the second intervenes in the immanent sphere (*tasbīḥa*),[28] our Naqshbandī authors turn to another important tradition often quoted by Ibn al-'Arabī and other great authorities:

> The relation between me [Muḥammad] and Adam was that of the spirit and the body. . . .
>
> I was a prophet when Adam was between spirit and clay. —*Ibn Ḥanbal,* IV, *al-Tirmidhī, manāqib* 1

and again

> Verily, I was the first among the prophets to be created and the last to be deputed. —*al-Ṭabarī: Tafsīr* XXI

The significance of such preliminary considerations consists not only in the author's intention to prepare the contextual framework for the following discussions, but aims moreover at focusing the attention on the immediate goal that must be envisaged by the novice determined to undertake the journey of spiritual realisation.[29]

→ by this *ḥadīth al-ṣaḥīḥ*: 'Allāh turned to His beloved and said: "Oh my dear! If you had not been I would not have created the heavens and I would not have brought into existence My Divine Being".' (related by Abī Imāma, Abū Huraira, Al-Tirmidhī and Allama Qasṭallānī, *Mishkāt* IV, *bāb-i faḍā'il*).

28. It is obvious that in order to fulfil his role as prophet (*nabī*) and legislator (*rasūl*), Muḥammad had to bear a relation with the transcendent order too, a relation established through the archangel Gabriel (*Jibra'īl*) who acts as mediator between the two spheres and hence as transmitter of the *Koran*. But on some particular occasions God is said to have spoken directly through His messenger, as transmitted in the *ḥādīth qudsī*, in spite of the fact that Islam, unlike Christianity, denies categorically the possibility of prophets having a double nature and stresses the entirely human nature of Muḥammad.

29. As far as I have been able to clear my doubts in regard during a meeting with the author of this treatise during Ramaḍān 1411/ February 1991. For most other clarifications and comments on this doctrinal section I am indebted to the nephew of the author and present head of the Mujaddidī *khānaqāh* at Quetta (Baluchistan), →

The whole sphere of existence comprised in the macrocosm is referred to by the Mujaddidīs as 'sphere of universal possibility' (*dā'ira-i imkān*)[30] since it contains the total sum of the possibilities in the realm of creation pertaining to the past, the present and the future. This sphere is ideally divided into two parts along the equatorial axis, each representing a peculiar existential condition termed for the sake of convention as 'world' (*'ālam*). The upper hemisphere corresponds to the 'world of order' (*'ālam-i amr*) and has received this denomination because it was brought into existence on a single order of God (*amr*) without any temporal succession (*muddat*) as sanctioned by the verse

> Verily, when He intends a thing, His command is: "Be!" and it is. — *Koran*, 36:82

This realm is essentially identical with the 'world of light' (*'ālam-i nūr*) that came into being with the first determination of the *rūḥ al-muḥammadī*. It designates the supra-individual states and contains the principles (*uṣūl*, pl. of *aṣl*) and inner realities of all those possibilities of manifestation (*ḥaqā'iq-i mumkināt*) which have already appeared in their formal existence in the lower hemisphere in the past, do bear existence in the present or will bear it in the future, representing their inner imperishable core (*al-bāṭin*).[31] The 'world of order' is moreover

→ Ḥaḍrat Abū Ḥafs 'Umar Fārūqī; cf. *MnS*, pp. 15-17/29-31. A more complete explanation of this complex relationship as described by the shaikhs of the Naqshbandiyya Mujaddidiyya would require an ample treatment of the whole doctrine known as *waḥdat al-shuhūd* as expounded by Shaikh Aḥmad Sirhindī in his works; cf. Y. Friedmann (1971), Muhammad Abdul Haqq Ansari (1986) and terHaar (1990).

30. This term has often been translated as 'sphere of contingencies' (see terHaar (1990, p. 95) which is equally correct as it indicates the contingent nature of everything included in that dominion in respect to the Absolute Being (*wujūd-i muṭlaq*) of Allāh. Circle or sphere are analogous terms, for the latter is nothing but a projection of the former into the third dimension.

31. All those contingent beings which are still to descend into the individual manifestation (implying the passage from potentiality to effective act) are said to correspond to the Divine archetypes (*al-* →

said to comprehend the realm of the spirits of all beings (*'ālam-i arwāḥ*) prior to their descent into formal creation.

Its has been defined as 'not positioned in space' (*lā-makāniyat*), a characteristic which along with the above mentioned absence of time leaves it beyond the co-ordinates that govern the ordinary world pertaining to the realm of form. On the contrary, time and space represent the modalities that determine the lower hemisphere, termed 'world of creation' (*'ālam-i khalq*) which, according to our author, bears this name because unlike the former it is subject to the creative process (*takhlīq*) that involves numerous causes (*asbāb*) and imperfections (*'ilāl*). It was brought into existence according to the laws of gradual development (*nashw wa irtiqā'*) as expressed in the Koranic verse:

> Your Guardian Lord is Allāh, Who created the heavens and the earth in six days. . . . —*Koran*, 7:54[32]

Since these two represent the limiting conditions of all individual creatures, it can be said that this hemisphere comprehends the whole dominion of individual existence further subdivided along the levels of gross (*kathīf*) and subtle (*laṭīf*) creation. Affirms Shāh Abūl Ḥasan:

> The individual souls (*ashkhāṣ*) and the bodies (*ajsām*) of all contingent beings are collocated in the world of creation, the same way as the Throne of God (*'arsh*), the well-preserved Tablet (*lauḥ-i maḥfūẓ*), the pen (*qalam*), paradise (*jannat*), hell (*dozakh*), the fix stars (*kawākib*), the heavens (*āsmānhā*), the earths (*zamīnhā*), the angels (*firishta*), the genii (*jinn*), men

→ *mithāl*) and constitute, form an analytica point of view, a particular dominion within the boundaries of the 'world of order'. These occupy an important position in the theories of the Shaikh al-Akbar and their mention by the Mujaddidī author shows the acceptance of these concepts even in the *shuhūdī* doctrine.

32. These days cannot be intended on a par with our human days but refer to a much vaster cycle of time, as hinted at in the verse: '. . . Verily a day in the sight of thy Lord is like a thousand years of our reckoning.' (*Koran*, 22:47).

> (*ins*), all animals (*jam'-i ḥaiwānāt*), plants (*nabatāt*), air (*hawā*), water (*āb*), fire (*ātish*), earth (*khāk*), heat (*ḥarārat*) and cold (*baraudat*) one part of it. . . .[33]

Hence, all categories of beings which populate the different regions of the universal share this major condition of individual existence in act. To complete the picture of this traditional cosmological concept, the 'world of creation' is further divided into two parts along a horizontal line: the superior dominion described as extending from the Throne of God (*al-'arsh*) down to the horizon of the sky (*āsmān-i duniyā*) comprising the lower heavenly regions is called 'world of sovereignty' (*'ālam-i malakūt*) characterised by the subtle or psychical level (*nafsī*), while the inferior part extending from the horizon of the sky down to the shoalest parts of the earth, called 'world of human sovereignty' (*'ālam-i mulk*), is characterised by the gross state that determines the physical bodies and corresponds to the world perceivable through the senses (*ḥawāṣṣ*).[34]

The upper limit of the *'ālam-al-khalq* consists of the Throne of God representing the projection of the creative principle that determines the existence of the Universal Possibility in this world, while the immediately adjoining limit of the *'ālam-i amr* consists of the subtle principle of the heart-organ (*maqām-i aṣl-i laṭīfa-i qalb*) the reflection of which resides in the cavern of the heart inside the human body. The ideal line which separates and simultaneously links these two hemispheres is referred to as *barzakh*, a Koranic term that indicates the line which separates and unites two oceans (*majma' al-baḥrain*), one

33. *MnS*, pp. 15/29.

34. The fact that the author attributes to both dominions the common denomination of 'corporeal world' (*'ālam-i ajsām*) indicates that the term 'body' is intended in a broader sense of an aggregate endowed with form, implying an entity composed of a number of parts or elements that confer a particular outer shape (*ṣūrat*) on the plane of existence in question. Only in this sense can one talk of a 'body of the angels' which implies that, though of subtle nature, their formal vehicle too consists in a combination of elements of which fire and its luminous quality is the dominant one.

containing salt water and the other sweet water.[35] According to Shāh, Abūl Ḥasan it is the *barzakh* itself as summerising these complemen-tary points of view. We derive, therefore, that according to the rigorously inverse analogy established before, what appears biggest because all-encompassing (*al-muḥīṭ*) in one dominion, viz., the Throne, corresponds to the smallest of all possibilities if contemplated from its complementary perspective.[36]

According to traditional cosmology, every creature in the realm of immanence (*'ālam-i khalq*) necessarily has its immediate cause or principle in the transcendent realm (*'ālam-i amr*), corresponding to its higher degree of reality between the dominion of contingency of the mere creature and the essential one pertaining to its Creator. In an esoteric perspective, the whole Universe represents therefore the stage for the display of the irradiations of the names and attributes (*jam'-i tajalliyāt-i asmā' o ṣifāt*) of the one Necessary Being, Allāh. Every contingent creature depends either directly or indirectly on the irradiation of one among the unlimited number of Divine attributes. The distinction between direct and indirect dependance stressed by the authors takes us to the peculiar Mujaddidī doctrine according to which the world does not represent a real descent of the Divine Essence into an increasingly contingent realm of existence, as propounded by Ibn al-'Arabī and the followers, of the *wujūdī* doctrine, but only a reflection or shadow

35. Cf. *Koran*, 18:53. In Islamic theology this term denotes the realm where the souls of the deceased ancestors reside during the interval that occurs between death and the day of resurrection (*qiyāmat*), for it separates the two dominions of life on earth and in the Hereafter. For a discussion of the deeper implications of this term in *taṣawwuf*, see Titus Burckhardt's article: 'Concerning the *Barzakh*', in *Review of Comparative Religious Studies* (1971), pp. 24-30.

36. This allows us to conclude that the Throne and the principle of the heart actually refer to one and the same reality which, according to the point of view, assumes the quality of one of these two entities. This is further corroborated by the assertion that what occupies the highest rank in the world of creation holds the lowest rank in the world of order. The *barzakh*, thus, acts as a mirror-like plane of reflection which inverts the image of the presences in one dominion and their derivates in the other.

(*ẓill,'aks*) in descending intermediate degrees of God's absolutely transcendent Reality. This change in perspective has important implications for the way the Sūfis of this *ṭarīqa* describe the initiatic journey. Accordingly, Shāh Abūl Ḥasan writes:

> . . . the principles of the common creatures, because of their languor, want of capacity and lack of strength cannot bear the radiance of the irradiations of the names and attributes; they rather develop a relationship with the shadows of these attributive irradiations (*tajalliyāt-i ṣifatiya*) reaping benefit from the lights of those reflections which confer upon them the power to fly and eventually reach the top of the veils of all radiances. . . .[37]

This paragraph describes the situation of the vast majority of common creatures, while for those who occupy a higher rank in the hierarchy of existence things are slightly different:

> . . . as regards the principles of the pure and sacred souls of the prophets and angels — peace be upon them! — because of their purity of nature, power of lustre and height of auspiciousness, they are not in need of any assistance on account of the reflections . . . nay they depend directly on the integral amount of irradiations. . . .[38]

The innate difference between those beings who inhabit the cosmic regions is, thus, sanctioned by their relatively lesser or greater adherence to the essence of the transcendent Principle (*al-Ḥaqq*). It is up to the elected ones alone to undertake the difficult path which will eventually lead them back to the original state of 'nearness to Allāh' (*qurbiyat*) hinted at in the Koranic verse:

> . . . We are nearer to him than his jugular vein.
>
> — *Koran*, 50:16

37. *MnS*, pp. 17/31.
38. *Ibidem*.

The constitution of the human being in the light of the science of the subtle centres

After establishing the principles that sanction the role of mankind in the universe, it is now necessary to analyse how the analogy traced between macrocosm and microcosm is reflected in the constitution of the human being. With this we enter more specifically the Mujaddidī teachings which propose an extremely elaborated picture in this regard. Although principles regarding some of the fundamental tenets of these teachings can be traced back to earlier Sūfīs such as Ālā al-Dawla al-Simnānī (*d.* 736/1336),[39] it is in India with Shaikh Aḥmad Sirhindī and his successors in the Mujaddidī lineage that there developed in great detail what came to be known as the 'science of the subtle centres' (*'ilm-i laṭā'if*).

Curiously, this important aspect of Mujaddidī doctrine has been little studied by modern scholars. Their interest has remained mostly confined to the socio-historical role of the Mujaddidī leaders and has preferred to focus rather on the position held by the *waḥdat al-shuhūd vis-à-vis* the purely unitarian view of the *waḥdat al-wujūd*.[40] This appears even more surprising in view of the fundamental importance this science assumes in the Indian context with its rich indigenous spiritual tradition based on similar presumptions. Elaborated by the 'Renewer of the second Millennium of Islam' and his successors,[41] this science has become one of the central aspects around which the *ṭarīqa*'s entire doctrinal edifice develops. While the available information does not allow any precise determin-

---

39. This prolific Sūfī author is sometimes described as the precursor of Sirhindī's *waḥdat al-shuhūd* because of his theories which stress God's absolute transcendence, as described in his *Arwah li ahl-i khalwa*. He elaborated the idea of seven subtle centres (*laṭā'if*) which apparently bears some resemblance with that of the Mujaddid. Cf. Henry Corbin: *En Islam iranien*, part III, pp. 274-355.

40. One of the very few exceptions is Marcia K. Hermansen whose study of Shāh Walī Allāh Dihlawī (*d.* 1176/1762) includes some attention to his version of this science.

41. For example, *Mak.* I:34, 58, 115, 196 and 257, *Mabdā o Ma'ād* (Urdu), pp. 183-6.

ation of a direct influence of the Indian or the Iranian environment on the development of this science, it nevertheless constitutes a most interesting feature of the order with interesting parallels to the *cakra-vidyā* known in Tāntric Hinduism. Indeed, the *'ilm-i latā'if* is fundamental for the Hindu initiates of the *silsila* who found no difficulty in adopting it from their Muslim preceptors while integrating it into their own doctrines bearing obvious signs of the indigenous environment. Its importance for the followers of Shaikh Aḥmad in India and elsewhere[42] is reflected by the considerable space dedicated to it in most doctrinal treatises, since it is on the subtle components of the human organism described by this science that the techniques taught by the shaikhs are meant to act. The subtle centres, thus, bear an inextricable relation with the Mujaddidī *sulūk*.

According to Shaikh Aḥmad Sirhindī's grandson Shaikh 'Abd al-Aḥad,[43] Man's eminent position in the world derives from his potential ability to perceive inside himself through the 'inner vision of knowledge' (*dīdah-yi bāṭin-i ma'rifat*) the subtle realities pertaining to the dominion of the Sacred, in accordance to the Tradition: 'Who knoweth his own self knoweth his Lord!' In the epistle titled *Kahl al-Jawāhir* he writes:

> One should aknowledge that Man who is a microcosm (*'ālam-al-ṣaghīr*) is composed of ten constituent parts

42. For a mention of the seven subtle centres of the Mujaddidī doctrine outside the Indian subcontinent, see the *Kitāb mustamil 'alā thalāth al-ṭarā'iq*, ascribed to a Syrian Sūfī master close to 'Abd al-Ghanī al-Nabulūsī (*d.*1143/1731) who was affiliated to both the Naqshbandiyya and the Qādiriyya, see Angelo Scarabel: *Il Kitāb Mustamil 'Ala Talāṭ Tarā'iq* in *RSo,* 53 (1979), pp. 95-119.

43. Shaikh 'Abd al-Aḥad, micknamed 'Shāhgul' (*d.* 1108) was the son of Shaikh Aḥmad Sirhindī's second son and *khalīfa* Khwāja Muḥammad Sa'īd (1005/1596-1070/1660), a renowned spiritual authority with a considerable following in the western Punjab. The initiatory chain of Shaikh Imām 'Alī Makānwī (1212/1797-1282/1865) of Makan-i Sharif (dist. Gurdāspur, Punjab) goes through him back to the *Mujaddid.* The insertion of this letter in the *malfūẓāt* of Mīrzā Jān-i Jānān suggest it was this shaikh who first gave a detailed account of the ten subtle organs which has since been accepted as the established doctrine by all the successors.

> whose origin lies in the macrocosm (*'ālam-i kabīr*), an expression that designates the sum of all existing things pertaining to both the world of creation and the world of order: among these, five pertain to the world of order, the heart (*qalb*), the spirit (*rūḥ*), the secret (*sirr*), the hidden (*khafī*) and the most hidden (*akhfā*), while the other five pertain to the world of creation, viz., the soul (*nafs*) and the four gross elements (*'anāṣir-i 'arba*). . . .[44]

Shāh Abūl Ḥasan specifies that the five subtle organs pertaining to the 'world of order' constitute the inner aspect of Man (*al-bāṭin*) while the five subtle organs pertaining to the 'world of creation' represent his outer aspect (*al-ẓāhir*).[45] Though from a different perspective, the science of the subtle centres, thus, reaffirms that the human being partakes of both, the individual level represented by the four gross elements that compose the gross body and the soul or psyche (*nafs*) contained in the *'ālam-i khalq*, and of the essentially supra-individual or spiritual realm of the *'ālam-i amr*.[46] However, the spiritual components of the *amr* bear a strong relation with the individual elements directly derived from them:

> When the glorious and most high Truth [=Allāh] desired to confer upon the frail structure of Man the dignity of the Trust and of His viceregency, He ordered that the five components of the world of creation be enforced and ennobled through their principles which are the five subtleties of the world of order; He thus established a relationship of affection between every principle or root

---

44. Quoted from Shāh Na'īm Allāh Bahrāichī's *Ma'mūlāt-i Maẓhariyya* (p. 76) which relates large parts of Shāh 'Abd al-Aḥad's epistle in the chapter dedicated to the ten subtle organs (pp. 76-81); this epistle is cited also by Shāh Walī Allāh in his *Intibāḥ fī salāsil-i awliyā'*, pp. 61-4.
45. *MnS*, p.17/32.
46. Shaikh Aḥmad in *Mak*. I:34 considers, against the philosophers, the faculty of reason (*al-'aql*) along with the psychical aggregate it governs as belonging to the realm of individuality contained in the world of creation, for it is through the five senses that it maintains a relation with the surrounding world; as such, it is defined as the *nafs-i nāṭiqa*, the rational faculty, comparable to the Hindu concept of *manas*.

> (*aṣl*) and its branch (*far'*) alighting them from above the Throne and implanting each of them inside the [human] breast which is the palace of knowledge and wisdom whence irradiates the light of the true faith. . . .[47]

The reference to the *Koran* already mentioned in connection with the 'offering of the Trust' (cf. *Koran*. 33:72 and 41:53) shows that the shaikhs of the Mujaddidiyya perceive the science of the subtle centres as being directly derived from the primary source of Islamic revelation. This is corroborated by the entirely Koranic terminology used in this context. It demonstrates the close link between the subtle parts of the two dominions and sanctions the superiority of the spiritual component over the temporal and individual one and reiterates the relation between the principle and its derivate as being one of cause and effect. The nature of this relationship, exactly like that of the primordial determination of the pure Being in the realm of existence, is defined as one of love and affection (*'ishq*), associated with the infusion of the Divine spirit into an earthen frame during the act of creation. The location of this spiritual treasure inside the human organism is indicated as the breast (*ṣadr*) in further Koranic references (i.e., 29:49, 40:19, etc.) which mention the breast, or the heart-region, as the place where the signs of knowledge become manifest for the elected ones.[48]

The exact location of these five spiritual organs (*laṭā'if-i khamsa*) can vary slightly in the descriptions given by the order's authorities, but the shaikhs of the Maẓhariyya branch unanimously adhere to the pattern elaborated by Shaikh Aḥmad Sirhindī.[49] Accordingly, the *laṭīfa-i qalb* is located on the left

47. *MnS*, pp.17/32; cf. also *MuM*, p. 77.

48. Cf. *Koran* 96; this *sūrah* describes the opening of the breast of Muḥammad by the two archangels that sanctioned the beginning of his prophethood.

49. Interesting graphical plans of the disposition of the subtle centres in the human breast according to the old scheme introduced by Khwāja Bahā al-Dīn al-Naqshband together with the new one introduced by Shaikh Aḥmad Sirhindī are given by the hagiographer of Maulānā Sayyid Ghawth 'Alī Shāh Qalandarī Pānīpatī, Maulawī Shāh Gul Ḥasan Qādirī, in his *Tadhkira-i Ghauthiya* (pp. 146-8), which includes also a detailed description of each single *laṭīfa* (see Appendix II).

side of the breast, two fingers beneath the nipple, in correspondence with the vital corporeal organ which the masters refer to as 'pinecone heart' (*qalb-i sanawbarī*) because of its resemblance to the fruit of the pine-tree whose shape resembles to a reverse triangle turned (*maqlūb*).[50] The *laṭīfa-i rūḥ*, associated with the element air (*bād*, *hawā*) occupies the same position on the right side of the breast. The *laṭīfa-i sirr*, associated with the element water (*āb*), is located on the left side of the breast between the heart and the exact centre of the breast. The *laṭīfa-i khafī*, associated with the element fire (*ātish*), is on the corresponding right side, while the *laṭīfa-i akhfā*, associated with the earth (*khāk*), regarded as the most beautiful and perfect of all spiritual organs and nearest to the Divine presence, has been located in the very centre of the breast.[51]

To each of these subtle organs is attributed a particular colour conventionally described as yellow for the *qalb*, red for the *rūḥ*, white for the *sirr*, black for the *khafī* and green for the *akhfā*.[52] Along with the subtle organ of the soul (*nafs*) located on the forehead between the two eyebrows[53] and that comprising the entire physical frame (*qālib*) composed of the four gross

---

50. It is important to note that the Arabic term *qalb* derives from the root *qalaba* with the meaning of 'to invert, to turn', with the intrinsic implication of a sense of inversion. It is noteworthy that in other traditions too, the geometrical symbol of the heart is represented by an inverted triangle pointing towards the ground. This symbolism is closely connected with the analogy between the two main dominions of the Universe and the reflection, from *amr* to *khalq*, of the images or celestial archetypes (*mithāl*).

51. *MnS*, pp. 17-18/32-3, *MuM*, pp. 77-9, *HdT*, pp. 8-9, *Majālis-i Ḥabīb*, pp. 174-8.

52. According to Shāh Abūl Ḥasan, it is to these subtle organs implanted by Allāh into the human breast in order to implement His desire to create Man similar to Himself that the verse 'On the earth there are signs for those of assured faith, as also given in your own selves: will ye not then see?' (*Koran*, 51:20-1) refers.

53. According to many Sufis, the *nafs* is located at a distance of about two fingers below the navel, while Shaikh Aḥmad Sirhindī situates it on the forehead. This apparent disaccordance led some authorities to the conclusion that while its root lies below the navel its head extends up to the forehead, thus comprising the entire intermeditate domain.

elements, these represent the seven subtle centres (*laṭā'if-i sab'a*) whose gradual purification enables the spiritual traveller (*sālik*) to traverse the stations of the initiatic path.[54] Through this process the initiate seeks to achieve the reintegration (*fanā*) of all seven subtle centres into their immediately superior principles that has become necessary because the five subtle organs lost their original luminosity during their descent into the world of creation caused by their link with the concupiscent soul (*nafs-i ammāra*) which is contaminated by its attachment to worldly objects. It, therefore, aims to restore their original situation and state of radiance in the 'pacified soul' (*nafs-i muṭma'inna*), a return which if interpreted from a different angle, corresponds to the re-conquest of the primordial condition of mankind's common ancestor Adam when 'the angels laid down their head in prostration acknowledging his excellence and eminence'.

Each of these five subtle organs is said to bear a relation with one of the degrees of sainthood (*wilāyat*) leading step by step to the vision of the pure Essence of Allāh (*mushāhada*). Simultaneously, each of these five degrees is also related to the essential nature of one of the 'prophets of right determination' (*anbiyā'-i ulū al-'azm*). During his passage through each subtle centre, the disciple is said to be guided by the prophet who governs and thereby, characterises that particular station. The initiate, thus, follows in the footsteps of these spiritual archetypes who have paved the way for those who are ready to follow them, thereby being endowed with the intimate nature of these prophets (*al-mashrab*).[55] Every subtle centre is, moreover, associated with a particular irradiation (*tajallī*), corresponding to one of the major Divine attributes which reflect different aspects of the Truth contained in God's Essence. According to individual capacity, every disciple partakes of one or more of these degrees during his ascent (*'urūj*) towards the

54. Cf. *MnS*, pp. 52/76.

55. This idea of following the footsteps of those who have shown the path bears some resemblance to the Buddha in his role as *tathāgata* (lit., 'he who has thus walked'), or to the Jain *tīrthaṁkāras* (lit. 'preparer of the ford').

peak that will grant him contemplation of the Divine essence (*al-dhāt*). The *laṭīfa-i qalb*, the nearest to the realm of creation and considered as the *barzakh* itself,[56] is related to the irradiation of the 'attribute of creative action' (*tajallī-yi ṣifāt-i takwīn wa fa'l*), qualified as one of the additional attributes of God (*ṣifāt-i iḍafiya*) on which depends the existence of all possible beings.[57] Whosoever acquires the perfection of this subtle centre presided by the prophet Adam and considered as the root of all the remaining centres will ultimately transcend any attachment to his own individual way of acting and instead accomplish everything in harmony with Divine action.[58] This stage corresponds to the 'extinction of the heart' (*fanā-i qalb*) and constitutes the result of the process of spiritual realisation termed as 'cleansing of the heart' (*taṣfiya-i qalb*) during which the disciple must concentrate his efforts on cutting his attachment to the transient world while focusing on God alone. The Mujaddidī teachings saction that the subtle heart is intimately connected with the 'subtlety of the soul' (*laṭīfa-i nafs*) which covers with the innumerable veils created by the numerous sensual impulses received from the outside world the direct vision of the essence of the heart.[59]

In order to correct the relationship between these two subtle centres, many later authorities have advised their disciples to consider the 'purification of the soul' (*tadhkiya-i nafs*) as an

---

56. With due precaution, it could be argued that the principle represented by the Throne of God on a macrocosmic level in the 'sphere of contingency', is represented by the spiritual organ inside the human heart on a microcosmic plane; it is this sense that justifies the analogy between the cosmic mountain (*jabal al-qāf*, Mount *Meru*) with the cavern in the heart indicated, e.g., the Gospel's mustard seed (Matthew 13:31-2, Mark 4:30-2, Luke 13:18-19) and the seed in the Upaniṣad said to be smaller than the smallest particle.

57. According to Shāh Abūl Ḥasan, the abode of the heart-principle is also referred to as 'the greater heart' (*qalb-i kabīr*), or the seat of the all-comprehensive Truth (*ḥaqīqat-i jam'*). Both terms hint at the heart as the symbolic centre of Being.

58. *MuM*, p. 77.

59. The root of *nafs* is *nafas*, literally, 'to desire greatly, to esteem', an indication of the state it commonly refers to.

important process leading to the transmutation of the carnal soul (*nafs-i ammāra*) which is pervaded by vices and distractions into a 'soul pervaded by peace' (*nafs-i muṭma'inna*) which reflects its inner purity outwardly through virtues and laudable qualities.[60] So, the purified soul outwardly reflects the brightness irradiating from the inner perfection of the heart. Major attention is given nowadays to these two subtle centres regarded as pivotal in the human organism. Many shaikhs maintain that the purification of these two alone is sufficient for the average disciple since it includes in principle that of the remaining subtle organs.

Such an attitude, however, seems to be the result of a simplification and reduction of the original method due to the peculiar circumstances of our epoch in which few people possess the capability to traverse the entire *sulūk*. However, on the basis of their own achievements, all great shaikhs of the Delhi lineage of the Mujaddidiyya, while admitting for this possibility in principle, give preference to the original method as taught by Shaikh Aḥmad Sirhindī which embraces the complete journey through all seven subtle centres.[61]

The *laṭīfa-i rūḥ* whose location in the *'ālam-i amr* lies above that of the *qalb*, is associated with the prophets Noah and Abraham. Its utmost perfection consists of the adherence to the irradiation of God's affirmative attributes (*tajalliyāt-i ṣifāt-i thubūtiya*). The disciple who has reached this second level of sainthood is said to be freed from all individual limitations. He, thus, remains completely connected with the attributes of his Lord.

Similarly, the *laṭīfa-i sirr* which lies one step higher is related to Moses. Its inner reality bears an intimate relation with the irradiations of the essential qualities of Allāh (*tajalliyāt-i shuyūnāt-i dhātiya*) which are one step closer to the pure Essence of God.

---

60. For a discussion of these two phases of the spiritual process, see Mir Valiuddin (1980), chapters I and II.

61. Cf. *MuM*, p. 77.

The essential nature of the *laṭīfa-i khafī* constitutes the fourth level of sainthood and is characterised by the prophecy of Jesus. Its full reintegration establishes the contact with the irradiations of the negative attributes of the transcendent plane (*tajalliyāt-i ṣifāt-i salbiya-i tanzīha*) and refers to the degree of non-existence (*'adam*) as complementary to that of existence (*wujūd*).

Finally, the fifth and most subtle among the spiritual organs, the *laṭīfa-i akhfā* which is the nearest to the pure Essence (*dhāt-i pāk*)[62] and is situated at the exact centre of the human breast (*wasaṭ-i sīna*), is associated to the 'seal of prophethood' (*khātm al-nubuwwat*) Muḥammad, considered the most perfect of all prophets.[63] The intrinsic nature of this subtle organ is connected with the irradiation of the universal reality (*tajallī-i shān-i jam'*) which the order's authorities describe as a *barzakh* between the plane of absolute transcendence (*martaba-i tanzīhī*) and that of Pure Unity (*aḥadiyat-i mujarrada*).[64] It represents for the Mujaddidīs the entrance gate to the degree of 'major sainthood' (*wilāyat-i kubrā*). In the language of the *wujūdīs*, this corresponds to the level of union (*ittiḥād*) and unification (*jam'*). Here the ascending 'journey towards Allāh' (*sair ilā Allāh*), comes to an end. Now the disciple will turn to the *laṭīfa-i nafs*, trying to rectify its corrupted state caused by the impressions left by the innumerable sensual desires and distractions, in order to achieve the definitive extinction (*fanā*) and permanent realisation (*baqā*) that will ultimately confer upon the disciple's inner state a lasting state of peace (*iṭmīnān*).

62. It must be noted that in the Mujaddidī terminology, there can be no question of identity between the Necessary Being and the contingent possibilities but only of proximity (*qurbiyat*) and of utmost proximity (*aqrabiyat*).

63. The hierarchy, thus, sanctioned among the prophets coincides with the chronological succession of their mission, cf. *Koran*, 2:253: 'Those messengers We endowed with gifts, some above others. . .'. It should also be pointed out that the association of Muḥammad with the source of all realities underlines his image as source of all spiritual bliss (*baraka*), the main reason that all spiritual orders of Islam trace their genealogy back to him.

64. *MuM*, p. 39 and *MnS*, pp. 20/37.

Hereafter, attention will be focussed on the subtle essence of three of the four primary elements pertaining to the realm of creation, namely the elements fire, air and water. This further advancement implies a gradual return to the outer world of form until the *sālik* eventually reaches the refinement of the subtle essence of the grossest of all elements, i.e., earth. His return to the world will be brought to perfection through the attainment of the prophetic perfections (*kamālāt-i nubuwwa*). The ultimate stage of the path will lead to the synthesis of the subtle organs of both dominions in an all-integrating subtlety (*hai'at-i waḥdānī*) which comprehends the entire physical frame (*qālib*).

This in sum is the path of gradual spiritual realisation conceived from the perspective of the science of the subtle centres as handed down by the authorities of the order till the present day. Its completion guarantees the attainment of the highest degree of perfection contemplated by the *ṭarīqa* and is reached by following the instructions left by Shaikh Aḥmad Sirhindī to his successors. The multiplicity of tracks implied in the knowledge of the various subtle organs is said to facilitate the task of aspirant adepts taking into account the different degrees of their individual qualifications and natures. The existence of such natural hierarchy among human creatures, including saints and prophets, is corroborated by a Divine sanction found in the *Koran*:

> To each among you have We prescribed a Law and an open way. If Allāh had so willed, He would have made you a single People, but to test you in what He hath given you. . . . — *Koran*, 5:48

But it is important to bear in mind that the assimilation of some major prophets to each of the quintuple degrees of sainthood cannot imply the identification of the seeker with the perfections of their essential nature, an impossibility in terms of Islamic orthodoxy which the authorities of the *ṭarīqa* repeatedly stress. Such a position would be in open contradiction with the teachings of the *Imām-i Rabbānī* according to whom the rank of prophethood (*nubuwwa*) constitutes an infinitely higher degree of perfection as compared to the degree of sainthood (*wilāya*).[65] In the *shuhūdī* perspective, it rather indicates the initiates participation at the shadow (*ẓill*) or reflection (*'aks*) of the prophetic perfection in question or, in other words, the *murīd's* effective assimilation of one of the manifold qualities characterising that particular prophet.[66] The qualitative difference between the two consists, according to our shaikhs, in the fact that while the nature of the prophets is in relation with and nourished by the totality of the respective Divine names and attributes, their spiritual heirs are related and nourished only by the shadows and single points on the rays of their irradiations. Hence, the individual's inner constitution is determined by only a fraction of these attributes and only those who can participate in the reflection of the prophet of Islam (*muḥammadī al-mashrab*) will be capable of crossing the 'straight royal highway' (*shāhrāh-i mustaqīm*) that leads through all five subtle centres up to the degree of Unity connected with the total sum of Divine attributes, at the very source of their irradiation.[67]

Since the essential function of the prophets and messengers is to convey a new Divinely revealed message to the world and its people, besides their innate spiritual perfections they too must participate in the elements of creation outwardly symbolised through their physical body. But only those few people endowed with exceptional spiritual insight are able to distingu-ish the prophets from other human beings, while most remain limited to the perception of their outer appearance altogether similar to that of common people. It is to the former that the verse '. . . . They are the Party of Allāh. Truly, it is the Party of Allāh that will achieve Success' (*Koran*, 58:22) refers,

---

65. Cf. *Mak.* I:95, 108, 260, 301 and II:46.
66. *Makātib-i Ḥaḍrat Shāh Ghulām 'Alī Dihlawī*, quoted in *Qāfila-i ahl-i dil*, p. 126.
67. In this sense, Muḥammad's central position among the prophets and legislators is analogous to the central position held by the *nafs* among the elements of the *khalq* and that of the *akhfā* among the spiritual components of the *amr*. Cf. Ibn al-'Arabī's idea that every *walī* is a heir to the prophethood of a particular prophet.

in a sense that may here be compared to those who have achieved the purification of their subtle organs. After being admitted into the company of the saints (*awliyā Allāh*), they contemplate the inner truth of all creatures through direct connection with the source of the Divine names and attributes which partakes of the radiance that illuminates the Universe as a reflection of the primordial *nūr-i muḥammadī*.

The stages of the path in the light of the science of the subtle centres

The different stages (*darjāt, marātib*) of the initiatory journey described by Shaikh Aḥmad Sirhindī and his followers are so intimately related to the subtle organs that both must be dealt with simultaneously. This close interrelation indicates the extent to which the science of the subtle centres (*'ilm-i laṭā'if*) permeates the entire doctrine of the order as the core around which everything else revolves and as the link between the *ṭarīqa*'s speculative (*'ilmī*) and operative (*'amlī*) aspects. Any attempt to describe the single stages of the inner journey, depicted as 'spheres' or 'circles' (*dawā'ir*, pl. of *dā'ira*), must, therefore, include some further aspects of this science from a different perspective. Hence, the subtle centres can be seen as signs of the Divine presence in the world shining through the innumerable veils of the soul which prevent man from witnessing the Divine Truth.[68]

The spiritual journey as conceived by the Mujaddidīs consists of two major phases. The first is ascending (*'urūj*) during which the disciple accomplishes an upward 'movement' (*ḥarkat*)[69] away from the apparent multiplicity of creation

---

68. Cf. *Koran*, 41:53. It is curious to note the parallel between the luminosity of the seven subtle organs and the seven colours of the rainbow which, as we know, are produced by the refractions of the colourless light of the sun, the luminous source that illuminates our world, in the intermediate space of the atmosphere.

69. In *Mak*. I:144, Shaikh Aḥmad Sirhindī stresses the fact that the terms *sair* and *sulūk* are more or less synonyms; both denote rather than a movement in space a qualitative movement from a lower stage of spiritual realisation to a series of progressively higher stages.

towards a unitarian experience achieved through a synthesised vision. This part of the journey is called 'journey towards Allāh' (*sair ilā Allāh*). By the end of this phase any individual consciousness (*anāniyyat*) whence arises the idea of being separated from the principle of generation will be annihilated (*fanā*). Once he has reached this stage, the spiritual traveller will be in contact with the source of the determinations (*ta'ayyunāt*) of all contingent creatures and will recognise the existence of the world as being a mere shadow of the names and attributes of God, the only One Necessary Being (*wājib al-wujūd*). This part of the initiatory process is called 'the journey in Allāh' (*sair fī Allāh*) because of the disciple's co-presence (*ma'iyat*) with God during this stage which signals the perfection of the ascending phase. At the same time it preludes to the beginning of the second, descending phase of the spiritual journey (*nuzūl*). That phase is referred to as 'journey from Allāh with Allāh' (*sair 'an Allāh bi Allāh*) and implies an apparent return (*rujū'*) from the Divine station towards the contingent reality of the world. It reaches its perfection when the adept, now endowed the with the innermost vision of Divine wisdom (*ḥikmat-i ilāhī*) penetrates the inner reality of every single object, of every single act accomplished by every single creature. This part of the path is called the 'journey through things' (*sair dar ashiyā'*).[70]

The first two phases of the ascending journey lead the *murīd* to the realm of the 'saints living in seclusion' (*awliyā'-i 'uzlat*) while the last two phases of the descending journey are said to open to the traveller the gates to the realms of the 'saints of social entertainment' (*awliyā'-i 'ishrat*).[71] These subsequent stages in the disciple's spiritual development are closely interconnected with the process of transmutation that uses the subtle organs as ground for action. For this reason and in virtue of the analogy between microcosm and macrocosm it is possible to

70. For a detailed description based on Shaikh Aḥmad Sirhindī, cf. terHaar (1990), pp. 93-4.

71. The connotations of *'ishrat* suggest analogies with the Hindu tradition important for the Kāyasth initiates of the order who consider this condition an essential ingredient of their spiritual discipline.

assimilate this interior process to a journey through the realms of the cosmos.[72] It is in this sense that the return of the *laṭā'if* from the spatial extension of the cosmos towards their contraction and finally extinction in the principles of the 'world of order' is at first described as a 'journey from the cardinal points' (*sair-i āfāqī*) and successively as the perfection of the 'journey through the inner selves' (*sair-i anfusī*).[73] In fact, the journey through the first of the seven spheres leads the 'traveller' through the 'sphere of universal existence' symbolically indicated by the four cardinal points which govern the spatial extension of the latter. Whenever any of the subtle centres is awakened through the use of precisely focussed techniques and thereby becomes aware of its origin, it 'bursts out into a flame of passion and takes flight towards its heavenly principle so as to unite itself with it'.[74] In the terminology of the Mujaddidīs this is called the 'opening of the gate' (*fatḥ-i bāb*).

The luminosity of the subtle organ continues to increase until it is perceived by the initiate as bursting out of its seat inside the body and departing in the guise of a column of light that continues to grow until it eventually reaches the world of order. The utmost perfection of the *sair-i āfāqī* includes the return of the five subtle organs located in the human breast plus the *nafs* to the intemporal reality of the celestial world (*'ālam-i quds*) through the central and most elevated of all five subtle centres, the *laṭīfa-i akhfā* situated in the very centre of the breast. According to the shaikhs, this transcendence of the

72. Cf. the work and description of the alchemists in the hermetic tradition whose efforts rested on the subtle transmutation of a series of elements into a higher order; the spiritual degree of a Sūfī like Ibn al-'Arabī was described as the station of 'red sulphur' (*al-kibrit al-aḥmar*).

73. The mention of these two journeys derives directly from the famous verse: 'Soon will We show them Our signs in the furthest regions of the earth (*fi'l-āfāqī*) and inside their own souls (*fī anfusikum*)'. (*Koran*, 41:53).

74. *MnS*, pp. 23/49. Interestingly, this 'extreme passion' that develops inside the subtle organ is described as a bright flame; the disciple is said to be pervaded by a 'strange feeling of heat' throughout his body. Both indicate the superior and inferior aspects of the subtle state represented by the element fire.

spiritual faculties from their individual wrapping to a supra-individual state first assumes merely the degree of a provisional state (*ḥāl*) and only later that of a permanent station (*maqām*).[75]At that moment, the individual aggregate of the initiate represented by these very subtleties and governed by the mental faculty residing in the *nafs*, truly reaches the degree of extinction (*fanā*) described by the *Koran* as a 'death before death' (*mūtū qabl an tamūtū*).[76] Once this stage is attained to, only the physical body remains present in this world as an outward sign of the initiate, so that common people are unable to distinguish it from other creatures.[77]

The representative function of the gross body (*jism-i kathīf*) is then said to be governed by the 'pinecone-heart' (*qalb-i ṣanawbarī*), an obvious symbolic analogy between the *laṭīfa-i qalb* as *barzakh* and axis of the macrocosm on a spiritual level and its vital function in the body of the microcosm, which guarantees the link between the residual elements of the physical body and the spiritual components now reunited with their heavenly principles. The prophetic tradition 'Verily, the heart of a true believer is placed between two fingers of Allāh' (*Mishkāt al-Tirmidhī*, part II, *bāl al-istighfā*) and many others are interpreted by Shāh Abūl Ḥasan in this sense.[78]

In one of his letters, Shaikh Aḥmad Sirhindī strongly rejects the opinion of Shaikh Shihāb al-Dīn 'Umar al-Suhrawardī (AD 1145-1234) expressed in his *'Awārif al-ma'ārif* that the

75. In Sūfi terminology, the *ḥāl* designates a momentarily acquired state of spiritual realisation from which it is still possible to fall back to the previous condition, while a *maqām* corresponds to a definitively acquired stage of realisation which cannot ever be lost.

76. Again, this case refers to the most perfect degree of extinction put in relation to the prophet Muḥammad and, hence, associated to the *laṭīfa-i akhfā*.

77. During my stay at the Mujaddidī *khānqāh*s at Delhi and Quetta, I was repeatedly told of the special faculty of the order's masters to fix and capture with a single glance the inner state of those sitting in front of them thus enabling them to recognise their degree of spiritual qualification and the progress made in the discipline.

78. *MnS*, pp. 25/42.

supranatural inspiration (*ilhām*) descends upon the saint's pacified soul (*nafs-i muṭma'inna*) concentrated in the place of the heart. He stresses instead the fundamental role played by the heart itself, citing the renowned Tradition 'No doubt, the body of Ādam contains a lump of flesh — if it is healthy the entire body is sound, but if it is corrupted the whole body is corrupted'.

After the reintegration of the possibilities contained in the 'sphere of contingency' along its four horizons,[79] the Naqshbandī doctrine teaches that the final extinction of the five subtle organs in their principles and the connected entrance into the 'journey of the inner selves' (*sair-i anfusī*) take the disciple to the 'sphere of minor sainthood' (*dā'ira-i wilāyat-i ṣughrā*), defined also as the 'abode of the manifestation of Divine unity and of the secrets of co-presence' (*maḥal-i ẓāhir-i tawḥīd wa asrār-i ma'iyat*) or as the 'sphere of shadows' (*dā'ira-i ẓalāl*).[80] The journey through this realm is described by Shaikh Aḥmad Sirhindī (*Mak.* II:99) as lying beyond that of the horizons and inner selves since it is only beyond them that it becomes possible to reach the shadows or reflections of the Divine names contained in the 'selves in guise of the horizons' (*anfus-i āfāq*), considered as the 'sovereign of all reflections' (*sultān al-adhkār*). This means that the disciple no longer contemplates the world in its single forms and their inner realities, but through a unique Divine reflection resulting

79. This explains the inverted position of the heart since every reflection casts an inverted image; cf. *Mak.* III:31 in which Shaikh Aḥmad Sirhindī defines the 'world of the celestial archetypes' (*'ālam-i mithāl*) as a mirror for the beings in the formal dominion who derive their existence from the reflection of their spirits in the *'ālam-i arwāḥ*.

    The term '*horizon*', previously translated as 'cardinal points', evokes the idea of an imaginary line along which heaven and earth apparently meet. The etymology of the word (from the Greek *horizein* 'to delimit') implies a linear extension along one level and, thus, complements a vertical extension which denotes a qualitative succession; the latter is associated with the axis that leads to the higher planes of this world and finally beyond towards the future worlds.

80. *MnS*, pp. 47/71. Cf. also *HdT* whose author points out that the 'journey along the cardinal points' regards the reintegration through the *'ālam-i khalq* while the *sair-i anfusī* leads through the stages of the *'ālam-i amr* (p. 26).

from his co-presence (*ma'iyat*) with its very source. The immediate principle of the shadow of the first sphere is, thus, reached and those capable of proceeding further must now focus on the original principle of those reflections, and so on. This movement of successive links (*musalsal*) from principle to principle until arriving at the source of all principles (*'ain-i uṣūl*) determines the journey indicated by the Shaikh as one whose course begins in the sphere of minor sainthood and goes on until the attainment of the final Goal.

It is said that at this stage the disciple is pervaded by the sense of encompassing all six directions of space (*shish jihāt*).[81] He who attains to the co-presence of the principle regains inside himself the link with that central point of the Universe which provides access to the superior states along the vertical axis passing through that centre and which is possibly identified with the *maqām-i amr* along which the prophets receive their heavenly communications. There, the purification of the heart (*taṣfiya-i qalb*) reaches such a degree that it can no longer be disturbed by any sensual perception pertaining to worldly affairs (*waswasa*), but remains continuously immersed in a feeling of intense longing for the sole object of its attention. In the language of the Sūfis, the process leading to this inner state is hinted at as 'cleansing the mirror of the heart from the dust and rust of forgetfulness'.

But the authorities of the Mujaddidiyya warn their followers of the dangers that can be possibly encountered in this station. The *murīd* ruins the risks of being overpowered by an excessive enthusiasm and state of inebriation (*sukr*) caused by his confusion and inability to distinguish between the principle and its reflection. We know of many renowned Sūfis who have lost control over themselves in the state of *fanā* often uttering senseless and apparently blasphemous sentences (*shaṭṭāḥāt*).[82] To avoid these dangerous slips, the disciple is strongly recommended to remain prudent and attentive, in order to check the state of enrapture caused by the sudden witness of the

81. *HdT*, pp. 14, 28.

82. Cf. *Mak*. I:95, 100, 152 and II:95.

dissolution of contingent existence in the shining light of the attributes of the Necessary Being.[83] Only he who has truly achieved the extinction of his individual condition (*khudī*) is really beyond any blame and reproach (*malāmat*), ready to join the company of the saints of Allāh and qualified to be included among the mad lovers of the Lord (*'āshiqān-i majdhūb*).[84] It applies exclusively to those who have traversed the 'sphere of minor sainthood' and its accompanying journey through the reflections of Divine names and attributes; for all others, it is strictly forbidden to pronounce any such phrases pertaining to the degree of 'unicity of existence' (*waḥdat al-wujūd*) and Divine unity (*tawḥīd*).[85] This danger, liable to be further increased by devotional music-sessions (*samā'*) and poetic recitals, can promote an inconvenient sense of emotional participation in these states which is described as provoking inner heat. Such descriptions reflect the typical Naqshbandī aversion for anything which might provoke an emotional imbalance in the *murīd*'s nature and underlines the importance attributed by the *ṭarīqa*'s authorities to a sober, purely interior process of spiritual realisation.

This is, however, far from being the abode of Unity (*maqām-i tawḥīd*) experienced at the stage of minor sainthood at the end of the 'journey through the details' (*sair-i tafṣīlī*). Those who have arrived at this degree of Unity must, therefore, try hard to advance to still higher levels until they attain the point of resolution (*nuqṭa-i ijmālī*) which corresponds to the primordial determination (*ta'ayyun-i awwal*) of the Divine being, identified

---

83. *MnS*, pp. 49/73.

84. In very similar allegorical terms to those used in the Śaiva context of the Hindu tradition, Shāh Abūl Ḥasan affirms that 'the fire of passionate love has reduced one's individual existence to ashes and the flame of love has incinerated the existence of this world and the harvest of life'. (*MnS*, p.45).

85. This is why the prophets characterised by a high degree of sobriety (*ṣaḥw*) invite us to the continuous contemplation of the Truth expressed in the formula of the *shahādat*, *Lā ilāha illā Allāh*, with its obvious reference to a projection away from multiplicity and towards Unity.

with the 'reality of Muḥammad'.[86] Rather, the 'sphere of minor sainthood' constitutes the beginning of the determination of all possibilities (*mabdā-i ta'ayyun-i mumkināt*), with the sole exception of the prophets and angels whose intimate reality is determined by a yet more essential participation in the Divine presence. Irrespective of their natural constitution, each individual receives its particular determination through a continuous effusion of Divine grace (*fuyūḍāt*, pl. of *faiḍ*) manifesting itself in an indefinite number of names and attributes in the contingent world, which simultaneously represents also its limit.

To illustrate this concept, Shāh Abūl Ḥasan quotes the widely known Sūfī maxim 'The roads and paths that lead towards God are as numerous as the souls of His creatures',[87] which in his opinion refers to these very points of reflection. Through the extinction and permanence reached by the subtle organs at this level, the individual actions (*af'āl*), attributes (*ṣifāt*),[88] essences (*dhāt*), negative attributes (*ṣifāt-i salbiya*) and virtues (*akhlāq*) of the initiate and of all other possibilities reveal themselves to the *murīd* as ultimately possessing no real degree of existence (*ma'dūb*). They, thus, vanish from the initiate's sight, and he perceives every action, attribute, negative attribute and virtue as manifestations and effects (*maẓāhir wa athār*) of the reflections and attributes of the one and unique Truth. Here the 'journey towards Allāh' ends and the traveller enters the 'journey in Allāh' (*sair fī Allāh*) that begins in the third of the

86. The use of a terminology identical to that of the Shaikh al-Akbar reveals the analogy of concepts behind the different doctrinal formulations with the *wujūdī* one maintaining a more metaphysical perspective focussed on the non-dual Principle if compared to the Mujaddidīs who deliberately contemplate the principle always in relation to its derivatives.

87. *MnS*, pp. 50/75.

88. Following the list of al-Ghazzālī (450/1058-505/1111) in his *Iḥyā al-'ulūm al-Dīn*, the author sanctions as the most important of these hearing (*sam'*), vision (*basr*), power (*qudrat*), will (*irāda*) and speech (*kalām*), which correspond to the first determination of God's essence into attributes.

seven spheres, the 'sphere of major sainthood' (*dā'ira-i wilāyat-i kubrā*).[89]

While minor sainthood is associated by the Mujaddidīs with the saints characterised by a state of inebriation and unification of existence (*tawḥīd-i wujūdī*), major sainthood is said to correspond to the nature of the great prophets, characterised by a state of sobriety (*ṣaḥw*) and lucid awareness (*hoshyārī*): it is at this stage that prophethood was revealed to them, i.e., it is there that the prophets received their particular individualisations (*ta'ayyūnāt*) in accordance with their peculiar prophetic function. Those qualified to ascend to this sphere transcend the level of reflections and, thus, come into direct contact with the Divine names, attributes and intrinsic qualities (*asmā' o ṣifāt o shuyūnāt*). Only then will the initiate attain the 'unicity of direct vision' (*tawḥid-i shuhūdī*), because only from this stage it is possible for him to witness the difference between the reflected existence of the contingent creatures based on the sum of non-existences (*'adam*) that cast their shadow into the realm of contingent existence (*wujūd*) through the veils of ignorance.[90] A new sense of apparent duality (*thanainiyyat*) arises in the consciousness of the initiate as he becomes aware of the difference between the reflected immanent reality of contingency and the original transcendant Reality of *al-Ḥaqq*, summarised in the difference implicit between the stages of co-presence (*ma'iyat*) and extreme closeness (*aqrabiyat*).

The subtle organ most directly involved at this stage of the alchemical process is the *laṭīfa-i nafs*, for it is on this plane that the transmutation of the sensual soul (*nafs-i ammāra*) into the pacified soul (*nafs-i muṭma'inna*) through the control and eventual arrest of the thought current is said to be completed. Therefore, the Mujaddidī doctrine identifies the place of descent

---

89. Cf. *MnS*, pp. 68/95; *HdT*, pp. 44-52.

90. *HdT*, p. 46. For a detailed discussion regarding the difference between *tawḥīd-i wujūd* and *tawḥīd-i shuhūd*, see Shaikh Aḥmad Sirhindī: *Mak*. I:272 and II:1. Cf. also Mir Valiuddin's article 'Reconciliation between Ibn al-'Arabī's *waḥdat al-wujūd* and the Mujaddidī's *waḥdat al-shuhūd*' in *IC* 25 (1951), pp. 43-51, terHaar (1990), pp. 119-20, Friedmann (1971), pp. 62-7 and Faruqi (1947), pp. 85-140.

for the effusion of the Divine grace (*mawrid-i faiḍ*) in this sphere with the *laṭīfa-i nafs* located on the forehead while the remaining subtle organs participate only passively at it. Since the superior part of the *nafs* is assimilated to the rational faculty located in the human brain, it is with this organ that the inner effusion of major sainthood will maintain contact until the stage is brought to conclusion. Once the *nafs* is permeated by a state of peace and stability, it will ascend to the abode of contentment (*maqām-i riḍā*), the tenth and last of the stations of the spiritual journey. This process is referred to as 'sitting in the royal gallery of the breast (*aiwān-i ṣadr*)', because for the Mujaddidī shaikhs it indicates the highest ascent of the subtle organs in the course of the *sulūk*. In keeping with the descending perspective typical of the *shuhūdī* doctrine, however, they warn their disciples against a premature belief in perfection since the total extinction of such base qualities as lowness, mutability and arrogance depends also on the purification of the four primary elements rather than exclusively on that of the *nafs* and is therefore obtained only at a later stage. This assertion implies that the total purification of the *nafs* (*tadhkiya-i nafs*), the quintessence (*khulāṣa*) of the other four elements, still has to await further refinement. Hence, the saying attributed to Khwāja 'Ubaid Allāh Aḥrār (*d*. 895/1490), that it is easy to pronounce the words *Anā'l-Ḥaqq*, while it is extremely difficult to eradicate completely the *anā* or ego.[91]

After completing this stage, the initiatory path leads the disciple into the sphere of supreme sainthood (*dā'ira-i wilāyat-i 'uliyā'*), also referred to as 'sainthood of the sublime assembly' (*wilāyat-i malā-i a'lā*). It is considered the stage where the determinations of the angels originated, and this accounts for their essentially luminous nature. The intensity of light is such that that those who enter this sphere are said to remain dazzled at first by the sun-like brilliance of its shining rays.[92]

---

91. For him, see H. Algar, 'The Naqshbandī Order: a preliminary survey of its history and significance' in *SI* 44 (1976), pp. 137-9, and Jāmī's *Nafaḥāt al- uns* (Urdu edition 1994), pp. 641-7.

92. It is to be noted that the close affinity between the angels of the Semitic religions and the gods (*devatā*) of the Hindu tradition, the →

These rays are described as consisting of the essential names and attributes of Allāh's pure Being, establishing an interesting relation between the seven solar rays and these sevenfold Divine attributes and the corresponding names in classical Islamic theology which qualify God's essence.[93] In this sense, the source of these rays — metaphorically indicated by the sun — is identical to the pure Being, with the rays emanating from It corresponding to Its names and attributes. Gradually, these rays are said to disappear from the sight of the *murīd* who, attracted by the desire for the only Aim of his quest, penetrates beyond the veils of these irradiations until he reaches the 'picture-gallery of the irradiations of the Essence' (*nigārkhāna-yi tajalliyāt-i dhāt*).

There, he has reached the level of the purification of the first three primary elements, viz., air, fire and water, as a result of the descent of the Divine effusion on them. The elevated states of the five spiritual organs expand from the breast to the whole body, thereby indicating the beginning of the re-descent of the elements pertaining to the world. If this apparent descent outwardly implies that the individual develops an increasingly intense relation with the attributes that characterise the human state (*basharīyat*), yet inwardly he is permeated by the celestial nature of the angels (*malakiyat*). In the metaphorical language used to describe the supra-individual states of existence, Shāh Abūl Ḥasan reiterates the descriptions of his predecessors when he defines the overcoming of the extreme limits of this sphere as 'the final flight towards the Sacred abode' achieved through 'the strength of the two wings consisting in the manifestations of the Divine names of Huwā al-Ẓāhir ('He is Apparent') on one side and Huwā al-Bāṭin ('He is concealed') on the other.[94] This

→ etymology of the latter clearly indicating their essentially subtle nature (from the root *div*, 'being luminous').

93. These seven names and the attributes they denote are: The Living One (*al-Ḥayy*, with life —*ḥayāt*), The Omniscient (*al-'Ālim*, with knowledge — *ilm*), The Omnipotent (*al-Qādir*, with power —*qudrat*), The Willing One (*al-Murīd*, with will —*irāda*), The Hearing One (*al-Samī*, with hearing —*sam'*), The Seeing One (*al-Baṣīr*, with seeing —*baṣr*) and The Speaker (*al-Mutakallim*, with the word —*kalīma*).

94. *MnS*, pp. 72/99.

'flight' indicates the passage to the superior states of the celestial regions and takes the disciple from the irradiations of the names and attributes to those of the Essence, while the wings allude to the angels who populate those intermediate regions. The reference to the two names, 'the Apparent' and 'the Concealed', must also be understood in this context. The contemplation of the apparent, exterior aspects of the Divinity (*murāqaba-i ism-i ẓāhir*) which began during the preceding sphere of major sainthood, remained necessarily limited to the attributes without yet being able to penetrate beyond the remaining veils covering the Essence. The contemplation of the concealed aspect (*murāqaba-i ism-i bāṭin*), an exclusive characteristic of the 'supreme sainthood', takes into account the Subject relating to these attributes,[95] or the divine Personality.

For example, if during the first contemplation the attribute of knowledge (*'ilm*) alone is considered, without yet allowing for any relation to its inherent reality, the second contemplation of the name of 'He who knows' (*al-'Ālim*) also reveals the essence that knows (*al 'Alīm*). The same applies equally to all other names and attributes. One applies to the absolutely transcendent reality of Allāh beyond the sphere of existence while the other pertains to the ideal determinations (*a'yān al-thābita*) of the pure Being and principle of existence; hence, the double names of *al-Ẓāhir* and *al-Bāṭin*. The extreme limit of 'supreme sainthood' coincides with the first of all determinations (*ta'ayyun-i awwal*) and sum of all names, attributes and qualities, perceived as the very source of all possible individualisations of the existing world.

In a letter addressed to his eldest son Muḥammad Ṣādiq (1000/1591-1025/1616), Shaikh Aḥmad Sirhindī explains that to distinguish the summit of this particular sphere it is necessary to transcend the stage of analytic knowledge (*'ilm-i ḥuṣūlī*) and move on to that of intuitive knowledge (*'ilm-i ḥuḍūrī*), the first being limited to the mental sphere and the corresponding senses, the second one being associated with the very source of

95. Cf. *Mak.* II:3 and III:11.

knowledge, in relation to the 'faculty of inspiration'.[96] The slightest reminiscence of the individual aggregate there finally disappears through the identification with the principle of all individuality. This stage is termed the 'journey in God' (*sair fī Allāh*).

Next follows the fifth plane, called the 'sphere of the triple perfections' (*dā'ira-i kamālāt-i thalāthā*), viz., the 'perfections of prophecy' (*nubuwwa*), the 'perfections of the Divine mission' (*risāla*) and the 'perfections of the prophets of right determination' (*anbiyā'l-ulū al-azm*). Here the journey leads the *murīd* through the everlasting irradiations of the Divine Essence (*tajalliyāt-i dhāt-i dā'imī*). The adept now contemplates the pure Essence of Allāh, bare of any contingent determination and far beyond any ephemeral degree of existence. At this stage, the effusion of God's grace descends directly from its source to the essence of the subtle organ of the element earth (*laṭīfa-i khāk-i pāk*). This completes the purification and reintegration of the ten subtle organs in their differentiated aspect, and the authors of the various treatises agree that from this moment onwards these assume a new, synthesised aspect (*hai'at-i waḥdānī*), whose nature is compared to that of different medical herbs each with different properties which, if mixed together, assume a new, combined property.[97]

At first, one perceives the Divine presence as bearing no relation to the spatial dimension (*be-jihat*) and one attains to the boon of certainty at its very root (*'ain al-yaqīn*) in front of which all previous doubts and incertitudes dissolve themselves. The Mujaddidīs assert that the perfections acquired on all previous levels of sainthood are null and void in comparison with those of a single point on the way of prophethood, since the former are considered to be mere reflections of the latter.[98]

---

96. For an interesting qualitative contrast analysis of these two types of knowledge, see Khaliq Anjum (1989), pp. 105-7.

97. *HdT*, p. 64.

98. The analogy is that between the limited (*maḥdūd*) and the unlimited (*ghair-muntahā*) which renders clearly the qualitative difference involved.

We, therefore, find here a direct application of the doctrinal assertion that attributes a higher degree to prophethood as compared to sainthood, and to the *nabī* a higher place than the *walī*, based on the assumption that the latter remains concentrated on Allāh alone while the former combines attention on both God and the world.[99]

As its name suggest, the sphere of the triple perfections is connected to the source of the perfections that characterises the various prophets and their legislative mission (*risālat*) embracing, moreover, the perfections of the saints. It is, therefore, legitimate to affirm a certain superiority of the *nabī* over the *walī*, the former re-descending from the Sacred abode of the Divine Essence beyond creation for the sake of conveying a particular message to the created world. This return (*rujū'*) from the transcendent to the immanent plane includes both an inward and outward participation at the Divine perception through which the *rasūl* will eventually reach total universal isation identifying himself with the *insān al-kāmil*.[100]

In fact, the author of the *Manāhij al-Sair* informs us that in the fifth sphere of the source of prophethood and divine mission there 'appears the existential prototype of the Perfect Man imbued with Divine virtues (*auṣāf-i ilāhī*), lord of his desires and of his self, none of whose actions are contrary to the pleasure of his Lord'.[101]

The reintegration of the ten subtle organs pertaining to the dominions of *khalq* and *amr* must be interpreted in this sense because the source of prophetic inspiration participates equally in both dominions. From this point begins the 'journey from Allāh with Allāh' (*sair an Allāh bi Allāh*) during which the 'traveller' partakes at the realities of creation through direct participation at the one Reality. This is evidenced through the

99. Cf. *Mak*. I:291, 337, 338 and II:89, 93, 191; see further Friedmann (1971), ch. IV, pp. 33-40 and terHaar (1990), ch. X, pp. 137-45.

100. The relationship of the *walī* and *nabī*, thus, bears notable similarities with that of the Buddha and the *bodhisattvas* in Mahāyāna Buddhism.

101. *MnS*, pp. 75/102, based on the descriptions of the prophet in *Koran*, 53:2-9.

knowledge of the Law (*sharī'at*), of the mysteries of the letters of the *Koran* (*muqaṭṭa'āt-i Koran*), of things pertaining to the unseen world (*al-ghaib*), the tomb (*al-qabr*), heaven and hell (*jannat wa dozakh*), all of which have been revealed to humanity through the message of the prophet Muḥammad by the certitude derived from direct intuition. This condition corresponds exactly to that of 'heir of the prophets' and pertains to the last of the triple perfections.

It is said that while the attainment of the previous stages depended on the initiate's active effort, entry into the sixth sphere depends entirely on the grace bestowed by Allāh upon those who pay their humble respects to Him, an expression that denotes a more passive attitude in the *murīd* who is now provided guidance by the interior guide awakened through the effect left by the Divine effusions. This sixth sphere is called the 'sphere of Divine realities' (*dā'ira-i ḥaqā'iq-i Ilāhī*) and comprehends altogether four planes: those of the celestial Ka'ba (*ḥaqīqat-i Ka'ba-i rabbānī*), of the Holy Koran (*ḥaqīqat-i Koran-i karīm*), of ritual prayer (*ḥaqīqat-i ṣalāt*) and of pure servanthood (*ḥaqīqat-i ma'būdiyat-i ṣarfa*).

The realities to which the adept gains access at this stage are described by Shaikh Abū Sa'īd and his descendants as waves if compared to the even surface of the triple perfections, an image drawn to underline the impossibility to conceive anything beyond the irradiation of the perpetual Essence which is separate from It[102] and a metaphor to denote a revelation of ulterior truths pertaining to that same metaphysical Truth from which they emanate. These truths reveal the intimate relationship that subsists between the outer, substantial form (*ṣūrat*) of the objects of worship, e.g., the terrestial Ka'ba, at Mecca and the innermost transcendent reality pertaining to its celestial archetype, a symbol contained in the *'ālam-i mithāl* that assumes the role of the Throne of God and of the *rūḥ al-muḥammadiya*.

The authors of these descriptions stress that given the

---

102. *HdT*, p. 70; *MnS*; pp. 76/106.

sublime spiritual nature they refer to these states can be described only through symbolic allusions (*ishāra*). These recall the symbolic descriptions of the polar axis (*al-rukn al-quṭubiya*) connecting the celestial regions with the various realms of the immanent world and passing through the centre of the Throne. It is along this axis alone that any contact and mediation (can between these hierarchically superseding planes (*maqāmāt*) can be achieved. Hence, derives Shāh Abūl Ḥasan's assertion that those who have reached this stage can now worship Allāh and prostrate to Him at every *maqām*.

The second level containing the truth of the Glorious *Koran* also partakes of the symbolism of the *rukn*, for it is there that there is manifested to the *sālik* the deeper inner meaning (*bawāṭin-i kalām-i pāk*) of the Divine message revealed to Muḥammad whose single letters are said to contain a 'boundless river' (*daryā-i be-karān*) reaching down to the Ka'ba. If the *murīd* recites the Holy Book at this stage, his tongue is said to 'manifest the burning tree of Moses', yet another symbolic hint at the axis, and his entire body appears 'like a tongue' uttering Divine truths.[103] Hit by the weight of the lights reversed upon him, the *'ārif* experiences a feeling of heaviness which reveals him the meaning of the verse: 'Soon shall We send down to thee a weighty word.' (*Koran*, 73:5). Here again, we notice the reference to the polar axis as the vertical channel of communication between the realms of the transcendent and the immanent.[104]

The third degree included in this sphere consists of the perception of the intrinsic truth of ritual prayer (*ḥaqīqat-i ṣalāt*) and reflects more openly the position held by the Mujaddidī doctrine stressing the inner benefits the true believer (*mu'min*) derives from adherence to this obligatory act of daily worship. Its performance, which in itself constitutes an expression of the believer's submission and perception of servanthood to the Divinity, is described as opening to the disciple the gates of the

103. *MnS*, pp. 78/106.

104. The polar symbolism and connected terminology is most elaborated by the *Shaikh al-Akbar* and his followers, while being less explicit in the doctrines of the Mujaddidiyya.

Divine bounties. There he attains the degree of extreme proximity (*intihā-yi qurb*), as expressed in the well-known Prophetic saying:

> The performance of the ritual prayer constitutes the ascension (*mi'rāj*) of the true believer.[105]

During the performance of the *ṣalāt* by those endowed with the particular knowledge contained in this sphere, their maximal closeness and 'the beautiful vision of the face of the Object of the quest' (*maṭlūb*) are said to bring about a wonderful feeling of inner peace which dissipates every sadness and ardent desire because there the lover (*'āshiq*) has finally reached his Beloved (*ma'shūq*). The various phases of the ritual prayer, thus, assume a new significance for the gnostic, who displays his inner humility in front of the Divine principle after having relinquished both the worlds while perceiving the presence of the Lord inside his own self. It is said that he who performs his prayers in this manner has definitively left this world behind and has entered the realm of the Hereafter (*nashāt-i ākhirwī*) while still alive.[106]

In the combination of a persisting duality implied in the relation between the knowing humble servant and Allāh on one side and the affirmation of identity through the continuous presence of the Divine in him on the other there lies resumed the entire perspective of the Mujaddidī doctrine, which links the stage of supreme realisation with the arising of an unprecedented awareness of the diversity between the servant (*al-'abd*) and his Lord (*al-Rabb*). Maintaining the perspective assumed during the preceding levels of this major sphere, the inner truth of the ritual prayer constitutes the link that connects

---

105. This famous sentence attributed to Muḥammad is calligraphically inscribed on the *mihrāb* of many mosques and *dargāhs*. It alludes to the passage to the superior regions along that same polar axis on which the prophet of Islam ascended to the Throne through the celestial spheres during his journey in the night of ascension (*lailat al-mi'rāj*, cf. *Koran*, 17:1).

106. Shāh Abūl Ḥasan relates this to the gesture of raising both hands to the head at the beginning of each *rak'ah* while pronouncing the *takbīr-i taḥrīr*. Cf. *MnS*, pp. 79/107.

the sincere and conscious worshipper with his Creator. It, thus, again suggests the idea of the *rukn*: along its vertical extension it is possible to ascend towards the heavens traversing the regions that lead towards the apex of the celestial hierarchy up to the Principle of all principles. At the same time, it is also possible to re-descend along the same path towards the multiplicity of creation, analogous to the descent of the Koranic message that manifested the power of the Lord to the heart of the Prophet of Islam during the night of Power (*lailat al-qadr*).[107] According to the interpretation given by Shāh Abū Sa'īd Fārūqī Mujaddidī of the *ḥadīth al-qudsī* 'He who prostrates himself to Me is close to Me', the entire prayer ritual is summed up in the act of prostration (*sijjda*), as it is this outward sign of supreme humility and submission reflects the highest degree of inner proximity that sanctious the *murīd*'s to participation in the assembly of the sublime ones (*jalsa-i a'lā*).[108]

The state of selflessness (*be-khudī*) attained during the time of prayer is directly connected with the fourth and last sphere of Divine realities, that of 'pure servanthood' (*ma'būdiyat-i ṣarfa*). This stage is described as a purely visual one (*naẓarī*), since it cannot possibly defined as a further step on the path of spiritual realisation. It is assimilated to that of the perfect spiritual realisation represented by Muḥammad who was asked in the course of his *mi'rāj* to stop at the stage of extreme closeness: 'O Muḥammad! Stop and sit down for a while for Your Lord sends you His blessings!'

This constitutes the degree beyond which no one can set his step and where only pure vision persists. In this *maqām*, the initiate is granted access to the hidden mysteries hinted at in the formula *lā ma'būda illā Allāh* (There is no object of worship except Allāh), the truth that every kind of worship can only

107. This also explains why these two nights are regarded as particularly beneficial for any sort of spiritual practice and supererogatory acts of devotion (*nawāfil*) including the *tahajjud* prayer. During these two nights the heavenly gates are open for sincere devotees to reverse the celestial influences on their hearts.

108. *HdT*, p. 78.

reach the absolute unicity of Allāh even if in the guise of His names and attributes. No possibility of unlawful association (*shirk*) remains as the journey of the Divine realities reaches its conclusion in the awareness of being separated from the unique Object of worship (*ma'būd*). Which while pervading everything remains essentially beyond everything. There, the adept acquires the highest degree of spiritual insight into the most intimate truth of being a true and upright servant of God.

Utmost perfection represented by the last of the seven spheres termed the 'sphere of the prophetic realities' (*dā'ira-i ḥaqā'iq-i anbiyā'*) which is further divided into six minor planes corresponding to six degrees of truth.

Progress in this most elevated sphere is characterised neither by any strenuous effort of the disciple nor by the descending of Divine grace (*faiḍ*), but is based entirely on love (*muḥabbat*), the first of all determinations of *al-Ḥaqq*. The centre and most sublime degree within this primordial determination is called *ta'ayyun-i ḥubb* where the ultimate identity or meeting between 'belovedness' (*maḥbūbiyat*) and 'true loving' (*maḥabbiyat*) occurs. It is described by the head of the Mujaddidī branch as the union of the metaphysical principle referred to as *ḥaqīqat-i muḥammadī* and its physical determination (*ta'ayyun-i jasadī*) in the shape of the historical figure of the prophet of Islam, Muḥammad.

Of a similar nature but at a slightly inferior level we find the 'reality of Moses' (*ḥaqīqat-i mūsawī*), characterised by 'pure lovingness' (*maḥabbiyat-i ṣarfa*), the focal point enclosed by a circumference or circle which in its symbolic implication consists of the true friendship (*khullat*) contained in the 'reality of Abraham' (*ḥaqīqat-i ibrahīmī*).

The relationship between the first and the last two prophetic realities is that between belovedness in view of the Divine attributes (*maḥbūbiyat-i ṣifatī*) and belovedness in view of the Divine Essence (*maḥbūbiyat-i ṣarfa*). Among these, the 'reality of Abraham' constitutes the first of the six levels. At this stage the disciple re-descends, turning his face towards the world while being endowed with the particular qualities of the prophet from the source of his specific determination. In the case of Abraham, this is intimacy and sincere companionship (*uns*) between God and His servant as expressed in the verse

> . . . Who submits his whole self to Allāh, does good, and follows the way of Abraham the true in faith?
>
> — *Koran*, 4:125

Though the relationship with Truth occurs at an extremely sublime level characterised by an indissoluble bond of friendship (*khullat*), the passage to the second sphere containing the 'reality of Moses' implies a still higher degree of perfection since it is characterised by the pure loving (*maḥabbiyat-i ṣarfa*) of the pure Essence, that loves Itself (*muḥibb*) for Itself. The masters affirm that in addition to the manifestation of love the quality of independence (*istighnā*) and freedom from want (*be-niyāzī*) also appear, and the secret of some daring expressions uttered by this prophet is revealed to the initiate.[109] Although the relationship between God and His creature has reached the most sublime level of love, a residual subtle veil of duality still persists between the object and the subject of this relationship.

This veil is finally lifted in the third stage of Truth, that of the 'reality of Muḥammad', where the distinction between 'belovedness' (*maḥbūbiyat*) and 'loving' (*maḥabbiyat*) does subsist only in the Essence of Allāh. This mingling with the pure Essence is, according to the Mujaddidīs, symbolically represented by the double *mīm* contained in the name of Muḥammad and enclosed by the letters *ḥe* and *dal* which, if joined together, form the word *ḥad* or 'extreme limit' of spiritual perfection reached by the 'seal of prophecy' (*khatima al-anbiyā'*). The implicit meaning of the prophet's name could, thus, be possibly rendered in its esoteric meaning as 'he who has reached the utmost limit of belovedness and loving', a description that refers to the sublime degree of his spiritual realisation. No one is superior to him in these two essential attributes.

So not even the *ḥaqīqat-i muḥammadī* constitutes the ultimate degree of Truth. Such an assertion differs from the

109. *MnS*, pp. 81/110.

earlier doctrinal elaborations of *taṣawwuf*. Shaikh Aḥmad Sirhindī describes it as a particular development of the second millennium of Islam.[110] This stage, reached at the fourth level and referred to as the *ḥaqīqat-i aḥmadī*, is considered as superior even to the primordial determination of the absolute Truth in the *ḥaqīqat-i muḥammadī* and represents an important reformulation and adaption of the esoteric doctrine for the second millennium of the Islamic era.

This newly described *ḥaqīqat* occupies the absolute centre in the conceptions of the Mujaddiyya. Its display takes the adept into the footsteps of the prophet Muḥammad leading him towards the 'abode of loneliness of the most hidden secret' (*khilwatkhāna-yi ghaib al-ghaib*) of pure belovedness (*maḥbūbiyat-i ṣarfa*). The letter *mīm* in the name of the prophet is seen as symbol of this station in which every remaining duality between the subject and the object of love is dissolved in the metaphysical Unity indicated by the *aḥad* of Aḥmad deprived of its letter *mīm*. At the same time, it designates in a descending perspective the unicity of the prophet of Islam in intensity and sincerity, devotion and worship, adoration and belovedness as the perfect servant of God. In the opinion of the Mujaddid, this stage bears an intimate relation with the *ḥaqīqat-i Ka'ba-i Rabbānī*[111] as being superior even to the 'Muḥammadan reality' for it is the object of worship in the latter stage (*masjūd*), not on the formal and individual plane but in the *'ālam-i mithāl*, where the greatness (*kibriyā'ī*) and glory (*'aẓmat*) of its inner Truth coincides with that of the beloved and adored, both terms applying to the prophet Muḥammad.

Both Shāh Abūl Ḥasan Zaid and Shāh Abū Sa'īd[112] list two further degrees of Truth which, strictly speaking, do not constitute a further prophetic reality but rather additional classifications of the *ḥaqīqat-i aḥmadī*. The fifth, denominated 'pure love of the Divine essence' (*ḥubb-i ṣarfa-i dhātiya*), evidently refers to the essential stage also at the last level

110. Cf. *Mak*. I:94; *Mabdā o Ma'ād*, *minhā* 48, pp. 204-6.

111. *Mak*. I:209; *Mabdā o Ma'ād*, p. 204.

112. *MnS*, pp. 112-13; *HdT*, pp. 89-90.

beyond the attributive stage of love which characterised the first four levels. Sublimity and non-qualification are mentioned as necessary characteristics of a stage in extreme proximity to the supreme Principle, identified with *Allāh Ta'ālā*. This pure love is described as a particular station of the beloved of the Lord (*maḥbūb*) and a primordial determination of the absolutely undetermined (*lā-ta'ayyun*) based on the authority of 'Allamā Qasṭallānī and Mullā 'Alī Qārī who have judged as authentic the *ḥadīth-al qudsī* in which Allāh addresses His beloved: 'If it were not for you I would not have created the heavens and I would not have manifested My haughtiness'.

If we accept the authenticity of this tradition, it becomes obvious that for the masters of our *ṭarīqa* this saying refers to the cosmological principle and purely spiritual dimension of Muḥammad, the *rūḥ al-muḥammadiyya*, starting point of creation (*mabdā-i khalqat*)[113] beyond the limiting co-ordinates of time and space. First his pure light came into being, and from it the Throne, the projection of the principle of creation into this world in the *'ālam-i mithāl*, and then the Pen (*qalam*) and the well-preserved Tablet (*lauḥ al-maḥfūẓ*) from which the cosmic duality of heaven and earth, the angels, the *jinn*, men and all other creatures ultimately derive their existence. The prophet, thus, becomes in his most essential reality the supreme manifestation of the Divine attributes, superseding the Supreme Principle which resumes *in nuce* the perfections of all contingencies. It was this light only which made Adam worthy to be adored by the angels and the Ka'ba to become the object of worship of all creatures.

---

113. This affirmation is enhanced by the historical figure of the prophet which acts like a terrestial reflection of this principle endowed with a further, corporeal determination, hinted at in his saying: 'I was already a prophet when Adam was still between spirit and body', Muslim: *Ṣaḥīḥ* 44, Bukhārī: *Ṣaḥīḥ* 78, *Kitāb al-Ādāb* 119. A slightly different version of this Tradition substitutes the two term as of body and spirit with those of clay and water. Its authenticity has been doubted by Ibn Tayimiyya and his fellow Hanbalites. It is noteworthy that the Mujaddidī authors chose to quote the more widely accepted version rather than the second one, often quoted by the *Shaikh al-Akbar* and his followers.

At his stage, the disciple has reached the degree of *insān al-kāmil*, participating at the very source of every perfection. He, thus, enters the sixth and final plane, that of the Infinite (*lā-ta'ayyun*) and Absolute (*ḥadrat-i iṭlāq*), unlimited and unconditioned, beyond any possible definition and description, where neither foot nor sight can reach. There, the *sālik* has attained to the perfection of beatitude while abiding in the everlasting presence of his boundless Lord.

Methods and techniques for spiritual realisation in the light of the science of the subtle centres

We shall now turn to the methods which allow the initiate to operate on his inner constitution in order to progress on the path whose different stages have previously been described. We are, thus, concerned with the operative (*'amlī*) aspect of the *ṭarīqa* that complements its speculative (*'ilmī*) side, both of which are necessary for an integral esoteric tradition qualified to provide its members with the means to rise towards the experience of Divine Truth (*ḥaqīqat*). These methods are designed to bring about the transmutation of the complex human aggregate. To achieve this goal, they intervene on its subtle component which constitutes the intermediate link between the gross body and man's purely spiritual component. In the specific case of the Mujaddidiyya, these techniques are, therefore, closely connected with the subtle centres adding yet a further dimension to the *'ilm-i latā'if*.

Shāh Na'īm Allāh Bahrāichī, Shāh Abū Sa'īd Fārūqī and Shāh Abūl-Ḥasan Zaid describe three principal categories of techniques.[114] The following section will deal with only two of these, namely *dhikr* and *murāqaba*, leaving the third, i.e., *rābiṭa*, for a subsequent sub-section in view of its close affinity to other important considerations.

An integral part of the Naqshbandī methodology is summed up in the so-called 'eleven technical principles' (*yāzdah kalimāt-i muṣtalāḥa*). The first eight are traditionally ascribed to 'Abd

114. See *MuM*, pp. 82-7; *HdT*, pp. 10-18; *MnS*, pp. 40-63/46-69.

al-Khāliq al-Gujdawānī (*d.* AD 575/1179 or 1220) while the formulation of the remaining three has been attributed to Khwāja Bahā al-Dīn al-Naqshband (717/1318-791/1389).[115] Since they represent the fundamental pillars on which the *ṭarīqa*'s methodology rests, they will be introduced in the appropriate context below.

DHIKR

The term *dhikr* embraces numerous meanings according to the specific context in which it is used. Derived from the Arabic verbal root *dhakara* bearing the meaning of 'to remember, recollect, mention', it can be applied to everything remembered or recalled and, therefore, mentioned.[116] In the specific religious context, this applies naturally to the sole Object of worship, i.e., Allāh. In the esoteric tradition, this term refers strictly to the perpetual remembrance of Allāh, and since for every believing Muslim the link with the Sacred is guaranteed by the Divine message as revealed to the prophet Muḥammad, it is again from the *Koran* and the prophetic Traditions that the Sūfīs derive the notions regarding the various techniques developed in this field.The *Koran* states:

> O ye who believe! Remember Allāh, with much remembrance; and glorify Him morning and evening.
> — *Koran*, 33:41-2

and also:

> Men who remember Allāh standing, sitting and lying down on their sides, . . . — *Koran*, 3:191

Both verses hint at the importance attributed by the Islamic tradition to the constant rememberance of God in order to maintain awareness of the world's ultimate Sovereign. The

115. For these two authorities' role in the early history of the order, cf. Marijan Molé, 'Autour du Dare Mansour: L'Apprentissage Mystique de Bahā'al-Dīn Naqshband', in *Revue des Études Islamiques* 27 (1959), pp. 35-66, and Hamid Algar, *art.cit.* (1976).

116. For a general introduction to *dhikr,* see Mir Valiuddin (1980), pp. 31-50.

second verse in particular is a reminder of the continuity which must be achieved in the act of recollecting which requires perseverance in every moment and in every act of the initiate's daily routine. In extension of this concept, Shāh Abūl Ḥasan states that every action performed in accordance with the legal prescriptions of the Divine law (*aḥkām-i sharīʿat*) constitutes a form of *dhikr*, including the transactions of buying and selling, since all these acts are ultimately accomplished in accordance with the primordial Divine command.

In its primary sense *dhikr*, therefore, denotes the conscious adherence of the individual to the Law (*al-Dīn*) which governs and maintains the cosmic order. In a derived sense, *dhikr* refers to every kind of religious and ritual performance, e.g., the recital of the *Koran* or the prayers, which are apt to promote the state of remembrance.[117] Only in a later derived sense did this term come to describe also the often elaborate techniques used by the different orders to recall Allāh through the repetitive rhythmic invocation of His names or through particular formulas with the aim of 'purifying the heart and to detach it from everything except Him'.[118] This corresponds to what the *Khwājagān*[119] intended by one of the eleven principles called *yād kard* (remembering) which, technically speaking, entails the removal of any forgetfulness (*ghaflat*) of God from one's heart achieved through the invocation of the 'noble formula of remembrance' (*dhikr-i sharīf*).

For the Naqshbandīs, this can be of two types: the recital of the name of the Divine Essence (*dhikr-i ism-i dhāt*), consisting of the constant repetition of the word *Allāh*, or the recital of the

---

117. *MnS*, pp. 44/67.

118. Madeleine Habib, 'Some Notes on the Naqshbandī Order', in *MW* 59 (1979), p. 42.

Naqshbandī tradition attributes the origin of this technique to the caliph Abū Bakr al-Siddīq, first link after the prophet in the *ṭarīqa*'s initiatic chain who was taught this technique during the flight from Mecca to Medina while hiding with Muḥammad in a cave from their Quraishi persecutors.

119. The *silsila-i khwājagān* constituted from the twelfth century AD onwards the lineage of what was later to become the Naqshbandiyya →

'formula of negation and affirmation' (*dhikr-i nafī wa ithbāt*), i.e., *lā ilāha illā Allāh*, also known as the 'formula carrying powerful blessings' (*kalima-i tayyiba*). While being engaged in the use of this technique, it is extremely important that no interruption should occur in the chain of repetitions. A peculiar characteristic of the *ṭarīqa* consists in its preference of the silent, purely mental invocation hidden from the perception of others (*dhikr-i qalb, dhikr-i khafī*) over oral recital produced with the tongue (*dhikr-i zabānī, dhikr-i lisānī*), because while the latter necessarily implies an interruption in the chain due to the intercurring phases of breath the former can be perpetuated continuously.[120] Once again, the ideal example to follow is that of Muḥammad who is said to have been immersed in a state of constant *dhikr* in his heart, as indicated by the Tradition: 'My eyes are at rest but my heart is alert.' (Bukhārī).[121]

The immediate purpose of this practice is to focus the disciple's attention entirely on God so as to lead him towards a constant awareness (*āgāhī-i dawāmī*) of the goal and instil in his heart a deep feeling of love and veneration that keeps him always conscious and attentive. As long as the removal of the state of forgetfulness continues to demand great efforts during the performance of *dhikr*, its effects remain precarious and do not take him beyond the stage of *yād kard*. For this reason, the order's authorities recommend during the initial stages of this

→ and consists of a series of authorities all hailing from the region of Bukhara: (1) Khwāja 'Abd al-Khāliq al-Gujdawānī (*d.* 617/1220), (2) Khwāja 'Ārif al-Riwgarī (*d.* 657/1259), (3) Khwāja Maḥmūd Anjīr al-Faghnawī (*d.* 670/1272), (4) Khwāja 'Azīzān 'Alī al-Ramitānī (*d.* 721/1321), (5) Khwāja Muḥammad Bābā al-Samnānī (*d.* 744/1354) and (6) Khwāja Sayyid Amīr Kulālī al-Bukhārī (d.772/1371).

120. *MuM*, p.74; *MnS*, pp. 36/58.

121. This state of maximal permeation of the *dhikr* refers to the most advanced stage to be attained by this technique and is said to bring about many blessings and spiritual benefits. It is, therefore, called by the Naqshbandīs 'sovereign of all invocations' (*sulṭān al-adhkār*), though it is not to be considered in this initial stage of *yād kard*. For a description of the intimate nature of this invocation and its secrets said to have been revealed to Khwāja 'Abd al-Khāliq al-Gujdawānī, cf. Stéphane Ruspoli, 'Réflexions sur la voie spirituelle des Naqshbandis', in Varia Turcica, *Naqshbandis* (1990), pp. 95-107.

spiritual practice the exclusive invocation of the *ism-e dhāt*, the simplest and most essential form of *dhikr*. Only once the recollection is firmly impressed in the *murīd*'s mind no longer requiring strenuous efforts, the initiate eventually accedes to the successive stage of *yād dāsht*, lit. 'preservation of remembrance', which allows for the use of different formulas.

Most Naqshbandī shaikhs follow the example set by Khwāja 'Ubaid Allāh Aḥrār (*d.* 895/1490) for whom the attainment of this advanced stage presupposed the application of two other principles, namely *bāz gasht* (post-remembrance) and *nigāh dāsht* (lit., preservation of sight).[122] The first of these prescribes the repetition of the additional invocation: 'O God! You alone and Your pleasure are my objective! Grant me Your love and Your knowledge!', sanctioning regular intervals in the recital of the main *dhikr* and meant to confer further emphasis on the sole aim on which every thought should be concentrated.[123] The second principle entails the safeguarding (*muḥāfaẓat*) of the state of awareness and mental presence attained through the practice of *dhikr* so that no thought should enter the *dhākir*'s mind except that of the absolute unity of Allāh (*aḥadiyat-i mujarrada*) intended as unqualified Principle without any considerations for His names and attributes.[124] *Nigāh dāsht* refers to a fairly advanced stage of *dhikr* practice that keeps in view the comprehension of the Divine essence. Its difficulty is attested by the statements of several authorities who affirm that the perseverance of such a state for a couple of hours or for a span of time that lasts from sunrise till mid-morning (*chāsht*) constitutes a very elevated degree of perfection reserved only to a very few particularly qualified persons.

In this superior interpretation, *nigāh dāsht* is said to lead to the 'direct witnessing' (*mushāhada*) of the luminous

---

122. *MnS*, pp. 33-4/59.

123. Most shaikhs affirm that the formula that should follow the invocation of the *dhikr-i nafī wa ithbāt* may nowadays simply be: 'I have no object of worship except the adored God because the Adored and the Goal are the same.' This practice is still in use among the inmates of the Delhi *khānaqāh*.

124. *MuM*, p. 75.

irradiations of the Divine Essence, while its more modest interpretation qualifies it as the protection of the heart from the vortex of mental consciousness and incessant current of distracting thoughts (*khaṭrāt*) during the recital of *dhikr*. The perfection of this practice leads eventually to *yād dāsht*, the most perfect state attainable by this technique, and corresponds to the realisation of the perpetual presence (*ḥuḍūr-i dā'imī*) of the unqualified Deity.[125] Variously defined as 'perfection of contemplation' (*kamāl-i mushāhada*), as 'presence without absence' (*ḥuḍūr-i be-ghaibat*), or as 'witnessing of Truth' (*shuhūd-i Ḥaqq*), it is said to be infused into the initiate's heart by the love the Essence nourishes for Its servant.

These are the degrees of spiritual progress achieved through the practice of *dhikr*. To reach them, correct execution of the prescribed method, constant application and total dedication to its performance by the disciple under the supervision of the spiritual preceptor are necessary.

The pivotal role the *dhikr* plays in the methodology current among the various *ṭuruq* results immediately from the fact that the disciple's initiation sanctioned by the vow of allegiance made to the shaikh (*bai'at*) is intimately connected with the transmission of the *dhikr*. In the course of this ritual, its subtle power is implanted like a germ into the heart of the novice who from that moment onwards must cultivate it in order to 'let it grow into a fruit-bearing tree'. This process guarantees the establishment of his spiritual link (*nisbat*)[126] with the entire

---

125. A chapter of Shaikh Aḥmad Sirhindī's esoteric treatise *Mabdā o Ma'ād* (*minhā* 30, pp. 169-71) distinguishes three levels within *yād dāsht*, between the outer form (*ṣūrat*), attained by those reaching the concentration of the heart (*jam'iyat-i qalb*), and its inner truth (*ḥaqīqat*), obtainable only after the 'cleansing of the soul' and the 'purification of the heart' are brought to perfection; but one must still distinguish between the degree of the presence of the necessary attributes (*martaba-i wujūb*) which constitute the sum of attributes, and the topmost degree regards the presence of absolute Unity beyond the names, attributes and qualities. We recognise here the stages of sainthood described in the previous chapter.

126. For its peculiar meaning in the order's technical vocabulary, cf. W.E. Fusfeld (1981), pp. 80-1.

series of spiritual ancestors of the lineage leading back to Abū Bakr and finally Muḥammad, generally recognised as the fountainhead of spiritual influence (*baraka*).[127]

The *dhikr* constitutes, thus, the first and primacy tool the disciple receives from his shaikh. Its formula as transmitted by the masters of the Mujaddidiyya initially comprises the most essential of all names (*ism-i dhāt*), i.e., Allāh. At this priliminary, stage, it symbolically represents the germinal condition of the disciple's inner part upon which the *dhikr* is meant to act. When the neophyte is ready to receive the bestowal of his master's spiritual allowance (*waẓīfa*) together with the accompanying method, he should sit down on his heels, turn his breast towards that of his master, keep his hands placed on his knees, close his eyes and mouth, press the tip of his tongue against the palate, clench his teeth and begin to invoke with utmost respect and reverence the name *Allāh*, following precisely the instructions received.

At the very beginning, the *dhikr* should be directed on the *laṭīfa-i qalb* while constantly bearing in mind the implicit significance of that sublime name; this process is called 'refinement' (*pardākht*).[128] During the invocation, the whole attention must remain concentrated on that Essence, otherwise the danger of being overpowered by evil inspirations (*waswasa*) increases and the efficacy of the performance is compromised.

Apart from the additional invocations interspersed at regular intervals between the recital of the main *dhikr*, Khwāja Bahā al-Dīn al-Naqshband introduced yet another fundamental principle to be followed during the practice of invoking, called *waqūf-i qalbī* or 'alertness of the heart'. According to Shāh Abūl Ḥasan, *waqūf-i qalbī* can be interpreted in various ways. In its

---

127. In considering the double function of Muḥammad as both historical 'seal of prophecy' (*khātima al-'anbiya'*) and universal spirit and principle of creation, the central position attributed to him by the esoteric tradition becomes evident. But the Naqshbandīs claim a parallel descent through 'Alī ibn Abū Ṭālib, through whom the cognisance of the vocal *dhikr* is said to have been transmitted.

128. *MnS*, pp. 44/68.

primary sense it denotes the awareness of and connection with the nominated Object, viz., the heart's alertness towards the Object invoked, also called 'contemplative witnessing' (*shuhūd*). In practical terms, it actually coincides with the stage of *yād dāsht*. The second meaning implies that the *dhākir* must revolve all his attention on the 'pinecone-shaped heart' (*qalb-i ṣanawbarī*), viz., the physical organ that constitutes the seat of the subtle organ bearing the same name and preserving in its innermost core the synthesised Reality (*ḥaqīqat-i jam'a*) of the human creature, so that even that 'piece of flesh' (*mudgha*) may participate in the reality of the *dhikr* thereby acquiring its distinctive consciousness. The third meaning goes back to Khwāja Muḥammad Ma'ṣūm (AD 1599-1668), the third son and principal successor of Shaikh Aḥmad Sirhindī, and reiterates what has already been said regarding *yād dāsht*, i.e., the necessity for the *dhākir* to remain watchful of his heart so that no distraction may divert its attention.[129] For the fourth and last meaning, the authors quote the authority of Khwāja 'Ubaid Allāh Aḥrār who interpreted *waqūf-i qalbī* as the heart's lasting awareness of the Sacred in such a way as to erase from it all other existences except Him.[130] All three authors agree, however, that this last interpretation bears no direct relation to the *dhikr* but refers rather to a particular spiritual state (*ḥāl*) attained during the 'cleansing of the soul' (*tadhkiya-i nafs*).

Yet another important Mujaddidī authority, Shāh Ghulām 'Alī Dihlawī, has defined this indispensable principle as the strict focusing of all spiritual attention (*tawajjuh*) on the organ of the heart for the sake of imprinting on it the image (*naqsha*) of the

129. Shaikh Aḥmad recommends those not receiving any benefit from this method to interrupt the performance for a while and try instead to focus attention on the *waqūf-i qalbī* until the state of awareness of the heart eventually permits to revert to the practice of *dhikr*. The pre-eminence given to this alertness over the *dhikr* emphasises the enormous importance of inner attitude as prerequisite for any success in the *ṭarīqa*.

130. *MnS*, pp. 39-40/62-3; *MuM*, pp. 70-1; *HdT*, pp. 11-12. For details of the order's eleven technical principles, see also Qāḍī Thanā Allāh Pānipatī's *Al-Kitāb al-Najāt 'an ṭarīqat al-Ghawāt*.

ism-i dhāt.[131] For the Naqshbandīs, this spiritual attention plays exactly the same role as the 'stroke' (*ḍarb*) in other Sūfī orders where the vocal invocation is practised in order to scan a continuous sonorous rhythm, and points to the emphasis placed on the interiorised attitude by this *ṭarīqa*.[132] While being hit by the *dhikr*, the heart should, thus, incline all its attention towards the Sacred abode from which the effusion of God's spiritual grace is expected, so as to create the preliminary conditions for the ultimate establishment of the spiritual link (*nisbat*) with the transcendent order.[133]

Once the subtle heart-organ is completely permeated by the vibration of the *dhikr* in tune with the primordial vibration contained in the name Allāh, the subtle invocation is focussed on the immediately following centre, the *laṭīfa-i rūḥ*, and so on through all seven subtle centres until the entire body, from the 'tips of the hair to the nails of the feet', reproduces the sound vibration contained in the name of the Essence. This stage, which corresponds to the ascent of the *laṭā'if* to the *'ālam-i amr* and from there to the celestial abode of the Supreme Principle, is called 'sovereign of all invocations' (*sulṭān al-adhkār*) for it represents the most perfect realisation of the *ism-i dhāt*. The process of reintegration of the five spiritual components located inside the breast has reached its conclusion restoring them to their original state prior to their link with the human body and bringing about their illumination. This leads to a stage where through the established *nisbat* the Divine presence situated in the very hidden mystery of the pinecone heart which has now taken over the role played previously by the subtle organs becomes Itself the interior *dhākir*.

---

131. *Durr al Ma'ārif*, note referring to Friday, 15 Rabī al-Awwal 1231/14 February 1816. The shaikh explains that the heart should be freed from all thoughts relating to either the past or the future but focus on the present moment alone.

132. For their techniques regarding the *dhikr* and in particular the method of beating the heart with the strokes of rhythmic invocation, see J.S. Trimingham, *Sufi orders in Islam*, and Mir Valiuddin (1980), pp. 51-9, with special reference to the Chishtiyya and Qāḍiriyya.

133. Cf. Khaliq Anjum (1989), pp. 101-4.

After the attainment of the benefits derived from this first type of invocation, in relation to the 'purification of the heart' (*tasfiya-i qalb*), the Mujaddidīs instruct their disciples in the practice of the *dhikr-i nafī wa ithbāt*, deemed efficacious for the successive process of 'cleansing of the soul' (*tadhkiya-i nafs*). The way this second type of *dhikr* is performed by the adherents to the *ṭarīqa* Mujaddidiyya is described as follows:

> The disciple should be in a state of ritual purity . . . and turn his face towards the *qibla*, either sitting or kneeling, put his hands on his thighs, concentrate all his senses on the heart while keeping his eyes closed, arrest his breath under the navel and while pronouncing slowly and respectfully the word *Lā* try to pull it from below the navel up to the forehead and brain and imagine that it has flown out of him. He should than concentrate on the term *ilāha*, pull it upwards until it reaches the right shoulder, and finally from there hit with utmost force the pinecone heart with the charge contained in the words *illā Allāh* in such a way as to leave the imprint of its vibration on all five subtle organs and perceive a sensation of heat pervading all limbs. . . .[134]

For the performance of this type of *dhikr* it is deemed auspicious to use an undefined number of invocations in odd numbers in accordance with yet another of the eleven principles, called *waqūf-i 'adadī* (numerical awareness). Although it has been considered an integral part of this technique in the earlier days of the order, in the opinion of most later Mujaddidī authorities, the retention of breath (*ḥabs-i nafas*) is not necessary for a successful performance of the *dhikr* though its utility is still recognised.[135]

134. *MnS*, pp. 52/76-7; *MuM*, p. 84; *HdT*, p. 12; the first two are based on themselves on Qāḍī Thanā Allāh Pānīpatī (cf. no. 130 supra).

135. The mental invocation of this *dhikr* in combination with the retention of the breath was the first teaching received by Khwāja 'Abd al-Khāliq al-Gujdawānī from *al-Khiḍr* as part of the divinely inspired *'ilm al-ladunnī*. According to the Naqshbandīs this *dhikr* brings about the revelation and comprehension of the mysteries of the *sulūk*. *Al-Khiḍr* actually instructs al-Gujdawānī to submerge himself in water while practising the *dhikr-i-khafī* so as to force him to retain his breath.

It is also maintained that there is no need to engage very frequently in the performance of this invocation; however, it should always be practised in a state of full alertness in order to reap the maximal benefit. The perfect execution of the *dhikr-i nafī wa ithbāt* is said to consist of 21 repetitions within one complete phase of respiration consisting of inspiration, retention and expiration, thus, scanning a rhythm of seven repetitions for each phase.[136] The effect of this method is said to consist of the rejection and ultimate dissolution of the practitioner's human individuality (*wujūd-i bashariyat*) while invoking the first part of the formula, viz., *lā ilāha*, and in the display and absorption of the effects of the totality of Divine influences on oneself during the pronunciation of its second, affirmative part comprising the words *illā Allāh*. In case of beginners (*mubtadī*), these effects are said to represent the first level of the *'ilm al-ladunnī*, communicated by God through *al-Khiḍr*[137] to the elected ones among the *awliyā' Allāh*. Thse mysteries are said to belong to a type of knowledge the essential meaning of which cannot be grasped by the human mind. For those more advanced on the spiritual path the recital of this *dhikr* leads to the awareness that the permeation of real Unity (*aḥadiyat-i ḥaqīqat*) reaches all degrees of cosmic multiplicity in the same

136. All authorities agree that if no effect is perceived on the inner sphere once the most perfect number of invocations is reached, the performance should be abandoned until later.

137. The mysterious figure who appears in the *Koran* as the spiritual guide of Moses (*Koran*, 18:60-82), although his name (lit. 'the Green one') is not mentioned in the Holy Book. He occupies a very important role in the spiritual development of many Sūfīs as the interior guide communicating the directly inspired science from the most sublime stage of Divine wisdom (*al-ta'līm al Rabbānī*). He is said to be the chief of the *afrād* holding an important position in the spiritual hierarchy independent even of the seven poles (*aqṭāb*) who govern the cosmos. Moreover, *al-Khiḍr* is closely connected to the spontaneous initiation (*nisbat al 'uwaysī*) conferred outside the regular pattern of transmission of the spiritual influence within a regular *ṭarīqa*. He is included also among the four immortal prophets. For him, see Hassan Elboudrari, 'Entre le symbolisme et l'Historique: Khadir Immemorial', in *SI* 76 (1992), pp. 25-39 and Irfan Omar, 'Khiḍr in the Islamic Tradition', in *MW* 83 (1993), pp. 279-91 or A.J. Wensinck, 'Al-Khadir' in *EI* (second edition), vol. 4, pp. 935-8.

way as the number one contains the entire series of arithmetically conceiveable numbers.

A further requirement for the correct performance of this method consists of its strictly mental performance, practised in absolute discretion and privacy. The phase of expiration should correspond to the recital of the final part of the *kalima-i shahāda*, i.e., *Muḥammad rasūl Allāh*, so as to lead the disciple eventually to a descending vision revolved towards the world. The pronunciation of the negative term *Lā* as meant to deny and finally annihilate the initiate's human component while all other contingent beings simultaneously appear without any real existence (*nīstī*). During the affirmative phase, the Creator must be envisaged as the only goal so that by the means of the *dhikr*. His presence can eventually penetrate into the *dhākir*'s heart with such vehemence that the *sālik* becomes oblivious of everything else around him. At this stage of advanced interiorisation of the *dhikr*, the number of invocations can be gradually raised from 21 to more than one thousand, and the heat and effusion that accompany it will extend to all subtle organs including those of the four gross elements. Hence, Shāh Abūl Ḥasan tells us that

> since the ascendance of the heart (*'urūj al-qalb*) includes the purification of all elements from haughtiness, pride, meanness and degradation . . . , they become balanced and uniformed.[138]

We, thus, learn that the utility of this *dhikr* extends to the erasure and removal of the negative qualities and vices rooted in the individual's nature and their gradual replacement with the Divine qualities and anglic virtues. Shaikh Aḥmad Sirhindī compares the recital of the negative syllable *Lā* to an axe which cuts mountains of attributes and ephemeral relations with the phenomenal world.[139]

---

138. *MnS*, pp. 53/67-8.

139. During the pronunciation of the negation, the term *ilāha* should be replaced with that of the vice whose extinction is envisaged before continuing in the usual manner until its obliteration from the soul is achieved. This should be done one by one with all negative attitudes →

It follows that this second type of *dhikr*, which bears a particular relation with the path of inner realisation by stages through the ten stations (*maqāmāt-i 'ashra*),[140] contributes to the gradual processes of 'soul-cleansing' (*tadhkiya-i nafs*). This constitutes its real aim, for it finally leads to the *murīd*'s continuous cognition and consciousness of the Divine presence after reaching the stage of *fanā-i nafs*. So, the utility of this *dhikr* remains largely connected with the ascending phase of the spiritual journey which culminates on the last level of major sainthood.[141]

In fact, as long as the disciple remains engaged in the first part of his spiritual journey, the use of *dhikr* combined with a sincere commitment to the legal prescriptions of the *sharī'at* and the injunctions of the *sunna* represent the sole requirements. Only after the total realisation of the 'synthesised state' (*jam' al-jam'*) at the apex of the ascending journey which signals the turning point in the Mujaddidī concept of the *sair* and in which the adept acquires knowledge of the difference between God and creation (*farq ba'd al-jam'*) and of the inner realities of Islam (*islām-i ḥaqīqat*) is achieved, is the practitioner advised to substitute or integrate the synthetic invocation with the performance of a series of supererogatory acts of devotion

---

→ until the soul is perfectly purified. This procedure exemplifies the use of the *dhikr* during the process of 'cleansing the soul'.

140. The first corresponds for the Naqshbandīs and most other orders to the 'station of repentance and penitence' (*maqām-i tawba wa inābat*) in which the disciple repents honestly for all sins and negligences committed in the past and seeking refuge in the service of a qualified master thereby symbolically returning to a state of primordial purity, while the tenth and last station, that of contentment (*maqām-i riḍā*) is concerned with the illuminations of the Divine Essence. For the ten stations, see *MnS*, pp. 29-32/48-52; *MuM*, pp. 50-4.

141. In *Mak*. II:95, Shaikh Aḥmad Sirhindī writes: 'The invocation of the formula *Lā ilāha illā Allāh* with the addition of *Muḥammad rasūl Allāh* for at least 100 times brings about the attainment of ascension and Divine attraction (*'urūj wa jadhba*); if one then proceeds to a repeated invocation of the formula *Muḥammad rasūl Allāh,* this will result in an ascent and descent (*'urūj wa nuzūl*), and if one recites continuously the entire *kalima-i tayyiba*, this will bring about the total descent (*jumla-i nuzūl*)'.

(*nawāfil*). These include prayers, the study of the religious sciences (*'ulūm-i dīniya*), the recital of the *Koran* (*talāwat*), the study of the Traditions, the blessing and salutation on the prophet, his family and the companions (*durūd-i sharīf*), the recital of the *tasbīḥa* (*sulḥān Allāh*), the *takbīr* (*Allāhu Akbar*) and the *taḥmīd* (*al-ḥamdu* Allāh), etc. At this stage, no difference between *sharī'at* and *ṭarīqat*, exoterism and esoterism, persists for the saint who now contemplates religious tenets, rituals and spiritual practice as different expressions of the one Truth (*ḥaqīqat*).

MURĀQABA

The Persian noun *murāqaba* is derived from the Arabic root *raqaba* bearing the meaning of to 'attend, to observe, to contemplate'. Its translation as 'visualisation, attentive observation, contemplation' conveys fairly well the range of conceptions implied by the term in the technical vocabulary of the Mujaddidiyya.

According to a letter written by Khwāja Muḥammad Ma'ṣūm, the term reunites two slightly different but complementary meanings both derived from the same root: one from *raqābat* meaning 'protecting, guarding, preserving', the other from *ruqūbat* meaning 'expecting, waiting for, looking for'.[142]

In the terminology of next Sūfī orders, *murāqaba* designates the inner attitude assumed while fixing the attention on an outer object with the aim of emptying the mind from all emerging thoughts while trying to remain fully concentrated on Allāh. In the vocabulary of the Mujaddidiyya Maẓhariyya, the term refers to a particular technique requiring the disciple to close his eyes and to attend to the descent of the Divine grace from its source (*mabdā-i faiḍ*) first on each single subtle centre and later on

---

142. Cf. *MuM*, p. 82; *MnS*, pp. 55/81. The closure of the eyes recommended for efficient execution of this technique is meant to facilitate the detachment of the senses from the objects of the phenomenal world and their introversion on the inner states eventually leading to the 'inner vision of beatitude'.

their synthesised aspect. This current of grace is initially perceived in the guise of one of the multiple aspects of the Divine (*wujūh*, pl. of *wajh*) and later on Its unqualified Essence. At first, the relation, thus, established between the visualising subject and the visualised Object must be enforced to such an extent that no distracting thought (*khaṭra*) can interfere in it, by creating a sort of psycho-mental shield around the disciple's mind which leaves him entirely focussed on his single aim. Khwāja Muḥammad 'Abd Allāh, the youngest son of Shaikh Aḥmad's spiritual instructor Khwāja Bāqī Billāh (971/1563-1012/1603), provides us with the following description of *murāqaba*:

> *Murāqaba* must arise out of the disregard for all spiritual states (*aḥwāl*) and merits (*auṣāf*) and one's capacity of endurance to wait for the encounter with the Lord, eagerly longing for His beauty (*jamālihi*) to manifest Itself while remaining fully absorbed in the desire and love for Him. . . .[143]

Some sources trace the origins of this method back to the master of Shaikh Junaid al-Baghdādī (*d.* 297/909) who reportedly used to compare the inner attitude required during the performance of *murāqaba* to a cat's intent fully absorbed in its attentive observation and concentration on the den of a mouse while patiently waiting to catch it.

These descriptions clearly convey the double, active and passive, attitude of the practitioner engaged in this method, although the whole process must be understood as an entirely interiorised practice with the aim of removing oneself from the sensory objects of the outer world. It expresses itself in an outer immobility (comparable to that of the hunting cat) that reflects the concentration of all potentialities on the interior self in an effort to focus on the desired object and to penetrate its inner reality. Once the *sālik* has reached an advanced degree of perfection in this performance of this method, he should finally be able to control, fix and eventually comprehend the quality

143. *Fawātiḥ*, quoted by Shāh Abūl Ḥasan in *MnS*, p. 56/81.

inherent to the contemplated object, thus, identifying himself with its essence. This state is expressed in the language of the shaikhs as 'effusion of Divine grace' (*mawrid-i faiḍ*) through which the passive seeker is said to gain the bounty of the Lord by becoming a beneficiary of His mercy.

The term *murāqaba* as used by the Mujaddidīs applies, therefore, to an entirely cognitive process (*fikr*) progressing from the mental perception of the prefixed object to the ultimate identification with it. If brought to utmost perfection it leads the *murīd* to participate in the Divine wisdom (*ḥikmat-i ilāhī*). It implies the passage from reflected knowledge (*'ilm*) on the rational plane to spiritual inspiration (*ilhām*, *kashf*) on an exclusively intuitional plane which provides access to the supra-individual, directly inspired knowledge or gnosis (*ma'rifa*). The term *fikr* (lit. 'thought, mental activity', and, by extension, 'mental discipline') is thereby used to qualify the whole method as complementary to that of *dhikr*.

At the beginning of the journey, however, the *sālik* remains exclusively concerned with the more contingent aspects of universal existence and the reflections of the transcendent principles in it. Since these are by definition indefinite in number, the shaikhs point out the impossibility of exhausting the journey while trying to contemplate the multitude of adjunctive names and attributes (*asmā o ṣifāt-i iḍafiya*) to which they correspond analytically. To prevent their followers from losing themselves in this endless chain of corresponding degrees of attainment (*marātib-i wuṣūl*), the ancestors of the *ṭarīqa* claim to possess the specific knowledge regarding the way that synthetically accomplishes (*ba ṭarīq-i ijmālī*) the journey through the names and attributes and quickly reaches in the presence of the Essence.[144]

Here again we encounter the often repeated Mujaddidī assertion of a unique and unprecedented method that facilitates considerably the disciple's task of gaining access to the hidden mysteries. This position is summed up in the principle of

144. *MnS*, pp. 56/82. Cf. also Shaikh Aḥmad Sirhindī's *Mabdā o Ma'ād*, *minhā* 53, pp. 212-13.

'including the end at the very beginning' (*indirāj-i nihāyat dar bidāyat*) which holds that the novice who enjoys the company of a perfect (Mujaddidī) shaikh can gain access to a preliminary experience of Divine unity during the very first steps of his inner journey.[145]

This principle finds its application in the division of the spiritual path into seven sections or stages (*madārij*). Each stage contains one or more particular 'visualisations' reflecting the point of view from which the disciple looks at his objective. However, in its immediate application *murāqaba* aims at the attainment of the composure of the heart (*iṭminān-i qalb*), the granting of the inner vision of magnificence (*'atā-i kubriyā*), the arrest of the thought-current (*jam'iyat-i khaṭrāt*) and the resulting attainment of inner peace (*ilqā-yi sakīna*). It can be practised either alone or be accompanied by the use of *dhikr*. The rigorous preservation of the disciple's inner attention at each successive stage on the source of effusion of the celestial influences and its respective place of arrival in his subtle aggregate is considered of foremost importance for the successful performance of this method, for these represent the two poles between which the entire process takes place.

The first stage, concerned with the *dā'ira-i imkān*, contains a single *murāqaba*, refered as the visualisation of 'pure unicity' (*aḥadiyat-i ṣarfa*) since it refers to that unique principle (*al-aḥad*) that governs this world and which comprehends the total sum of all contingent possibilities. During this part of the journey the spiritual influence descends upon the *laṭīfa-i qalb*, considered to be the centre of the microcosm and seat of the spiritual principle. This interior performance in the 'sphere of possible existence' is said to reach its conclusion when the disciple's mental current remains constantly focussed for about twelve hours on the 'fountainhead of all graces' and when the object of his meditation has been assimilated to a satisfying

---

145. For ample discussion, see, e.g., Shāh Rauf Aḥmad Rāmpurī, *Durr al-Ma'ārif* (note on 13 Sha'bān 1231/1816). A detailed account of this important aspect bearing notable relevance in the order's Hindu sub-lineage will be given in the next chapter.

extent. The authors of our treatises report that the inner perception of lights represents an infallible sign of the attainment of this stage, during which many other marvellous things including Divine attraction (*jadhba*) and occasional spiritual accidents (*wāridāt*) may occur.[146]

During the following stage of minor sainthood, the disciple's visualisation consists of the *murāqaba-i ma'iyat*,[147] the contemplation of co-presence with the principles of the determinations of all common creatures, or that aspect of the Deity in which God's presence is felt in every single particle of the created cosmos, succinctly expressed by the formula *Huwā al-Ẓāhir* (He is Manifest).

At this stage, the disciple recognises that everything exists only because of *Allāh* Who manifests His perfections in the world. The *murīd*'s heart as receptacle of spiritual influences simultaneously experiences a feeling of expansion into the six directions of space until it is perceived as encompassing the entire Universe. This perception announces the attainment of the 'extinction of the heart' (*fanā-i qalb*) and represents from a microcosmic point of view the overcoming of the limiting conditions of individual existence at the same time as it denotes a reflected participation in the principle of creation from a macrocosmic perspective, rendered possible on behalf of the analogy between the two dominions. Hence, the correspondence between the physical heart (*qalb-i ṣanawbarī*) and the all-comprising Universal heart (*qalb-i kullī*) identified with the Throne situated at the centre of the *'ālam-i kabīr*, which reveals to the disciple the secrets of the *waḥdat al-wujūd*.

Part of these first stages of the ascending journey is also the 'visualisation of the five spiritual organs' (*murāqaba-i laṭā'if-i khamsa*), which function as landmarks against which the

146. The Koranic reference quoted by the masters is: 'Allāh is with you wherever you are.' (*Koran*, 5:76).

147. Mīrzā Maẓhar Jān-i Jānān, for instance, expressly warns his disciples not to pay any attention to these lights as they distract the 'traveller' from focusing on the progress along the straight path. Cf. *MuM*, p. 82.

disciple can check his progress. We have already described the Mujaddidī association of each of these five organs with one of the great prophets whose particular qualification is put in relation with different kinds of Divine irradiations. The procedure is very similar for each of the subtle organs and consists of the imaginary placing one's subtle organs in front of those contained in the breast of the prophet Muḥammad, invoking Allāh with the request to grant through His immediate intercessor and the chain of spiritual ancestors part of the grace of the irradiations pertaining to that particular *laṭīfa*. Once the boon is granted and the link established, the *murīd* partakes of the inherent nature, temper and reality of the prophet who governs that particular plane (*mashrab*).

The hierarchy among the subtle organs corresponds to that of the various prophets, so as to enable the *sālik* to penetrate gradually the veils of the superseding irradiations, thereby enhancing the power of his spiritual vision. This whole interior process which includes both the mental and the vibrational sphere pertaining to the psychic constituents of the human individual can be defined in this context as a sort of human and cosmic alchemy aimed at transmuting the elements pertaining to the subtle state into an increasingly more sublime degree of reality the closer one gets to its principles and governing causes. Such an interpretation also accounts for the luminosity of the subtle organs which indicate their ascent to the higher regions of the intermediary world. The disciple reiterates within himself the entire cosmological process in a direction inverse to that of its gradual unfolding, from the point of maximal expansion to that of contraction (*qabḍ*) into the principal point whence everything originated. The Mujaddidīs call this the 'journey through the cardinal points' (*sair-i āfāqī*). It lasts for the entire duration of the journey through the realms of major sainthood when it assumes the denomination of 'journey through the inner selves' (*sair-i anfusī*).[148]

---

148. But until arrival at the final stages of the *sulūk*, we are still exclusively concerned with the reflections of the names and attributes in the minor sainthood and the names and attributes in the major one, i.e., although central in respect to our world, this stage is still contingent in regard to the Essence and its essential attributes.

Major sainthood is the next stage of the spiritual journey and is described as including altogether four *murāqabāt* the most important of which is the 'visualisation of extreme proximity' (*murāqaba-i aqrabiyat*) that goes back to the inner meaning of the Koranic verse: '. . . We are nearer to him than his jugular vein. . . (*Koran*, 50:16). On that plane the five subtle organs attain to their maximal ascension and bring the 'journey towards Allāh' to conclusion. The previous stage led the *sālik* from the concentration, meditation and finally contemplation of his co-presence with Allāh culminating in the experience of union (*ittiḥād*) and, consequently, in a synthetic vision of God and the world (*tawḥīd-i wujūd*) characterised by a condition of inebriation (*sukr*). This stage leads to a state of extreme proximity, indicative of a subsisting degree of duality (*du'ī*).[149] Here, the initiate returns to a state of sobriety (*saḥw*) accompanied by a new vision of the world's reality (*tawḥīd-i shuhūdī*), which allows him to perceive the entire Universe as a mirror (*a'īna*) in which the beauty of the Beloved is reflected on a plane of minor reality. During this part of the journey, the subtle organ concerned is the *nafs*. We may, thus, partially identify it with the process referred to as 'cleansing of the soul', that wants to refine the vicious qualities of the disciple's soul into virtues while conveying upon his inner self a state of peace that enables it to partake at the current of God's mercy (*al-rahmat*).[150]

Consequently, the perfection of this level coincides with the 'extinction of the soul'. It is attained, however, only after having gone through the other sub-degrees comprised in the stage of 'major sainthood', all focussed on the 'visualisation of love'

---

149. These three degrees show a great affinity with the stages listed by Patañjali in his *Yoga-Sūtra* as *dhāraṇā*, *dyāna* and *samādhi* and define an increasing intensity in the relationship between the subject that focusses and the object focussed, eventually leading to the identification between these initially separate entities. All are implicitly comprehended in the term *murāqaba* as used by the Mujaddidīs. For this reason, I have preferred to render the term with 'visualisation' rather than with 'contemplation' since only the more advanced stage of this method effectively corresponds to the latter.

150. *MnS*, pp. 68/95.

(*murāqaba-i muḥabbat*).[151] Through meditation on this particular aspect of the Divine, a deep reciprocal relationship of love arises between the longing disciple who assumes the role of lover (*maḥbūb*) and his Beloved one (*ḥabīb*). The remaining three sub-levels derived from each other in a descending order apparently only mark increasing degrees of intensity of this relationship, although they do bear a degree of qualitative difference.[152]

This process is accompanied by a gradual penetration into the knowledge of the Divine names, attributes and qualities in the measure corresponding to the extinction and transmutation of the individual vices or imperfections into the angelic virtues of the *'ālam-i malakūt*.[153] The traversing of these spheres is said to resemble a journey through the radiant circle of the sun which appears increasingly luminous the more parts of it are acquired leaving the remaining parts obscure like those of the solar disk during an eclipse. Other authors point out that the disciple begins to feel his own existence as entirely dependent on its source, the sum of Allāh's pure Being.[154]

---

151. Based on: '. . . When He loves them as they love Him . . .' (*Koran*, 5:57)

152. Maulānā Ḥāfiẓ Ghulām Ḥabīb, a contemporary Mujaddidī shaikh of Sindh and author of *Majālis-i Ḥabīb wa musamma ba Irshād al-Mursalīn*, specifies (pp. 187-9) that to each of the four degrees contained in the sphere of major sainthood corresponds a particular category of ranks.

153. It is said, for instance, that in the stage of major sainthood the mean qualities of the soul, viz., envy (*ḥasad*), avarice (*bukhl*), avidity (*ḥarṣ*), rancour (*kīna*), pride (*takabbur*), vanish and their place is taken instead by the laudable attributes like patience (*ṣabr*), gratitude (*shukr*), reticence (*wara'*), pious devotion (*taqwā*), continence (*zuhd*), etc. Cf. also *Majālis-i Ḥabīb*, p. 189.

154. *MnS*, pp. 69/97. The solar symbolism here employed by the authorities to describe the transcendent source of all supra-individual knowledge finds its parallel in the Hindu tradition too where the reflected, indirectly perceived knowledge pertaining to the sphere of *manas*, the mental plane is assimilated to the silver radiance of the lunar light while the transcendent and direct knowledge pertaining to the superior intellect or *buddhi* is assimilated to the golden light of the sun.

Perfection or 'major sainthood' and the simultaneous entry into the 'sphere of supreme sainthood' are obtained when the *sālik* no longer perceives the Divine grace descending on his cerebral region, the seat of the *laṭīfa-i nafs* which is now perfectly balanced and permeated by a lasting feeling of absolute peace, and the individual limits set by the apex of the rational sphere are definitively transcended. After the liberation of the individual soul from the limiting summons sanctioned by the Divine decree (*aḥkām-i qaḍā*), the *nafs* ascends to the station of contentment (*maqām-i riḍā*), the tenth and most sublime of the *maqāmāt*. The disciple now contemplates the expansion and opening of his breast (*sharḥ-i ṣadr*), which is the receptacle for the comprehension of the Divine mysteries, having been sanctioned as the seat of man's spiritual component by Muḥammad's experience when the two angels Jibra'īl and Mika'īl opened his breast in order to extract a black clot of blood representing the corrupted human nature (cf. *Koran*, 96).[155]

Once again, the corresponding mode of procedure for this *murāqaba* consists of the visualisation of the idea of putting one's breast before that of the prophet praying to God to be allowed to participate in the blessings of this station and reciting the *ṣūrat al-inshīraḥ* (*Koran*, 94). In its uttermost perfection, this visualisation is said to reveal the secrets of the Divine promises (*mawā'id-i ilāhī*) which grant access to the degree of perfect certitude (*yaqīn-i kāmil*) and to the inner comprehension of the sum of injunctions comprised by the *sharī'at* without need of further proofs. The removal of individual boundaries separating the *sālik* from the vision of the perpetual presence (*ḥuḍūr-i dā'imī*) of the Divine law, allows him to adhere to the inner truth of Islam (*ḥaqīqat-i Islām*) and God's signs in the world are sufficient for its comprehension.

The following stages are described in close association with the doctrinal perspective held by the Mujaddidīs. As such, they had not been explicitly developed by the earlier leaders of the

155. See also D. Giordani, 'Al-Inshīrah: la sura dell'apertura' in *'Ayn al-ḥayāt, Quaderno di Studi della Tariqa Naqshbandiyya*, Roma, 1995, pp. 31-45.

Naqshbandiyya but reflect the Mujaddidī's anxiety to modify the *ṭarīqa* view of the requirements of the second millennium of Islam when both the *umma* and the Sūfīs were in need of further explanations in order to strengthen their comprehension of the hidden realities contained in the Koranic message. What had previously been included in the degree of 'major sainthood' now required further specification, although the aim of the proposal remained unchanged. This position at the base of the entire Mujaddidī doctrinal perspective resulted in its peculiar vision of the world which contemplates the ultimate perfections of spiritual realisation as a reflection of the role of the prophets in charge of the task of conveying a Divine message (*risāla*) to humanity in need to be led back to the right path.[156] In line with this perspective, the Mujaddid concentrated his efforts on explaining in most detail those truths contained synthetically in the *ḥaqīqat-i Islāmī* by setting out their relationship with the higher stages of the *sulūk*.

There follows the stage of supreme sainthood (*wilāyat-i 'uliyā*) said to correspond to the station of the angels and other lofty celestial beings. During this part of the celestial journey, Allāh is contemplated in His inner, non-manifest aspect (*murāqaba-i ism-i bāṭin*). It is concerned with the purification of the three elements air, water and fire, back on the plane of differentiated existence though now on a more subtle plane. The oral invocation of the *tahlīl*,[157] a prolonged immersion in voluntary prayers and the punctillous observance of the *sharī'at* are considered very efficacious for gaining the celestial state which is said to be reached with the help of the two wings representing *Allāh*'s double aspect as the Manifest and the non-manifest. By now the seeker of Truth has acquired the knowledge pertaining to both, the stage of the manifest *'ālam-i khalq* and the non-manifest *'ālam-i amr* and is, thus, ready to

156. For some important aspects of the Mujaddid's role in the view of himself and his followers, see Friedmann (1971), pp. 153-60 and terHaar (1990), pp. 13.

157. The *tahlīl* refers to the formula of the *dhikr-i nafī wa ithbāt*, but seen from a different perspective, *tahlīl* meaning literally 'to proclaim the truth of God'.

be accepted as a member of the Sublime Assembly in the *'ālam-i quds*. Notwithstanding the prophetical perspective that culminates in the concept of the 'pole of Divinely inspired instruction' (*quṭb al-irshād*) designed to illuminate the world (*munawwar-i 'ālam*),[158] which is obtained in the station of perfectioning (*maqām-i takmil*), the total realisation of the spiritual path implies the passage to the superior realms of Being symbolically indicated by the celestial spheres. There the initiate is said to encounter all sorts of angelic beings (*malā'ika*), thus putting emphasis on the idea of an ascent along a vertical axis.[159]

Indifferent of the journey's definition as a descent (*nuzūl*) or as the beginning of the ascent along the vertical axis connecting the *'ālam-i mulk* and the *'ālam-i malakūt* with the *'ālam-i mithāl* and other still higher realms, from this moment onwards only the unqualified aspect of the Divinity is contemplated.[160] Whether at the stage of the triple perfections (*kamālat-i thalātha*), that of the Divine truths (*ḥaqā'iq-i ilāhī*) or that of the prophetic realities (*ḥaqā'iq-i anbiyā'*), the *sālik* remains throughout inspired directly from the fountainhead of Divine wisdom pertaining to the *'ilm al-ladunnī*. After accomplishing the purification of the element earth in the sphere of the triple perfections, the effusion of spiritual influences occurs on the synthesised aspect of the ten subtle organs.

During the visualisations that are part of these last three levels of the Mujaddidī path, the initiate gains understanding of the manifold prophetic perfections, although it must be remembered that he experiences these details in the reflected guise of sainthood rather than directly participating in prophethood, since the gates of prophecy have been definitively closed with the delivery of the message of Islam. This particularised

158. Cf. Shaikh Aḥmad Sirhindī's explanations given in *Mabdā o Ma'ād*, *minhā* 2 and 3, pp. 99-102.

159. *MnS*, p. 71/100.

160. Many interesting parallels could be traced between these concepts and the Hindu theories regarding the contemplation of the qualified Deity, *saguṇa Brahman*, and the unqualified Principle, *nirguṇa Brahman*.

knowledge pertaining to the celestial archetypes contained in the *'ālam-i mithāl*, like the inner realities pertaining to the celestial Ka'ba, the Holy *Koran* and ritual prayer, which reveal the hidden truth of the Divine secrets, is accompanied by a state of bewilderment (*ḥairat*) said to befall the aspirant adept when he realises his inability to comprehend the Divine Essence. It is, therefore, also referred to as the state of supreme negligence (*ghaflat*). The inner side of the disciple reaches with it a state of colourlessness and non-qualification (*be-rangī o be-kaifī*) which goes along with a perception of all the laws pertaining to the series of legislators (*'anbiyā'-i ūlū al-azm*) preceeding the mission of Muḥammad.

Only minor importance attaches to the slight divergencies among the later authorities regarding the order in which these last spheres should be crossed, some giving preference to the Divine realities others to the prophetic ones. According to Shāh Abūl Ḥasan, it is the unified aspect of the initiate's subtle aggregate that confers upon him the rank of *insān al kāmil* who reunites in himself not only the perfection of the human condition but also that of all other possible existences, thus, giving credit to the Tradition: 'Allāh has created Man according to His own image'.[161] It corresponds to the sublimest degree of spiritual perfection so that the attainment of the last realities contemplated on the *sulūk* seems implicit for those able to get there. Hence, it is often stressed that during those highly advanced stages of the path no further effort is required since the Divine grace alone can bestow the vision of these stations which are no longer part of the walkable journey (*sair-i qadamī*) but can only be visualised (*sair-i naẓarī*).

The techniques used during the preliminary phases now become obsolete and the disciple suddenly recognises his position of being a mere servant (*murāqaba-i ma'būdiyat-i ṣarfa*) in front of Allāh. This transcends both perceptions, identity between the possible (*mumkin*) and the Necessary (*wājib*) and that of 'adumbration' (*ẓilliyat*) between these two. Imbued with love, the *murīd* spontaneously adheres to the legal injunctions

161. *MnS*, pp. 75/102. Cf. Abū Ḥuraira, *Mishkāt*, III.

prescribed by the *sharī'at* and exceeds them in the performance of supererogatory acts of worship and the prolonged recital of the Holy scriptures. As an example of perfect behaviour, he, thus, becomes a true heir of the prophet and shows the way to a multitude of others without being tied to the individual characteristics perceived by those whose vision is limited by numerous imperfections. This is the station of pure and infinite love (*ḥubb-i ṣarfa-i dhātiya*) from which the perfect adept shares his love for creation in perfect harmony with the love of his Lord in the abode of eternal transcendence.

The master-disciple relationship

The relationship between the spiritual guide and preceptor (*pīr-o murshid bar Ḥaqq*) on one side and the seeker of Truth (*murīd, ṭālib-i Ḥaqq*) on the other revests utmost importance in all esoteric traditions.[162] Its importance derives from the essential role played by the master in transmitting the spiritual influence (*baraka*) into the disciple's innermost part in the course of the initiatory rite (*bai'at, waẓīfa*)[163] thus, legitimising his membership in and sanctioning his indissoluble link with the spiritual tradition in question.[164] Through this permanent bond, the shaikh assumes the role of mediator between the effusion of Divine grace from the transcendent plane and those

162. Although true in principle, practically speaking the concept of this relationship remains nowadays confined to the Eastern traditions where the esoteric part of the tradition has remained accessible and is, moreover, guaranteed through the existence of a regular chain of transmission perpetuated from master to disciple.

163. Actually, the transmission of spiritual influence may also be regularly performed by a simple *khalīfa* possibly unqualified to impart spiritual instructions on a higher level.

164. The Islamic esoteric tradition also allows for the spiritual influence to be transmitted without the physical presence of a shaikh. This type of initiation, referred to as *'uwaysī* in memory of the Yemenite saint 'Uways al-Qaranī (*d.* 18/639), is significant for some of the most renowned authorities of the spiritual hierarchy in Islam, such as Ibn al-'Arabī and many major authorities of the Naqshbandiyya Mujaddidiyya. For details on 'Uways al-Qaranī, see the article of A.S. Hussaini: " 'Uways al-Qaranī and the 'Uwaysi Sufis" in *MW* 57 (1967), pp. 103-13.

individuals eager to receive it, thus, assuming the responsibility for the rebirth and inner transmutation of the disciple. Unfortunately, the indispensability of the preceptor's presence and the necessity of absolute obediance to the master's orders has often been misinterpreted and has raised suspicion among outer observers since it contrasts strongly with the exaltation of individual freedom so dear to the modern mentality.

The importance of the shaikh for the spiritual rebirth and growth of his protegé, continuing during the following period of apprenticeship and spiritual emancipation (*tarbiyat*), is invariably stressed by all Sūfī orders.[165] In some esoteric circles, especially in the Suhrawardiyya and the Kubrāwiyya, the role of the shaikh has been assimilated to that of a second father and mediator of heavenly influences responsible for the inner growth (*wilāda-i ma'nawī*) of the novice. He is concerned with the inner kernel of the disciple's constitution (*ifāda*) whereas the biological father (*wilāda-i sūrī*) holds responsibility for the education of the *nafs*.[166] The shaikh, therefore, occupies a higher rank than the physical father whose importance remains limited to a more contingent realm, and although both must be objects of the disciple's love and respect, the love for the shaikh is considered to hold pre-eminence over that of the father.[167]

165. This idea of a rebirth obviously implies a preceding symbolic death, i.e., the passage from a profane condition of existence that keeps the world in view only to a higher existence with access to the realm of the sacred that, from a theological perspective, keeps in view the posthumous world in the Hereafter (*ākhira*). This concept becomes particularly evident with high caste *dvījā* Hindus.

166. Cf. Fritz Meier, *Zwei Abhandlungen über die Naqšbandiyya* (1994), part I: *Die Herzensbindung an den Meister*, p. 19.

167. The physical continuity from one generation to another is guaranteed through the link perpetuated between father and son and constitutes, thus, a sort of generational *silsila* apt to preserve the continuity of the clan and the longevity of the ancestors which play an important in most traditional cultures.

Shāh Na'īm Allāh quotes Muḥammad Parsā as having said that the common folk aspire to reviving the body (*iḥyā-i jasādī*) while the élite aspire to the revival of the heart (*iḥyā-i qalbī*).

Shaikh Aḥmad Sirhindī writes that while the exterior birth leads to an existence restricted in time the inner birth is meant to lead towards immortality (*ḥayāt-i abādī*). Cf. *MuM*, p. 61.

In the history of the Naqshbandiyya, the relationship between shaikh and disciple has been developed and interpreted in its own peculiar way which distinguishes it from that of other orders in some aspects. As outlined by the Dutch scholar terHaar, two of its main features consist of the importance and frequency of the *'uwaysī* type of initiation and the connected transmission of knowledge on one hand and the necessity for a strong and intimate tie with the living shaikh on the other.[168]

In the context of the more recent treatises examined for this study, however, the first component is less relevant and the authors prefer to stress the importance of the presence and company (*ṣuḥbat*) of a living shaikh.[169]

The reason for this attitude lies in the secret nature (*poshīda amr*) of that part of the doctrine concerned with the hidden master. It calls for a high degree of spiritual insight and an innate disposition for receiving this sort of spontaneous guidance and transmission of knowledge which occurs directly from one spiritual component (*rūḥāniyat*) to another.[170] It is, however, undeniable that the specific form the teachings of this order have assumed over the centuries owes much to the elaborations and ideas derived from those personalities who claim to be connected to a 'spiritual presence' of the *'uwaysī* type.

According to a widespread opinion in contemporary traditional circles related to the *ṭarīqa*, the Naqshbandī way indicated in particular by Khwājā Bahā al-Dīn and Shaikh Aḥmad Sirhindī remains nowa-days the shortest and easiest and,

168. J.G.J. terHaar, 'The importance of the Spiritual Guide in the Naqshbandi Order' in *The Legacy of Mediaeval Persian Sufism* (1992), pp. 311-21.

169. The extent to which the stress laid by more recent authorities on this second aspect of the *pīr-murīdī* relationship is influenced by modern circumstances, would require a detailed analysis; we limit ourselves here to a few considerations, mostly in relation with the Hindu sub-lineage of this order.

170. According to Shaikh Aḥmad Sirhindī who himself was a known benficiary of the *'uwaysī* link, it is exactly this type of knowledge that refers specifically to the *'ilm al-ladunnī* often mentioned in the texts of the *ṭarīqa*'s authorities.

therefore, most accessible method for the achievement of spiritual realisation, the only one that can guarantee access to the esoteric mysteries for a large part of people in our times.[171]

Though it is tempting to diminuish the significance of such assertions in view of the sort of exclusiveness that often accompanies the vision of those who are firmly rooted in their tradition, it nevertheless represents a curious continuum in the teachings of this order, much stressed also in the Hindu sub-branch that developed from it.

As a matter of fact, the bond between disciple and living master assumes great significance for the average disciple for it is a distinctive feature of this *ṭarīqa* to charge the *murshid* with an increasing responsibility and an active inner effort with regard to the disciple who has sought refuge at his feet. It is, therefore, important for the disciple to find a perfect and perfectioning master (*pīr-i kāmil o mukammil*) suitable to his nature and ready to fulfil the task of providing him guidance on the path and assistance in every circumstance and at every station (*irshād*).[172] The responsibility and acute sense of discrimination this preliminary step requires is, thus, described by one of the order's authorities:

> The method of discerning a perfect and adequate shaikh should not remain confined to his ability to display extraordinary deeds, his awareness of the distractions that can befall one's heart or that attainment of a state of trance (*wajd*) and spiritual state (*ḥāl*) because many among these things can be found also among the Jogis and Brahmins; so these matters do not represent any auspicious proof, nay the sign and authentic proof for recognising a perfect shaikh consists first of all

171. Cf. *MnS*, p. 28/46.

172. The station that qualifies one for leading others to perfection (*maqām-i takmīl*) occupies a high rank in the order's perspective and is, therefore, accessible only to the most perfect among the spiritual masters who are far superior to those who have acquired perfection only for themselves; hence, the pre-eminence attributed in this order to the *awliyā'-i ishrat* over the *'awliyā'-i uzlat*.

> outwardly in his resolute adherence to the *sharī'at* and his acting in accordance contained in the Holy Book and the Sunnat, so that it may be possible to devote oneself eagerly to him, for Allāh has disguised sainthood in the attitude of fear of God (*taqwā*) . . . one should avoid any place where likely harm is perceived. Whoever outwardly appears pious and devout, his company should be sought for no inconvenience will derive from joining one's hand with his . . . if ever one may derive profit or not from him; . . . if his company grants the effects recognised by both exoterists and esoterists as authentic, one should consider the company of such a man as red sulphur and a Divinely-sent boon, but if his company may provoke no effect or the respectable authorities do not recognise him, one should leave him, maintaining nevertheless a favourable judgement of him while turning to whatever place may be appropriate to provide guidance, for the only goal consists in Truth not in that particular individual. . . .[173]

The author of this passage, identifies these positive aspects as consisting of the detachment of the heart from all worldly ties, the revival of the disciple's dead heart, refraining from commiting sins, indigence from the desire to accomplish virtues and favourable actions (*a'māl-i ṣāliha wa ḥusnāt*), the recollection of God, etc.[174] The importance of joining the company of the appropriate shaikh, thus, represents an indispensable condition. It is a significant symptom of the sober attitudes assumed by the Mujaddidīs to stress the importance of correct outer behaviour in conformity with the *sharī'at* and the *sunna* and assign to it a preeminence over the ability to intervene on

---

173. Quoted from Qāḍī Thānā Allāh Pānīpatī on Shāh Walī Allāh's *Al-maqālat al-radhiya fī'l-naṣīḥhā wa al waṣiya* in *MuM*, p. 35.

174. Mīrzā Maẓhar Jān-i Jānān used to test the sincerity and firmness of those who approached him by trying to dissuade them by advancing all sorts of excuses and trying to convince them to go the numerous other shaikhs than present at Delhi (*MuM*, p. 38). But this strict attitude of the masters seems to have been relaxed by the reduced number of aspirants who would nowadays meet such high standards.

the subtle state and to provoke spontaneous spiritual experiences or to perform miracles.

But the shaikh too has to show his availability while selecting and accepting those seeking refuge at their service. Before reaching such a decision, the shaikh will first of all carefully scrutinise the innate qualifications of the aspirant, judging the degree of his sincerity and right determination and submitting him to one or more proofs of his resolve.

Once the shaikh has ascertained the suitability of the aspirant, the latter should entrust himself to the shaikh's disposal who will choose the auspicious moment to grant him initiation into the spiritual family (*khāndān*) by asking him to pay a vow of allegiance to him and the ancestors of the lineage (*bai'at*).[175] The ritual act of spiritual initiation thus consists of the conclusion of an indissolvable treaty between master and disciple which sanctions the establishment of a lifelong bond. At the moment chosen for formal initiation into the order, the disciple is asked to kneel down before the shaikh, join his right hand with that of the master and express his regret and repent (*tawba*) for all sins and negligences committed in the past (*istighfar*).[176] He is then asked to pronounce three times the *kalima-i shahāda*, followed by a vow to observe faithfully the five Islamic pillars (*arkān-i khamsa*) and the *sunna* of the prophet Muḥammad, to abstain from any unlawful innovations (*bid'āt*) or associating anything to the rank of God except Allāh (*shirk*). In short, the novice symbolically leaves behind the slags

175. Until the times of Mīrzā Maẓhar Jān-i Jānān and his successors it was customary for the shaikh to ask the newly arrived seeker to look for an auspicious Divine sign, often sought from the *Koran*, to confirm the righteousness of the decision to join in the order (*istikhāra*) and than to wait for a period of about seven days until the decision had fully matured in the applicant.

176. It should be noticed that the modalities of this initiatory rite imitate the ancient Arab tribal custom according to which the vow of allegiance sworn by many newly converted Muslims during the negotiations with the Quraish at Hudaibiya (*bai'at al-ridhwān*) acts as the prototype for all successive treaties and pacts; outside the Naqshbandiyya it is found with minor alterations in almost all esoteric orders.

of his previous profane existence and prepares himself for his rebirth in a new life as member of the spiritual family of which the shaikh represents the nearest and most immediate link.

Soon afterwards the neophyte receives for the first time the spiritual attention (*tawajjuh*) of his new shaikh, combined with the instructions in the method of focusing the mind on the *laṭīfa-i qalb* in order to prepare it for the reception of the spiritual grace (*faiḍ*). The impact created on a subtle level through the transmission and infusion of the master's *tawajjuh* aided by the repentant attitude of the novice creates a favourable condition for leaving an immediate imprint on the latter's subtle heart-organ (*naqshband*) which opens the gates for the reception of the Divine effusion and participation at God's mercy (*abwāt-i rahmat*).

The vehicle through which this spiritual attention is channelled towards the subtle heart-organ of the novice consists of the name of the Essence (*dhikr-i ism-i dhāt*). More precisely, the vehicle is in the subtle vibration produced by the repeated mental invocation of the word *Allāh*, which indicates the eminent role the *dhikr* plays especially during the initial stage of the spiritual career.

The enormous importance the transmission of the shaikh's *tawajjuh*[177] revests among the current techniques of the Mujaddidiyya is often said to date back to Khwāja Bahā al-Dīn al-Naqshband[178] and must be considered as part of his wider effort to make the the spiritual disciples more accessible to his contemporaries. It underlines the shift towards a growing responsibility of the preceptor in the disciple's spiritual upbringing (*tarbiyat*), a tendency that can be observed throughout the past centuries till the present day. This goes far beyond the merely educational aspect (*ta'līm*) of transmitting

177. The term is derived from the Arabic root *wajah* implying the meaning of 'to turn the face to'.

178. terHaar suggests that the emergence of *tawajjuh* as an essential part of the Naqshbandī methodology goes back to the *khalīfa* of Bahā al-Dīn, Khwāja Alā al-Dīn al-'Attār (*d.* 802/1400). Cf. *Mediaeval Persian Sufism*, p. 321.

the doctrinal knowledge, which had previously left the entire effort necessary for progress on the shoulders of the *sālik*. The importance of the spiritual attention gradually shifted more and more from the original attempt to enter into contact with the presence of a deceased person to the outright nourishing of the disciple's inner states by the *pīr*. The shaikh came to occupy the role of a mediator (*waṣīla*) between the spiritual presence of the ancestors of the lineage all the way back to Muḥammad and eventually to the unqualified Divine Essence, and the novice as last and most feable link in the spiritual chain. This concept is based on the traditional concept of a current of spiritual influence (*baraka*) that originates from Allāh passing through His messenger to the various intermediaries and members of the multiple chains spread throughout the Islamic world.

Conceived as effusion of Divine grace (*faiḍ*) it is the subtle energy of this spiritual current that ultimately nourishes the inner side (*al-bāṭin*) of the *murīd* and that contributes thereby to the growth of the inner guide. This idea stands at the base of the gradual elaboration of the concept of *tawajjuh* that gained increasing importance during the centuries from the *imām* of the order down to Mīrzā Jān-i Jānān, and that was to become the dominant feature in the teachings of masters of the *ṭarīqa* after him, both in the Islamic and in the Hindu environment. It sanctioned an increasingly active participation of the shaikh as transmitter of these influences to the benefit of a more and more passive disciple and must be understood in the context of the growing difficulties in modern times in gaining spiritual sustenance through one's own efforts. With this development, the relationship between *pīr* and *murīd* acquires a new dimension that helps to explain the value attributed to the submission of the 'spiritual child' to his mentor. For this reason, the authors we are here concerned with underline the necessity for the shaikh to follow with utmost attention every single step made by the disciple while proceeding on the path. As we have seen, this attention consists basically of imprinting the subtle vibration of the *dhikr* one by one on each of the disciple's subtle organs beginning with the *laṭīfa-i qalb*. To achieve that goal, the shaikh must first of all fix his attention on the ancestors of the *ṭarīqa*'s genealogy and seek their intercession in asking

Allāh to open the gates that grant access to the ocean of His endless bounty, called *fatḥ-i bāb*.[179]

Particular importance for the successful establishment of an efficient spiritual connection (*nisbat*) of this type is once again attributed by the author to Khwāja Bahā al-Dīn, the Naqshbandī, who bears the significant title of *mushkil-kushā* or 'remover of difficulties'. He is followed by Khwāja 'Ubaid Allāh Aḥrār, Shaikh Aḥmad Sirhindī and Mīrzā Maẓhar Jān-i Jānān.[180]

Once the connection is fully established, the shaikh's *tawajjuh* now loaded with the spiritual power of the entire *silsila* hits the inner states of the disciple, thus, accelerating the process of impressing the Sacred name on the subtle organ concerned thereby facilitating the practitioner's own efforts. While turning the attention on the subtle organs concerned, the shaikh is said to be in a position to recognise and check the extent to which the subtle vibration transmitted by the impact of this current has penetrated into the seeker's *laṭīfa*, a capacity that allows him to decide when and how to proceed in the practice.[181] This gift of spiritual insight and the connected ability to establish the condition of the inner states even of a complete stranger are frequently mentioned among the peculiar faculties with which the masters of this order are endowed and they constitute an important criteria for the qualification of its masters.[182]

---

179. *MnS*, p. 41/63.

180. If the disciple is physically absent, the use of a mental image in support of this technique is said to allow the master's spiritual attention to reach its destination over great distances. The wide use of this device is reflected in numerous letters of Mīrzā Jān-i Jānān, Shaikh Muḥammad Ma'ṣūm and Shāh Ghulām 'Alī. The duration fixed for a successful session may vary but is given as an arch of time that embraces one hundred breaths. *MnS*, pp. 87-8/116.

181. The procedure at the very beginning of the spiritual journey is also described by Shaikh Aḥmad Sirhindī who mentions his own first experience while joining at the service of his preceptor Khwāja Bāqī Billāh. Cf. *Maktūbāt* I, no. 290.

182. Shāh Abūl Ḥasan describes the particular faculty of his father and spiritual guide, Shāh Abūl Khair, who could focus his spiritual →

This process lasts from the very beginning until the substitution of the outer physical master with the inner, non-human guide said to reside in the innermost part of the heart and to which corresponds the rise of virtuous faith.[183] In its course the task of the aspirant adept is to elaborate an inner readiness for the reception of this current of grace, sometimes described as 'emptying the vessel of the heart'. In order to achieve this goal he must concentrate on the face and outer appearance (*ṣūrat*) of his master trying to fix and preserve his image in his heart. In the technical vocabulary of the order, this method is referred to as *rābiṭa*, a term derived from the root *rabaṭa* bearing the meaning of 'to tie, to fix, to fasten', alternatively refused to as *taṣawwur-i shaikh*. More precisely, it denotes more precisely the application of the spiritual attention on the relationship between master and disciple whereas *tawajjuh* in its general definition can imply a manifold direction, either of the shaikh towards his disciple or the other way round or of both towards either the spiritual ancestors and the prophet or even directly towards God.[184]

The glance (*dīdār*) received during the association with a perfect saint who has himself attained to the degree of direct contemplation of the Divine Being (*maqām-i mushāhada*) and who has, therefore, had experience of the irradiations connected to It, that can be safely chosen by the seeker of Truth for the realisation of this sort of bond with the aim of being immersed in the perpetual remembrance of Allāh.[185] It is the company of

---

→ attention on the eyes of his disciples in order to ascertain their inner lights, revealing the condition of their inner states. The impact of this current is described as so intense as to provoke an immediate agitation and trembling of the limbs of the person concerned. Cf. *MnS*, pp. 87/116.

183. The author of the *Ma'mūlāt-i Maẓhariyya* quotes a passage from Khwāja Bāqī Billāh's *Raka'āt* in which the latter lists a series of progressive degrees of *tawajjuh* meant to transmute the disciple's sins and vices caused by the lack of real faith (*kufr*) into beautiful virtues. *MuM*, p. 41.

184. Cf. Fritz Meier (1992), p. 45.

185. *MnS*, pp. 41/63.

such a saint to whom the tradition attributes the prophetic saying of 'those who are the companions of Allāh'[186] which is perceived as a preliminary condition for reaching the station of those who sit next to Allāh. So, the concept of association (*ṣuḥbat*) with a particular saint which may be intended both as a loose relationship with a group of saints, for instance at a holy place or a mosque, and as the close and intimate relationship between *pīr* and *murīd* in the context of an institutionalised order, appears to bear close resemblance to the concept of *satsaṅg* known in the devotional tradition of the *bhakti*-movement of mediaeval and more recent Hinduism. In both cases it includes the idea behind the Sūfī concepts of *tawajjuh* and *rābiṭa* for which it represents the necessary precondition, as the following sentence suggests:

> *yak zamāna ṣuḥbat bā awliyā'behtar az ṣad sālhā-yi ba-riyāz.*
>
> To enjoy the company of the saints for a single moment is better than one hundred years of austerity.

The shaikhs describe the performance of this method thus:

> . . . [the disciple] should focus his sight on a spot between the two eyebrows on the front of the spiritual perceptor's face and imagine that nothing else exists; trying to erase one's own self, the disciple should imbue himself with the qualities of the shaikh's blessed existence. As long as he remains at the feet of his master, he should equally try to maintain this mental bond (*rabṭ-i khayālī*) until the quality focussed on is fully acquired and the shaikh's outer picture (*ṣūrat*) remains impressed in [the disciple's] power of imagination (*quwwat-i khayālī*) even during the former's physical absence. He should either imagine [the master's] outer form in front of his heart or maintain his vision inside the chamber of the heart or try to project one's own outer form into that of the shaikh. . . .[187]

186. Related in *Ma'nāh al-Quds*, on the authority of Abū Huraira, *Mishkāt,* II.

187. *MnS*, pp. 41/64.

Well aware of the danger of being accused of *shirk* and *bid'at* which have frequently been hurdled against them by the exoterists and by scriptural literalists, the Naqshbandī authorities have always tried to defend their position pointing out the qualitative differences between the spiritual method of *rābiṭa* and *taṣawwur-i shaikh* and profane attempts to represent the transcendent principle through outer images. However, the extremely subtle difference intercurring between the two often escapes the attention of superficial observers, and the interesting hints made by Mīrzā Jān-i Jānān regarding the Hindu way of idol-worship prove the subtle approach adopted by some Naqshbandī leaders towards this delicate problem was well grounded.

3

Doctrine and Methodology of the Hindu Sūfīs at Fatehgarh and Kanpur

Continuity and Gradual Assimilation

Socio-political circumstances and religious environment

THE shift of this particular branch of the Naqshbandiyya Mujaddidiyya Maẓhariyya from the original Islamic environment into a Hindu context occurred at a time when many parts of Indian society had begun to feel the impact of European colonial rule in numerous fields. The agressive mentality of colonial rulers who aimed at establishing a political, material and cultural hegemony over the indigenous environment caught large segments of the traditionally educated Indian urban class unprepared and challenged its ability to react against this domination trying to provide concrete answers to the impact with modernity.

The new system and the internal tensions it caused led to the rise of a series of social and religious movements, each reflecting different shades of intellectual response to Western influence. These reactions ranged broadly from the call for profound social and religious reforms ready to sacrifice many essential aspects of the inherited tradition on the altar of rationalism typical of the vision imported by the British colonialists and mostly Protestant missionaries to an integral traditionalism rejecting any kind of innovation considered incompatible with the ancient indigenous values. Typical examples of the former are represented by the Brahmo-Samāj, founded in 1828 around the Bengali intellectuals Ram Mohan Ray (1772-1833) and Dwarka Nath Tagore (1794-1846) in the Hindu upper class environment of Calcutta,[1] by the Ārya-Samāj founded in 1875 by the Gujarātī brāhmaṇa Dayananda Sarasvati (1824-83)[2] and by the reform movement initiated among Muslims by Sir Sayyid Aḥmad Khān (1817-98).[3] Worth mentioning leading figures on the other side of the spectrum include Śrī Rāmākr̥ṣṇa Paramahaṁsa (1834-86) and some regional movements including that promoted by the Śaṅkarācārya of Puri or the Go-rakṣā ('Defence of the cow') movement initiated by Svāmī Kārpatrījī at Benares.

Significantly, most of these reform movements were promoted by high-caste Hindus who identified the cause of India's weakness *vis-á-vis* modernity in the degeneration of its sacred traditions into superstitious idol-worship and the corrupt ritualistic monopoly held by members of the orthodox priestly class. In many ways similar to their Muslim counterparts at Deoband, Delhi and other parts of northern India, they, pledged for a return to the original purity of the presumed golden age which somehow reflected the ideas predominant during and after the European Reformation of the sixteenth and seventeenth centuries and which lay at the base of the attitudes of the very colonial class they often so vehemently opposed.

Although the criticism of there reformers was outwardly similar to that advanced by many renowned saints and other traditional religious authorities in previous centuries, the

---

1. Cf. David Kopf, *The Brahmo Samaj and the Shaping of the Modern Indian Mind* (1979).
2. An extensive account of this major North Indian reform movement that lives on till the present day is given by J.N. Farquhar, *Modern Religious Movements in India* (1918), pp. 101-26.
3. For a fairly detailed analysis regarding the different ways of responding to that challenge in the Muslim environment, see among others Barbara Metcalf, *Islamic Revival in British India: Deoband 1860-1900* (1982) and Usha Sanyal, *Devotional Islam and Politics in British India: Ahmad Riza Khan Barelwi and his Movement, 1870-1920*, Oxford University Press, New Delhi, 1996.

reaction promoted by these new leaders was itself often imbued with elements of that very modern mentality which it so vehemently denounced. The attempt to combine both religious and social reform on a scale beyond the limited context of a particular tradition or social group, involving indiscriminately all sections of Hindu society, was an unprecedented phenomenon which proved too sharply opposed to the traditional spirit of Indian culture to successful in the long term, at least beyond the restricted sphere of the high-caste Westernised bourgeoisie living in the greater urban centres.

It is on the background of this religious and social ferment characteristic for late nineteenth-century India that the passage of the esoteric heritage of the Naqshbandiyya Mujaddidiyya into a particular Hindu environment must be at least partially envisaged. An exhaustive analysis of the socio-historical background that accompanied this development is complicated by the scarcity of reliable contemporary written sources and is further rendered difficult by the reluctance of the present authorities to disclose details of the order's history during that period. It is, however, possible to detect a series of factors favourable to this encounter of Islam and Hinduism at a time when the relations between the two communities were becoming increasingly strained as a result of the *divide et impera* policy persued by the colonial government.

Mahātmā Rāmcandra Saksenā, the charismatic leader of the Hindu Naqshbandīs, as well as most of his successors in that line, were born into one of the twelve subcastes of the north-Indian Kāyasth community whose members had for centuries served in the administrative and military service of India's ruling Muslim dynasties, especially during the Mogul era.[4] Prolonged contacts with the Muslim aristocracy both in the courts of the important centres of power and in the countryside saw the Kāyasths acquainted not only with Persian, the official language and administrative medium till 1837 and its associated

4. It was during the reign of the Mogul emperor Akbar (*r.* 1565-1605) that his ancestors were officially rewarded for their loyal services. Cf. *Bhogāv — atīt se vartamān*, pp. 77-9.

literary culture, but also acquire familiarity with the funda mental concepts of Islam.

We know that both, Rāmcandra and his brother, Raghubar Dayāl, underwent in their childhood a period of training with a Muslim scholar who instructed them in Persian and Urdu besides the fundamental skills of the art of poetry and the basic tenets of Islam. These essential requirements of a young Kāyasth under the old order prior to the imposition of European rule were integrated with an acquaintance with the customs of their caste[5] and the associated rituals regarding domestic worship. The biographies reveal that Rāmcandra's family was firmly embedded in the Ramaite devotional tradition prevalent in Awadh the scriptural authority of which was based on the *Rāmāyaṇa* and the *Rāmacaritmānasa*.[6]

Notwithstanding their Hindu heritage, the young Kāyasths were, therefore, acquainted with many aspects of Islamic culture and way of life and were, thus, facilitated in the reception and assimilation of an esoteric component from the latter. Although they belonged to a formerly respected and prosperous social class thanks to their privileged relations with the local Muslim aristocracy, their ritual status in the orthodox Hindu hierarchy did not qualify them for apprenticeship in the sacred sciences, leaving them dependant for the completion of their often elaborate rituals on the services of the priestly class. The rapid decline of Muslim power which was sealed by the formal abolition of the Mogul empire in 1857 and the consequent

---

5. Although the Kāyasth community occupies a somewhat ambiguous position in the Hindu ritual hierarchy derived from their obscure origin, the peculiar rituals, i.e., that pertaining to the *vivāha* nuptial rite are extremely elaborate and require the services of a highly esteemed *hotra* of Kannaujī brāhmaṇas.

6. The names of the two Kāyasth brothers, Rāmcandra and Raghubar Dayāl, suggest the family's adherence to the Ramaite devotional tradition current among most Kāyasth families in the eastern Ganges plains. A shift in the clan's devotional tradition may, however, have occurred with its migration during the sixteenth century from the Braj-deśa, heartland of the Kr̥ṣṇa cult, to Awadh, associated with Lord Rāma.

passage of the country's administrative system to British control deprived many north Indian Kāyasths of their traditional social function. As a result, many of them were compelled either to migrate from their homeland Awadh and in the Doāb to one of the nominally independent princely states in the west or the south (e.g., Gujarat, Sind, Hyderabad) which still largely preserved a traditional Muslim administration,[7] or to gradually adapt themselves to the circumstances under the new system while losing many of their former privileges.

The consequences the latter alternative implied are impressively documented in the case of Rāmacandra's ancestors, who witnessed the loss of their inherited *jāgīr* around the town of Bhogaon in the Mainpuri and Farrukhabad districts of the United Provinces during or shortly after the 1857-8 War. This was followed by the subsequent loss of the family's remaining privileges and belongings during the final years of the last century as a consequence of a legal dispute over the repayment of accumulated debts to the former chief of Mainpuri. The sudden lack of a guaranteed income and the contemporary change in the requirements for qualifying for a post in the colonial administration had a serious effect on the life of this once wealthy family and plays a non-indifferent role in the early history of this Hindu Sūfī lineage.

Rāmcandra Saksenā, provided only with a degree from the local English medium school, struggled to obtain a post as clerk in the town's tax excise department which hardly allowed him to provide his family with the bare minimum of subsistence. Even more modest was the situation of his younger brother Raghubar Dayāl who could never hold a fix position anywhere forcing him and his family into a life of utmost poverty and hardship. Only from the second generation onwards, with Raghubar Dayāl's son Bṛj Mohan Lāl and his nephews Oṁkār Nāth, Rādhe Mohan Lāl, etc.,[8] it is possible to observe a gradual

7. For Kāyasth migration to Hyderabad, see Karen Leonard (1977).

8. Encouraged by his paternal uncle Rāmcandra to pursue his studies, Bṛj Mohan Lāl became a highly ranking officer in the Police Department of the United Provinces while his eldest son and present- →

improvement in the social and economical background of this Saksenā family which reflects their successful adaption to the newly introduced standards of education and the perpetuation of the Kāyasth's traditional role under the changed circumstances.

The question as to how far the transition from pre-colonial social patterns to the modern age is relevant to the development of the spiritual discipline these Kāyasths inherited from the Mujaddidī shaikhs is complex. It combines with the more general question as to how far the very impulse for transmitting initiation into an orthodox Sūfī order to Hindus should be understood within the historical frame during which it occurred. The first explicit sign of a departure from the strictly orthodox Mujaddidī positions that had hitherto guaranteed the continuity of the *silsila*'s tradition within the folds of Sunni Islam came from Sayyid Abūl Ḥasan Naṣīrābādī during the first half of the nineteenth century when he entrusted one of his disciples with the task of opening up the *ṭarīqa* to Hindus. Although the available sources do not reveal details about this pivotal figure in the Na'īmiyya lineage which would allow for definite conclusions regarding the possible grounds inducing this leader to take such an unprecedentedly bold step, it is noteworthy that it occurred at a time of radical political and cultural transformation.

The second half of the nineteenth century not only witnessed the rise of many of the above mentioned social reform movements more or less directly derived from contact with modern thought, but also saw the revival of earlier established spiritual traditions in northern India. Many of these bore close affinities with the mediaeval *sant* traditions that had contributed considerably to the spiritual history of northern India since the times of Kabīr and Gurū Nānak.[9]

→ day authority (*ṣāḥib-i waqt*) of the lineage retired in 1994 from his higher administrative post in the Kanpur branch of the State Bank of India.

9. For the term *sant*, see Parashuram Caturvedi, *Uttarī Bhārat kī sant paramparā* (1964), pp. 1-22 and L.P. Mishra, 'Di certi termini →

The *sant*s are known in the West more for their prevalently humble social background and their open defiance of orthodox religious authority expressed through the powerful means of fervently devotional verses, rather than for the sometimes elaborate doctrines that developed into an institutionalised body of esoteric teachings under their successors. Mostly hailing from the Vaiṣṇava background within the Hindu tradition, they appeared almost contemporarily in various regions of the subcontinent, proclaiming a simple and direct approach towards the Sacred through sincere devotion (*upāsanā*) and loving surrender to the Supreme Lord (*prem-bhakti*).[10]

Later, a series of outstanding figures of this current whose spiritual affiliation remains in most cases shrouded in mystery, came to be regarded by their disciples and followers as the fountainhead of a distinctive esoteric tradition each of whom developed over the next generations a peculiar doctrinal body, methodology and regular lineage for the transmission of spiritual authority (*paramparā*), generally known as *panth*s (lit. 'spiritual paths', very similar to the Sūfi concept of *ṭarīqa*).

As such, the Kabīr-panth in the eastern Gangetic plain and the adjacent Vindhya mountain range, the Nānak-panth in the Punjab, the Dādū-panth which developed around Dādū Dayāl (1544-1603) in Gujarat and southern Rajasthan, but also the successors of the renowned Bengali sant Mahāprabhu Śrī

→ ricorrenti nella letteratura mistica dell'Hindi Medioevale' in *Annali di Cā Foscari* X (1971), pp. 39-49. If at all needed, I would propose the translation of *sant* as 'devotee of Truth'.

The first expressions of this sincere devotion which was to send new impulses to the whole of India, date back to the first recognised *sant*, Nāmadeva (1269-1350) of Maharashtra from where the medieval revival of Hinduism was to reach the north with renowned saints like Rāmānanda (1400-70) at Benares. For the controversial theories regarding the origins of this newly emerging devotional current, see P. Caturvedi (1964). For Nāmadeva, see Prabhakar Machave, *Namdev: Live and Philosophy* (1968).

10. Apart from Kabīr, a member of the recently converted Muslim weaver caste (*julāhā*), his contemporary Rāidās of Benares was a cobbler, Sena was a barber and Dādū probably a weaver. Cf. K.M. Sen, *Mediaeval Mysticism of India* (1930).

Caitanya (1485-1533) in Bengal and Orissa, and later in the Braj-Deśa around Mathurā and Vṛndāban to name only some of the best known examples, were largely successful in revitalising the appeal of India's spiritual heritage from within while extending their message of unconditioned and unrefrained love for the Divine down to the humblest strata of Hindu society.

The call for participation of all social classes in the transcendent truths through an immediate passionate longing and total self-surrender either to the chosen divinity in the guise of its personal attributes (*saguṇa*) or to the unqualified abstract Supreme Being (*nirguṇa*), as in the case of the above-mentioned *panth*s continued under such later figures as Tukārām (1598-1649) in Maharashtra, Palṭū Sāḥib of Ayodhyā (1757-1825) and Cārandās (1703-82) at Delhi.[11] The latter, although originally hailing from the Mewāt region in northern Rajasthan, was a contemporary and fellow citizen of Shaikh Mīrzā Jān-i Jānān.

These figures were in time followed by other generations of *sant*s. Amonge these, we find Tulsī Ṣāḥib Hāthrasī (1763-1843) the sant of the Braj region. According to tradition, he was the son of a high-ranking aristocrat in the Marāṭhā empire who decided to abandon his worldly career in search of a spiritual guide finally settling down in Hathras, a small town between Agra and Aligarh, where he soon rose to the rank of a revered saint among the local population.[12]

As far as we can ascertain from the abundant though often heavily hagiographical literature that has developed around the leading authorities, it was through Tulsī Ṣāḥib that Lālā Śiva Dayāl Singh (1818-78), the founder of the Rādhāsoāmī Satsang which was the last great *sant paramparā* to insert itelf into the precedent tradition, was awakened to the message and

11. See Daniel Gold, *The Lord as Guru: Hindi Sants in North Indian Tradition* (1987), pp. 67-77, and K.M. Sen (1931), pp. 130-2 and pp. 146-50 for the life and background of many of these *sants*, see *Sant Malātmāon kā Jīvan-Charitra Saṁgraha* Belvedere Printing Works, Allahabad, 1999.

12. For him, see Caturvedi (1964), pp. 775-86. Other sources include Rādhāsoāmī works, like S.D. Maheshwari, *Param Sant Tulsi Sahib*, Soami Bagh, Agra, n.d.

teachings of a living *sant*. A member of the Punjābī Khatrī community[13] whose ancestors were linked to the Nānak-Panth based on the teachings of Gurū Nānak, Śiva Dayāl Singh was to establish a newly shaped devotional tradition in the second half of the nineteenth century. The instructions he began to deliver from 1861 onwards to the members of his small *satsang* at Agra were collected and posthumously edited by his successor Rāī Śaligrām (*d.* 1898) in a work comprising two-volume and entitled *Sār Bacan* (The essential message), written in Hindī prose and verse, which remains the most important Rādhāsoāmī scriptural authority recognised by all branches till the present day.[14] Although soon after his death the lineage began to witness a number of schisms that led to the offspring of numerous independent and rival branches, each with its own doctrinal elaborations and peculiar methodology, the organisation and its teachings as a whole have preserved a degree of homogeneity that justifies its inclusion *in toto* in the mainstream *nirguṇa* devotional context, albeit as a more recent adaptation of its mediaeval forerunners.[15]

---

13. Many members of this caste derive the term *khatrī* from the Sanskrit kṣatriya, thus, claiming a noble descent as warrior-aristocrats. This claim, however, contrasts with their main occupation as merchants, traders or money-lenders, reason for which they are often associated with the vaiśya or baniyā caste. Their social background, thus, resembles closely to that of the Kāyasths.

14. The first edition was published at Allahabad by the Prayag Press Company in 1864. For an English version, see S.D. Maheshwari as: *Sār Bacan Rādhāsoāmi: Poetry* (vol.I) and *Sār Bacan Rādhāsoāmi: Prose* (1970).

15. Regarding the historical background and the teachings of this spiritual tradition from a scholarly point of view, see M. Juergensmeyer, *Radhasoami Reality: the logic of a modern faith* (1991), and Daniel Gold (1987). Cf. also Caturvedi (1964), pp. 789-818. Rāī Śaligrām Ṣāḥib Bahādur, a Kāyasth by birth was a government official in the Post Service and the first Indian to reach the position of Postmaster-General of the United Provinces; he is said to have turned towards spiritual life after witnessing the cruelties of the 1857-8 War. He finally recognised his master in Svāmī Mahārāj, the title attributed to Śiv Dayāl Singh by his followers, and served him until the latter's death when he himself assumed the charismatic leadership of the order, organising and invigorating the *satsang* into an efficient →

Such connections are strikingly put in evidence by Kabīr's frequent representation as archetype of a perfect *sant* and alleged *avatāra* of a spiritual principle which manifests itself from time to time to a few extraordinary human beings, and by the close similarity encountered in several key issues of the Rādhāsoāmī teachings with those prevalent in the Dharmadāsī branch of the Kabīr-panth.[16] Juergensmeyer shows the resemblance in style and content of Tulsī Ṣāḥib Hāthrasī's main work, the *Ghaṭ Rāmāyaṇa*,[17] the reading of which is strongly recommended by many Rādhāsoāmī authorities, to a treatise very popular among the Dharmadāsīs, the *Anurāg Sāgar* ('Ocean of Love'),[18] as well as to the poetry of Dariyā Sāḥib Bihārī (1674-1780), a poet-saint related to the Kabīr-panth who is highly revered by the Rādhāsoāmīs. This closeness leads him to presume a direct link between the medieval *sant*-tradition and what he calls 'esoteric santism' of more recent region, even if admittedly 'important differences between the two remain'.[19]

There are also other elements favouring the idea of continuity between the ideals of the mediaeval *sant*s and the

---

→ spiritual network with precise rules and methods. For him, cf. J.N. Farquhar (1918), pp. 163-4 and Juergensmeyer (1991), pp. 37-47. The main schism within the *satsang* occurred shortly after the death of Lālā Śiv Dayāl Singh and was apparently caused over a dispute regarding his succession as the founder had left no clear statement at this regard. The main contenders, Rāī Śaligrām and the retired Punjābī Army officer Jaimal Singh, came to stand thus at the head of the order's two main lines of descent, the Agra line and the Punjābī one based at Beās which later fragmented into numerous sub-branches.

16. For a short but comprehensive description of the cosmological doctrines of this second main branch of the Kabīr-panth derived from Kabīr's disciple Dharmadās, see F.E. Keay, *Kabīr and his followers* (1995), pp. 135-49.

17. The Hindī edition of this work has been published from the Belvedere Press, Allāhābād, in 1911.

18. This work originally written in Hindi, is available also in English, tr. by R.K. Bagga and ed. by Russell Perkins under the title *Introduction to the Ocean of Love: The Anurag-Sagar of Kabir* (1982).

19. Juergensmeyer (1991), pp. 26-9; for the Dariyā-panth, see Caturvedi (1964), pp. 651-63 and Sen (1931), pp. 133-6.

more recent manifestations of this sort of piety. These include the stress on the possibility of gaining access to the path of Truth while outwardly remaining involved in the worldly affairs as a householder (*gṛhasthī*), even if the choice to cut all worldly ties in order to dedicate one's entire attention to devotional exercises is seldom outrightly rejected, nay sometimes openly tolerated, as in the Dharmadāsī branch of the Kabīr-panth. In this context, the Vaiṣṇava background of most *sant*s is likely to play a certain role since, unlike its Śaiva counterpart, it lays a stronger emphasis on a direct involvement in worldby action that contributes to the maintenance of the cosmic order (*dharma*), thereby, reflecting the role of the *avatāra*s.

The attitude of these *sant*s comes curiously close to that assumed by the Naqshbandīs summoned up in the formula of 'solitude amidst the crowd' (*khilwat dar anjuman*). This principle was first sanctioned around AD 1200 as one of the *ṭarīqa*'s fundamental pillars by Khwāja 'Abd al-Khāliq al-Gujdawānī who claimed, that his innovative methods had been inspired by al-Khiḍr, and culminates in Shaikh Aḥmad Sirhindī's emphasis on the prophetic principle that found numerous imitators since the beginning of the second millennium of Islam. It reflects itself, moreover, in a number of peculiar techniques, like that of the silent invocation of the sacred name (*dhikr-i khafī*), which not only constitutes a distinctive of the Naqshbandiyya among the esoteric orders of Islam, but also shows some curious similarities with the *ajapa-japa* method of inner meditation on the name of the Supreme Principle which is current in the Kabīr-panth and Dādū-panth.[20]

All these considerations lead us back to the Hindu *gṛhasthī*s at Kānpur and Fatehgarh whose lineage reunites the esoteric heritage of both Islamic *taṣawwuf* through the initiatory link with the Naqshbandiyya Mujaddidiyya and the *sant paramparā* by means of their authority in the Kabīr-panth received through Svāmī Brahmānanda. The first link of this particular lineage consists of the figure of Mahātmā Rāmcandra Saksenā,

---

20. For the nirguṇa use of this method, see Savitri Shukla, *Sant Sāhitya kī sāmājik evam sāmskṛtik pṛṣthabhūmi* (1963), p. 281.

affectionately referred to by his followers as Lālājī Mahārāj,[21] who holds the rank of primary authority and initiator of this new spiritual tradition. At the same time, his death constitutes the point of departure for a successive fragmentation and ramification, frequently encountered among similar lineages. Author of a number of booklets, treatises, letters and other texts which still occupy a fundamental position among the Hindu initiates of the order's various branches, it was Rāmcandra who, on the explicit request of his Naqshbandī shaikh,[22] began to elaborate the shape of a spiritual discipline that reunites components of both traditions into an allegedly universal message suitable to the particular circumstances prevalent in our times.

As emerges from the sources, Rāmcandra perceived this task as just one further step in a natural process that tries to counteract the gradually decreasing intellectual capacities and spiritual qualifications of humanity through a gradual but continuous externalisation of the ancient esoteric wisdom in order to guarantee its preservation for the generations to come. An important element in this general development is represented by the 'science of the subtle centres' (*'ilm-i laṭā'if*, *cakra-vidyā*), the fundamental cornerstone of the Mujaddidī tradition whose authorities consider it a major contribution of the *ṭarīqa*'s ancestors, especially of Shaikh Aḥmad Sirhindī.[23]

In the introductory chapter of one of his major works that deals with various aspects of this science, Rāmcandra states:

---

21. This honorific title, together with that attributed by the Hindus to Shāh Faḍl Aḥmad Khān (*Ḥuḍūr Mahārāj*), recalls the titles of the Rādhāsoāmī masters and is probably a reverential imitation of this order, which may have acted as example in many other ways.

22. It may be recalled that Shāh Faḍl Aḥmad Khān himself maintained regular contacts with the Svāmī of the Kabīr-panth.

23. It is interesting to note that even the masters of the Rādhāsoamī Satsang mention Shaikh Aḥmad Sirhindī, referred to as *Mujaddid Alf-i Thānī*, as one of their predecessors in the *sant* tradition; cf. *Sar Bacan: Prose* (Dayal Bagh version), pp. 29-30. Other authors mention the Chishtī shaikh Mu'in al-Dīn Chishtī (d. AD 1236) among other Muslim authorities as manifestation of the supreme spiritual principle.

> The great spiritual authorities of both [Hindu and Muslim] traditions who after careful investigations have transmitted the knowledge of this science, had long since practised its perfectioning realisation; but on one hand its transmission at that time did not require a detailed explanation regarding the colour, form, name, sound vibration and effect of each of these [subtle organs] by leaving any written testimony of it to their disciples or to those coming after them, on the other hand due to their particular virtue they did not discuss any of its related aspects through words; nay rather they taught it to their present disciples through direct experience and, wherever necessary, assisted them through subtle hints since it had been an established custom for disciples during ancient times to remain for sometime with their master in order to receive his practical instructions, as appears from the Upaniṣads. . . .[24]

In this passage, the Rāmcandra hints at an underlying parallel in both traditions of the ancient methods of transmitting esoteric knowledge through subtle allusions and direct experience. These, it is claimed, did not yet call for an explicit description of any contingent details regarding this science due to the innate 'particular virtues' (*khāṣṣ maṣlaḥāt se*) of those concerned with it. Interestingly the author, moreover, asserts the existence of two independent traditions regarding the science of the subtle centres within both Hinduism and Islam, maintaining that its investigation had been carried out by the leading spiritual authorities of all sacred traditions (*har mulk ke mahātmāon aur buzurgon ne . . .*).

The means of transmission of this subtle science and, further, of the entire spiritual path were, according to the author of these lines, originally of an exclusively inner nature. Here and there they were integrated by oral explanations which did

---

24. *TP*, pp. 23-4. This work, originally compiled in Urdu, was first published in Hindī in 1941 by Rāmcandra Saksenā's son Jag Mohan Nārāyaṇ and has since been republished twice in the limited number of 1,000 copies in 1964 and 1971.

not, however, require any written record. As an example of this ancient method he cites the authors of the Upaniṣad who formulated the metaphysical doctrine according to the pattern of question-and-answer passing it on from master to disciple through the generations. The sacred knowledge they contain is defined as *brahma-vidyā* (lit. knowledge of the Supreme) and constitutes the core of the Veda, the Vedānta, which consists of the final and spiritually most elevated part of that ancient tradition.

According to Rāmcandra, this pattern remained valid and efficacious for a very long time in history and confirms the unaltered perpetuation of this practice down to the next important stage in India's spiritual history which simultaneously provides us an indication of his own affiliation:

> In the Upaniṣads, the entire transmission of knowledge occurred through subtle hints (*ishāra*) expressed in the form of question and answer between master and disciple. The oral teachings of Janāb Kabīr Ṣāḥib, Nānak Ṣāḥib, Dādū Ṣāḥib and Tulsī Ṣāḥib of Hathras still consist entirely of these subtle allusions. . . .[25]

Here the Hindu master indicates the link he perceives between the encient Vedic tradition preserved by brāhmaṇa orthodoxy with the mediaeval *sants* down to the more recent examples of *sant* piety. It also provides evidence for the other source from which he derives his inspiration and confirms his contacts with the Hindu environment beyond the well documented connection with authorities of the Mujaddidiyya.

According to Rāmcandra, despite the highly allusive language used by these illustrious saints, who were seldom bothered about preserving any records of their teachings, their disciples began to collect the sayings and oral instructions of their teachers in order to preserve them as authoritative guidelines for later generations.

Further on, Rāmcandra describes a third step in the

25. *TP*, p. 24.

unfolding of the initiatic doctrine undertaken by later authorities:

> . . . thereafter, the process of disclosing in major detail through explicit explanations the hitherto hidden secrets [of the sacred doctrine] has been undertaken by the blessed personalities of Janāb Ālīmaqām Rāī Ṣāḥib Śaligrām Sant, Janāb Devī Ṣāḥib Sant Murādābādī and Pandit Brahmaśaṅkarjī Ṣāḥib. . . . But the way Mahārishi Śivbratlāl — may the *paramātmā* grant him the fruits of his efforts! — has taken up the challenge of unfolding [it] in an extremely detailed way presenting its sacred and hidden secrets (*muqaddas o poshīda bhed*) without any hindrance in front of the whole world has so far remained unmatched.[26]

Presumably, the series of names listed in this paragraph indicates those authorities to which the author feels most immediately indebted for authentic first-hand information regarding the late *sant* tradition. The first of these, Rāī Śāligrām *alias* Ḥuḍūr Mahārāj (1828-98), was the Kāyasth successor of Śiv Dayāl Singh (Soāmījī)[27] and organiser of the Rādhāsoāmī Satsang at Agra. Credited with building up an efficient administration, he elaborated numerous rules that regulated the devotional practices of the *satsang* and published the recorded oral teachings of his *satgurū* amplified by his own comments, thus providing a solid doctrinal base for the growing numbers of the order.[28] When Rāī Śāligrām passed away in 1898 Rāmcandra Saksenā was just 25. Although it is nowhere recorded in the sources available to us, a personal encounter

---

26. *TP*.

27. Interestingly, Śiv Dayāl Singh mentions among his spiritual predecessors many of the mediaeval Indian saints including Kabīr, Tulsīdās, Jagjīvan Singh, Gharīb Dās, Palṭū, Gurū Nānak, Dādūjī, etc. Cf. Juergensmeyer (1991), p. 21, footnote 21, and *Sār Bacan* (Prose), pp. 29-30.

28. Cf. *supra*, p. 276 and Juergensmeyer (1991), pp. 36-44. The first Hindī edition of this text is dated 1884, published from the Prayag Press at Allahabad where Ḥuḍūr Mahārāj was stationed before his retirement in 1887.

between the two cannot be altogether excluded in view of the latter's early acquaintance with Svāmī Brahmānanda, the *Kabīr-panthī* he regularly met at his hometown, and his well documented first encounter with Shāh Faḍl Aḥmad Khān in 1891. Both events confirm his early spiritual inclination and suggest that the young Hindu may have well looked for inspiration among the authorities of the Rādhāsoāmī Satsang.

However, it is more likely that Rāmcandra's contacts with the leaders of the Rādhāsoāmī family occurred with the third link in the *satsang*'s main Agra line of succession (Soāmībāgh), Paṇḍit Brahmaśaṅkar Miśra (1861-1907), reverentially titled *Mahārāj Ṣāḥib* among his followers. A brāhmaṇa by birth working as a government official in his hometown Benares, he joined the *satsang* in 1885 and emerged as one of its leading figures thirteen years later following the death of Ḥuḍūr Mahārāj.[29] After having spent sometime at Karachi and Hyderābād (Sind), he assumed the leadership of the spiritual community from Allāhābād where he was posted in the local accountant-general's office. Following his retirement, he spent the rest of his life in his hometown Benares.[30]

Finally, Maharṣi Śivabratalāl (1860-1940), to whom Rāmcandra was apparently very closely linked given the great reverence expressed for him and his work, was yet another disciple of Rāī Śāligrām. He established his own *satsang* at Gopiganj near Benares in 1922. The *maharṣi*, a contemporary of Rāmcandra considered by Caturvedī a 'very able and intelligent person', is said to have spared no efforts to clarify some of the complicated aspects of the spiritual doctrines by giving simple explanations of them.[31] Author of numerous works published as small pamphlets or in the shape of essays that

---

29. Cf. Caturvedī (1964), p. 799 and Juergensmeyer (1991), pp. 44-6; his unfinished English version of the *Discourses on Rādhāsoāmī Faith* deals extensively with a series of doctrinal questions; 5th edn. Agra, Rādhāsoāmī Satsang (Dayālbāgh), 1973.

30. At his former residence near the Kabīr-Caurā at Benares, a *samādhi-sthāna* was erected after his death set in a beautiful garden where his affiliates use to gather on the occasion of the annual *bhanḍārā*.

31. Caturvedī (1964), p. 801.

used to appear in periodicals such as *Sādhu*, *Faqīr*, *Sant* and *Santsamāgam*, he also wrote an extensive commentary on Kabīr's *Bījak* besides compiling a series of biographies of many renowned saints, using short tales to bring their concealed instructions closer to the common people's reach.[32] His works, written mostly in Urdu, have, however, not attracted much attention beyond the restricted circle of his followers and have been largely ignored by the mainstream Rādhāsoāmī authorities his works being nowhere explicitly quoted. From the available sources it appears likely that Rāmcandra drew much inspiration from these nineteenth century *sants* regarding the method of exposing his particular understanding of the inherited doctrines and methods.[33]

The only name mentioned by Rāmacandra in relation to the last stage of open display of the spiritual doctrines who is not directly related to the Rādhāoāmīs is Bābā Devī Ṣāḥib Murādābādī (1841-1919) considered by Caturvedī as the first promulgator of the *santmat-satsang* adaptation of the older *sant* tradition.[34] This enigmatic figure too seems to be in some way related to Tulsī Ṣāḥib Hāthrasī although, if the biographical data given for these two are correct, it is impossible that the two ever met. But, as Caturvedī asserts, many of his compositions show a close similarity to the concepts expressed in Tulsī's *Ghaṭ Rāmāyaṇa*, to whose first published edition the Bābā wrote an extensive preface, and which also include a commentary on Gosvāmī Tulsīdās' *Rāmacaritmānasa* entitled *The origins of the Bāla-kāṇḍa and the end of the Uttara-kāṇḍa*.[35]

---

32. Caturvedī, (1964), p. 801.
33. Daniel Gold's *The Lord As Guru* traces the lineage of Pandit Faqir Chand (1886-1981) of Hoshiyarpur (Punjab) back to Svāmī Śiva Dayāl Singh through Rāī Śāligrām and Maharṣi Śivabratlāl (pp. 164-6 and p. 217). Probably the Maharṣi's best known disciple, his teachings differ slightly from those transmitted by the masters of the main Rādhāsoāmī Satsang.
34. For more details regarding this saint and the lineage that developed from him, see Caturvedī (1964), pp. 811-18.
35. *Ibidem*, p. 812. The first edition of this work was published from the Naval Kishore Press in Allahabad in 1896.

It is in line with the *sant* tradition that the spiritual affiliation of Bābā Devī Ṣāḥib remains obscure, while the hagiographic sources somewhat ambiguously assert that he felt equal devotion towards all major *sants*. Apparently, he was the first to use the term *santmat* to describe the whole edifice of his teachings and methods and to declare its purpose of exhortation towards the devotion of God as *satsang*, a term that at any rate had already current in earlier periods among the members of the Nānak-panth. Both were later adopted by the Rādhāsoāmī masters and also by the Hindu Naqshbandīs at Fatehgarh and Kanpur.[36] Quite significantly, Bābā Devī perceived his *santmat* as open to the followers of all religions and spiritual affiliations to whom he recommended, without any need to abandon their original creed, the inner practice of his version of Kabīr's *dr̥ṣṭi-yoga* and *sūrat-yoga*, two fundamental issues in his teachings. Among his numerous disciples, four are nominated by Caturvedī out of which Paramahaṁsa Menhīdās (1885- 19?), a Bihārī Kāyasth occupies a pre-eminent position not only for his role in the diffusion of his *guru*'s message but also for the authorship of many of Bābā Devī's recorded teachings which include his own additional doctrinal elucidations, especially his blend of concepts found in the ancient sacred texts with those obtained from the earlier mediaeval *sants*.[37]

As one can notice, the names of Rāmcandra's four contemporaries listed in the last paragraph quoted all lead back to the

36. Though the use of these words is not unprecedented in the technical vocabulary of the *sants* — Kabīr frequently used the term *santmat* in his verses and among *sādhus* the term is nowadays diffusedly used to indicate the virtuous company of holy men — it is their technical connotation in this new context probably adopted from the *Nānak-panthīs* that constitute an innovative aspect; some masters of the Rādhāsoāmī lineage ascribe it, however, to Tulsī Ṣāḥib Hāthrāsī. Cf. Juergensmeyer (1991), p. 22 footnote 22.

37. On page 814 of his encyclopaedic work *Uttarī Bhārat kī Sant Paramparā*, Caturvedī presents a list of nine major works ascribed to Menhīdās out of which the first three, *Rāmacaritmānasa sār saṭīk, Vinayapatrikā sār saṭīk* and *Bhāvārth sahit Ghaṭ Rāmāyaṇa* are directly related to the works of the saint from Hāthras, while others, such as *Veda Darśana Prakāśa*, *Gītā Yoga Prakāśa* and *Satsang Yoga* are closely concerned with the exposition of the *sādhanā*.

figure of Tulsī Ṣāḥib Hāthrasī whose name had appeared earlier in relation to the previous stage of doctrinal explication along with Kabīr, Nānak and Dādū. This somewhat enigmatic figure, regarded as the spiritual instructor of the founder of the Rādhāsoāmī tradition, thus, appears as representing the principal nexus in the transition from the mediaeval *sant* tradition to its revival in the eighteenth century which reunites most of these modern *sant*s.

Unfortunately, yet again no reliable information regarding the sources of inspiration of this *sant* nor any regular affiliation to one of the established *panth*s or any other *sampradāya* is available that would sanction the continuity in the transmission of this spiritual heritage. Also the link between the later members of this revived *sant* tradition whose teachings bear evident signs of a previous *sant* matrix, and Tulsī Ṣāḥib or any other authority within a regular *paramparā* remains as mysterious as that of their early predecessors in the mediaeval period.

In this sense, the extremely scarce information one can gather from the available sources regarding Rāmcandra's affiliation to the Kabīr-panth expressed through indirect hints rather than by any univocal statement do not represent an exception but put him in line with the commonly repeated pattern that wants the *sant*s to appear on the scene almost out of nowhere, legitimised by a sort of spontaneous initiation into the mysteries that claims to draw directly from the very source of Divine wisdom. But, as compared to other renowned *sant*s, both in the mediaeval period and in more recent times, there is one important difference between the *paramparā* initiated by Rāmcandra and the many other traditions which developed along similar lines: the ascertained direct affiliation to a Sūfī *silsila* that not only provided its initiates a vital tie with a living spiritual heritage pertaining to Islamic esoterism, but moreover furnished its leaders with the background for the elaboration of a true spiritual synthesis between the subcontinent's greatest and most widely diffused sacred traditions. It provides us, therefore, a tangible proof of the often supposed direct encounter between Islamic and Hindu spirituality within the folds of the *sant* tradition that sanctions the validity of this kind of assimilation and which accounts for the numerous elements encountered in many *sants*' teachings pleading in favour of such a theory possibly extendable also to other lineages.

This double affiliation accounts for the fact that, after delineating the process of progressive disclosure of the secret science in the Hindu environment, Rāmcandra describes a parallel development among the authorities of Islamic esoterism. Beginning with Abūl-Qāsim Junaid al-Baghdādī (*d.* 297/909) and Abū Yazīd al-Bisṭāmī (*d.* 261/875), two prominent Sūfis of the early period of Sufism and often considered as prototypes respectively of the ways of *sulūk* and *jadhba,* Rāmcandra includes in this first period also Shaikh Shams al-Tabrīzī (*d.* 639/1240), the spiritual preceptor of Maulānā Jalāl al-Dīn al-Rūmī. In his understading this is the period it is characterised by the use of a purely allusive language expressed in metaphors not intelligible to non-initiates.

The second period includes 'Abd al-Qādir al-Jīlānī (471/1079-561/1166) whose works are described as 'extremely subtle' and 'containing deep secrets' in front of whom 'contemporary *ulamā*' and *faqīh* had to acknowledge their impotence'. The *imām* of the Qādiriyya is followed by the Shaikh al-Akbar Muḥy al-Dīn Ibn al-'Arabī (560/1165-638/1240) who 'spared no effort in expounding the mysteries of the *'ilm al-ilāhī* in great detail discussing according to a well constructed pattern the relation that subsists between the absolute Being and the contingent Universe and its creatures'. According to Rāmcandra, the principles set out by Ibn al-'Arabī served most later authorities as base and guideline for the description of their own spiritual experiences and teachings. Last of the renowned Sūfis mentioned for this intermediate period are Maulānā Jalāl al-Dīn al-Rūmī (604/1207-672/1273) and the author of the celebrated *Iḥyā-i 'Ulūm al-Dīn*, Imām Abū Ḥamīd al-Ghazzālī (450/1058-505/1111), whose elucidations in the respective fields of *taṣawwuf* and ethical conduct (*'ilm al-akhlāq*) represent for Rāmcandra an extremely useful assistance in the quest for Truth by members of later initiatory orders (*firqa o panthvāle*).[38]

38. *TP*, p. 26.

The third stage seen as representing a decisive breakthrough towards the elaboration of new ways of transmitting the esoteric knowledge is described thus:

> Finally, the immeasurable treasure of explaining most painstakingly every single detail regarding the science of the subtle centres left behind for posterity by Ḥaḍrat Imām-i Rabbānī Shaikh Aḥmad Sirhindī Mujaddid Alf-i Thānī — the mercy of Allāh be upon him! — cannot possibly be expressed through words. Those who have investigated [the spiritual path] before him have not gone beyond the extent of using subtle metaphors without apparently taking any care in following any kind of logical order; but the deeply hidden mysteries disclosed by him stand yet uncompared never again to be reached by any other learned scholar or expert *faqīr*. The reason for which his blessed name has been decorated with the title of 'renewer of the second millennium [of Islam]' consists solely in the result of his new method of investigation (*taḥqīqat-i jadīd*). The task of investigating and commenting this subtle science which had never been inquired into before has been undertaken by him in a very ample way.[39]

This paragraph shows a reverence and respect for the founder of the Mujaddidiyya which does not fall short of that of any Muslim member of the *ṭarīqa* and suggests its original authorship with our Hindu's Muslim shaikh. It attributes to the 'Divinely inspired leader' a role very similar to that ascribed to some of the later *sant*s and pleads in favour of the idea of a historical process traceable in the great spiritual traditions that develops naturally and independently from each other. However, the most interesting affirmation follows in the immediately subsequent paragraph:

> . . . we can hence conclude that the *paramātmā* has granted the knowledge regarding this science of the

39. *TP*, pp. 26-7. Interestingly, also Shaikh Aḥmad Sirhindī figures among those great saints of the past mentioned by Śiva Dayāl Singh in *Sār Bacan*.

> subtle centres to those great authorities of every spiritual affiliation and distinctive sacred tradition of every culture who have appeared during the last period in the history of mankind (*zamāna-i ākhirī*). . . .[40]

According to this statement, the science of the subtle centres, constitutes the latest step so far in the gradual externalisation of the way the sacred knowledge is revealed to those particularly gifted saints whose role consists of transmitting it to a sufficient number of qualified initiates in order to ensure its survival for posterity. Such a conception reflects the author's traditional perspective which, in line with other contemporary *sant* authorities, sees the course of human history as a process in which the natural capacity of gaining deep spiritual insight among most people decreases at the same rate as the distance between them and the original source of it manifested from time to time in guise of a reviving spirit or founder of a new Divinely revealed message increases.[41]

In this sense, Rāmcandra's position agrees with the fact that the *cakra-vidyā* belongs, within the Hindu environment, to the Tāntrik doctrines of Laya-Yoga and Kuṇḍalinī-Yoga[42]

---

40. *TP*, p. 27.

41. This idea is closely connected with the cyclical conception of time expressed in the Hindu doctrine of the four cosmic eras (*caturyuga*) or the fourteen *manvantara* and the related doctrine of the *avatāra*s or descents of the Divine into the world with the purpose to re-establish the cosmic order or to deliver a message. The second function comes close to the Semitic concept of prophecy according to which man beginning with Ādam is rescued from oblivion of his Divine origin by a series of prophets culminating with the prophet of Islam who delivered the final legislation to the present cycle that will be abolished only by the apocalyptic cataclysm.

42. The main conception of this variety of Yoga consists in the idea that the supreme power or *kuṇḍalini-śakti* lies asleep in a state of latency, like a coiled snake, in the lowest of all subtle centres inside the human body the number of which is either seven, nine or more. Once this current of cosmic consciousness is awakened through the use of a series of techniques, it begins to rise step by step through a narrow channel (*suṣumnā*) connecting each of the subtle centres encountered on its way until reaching the union with its Lord and ultimate master, Śiva Parameśvara.

which developed among the Buddhist *siddhas* and Śaiva *nāths*, the latter tracing their origin to Gorakṣa-Nāth (eleventh century AD) through his non-human master Matsyendra-Nāth, i.e., at a much later stage than the original Vedic tradition and the completion of its metaphysical component in the Upaniṣad. The Nāth doctrines on the other hand constitute one of the authentic sources of earlier *sants* like Kabīr and Nānak and hence represent the core tradition which developed in various forms over the centuries and to which ultimately also Rāmacandra apparently indebted.

Curiously, the last Sūfī leader to whom Rāmcandra attributes the rank of extraordinary authority in the field of the 'science of the subtle centres' does not belong to his own Maẓhariyya sub-lineage, although he was linked to another branch of the Mujaddidiyya: Shāh Walī Allāh Dihlawī (1114/1703-1176/1762), the renowned contemporary of Mīrzā Jān-i Jānān at Delhi, although being praised for the thorough investigation of aspects of this science in some of his numerous works,[43] is nevertheless criticised for using a language and technical vocabulary (*istilāḥat, paribhāṣā*) too abstract and removed from common people's understanding to be useful for infusing new vigour into the propagation of this important doctrine. As Rāmcandra argues, this renders the comprehension of his works extremely difficult if not impossible for exoteric scholars and for those less acquainted with the Islamic sciences. It appears, however, that Shāh Walī Allāh's most important contribution to the reinterpretation of the doctrines of the Imām-i Rabbānī, in particular his revised model of the location and disposition of the subtle organs, played some role in the assimilation of the Hindu initiates into the lineage of Shāh Faḍl Aḥmad Khān and his works were certainly available to them.[44]

---

43. The work most specifically concerned with the science of the subtle centres is the *Tafhīmāt al-Ilāhīya*; its contents are analysed in the article of the American scholar Marcia K. Hermansen bearing the title 'Shāh Walī Allāh of Delhi's arrangement of the Subtle Spiritual Centres (*laṭā'if*)' in *StI* (1982), pp. 137-50.

44. For a general introduction to Shāh Walī Allāh, his works and his thought, see A. Bausani's article 'Note su Shāh Walīullah di Delhi' in →

After this enlightening insight into the two-fold spiritual heritage into which he inserts himself as the last link of a chain of illustrious figures operating the a continuous synthesis of transcendent unity beyond the diversity of different religious experiences, Rāmcandra begins to develop his own exposition of this science and the connected methodology. Purportedly, this is based largely on the instructions received through the 'fortunate occasion of attending the company of my *murshid*' ' and after a period of 'deep going reflections on the hints' they contained regarding the concealed mysteries and subtle points of *taṣawwuf*.[45]

The bulk of these elaborations are contained in two works, entitled *Tattva-Prabodhinī* ('The awakening of the essential elements') and *Kamāl-i insānī* (The human perfection), both originally compiled in Urdu in the late 1920s.[46] Besides these two texts which, as stated by Rāmcandra himself, remain largely focussed on aspects of the esoteric doctrine and methods taught in the Maẓhariyya Na'īmiyya line of the Mujaddidiya, he also composed a small treatise entitled *Vedānta-Sāgara*[47] which sets out some of the order's doctrinal fundamentals said to be based on the Vedāntic legacy of the Upaniṣad. Yet another small but important work is the *Santmat Darśana*[48] which delineates in

→ *AIO* (1961), pp. 93-147, and G. Jalbani, *The teachings of Shāh Walī Allāh* (1986).

45. *TP*, p. 28.

46. Later, these two works were translated into Hindi and published by his son Jag Mohan Narāyaṇ and his grandsons Akhileśa Kumār and Dineś Kumār in order to make them accessible to all those Hindu disciples who were not acquainjted with the Urdu script. The versions used for the present study are: *Tattva-Prabodhanī,* Sri Ramcandra Publication League, Fatehgarh (U.P), 1971 (second Hindi edition) and *Kamāl-i insānī,* Adhyatmik Dhara Prakashan, Fatehgarh/ Farrukhabad, 1973 (second Hindi edition).

47. *Vedānta-Sāgara*, Akhilesh Kumar Publications, Fatehgarh, 1964. This work has been translated into Hindī by a certain Thakur Karan Singh, a disciple of Rāmcandra, and its introduction has been written by his grandson, Akhileśa Kumār Saksenā.

48. *Santmat Darśana*, Naqush Mum Ramchandra Mission, Fatehgarh, 1986. This work has been translated from Urdu into English (*sic*!) for the numerous disciples from areas other than the north-Indian Hindī belt, by Dr. Har Nārāyaṇ Sakenā, Fatehgarh, 1974 (third edition).

perhaps the most original way the ideas of Rāmcandra as an authoritative exponent of a twentieth-century *sant* doctrine. In addition to these, some notions regarding his thought and method of teaching can be obtained, here and there, in the posthumously assembled letter collection entitled *Śrī Rām Sandeśa* ('The message of Lord Rām'),[49] containing excerpts from about fifty selected letters addressed either to his shaikh or to his disciples during the period from 1922 to his death in 1931.[50]

An attentive look at Rāmcandra's written legacy suggests that it belongs to the final period of his life, i.e., long after his shaikh's death in 1907 when, after a prolonged period of inner growth, absorption and elaboration of the instructions received,[51] he finally felt ready to deliver his own guidelines for the spiritual discipline and to fix it in written records. Worried about the future of the *paramparā* in view of his approaching death, it was during those last years of his life that most of these works acquired their definitive shape, at a time when Rāmacandra felt the urgent need to provide his growing spiritual community with a coherent doctrinal corpus containing the essential tenets of his message.

The descriptions of Rāmcandra's biographers and hagiographers[52] regarding the oral teachings imparted in the

---

49. *Śrī Rām Sandeśa*, a collection of letters ascribed to Rāmcandra and edited by Akhileś Kumār Saksenā, Adhyatmika Dhara Prakashan, Fatehgarh, 1974 (third edition).

50. There are, moreover, a few minor compilations attributed to this author, such as the *Bālkāṇḍa ke muta'alliq rūḥānī tashrīḥ*, a spiritual interpretation of the first part of the *Rāmāyaṇa* written in evident imitation of Tulsī Ṣāḥib Hāthrasī's *Ghaṭ Rāmāyaṇa*.

51. As mentioned earlier, it was not until 1914 that Rāmcandra, instigated by Shāh 'Abd al-Ghanī Khān to whom he still looked as ultimate authority, began reluctantly to organise his *satsang* at his residence at Fategarh. In 1923, the first annual *bhanḍārā* was held there during the Easter week, an indication that by that time the *satsang* had acquired some consistency, both in terms of number of adherents and organisation.

52. See, for instance, *Brij Mohan Lāl Saksenā: Jīvan-Caritra*, Sant Prakashan, Kanpur, 1993 (second edition).

course of his daily *satsang* reflect the image of an authoritative spiritual leader from a much earlier period. These show him to be well acquainted with the stories and teachings of the mediaeval saints as well as with the details regarding the Mujaddidī *ṭarīqa*. Although they lack the sort of systematic exposition useful for the uninitiated reader, these writings provide an indirect indication of the extent to which oral teachings still preserve their primary importance in the transmission of the sacred sciences. In fact, Rāmcandra and his descendants repeatedly condemn the alleged sterility of bookish knowledge and erudition, no matter how elevated their content, in the absence of the oral instructions imparted by a living master which infuse them with life.[53]

This attitude reiterates the essential difference already described by Mīrzā Jān-i Jānān, between the *'ilm-i ḥuṣūlī* and the *'ilm-i ḥuḍūrī*.[54] It also accounts for the fact that none of the mediaeval ancestors of our Kāyasth *sants*, who were themselves often illiterate, ever bothered to provide a definitive frame of their teachings the shape of books and written records, in the manner more typical of their Sūfī counterparts. Such a tendency begins to prevail only among much later Hindu masters and indicates an increasing anxiousness to preserve their message in an epoch of growing dispersion and increasing centrifugal tendencies.[55] Rāmcandra's writings can, therefore, rightly be

53. This genuinely traditional attitude provided the main difficulty during my research of written material since I was repeatedly reminded of the uselessness from the master's point of view of such written records for any real comprehension of the spiritual discipline, an attitude that occasionally resulted in open refusal to allow me access to these works, which usually circulate only among a limited number of initiates.

54. Cf. Khaliq Anjum (1989), letter no. 4, pp. 105-7.

55. As member of the Kāyasth community, Rāmcandra as well as his contemporary Maharṣi Śivbrat Lāl were naturally inclined towards writing records as part of their traditional occupation since time immemorial. A striking example of this attitude is furnished by the various Rādhāsoāmī masters, almost all of whom have compiled huge amounts of works, in particular Maharṣi Śivbrat Lāl who has written hundreds of books and pamphlets explaining in every detail his and his masters' teachings. →

considered as his spiritual testament, meant to be circulated among his intimate disciples after his death in absence of a living source of instruction, and as such they can be regarded as the gist of his spiritual career.

Rāmcandra's teachings, can be roughly divided along two principal lines, thus following the classical pattern prevalent in the past. One covers the doctrinal background consisting of metaphysical and cosmological concepts which develop mainly along Hindu lines of thought, while the other is concerned with technical and methodological questions clearly recognisable as being derived from the heritage of the Mujaddidī tradition. Although these two aspects are occasionally intermingled with one another, they constitute an interesting example of an attempt to apply the methodology provided by a particular tradition to a doctrinal background belonging to another tradition, an experiment which, if successful, would justify the claims of universality advanced by this modern *sant*.

In the following sections, Rāmcandra's works are, therefore, examined first for their doctrinal content and background. Thereafter, an effort is made to integrate this with the methodological aspect of his *sampradāya* in order to gain a comprehensive picture of this modern *sant*'s teachings.

The perception of metaphysical reality

The Hindu Rāmcandra turns to the sacred texts of his native tradition to set out a series of fundamental metaphysical and cosmological issues. His approach towards these fundamental doctrinal aspects largely follows the teachings of the *nirguṇa sant*s who do not regard the Supreme Divinity as qualified by any personal attribute, although many of the concepts treated in his works betray his acquaintance with the classical texts of the Hindu tradition, mainly the Upaniṣad and the *Bhagavad Gītā*.

The *sant* doctrines are to a large extent a continuation and further adaptation of the ancient concepts expounded in the

→ See Khaliq Anjum (1989), letter no. 4, pp. 105-7.

Upaniṣad and the *Vedānta-Sūtra* through the Tāntrik perspective of the Nāths.[56] Rāmcandra appears to confirm this continuity, for he starts his discussion in the *Vedānta-Sāgara* comment on the fundamental tenets held by the Vedānta, and hinting at the slightly diverging interpretations propounded by the founders of the different branches of the Advaita School, such as Srī Śaṅkarācārya's (AD 788-820) kevalādvaita, Śrī Rāmānujācārya's (AD 1017-1137?) viśiṣṭādvaita, Madhvācārya's (AD 1197-1276) dvaitādvaita[57] and Śrī Vallabhācārya's (AD 1479-1535) śuddhādvaita.

It is the underlying concept of non-duality (*advaita*) as a negative description of the inexpressable all-transcendent metaphysical reality summarised in the Upaniṣadic formula *neti-neti* that constitutes for Rāmcandra the thread of continuity between the doctrines that constitute the *jñāna-kāṇḍa* of the śruti and its later re-elaborations in the Tāntrik environment on one side and the affirmation of absolute Divine unity (*tawḥīd*) as conceived by the Sūfis on the other. Elaborating on this concept of an all-transcending principle, alternatively referred to in the impersonal perspective of the *nirguṇa-sant*s as *paramātmā* in the Sūfī perspective as *Allāh Ta'ālā* and the impossibility of describing it in positive terms without falling into the dilemma of simultaneously contradicting or limiting its underlying reality (*tawhīd kī dalīl khud radd-i tawḥīd hai*),[58] Rāmcandra concludes that to comprehend the highest level of Truth one must presuppose Its reflection in every human being as a practically acknowledgeable experience (*anubhava jñāna*) rather than a purely speculative nation. These two entities, viz., the subject that affirm Truth and Truth by itself, appear initially separated by the veil of imaginative thought (*wahm*), a

56. For the Nāth influence on Kabīr and the Kabīr-panth, see R.K. Varma, *Kabīr: Biography and Philosophy* (1977), pp. 43-6 and the article of G.G. Filippi, 'Des composants culturels dans le Granthāvalī de Kabīr' in *Indologica Taurinensia* VI (1978), pp. 137-41.

57. According to the author, it is from this particular school that the elaborations of Dayānanda Sarasvatī, the founder and organiser of the Ārya-Samāj, are derived.

58. *VS*, p. 12.

characteristic faculty of the human mind subject to the mental fancy of *māyā*, thus, providing an answer as to how the apparent duality between the subject that affirms unity and Unity in Itself came into being. In line with Kabīr who perceives the Supreme Reality as essentially impersonal and non-qualified by any contingent attribute (*nirguṇa Brahman*), Rāmcandra maintains that the Principle assumes Its imaginary qualification only when the human perception is covered by the veils of *māyā*, a condition that sanctions man's peripheral position in the manifested world. According to the author of the *Vedānta Sagara*, this condition accounts for the initial bewilderment (*udheḍ-bun*) that befalls the mind on which this veil has fallen and which 'revolves around the apparent existence of the universe (*jagat*) to his glance'.[59]

These follows a discussion that asserts the ultimate futility of all speculative discourses aimed at describing the metaphysical Reality. In the typical mode of Kabīr and other *sants*, Rāmcandra and his followers repeatedly emphasise what they see as the deceitful vanity (*mithyā*) of such speculations. Stress is consequently laid primarily on the practical aspect of the spiritual discipline (*sādhanā*) imparted as a preliminary step towards gaining access to this Truth through an inner direct experience of the transcendent sphere which will eventually dissolve the apparent discrepancy between the viewpoint of the Vedānta and personal experience.

Like Kabīr, Rāmcandra, therefore, does not conceive an ultimately subsisting difference between the purely intellectual approach of the *vedāntin*, which envisages direct knowledge of the infinite nature of the Supreme (*jñāna-mārga*) through the thorough comprehension of the doctrine of non-duality, and the position held by the Tantra-Yoga which perceives the Supreme through a more indirect vision that takes account of the contingent position of the individual through the projection of the attributive modalities of the Supreme into the realm of contingency.

---

59. *VS*, p.12.

Yet another interesting hint at the link between the ancient metaphysical doctrines through those of Kabīr and his followers is provided by the author's mention of the concept of *śūnya*. Rejecting the negative interpretation current among many Buddhist schools who interpret this term as a mere 'void', Rāmcandra asserts that it is intended among *sant*s as *sun* or *mahāsun*,[60] i.e., the final goal beyond the realm of duality in the abode of *Nirañjana* or *Narharī*. Therefore, its implications again lie beyond any possible verbal description due to its essentially transcendent nature. Most interestingly, the author also disagrees with the Mujaddidī concept of 'non-existence' (*'adam*), an essential tenet in Shaikh Aḥmad Sirhindī's *shuhūdī* doctrine, as a possible equivalent of the term *śūnya*, since if it is intended as an ultimate degree of achievement, it still implicates the correlative state of existence (*hastī*, *wujūd*) whereas Kabīr's sun ultimately transcends any such residual trace of duality.

Rāmcandra's extremely synthetic account here touches on the doctrines of Śrī Rāmānujācārya and Śrī Śaṅkarācārya who both acknowledge the unicity of the metaphysical Principle differing only nominally between each other due to an ultimately unreal spirit of opposition which does not subsist on the highest plane pertaining to the Supreme Identity.[61]

Major attention is given by Rāmcandra to Śrī Rāmānuja's viśiṣṭādvaita and to the doctrinal perspective of the later

---

60. For *śūnya* in Buddhist Mādhyamika and Yogācāra schools, see M. Gopinatha Kaviraj's article, 'Śūnyavāda aur Vijñānavāda' in *Kavirāj-Pratibhā* (collection of selected articles) (1984), pp. 204-14.

    The term had already changed its negative connotation among the *siddha*s who followed the Vajrayāna current of Buddhism, from where it was presumably adopted in a gradually more positive assumption by the Nāths and later on by Kabīr for whom the term, often used in association with the term *sahaja*, indicates the realisation of Supreme Identity. Cf. *Kabīr Granthāvalī, pāda 154* and *164* and *sākhī 5.*

    The terms *sun* and *mahāsun* have acquired major importance also in the Rādhāsoāmī doctrines expounded in Śiva Dayāl Singh's *Sār Bacan* where they designate, however, a lower position in the universal realms in correspondance to a state still subject to the law of birth and death. See M.G. Gupta (1994), pp. 154-6.

61 *VS*, p. 13.

chāyāvāda, both of which are more consonant with his own Vaiṣṇava background and certainly more compatible with the *shuhūdī* perspective held by the Mujaddidīs. These elements were certainly essential for the formation of his own position, which leads him finally to Rāmānanda (*c.* 1400-70?).[62] This renowned Vaiṣṇava saint who spent most of his life at Benares is traditionally considered to have been affiliated to Rāmānuja's *Śrī-sampradāya* and is credited with having spread the *upāsanā-mārga* from his native southern India to the north.[63] Often regarded as the wordly *guru* of Kabīr, he certainly played an important role in divulging the Rāma-*bhakti* among the humbler strata of the city's Hindu society, as the list of his main disciples given by Nabhadās' *Bhaktamālā* suggests.[64] Rāmcandra, himself an affiliate of the Kabīr-panth, maintained the heritage of the *Rām-nām* as Kabīr's favourite method of personal devotion. However, he does not hesitate to assert the ultimate superiority of Kabīr over the followers of the *Śrī-sampradāya*. Quoting some of the verses attributed to Kabīr, chosen from the *Kabīr-Vāṇī* and the *Anurāg-Sāgar*, he supports this alleged superiority by pointing out Kabīr's repeated hint at the most sublime level on which Rāma is ultimately conceivable. This transcends all qualified conditions of the universal existence (*triguṇa se niyārā*) beyond the secrets known to the gods in the *deva-loka*[65] and constitutes the perennial metaphysical principle (*nij sār hai*) that governs everything. The allusion to the fourth degree of Rām beyond the three levels

---

62. For Kabīr, see G. Grierson, 'Rāmānandis, Rāmāwāts in Encyclopaedia of Religion', *Ethics* X, pp. 569-71. For an extensive discussion on his biographical dates, see David N. Lorensen, *Kabir Legends and Ananta-Das's Kabir Parachai* (1991), pp. 9-13.

63. See, R.G. Bhandarkar, *Vaiṣṇavism, Śaivism and Minor Religious Systems* (1965) and H.P. Dvivedi, *Kabīr: A study of Kabīr, Followed by a Selection from his Poems* (1953).

64. Nābhajī, *Bhaktamālā* (1965).

65. The hint at the fourth plane refers to the *āloka* or the sphere nowhere situated in space which lies beyond the triple division of the cosmos common in Islamic esoterism and hinted at by the Hindu *Gāyatrī-mantra* as *oṁ bhur bhuvaḥ svaḥ*.

of cosmic existence points to the *nirguṇa Brahman* contemplated by the Vedānta[66]

> *tīna lok ko sab koī dhāve, cauthe dev kā marm na pāe* ।
> *cauthā choḍ pañcam cit lāe, kahen kabīr hamre dhing āe* ।।
>
> Three realms are invoked by everyone, the fourth lies beyond the mysteries of the gods,
>
> leaving the fourth while penetrating the fifth, this is the method of Kabīr.[67]

The firm conviction of possessing the keys to a doctrinal vision widely diffused in the *sant* tradition from Kabīr to the Rādhāsoāmīs, regarded as superior to that held by the classical and post-classical schools that preceded them, leads Rāmcandra to assert that the followers of Rāmānuja's viśiṣṭādvaita remained entangled in the comprehension of the first three levels, the stages corresponding to the qualified aspect of the Supreme (*saguṇa Brahman*) and its hypostasis as Lord of the manifested universe (Prajāpati or Īśvara). In reference to the *dohā* quoted that mentions a fifth level of intending Rāma as peculiar to the method of Kabīr, Rāmcandra declares that this fifth plane (*pāda*) corresponds to the *satnāma*, that is to say the highest aspect of Truth contained in seminal form in the Sacred Name identified with the *akṣara*, the unpronounc-eable syllable containing the ultimate synthesis of all sounds.[68] Nevertheless, even the very perception of the Name envisaged by both *Kabīr-panthīs* and *Nānak-panthīs* as *oṁkāra*, is

66. Cf. *Maitrī Upaniṣad* VII.11; *Bṛhadāraṇyaka Upaniṣad* V.14.3.

67. *VS*, p. 15.

68. Rāmcandra describes the *satnām* as 'the real name of the true master', aimed at the ascent to the *iṣṭapāda* which can be perceived only through the *guru*. This name constitutes a sign of the Divine power which resounds in the innermost part of every human being. Its perception through the audible subtle sound-current is said to open the gates for a real spiritual ascent. Cf.*VS*, p. 16. For identification of the *Brahman* with the *akṣara*. Cf. *Bṛhadāraṇyaka Upaniṣad*, III.8.8.

regarded as representing a subtle veil between the contingent and the original uncontaminated Essence.

But the most surprising feature of Rāmcandra's exposition is that in his opinion the Supreme Unity eventually transcends even the last possibly perceivable duality between the unqualified (*nirguṇa*) as in a sense still complementary to the qualified (*saguṇa*) along with the four planes mentioned in precedence. These planes are then assimilated to the five *pāda*s described by the Upaniṣad in connection with the 'knowledge of the quintuple fire' (*pañcāgni-vidyā*), a science regarding the course of the human soul after death traditionally reserved to members of the kṣatriya caste.[69]

Among other things, this science describes the gradual descent of the *paramātmā* into the sphere of contingent existence represented by the quintuple oblation to the fire. In the specific context, this descent constitutes the inverse process to that of the ascending path of spiritual realisation that has to be undertaken by the individual in order to achieve liberation (*mukti*), the most sublime human goal (*paramārtha*).[70]

The author's assumption leads to numerous further assimilations and underlines impressively the intellectual acuteness at the base of the spiritual tradition represented by the *gṛhasthī faqīr*s of this *paramparā*. It proves, moreover, that the aim of the many hints provided in the opening pages of the *Vedānta-Sāgara*, none of which is discussed in explicit detail, is

---

69. Cf. *Chāndogya Upaniṣad*, V.4-9.

70. In a later description by Rāmcandra's grandson, Bṛj Mohan Lāl, the discussion returns once more to the *pañcāgni-vidyā* connecting the heart as the seat of knowledge (*jñāna*) and experience (*anubhava*) of the quintuple light of the *ātmā* attaining to which one realises the Supreme Identity between *ātmā* and *paramātmā*. This final goal is also identified with the pure Essence (*dhāt-i muṭlaq*) described by the Mujaddidīs whereas the quintuple light and its corresponding name (Rāma) is associated with the quintuple planes of irradiation (*tajalliyāt*) introduced by the Ibn al-ʿ Arabī mentioned also by the authorities of the Mujaddidiyya. Cf. *AY*, pp. 162-3. Cf. also Rūmī's description of the different stages in the process of creation culminating in the human condition permeated by the Essence of the Divine.

to point towards the inherent unity that lies beyond the different language and forms of expression employed by various schools and traditions in the course of history. In this sense, any superiority or inferiority of these, rather than being implicit in their respective doctrinal perspectives, remains ultimately confined to the varying individual capacity of their followers to penetrate the hidden meanings they contain.

It also provides a basis for understanding how, once Rāmcandra leaves the metaphysical domain for a more contingent vision of the world, Sūfī, *yogī*, *Kabīr-panthī* and other notions are used alternatively in order to weave, in imitation of the renowned *julāhā* from Benares, the subtle tissue affecting a real spiritual synthesis between these different threads.

The coming into being of the universe

The cosmological doctrine begins for Rāmcandra exactly where the realm of metaphysics intersects with that of contingent existence or, in his own words, where 'the veil of fanciful imagination prevents the direct perception of the transcendent Principle'. On the authority of the Upaniṣad but immediately recalling to memory a famous saying of the prophet of Islam (*ḥadīth*), he affirms that first there was only Truth which remained hidden to Itself.[71]

At once, the veil of concealment (*parda-yi ikhtifā*) was cut open by the impulse of the hitherto hidden Truth manifesting itself in the guise of the *ādi-puruṣa*. This was the origin of Cosmic Man.[72] Both traditions are invoked to show how the treasure-

71. This description clearly refers to the state of non-manifestation (*avyakta*) which, in this sense, possesses a certain degree of superiority over that of manifestation. Interestingly, the author though claiming to describe his doctrine based on notions in the Upaniṣad, uses a language that appears much closer to the Islamic context, an idea enhanced by the use of a Sūfī terminology instead of its Sanskrit correspondent used in the Upaniṣad. It hints at his primary acquaintance with the latter doctrines, only at a later stage integrated by a study of the former ones, and his own educational background more familiar with the Urdu-Persian vocabulary.

72. *VS*, p. 18. This rather enigmatic statement becomes clear if we accept the idea that the concept of *puruṣa* in this particular context translates →

house of Supreme Truth is borne in his inmost being by mankind, earlier defined according to a purely Islamic perspective as a perfecting 'particularisation and individualisation' (*juzwiyat wa shakhṣiyat*) of the Divine Omnipotence (*al-qudrat*) Whose essential Reality lies beyond the limiting condition (*ḥaddiyat*) of the human qualities. But since the existentialisation of the Supreme Being took place as the result of Its primordial impulse to display Itself in the world, the *puruṣa* must from that initial moment onwards be envisaged in its cosmic projection inside the derived multiple degrees of existence, where it remains present in the guise of the individual human aggregate. It thereby assumes a specific form (*rūpa*) that characterises its existence in the dominion of the sensible world as a substantial determination of its new state. For the same reason it also bears a name (*nāma*) recalling its original state prior to manifestation,[73] i.e., *satpuruṣa* or, alternatively, *insān al-kāmil*. Both are assimilated to the very principle of manifestation conceived as the externalisation of the Divine power which is the ultimate source of the Universe and therefore assimilated to the 'Spirit of Muḥammad' (*rūḥ al-muḥammadī*) of classical Sūfī doctrines.[74]

Such a description suggests the parallel Rāmcandra draws between the Hindu doctrines taught by the Vedānta and the Kabīr-Panth on one side and the esoteric interpretation of the Islamic concept of creation on the other. *Sat-puruṣa* or 'True Man' and *insān al-kāmil* or 'Perfect Man' represented by the 'spirit of Muḥammad' are considered as synonyms in their role

---

→ to a fair extent the Sūfī concept of *rūḥ al-muḥammadī* as the primordial determination of the Necessary Being and creative principle of universal manifestation.

73. *Rūpa* along with *nāma* constitute the two co-ordinates describing the principal determinations of the individual condition, one corresponding roughly to the substantial determination and the other to its more essential one. *Nāma*, however, implies in its superior sense also the eternal archetype or 'idea' in the Platonic sense, inherent in every manifested creature, that constitutes the immediate principle of the other.

74. *VS*, p. 18.

of sovereigns or principles of the entire universal display; according to this perspective, they can be also associated with the Hindu concept of Īśvara, the personified principle of universal existence, or Prajāpati, the Lord of all creatures, and Allāh in his aspects of *al-Bārī* or *al-Khāliq* (the Creator), which from a more esoterical point of view can be identified with the 'Muḥammadan spirit'.

We must be careful to avoid confusion between the double application to which these terms are liable, either from the metaphysical point of view as designating the highest stage of Ultimate Reality (the terminology of the Vedānta employs the term *puruṣottama*), or in relation to relative unity if intended as the cosmic principle and the multiplicity it contains. They are nevertheless analogous since both designate in their respective traditions the first step from 'Pure Unity' or 'non-duality' (*aḥadiyat*, *advaita*) to its hypostasis, from pure Essence to the first Being characterised by the attribute of existence of a personal God (*saguṇa Brahman*, Īśvara or Allāh in its theological interpretation).[75]

According to Rāmcandra, this personal God is the Creator of everything, due to Whom the entire creation (*khilqat*) has come into existence and on Whom everything depends, because He is the Ruler of the Universe and the axis (*madār*) around which the entire cosmos develops. Rāmcandra's technical vocabulary here assumes a distinctively Islamic connotation in which we recognise the descriptions of the Naqshbandī shaikhs of Delhi: the all-powerful God to which all creatures should bow in sign of reverence and recognition of their dependence, and the concept of the Lord seated on the 'all-encompassing Throne' (*al-'arsh, al-muḥīṭ*)[76] at the centre of the Universe whence the Divine spirit descends into the realm of existence in order to

75. The validity of this double perspective is enhanced by Rāmcandra's later observations that if on one hand He is the producer of creation, on the other He is also not that, for the meaning of *sat* apart from meaning 'truth' comprises also the second meaning of 'essence', embracing both 'being' and 'not-being'.

76. *VS*, p. 18.

confer His command on the primordial indifferentiation.[77] Even more interesting is the occasional combination of Mujaddidī and *Kabīr-panthī* elements, as in the following passage:

> All around the *satpuruṣa* . . . , a subtle substance circulates [inside the universe] assuming manifold aspects. Like the light of the sun that irradiates everything around its source, this rapidly flowing substance expands in every direction around the Divinity which, like the top of the thunderbolt (*hīra*), remains motionless and unperturbed at Its place at the centre. The rapidly flowing substance expanding from the *satpuruṣa* is referred to as *ādimāyā*, the primordial substance. It continues to revolve around its centre at every time. When the reflection of the *satpuruṣa* falling into this whirlpool mingles itself with this substance, It thus manifests Itself in the form of a particular kind of individuality whose nature is similar to that of our shadows (*sāyā*). . . .[78]

The concept of reflection (*'aks*) and shadow (*sāyā*, *chāyā*) described in this passage as emanating from the primordial source of existence is reminiscent of Shaikh Aḥmad Sirhindī's *waḥdat al-shuhūd* which maintains a rhetorical difference in the degree of reality inherent to the different realms of contingency and the principle from which they derive. Each derives its existence from the reflection of the immediately preceding stage, thus, gradually descending into a lower degree of reality. This idea is assimilated to the *sant* concepts of *māyā* and *ādi-māyā* which, especially in the cosmological doctrines of the Kabīr-panth, bears a fundamental importance in explaining the interaction between essence and substance that gave rise

77. Rāmcandra defines the principle as *nirālamba*, 'absolutely independent', and *nirādhāra*, 'self-supporting', two designations which although of Sanskrit origin apply very well to describe the Divine attributes in Islamic theology. They appear deliberately chosen to bring the two doctrines closer in the understanding of his Hindu followers.

78. *VS*, p. 19.

to the universal manifest-ation.[79] From the intercourse between these two entities are produced the various degrees of individual existence (*shakhṣiyat*) in form of a series of shadows, hence, defined by Rāmcandra as 'congenital' (*ham-zād*).[80]

When this congenital shadow came into existence it turned its attention towards the *satpuruṣa* whence it derived its peculiar existence. Recognising his supremacy, it began to affirm its own, separate existence, expressed through the formula 'I am!' It signals the rise of the principle of individual consciousness (*ahaṁkāra*, *gharūr kā mādda*) regarded as the primordial element (*tattva*) of universal manifestation and identified by Rāmcandra in conformity with the *Kabīr-panthī* doctrines with *kāla* or *kāla-puruṣa*.[81]

This principle of individualisation is hence the final product of the primordial substance and signals the entrance into the temporal and spatial dimension of contingency through the non-acting presence and non-involved influence of the *satpuruṣa*, associated by Rāmcandra with the Islamic concept of the Omnipotent (*al-'Azīz*).

Therefore the *kāla-puruṣa* represents from a macrocosmic point of view the temporal principle that governs all contingent beings subject to the conditions of time, of birth, and of death, analogous to the role of Yama, the Hindu god of death. It also shows some parallels with the distinction made in the *Koran* between the primordial order issued by Allāh (*al-amr*) and the successive process of existentialisation in the *'ālam-i khalq* spanning over a period of six days, which embraces the entire creation. This dominion ultimately is subject to the all-devouring *kāla-puruṣa*, the lord of birth and death.

In many respects Rāmcandra's vision recalls the elaborate

---

79. Cf. F.E. Keay, *Kabir and his Followers* (1995, reprint of first edition 1931), pp. 135-49.

80. In the Islamic tradition, the term *ham-zād* defines the *jinn* of the clan which appears when a child is born and which accompanies it throughout the life. Cf. John T. Platts, *A Dictionary of Urdū Classical Hindī and English*, 1977 (first Indian edition), p. 1234.

81. *VS*, p. 20.

cosmology of the later *Kabīr-panthīs* and of the Rādhāsoāmīs which combines features of Vedānta and Sāṅkhya-Yoga with additional elements of different origin. His entire doctrinal edifice rests upon the introduction of an intermediate degree between the transcendent *paramātmā* or *para-brahma* as envisaged by the Vedānta, Its hypostasis and principle of manifestation (*īśvara*, *apara-brahma*), the attainment of and union with which is envisaged by the different schools of Yoga, and the primordial duality of *puruṣa* and *prakṛti* which ultimately determine the process of universal manifestation into multiplicity. At the same time it asserts its supremacy over other doctrines by claiming to go one step further towards the attainment of ultimate Truth.

This intermediate degree consists of the concept of *kāla-puruṣa* that traces its origin from the apparent duality arising the *ādi-māyā* and the reflection of the *satpuruṣa* on it. But duality is only apparent if contemplated from a contingent perspective, because this primordial substance is ultimately nothing but an irradiation of the *satpuruṣa* itself and essentially partakes of Its nature.[82] As such, the *kāla-puruṣa* is nothing but the projection of the *satpuruṣa* into a lower degree of reality. Only if perceived as the separate cause of the *ādi-māyā* does it appear complementary to the rise of the *kāla-puruṣa*, as an effect of the first veil constituted by the *ādi-māyā*. Such a formulation appears to be the outcome of an attempt to reconcile two different points of view, held in the Islamic context by the *waḥdat al-wujūd* and *waḥdat al-shuhūd* respectively, which juxtapose the concept of reflection and of irradiation as two different connotations of the same reality.

Rāmcandra stresses that from a microcosmic perspective the dual aspect inherent man's nature is uniquely a manifestation (*iẓhār*) of the imaginary consciousness (here termed as *tawajjuh*) of possessing an individual existence that confers a sense of separation from that of the principle, caused by that very shadow that has attained life through the deceitful intervention of the *kāla-puruṣa*. But, in reality, there was

---

82. Cf. *Bhagavad Gītā*, XV.16-18.

nothing in the beginning to declare either the existence (*hastī*) or non-existence (*nīstī*) of the Divine Being because these are two correlative terms (*nisbatī kalām*), whereas Truth must necessarily lie beyond relativity. To affirm such relativity even if intended as the highest of all complementaries, is possible only from the point of view of manifestation, that is to say from a degree of contingent existence.

Rāmcandra draws once more from the Upaniṣad to clarify his point: at the beginning there was only the Supreme darkness of non-manifestation in coincidence with the primordial chaos in which everything remained concealed. Nevertheless, this darkness it contained a marvellous brilliance irradiating a stream of pure light whose nature cannot be perceived by ordinary mortals.[83] For convenience, Rāmcandra calls it 'primordial impulse' (*chave mauj*, *mauj-i aṣlī*), whence both the *satpuruṣa* and *kāla-puruṣa* polarise themselves. While the former acquires luminosity and maintains his residence in the most sublime region, the latter, owing to the light irradiated from the former, assumes a separate identity as a shadow in the lower regions of contingency.

It follows that while both ultimately owe their origin to the *paramātmā*, the distinctive existence of the *kāla-puruṣa* depends on the *satpuruṣa* whose luminous projection on a lower plane of reflection casts a shadow onto the Divine fabric of the universe. This ray of projection is called by Rāmcandra *mahā-tawajjuh*. It is closely analogous to the *rūḥ al-muḥammadī* produced as a result of the Divine command described by the *Koran*, which finds its equivalent in classical Hindu doctrines in the projection of *buddhi*, the cosmic intelligence and first differentiation of *prakṛti* contemplated by the Sāṅkhya doctrine. Interestingly, Rāmcandra's account of this luminous projection and its

83. *Śvetāśvatara Upaniṣad*, VI.14, *Kaṭha Upaniṣad*, II.5.15. Cf. also *Bhagavad Gītā* XV:4-6. Rāmcandra remarks that this light must be intended not in a literal but in an allegorical sense since the state of the Supreme Principle cannot be possibly described as darkness or brilliance as such a distinction would imply a relapse into an underlying duality. Later, this process is compared to the light of a candle and the smoke produced by it.

reflection, which show a certain compatibility with the *shuhūdī* doctrine, is accompanied by a consideration of the primordial impulse co-present in this original luminosity which simultaneously expands between these two realms, thus, assuming a reflected existence or 'transmitted vibration' (*naqlī ḥarkat*).

These two subtle manifestations of light and sound consequently assume a primary significance in the spiritual discipline of Rāmcandra since they respectively correspond to the most elevated among the interior sensual faculties, light being associated to the sense of vision (*cakṣus*) and its corresponding organ, the eye, and sound to the sense of hearing (*śrotra*) among the five sensual faculties (*jñānendriya*) and to the faculty of speech (*vāc*) among the five faculties of action (*karmendriya*).[84]

Rāmcandra's description of the gradual process of manifestation follows closely the account provided by the Sāṅkhya *darśana:* at the due moment, the *kāla-puruṣa* divides itself into two parts: *puruṣa*, the essential or spiritual (*rūḥānī*) component and *prakṛti*, the substantial (*maddānī*) component, through which the process of cosmic generation is gradually enacted.[85] But since the degree of existence of these two entities is only that of 'mere shadows' (*sāya-i maḥẓ*) of the *kāla-puruṣa*, they lack of their own power of action, so that the initial push (*tawajjuh*) that leads from a state of pure potentiality to its effective enactment must directly derive from the *satpuruṣa*. Thereafter, *prakṛti* begins to originate out of herself the entire series of elements (*tattva*) that constitute the Universe.

The mention of the *satpuruṣa*'s influence on *prakṛti* underlines Rāmcandra's position concerning the cosmological

---

84. Cf. *Mānavadharmaśāstra*, II.89-92. For an explanation of their role in the *sādhanā*, see Bṛj Mohan Lāl Saksenā in *AY*, pp. 91-3.

85. *VS*, p. 22. Rāmcandra compares this to the two split halves of a pea that out of themselves give gradual rise to a new generation of plants. Similarly, *prakṛti* is described as *mūla* or root of all manifestation in the *Sāṅkhya-Kārikā*, while Rāmcandra defines it as *jar*, a term bearing the same meaning of root.

process, for he never loses sight of the transcendent Principle inherent in the *puruṣa* as compared to its derivatives. While the Sāṅkhya describes the initial intervention on *prakṛti* as coming from the *puruṣa* conceived as correlative of *prakṛti* and, therefore not transcending the plane of duality between these two entities, Rāmcandra emphasises the fact that ultimately there subsists no other principle than the absolute and supreme *satpuruṣa*.[86] Hence, a co-relationship of *puruṣa* and *prakṛti* is impossible unless perceived from an inferior degree pertaining to the plane of relativity.

It follows that all the different levels included under the common denomination of *puruṣa* hitherto described as separate entities (i.e., *satpuruṣa*, *kāla-puruṣa* and *puruṣa*) complementary to *prakṛti* ultimately exist only as fanciful products of the power of imagination inherent in the mind of the individual. The human mind perceives the world from its limited and contingent point of view subject to the power of *māyā*, the creative aspect of the Divine intellect, as mere reflections of the one beyond description (*alakh*) Reality, which are solely meant to explain the way leading to the original source. Only in this sense can *puruṣa* be described as analogous to the *insān al-kāmil* and, hence, be assimilated to the *ḥaqīqat-i muḥammadiya*.[87]

Considering now only *prakṛti*, also referred to as *pradhāna*,[88] Rāmcandra explains that the process of its self-diversification

---

86 On the other hand, the Sāṅkhya whose purpose does not lie beyond that of enumerating the single steps of the cosmological process, nevertheless hints at the essentially transcendent nature of *puruṣa* affirming that He is not directly involved in the process of manifestation, His only contribution to it consisting in His non-active disinvolved intervention on *prakṛti*.

87. *TP*, p. 33.

88. Literally 'pre-eminence', 'principal thing', *pradhāna* also bears the meaning of 'attendant of a king', which precisely renders the double position held by *prakṛti* as pre-eminent in relation to distinctive manifestation on one side and its subordinate rank in front of the Sovereign (*al-Mālik*) on the other, viz., *puruṣa*. It is hence conceived as feminine in relation to the latter and masculine in relation to the former.

which gives rise to the separate existence of multiple elements is analogous if on an inferior to the generation of the *kāla-puruṣa* by the *satpuruṣa* as a part (*anshā*) of his own. This affirmation hints at their ultimate identity with the Principle.[89] Thus, *prakṛti*, the primordial and undifferentiated substance assumes the quality of *vṛkṛti*, i.e., nature in its differentiated condition, similar to the difference described in Islamic doctrines between *fiṭrat* and *tabī'at*. It contains in a state of absolute harmony and equilibrium the qualities (*auṣāf*, *guṇa*) of all elements which are contained as latent possibilities in the cosmos. But once this inner balance is shaken by the intervention of *puruṣa*, it is brought into motion and the process of manifestation takes its unstoppable course.

Rāmcandra specifies that this initial movement occurs in form of a concentric expansion from a central point analogous to the expansion of the sound vibration in the ether (*ākāśa*). In this initial movement he detects the reason why all things contained in the universal workmanship (*racanā*)[90] including the sun, the moon, the stars and even the *satpuruṣa* are perceived as circles or spheres (*dā'ira*), being the sphere the projection into space of the aspacious point. This image closely reminds us of the seven spheres symbolically used by the Mujaddidī authorities as images of the planes of existence and degrees of spiritual realisation and illustrates the universal value of symbolism in different traditions.

Through the intercourse with *puruṣa*, *prakṛti*, often identified with *māyā*, modifies its own distinctivelessness and gives origin to a manifold series of determined states of existence (*ṣūrat-i tamīzī*). A similar concept is found in the Tāntrik doctrines which develop around the primordial couple Śiva-Śakti, apparently separated from each other holding the rank of poles

89. Cf. *Brahma-Sūtra*, II.3.43.

90. The use of the term *racanā* for the manifested world suits well to the underlying Hindu concept of the Divine carpenter and architect of the universal edifice, Viśvakarman, that represents the constructive aspect of *saguṇa Brahman*, similar to the function held by the *insān al-kāmil* in relation to creation and also to that of the universal architect conceived by Western free-masonry.

of universal existence which has to be brought together in order to gain access to the transcendent sphere.

As for the order of succession of these manifestions, Rāmcandra differs slightly from the doctrinal pattern laid out by Kapila's *Sāṅkhya-Sūtra* and *Sāṅkhya-Kārikā*, in identifying the first determination of *prakr̥ti* as *ahaṅkāra* instead of *buddhi*, since in his view

> the stages of [*prakr̥ti*'s] productions can become known only once the apprehension of individual perception (*idrāk*) has acquired a definitive shape.[91]

Hence, *ahaṅkāra* holds the rank of primary determination from which derive the different functions of *manas*, the mental faculty that governs 'the inner cause' (*antaḥkaraṇa*), that is to say the psychological dominion of the individual state. For Rāmcandra, it comprehends *buddhi* associated to the concept of '*aql* considered as the seat of the faculty of discriminative knowledge and of correct judgement, and *citta*, the common consciousness comprising the faculty of thought that gives rise to ideal concepts and the ability to link them.

These are the first four *tattvas* to which Rāmcandra adds the *tawajjuh* of the *puruṣa* as the fifth.[92] The pre-eminence of this fifth *tattva* over the other four is supported by the assertion that these latter ones came into existence only at the moment when the *kāla-puruṣa*, himself a projection of the *satpuruṣa*, gained consciousness of himself, which was the point of

91 *VS*, p. 23.

92. If conceived from this angle, *tawajjuh* earlier described as a luminous irradiation of the *satpuruṣa*, assumes the rank of *buddhi* as intended by the Sāṅkhya, that is to say as the Cosmic intelligence that irradiates, like a solar ray, as colourless light from the Supreme Being onto a plane of reflection situated at the centre of the plane of Its primordial determination in *puruṣa* and *prakr̥ti* where it is than perpetuated as the primary impulse on *prakr̥ti*. These two levels had been mentioned earlier as *mahātawajjuh* and *tawajjuh*. This fifth *tattva* is recovered in this context by the affirmation that the coming into existence of the other four named *tattvas* coincides with that very instance of self-diversification.

departure of the impulse exercised on *prakṛti*. In distinction to the Sāṅkhya, the *tawajjuh* is not a production of *prakṛti* but of the *kāla-puruṣa* who stands beyond this immediate duality and collaborates in its production. Strictly speaking, *puruṣa* and *prakṛti* must therefore themselves be regarded as *tattvas*, including the *tawajjuh* that gave origin to their separate existence.

The difference between Rāmcandra's position and the classical doctrines, thus, reduces itself to a merely formal one based on slightly different perspectives. It reflects his attempt to reconcile the different elements pertaining to the Hindu cosmological doctrines current among the *sants* with those expounded in the Sūfī teachings, particularly those of the *Mujaddid* who reiterated the absolute transcendence of the Divine essence and the impossibility of its direct involvement in the creative process by introducing the idea of shadows and reflections.

It is therefore especially in the relation the *paramātmā* bears with the realm of individual manifestation that a synthesis is required between the underlying formal differences in the perspectives held by the two traditions. Once this point is clarified Rāmcandra's enumeration of the various degrees of existence and their respective order of production presents fewer difficulties and develops in conformity with the pattern set out by the Sāṅkhya without incurring into any major discrepancies.

Ahaṅkāra goes rise to *śabda*, the auditive quality. As the first of the quintuple series of subtle principles of the corporeal elements (*tanmātra*), it gives rise to the element ether (*ākāśa*), the first most subtle of the five corporeal elements (*bhūta*). These two belong respectively to the planes of subtle and of gross manifestation, and as the first and most subtle of the series they are the leading productions in their respective degrees of existence, containing the following four synthetically in their folds. From the *śabda* there originates the touch (*sparśa*) and principle of the element air (*vāyu*, *hawā*); from the *sparśa* there springs the *rūpa* (lit. 'form', associated with the visible quality) which goes rise to the element fire (*agni*, *ātish*); from the *rūpa* there springs the *rasa*, the quality of savouring which manifests the element water (*ap*, *āb*); and finally, the *rasa* gives origin to *gandha*, the quality of smell that bears a relation with the element earth (*pṛthvī*, *khāk*), last and grossest in the series.[93]

Although they may be referred to most living beings, these determinations of individual existence covering the subtle (*sūkṣma*, *laṭīf*) and the gross planes (*sthūla*, *kathīf*) bear a particular relation to the human state. Man's superiority, the sanctioning of which in the Islamic tradition has been already described, finds its analogous expression in Hindu teaching in the very designation of the term *puruṣa* that includes the Supreme Being or *satpuruṣa*, the governor of this particular world, or *kāla-puruṣa*, and finally both humanity as a whole and every single human individual.[94]

In the impersonal perspective of the Vedānta adopted by the *nirguṇa* tradition, *puruṣa* stands in its highest rank as *puruṣottama* down to the single human individual for the perpetual presence of the Supreme Principle in all the degrees of existence.[95] It is in this sense that the reading of the *Koran* and the prophetic Traditions according to which Allāh has infused His essence into the earthen mould of Ādam before appointing him His *khalīfa* on earth, was interpreted by many Sūfis in its gnostic dimension as expressed in such doctrines as the *waḥdat al-wujūd* and the *waḥdat al-shuhūd*. In their

93. *VS*, p. 24. The Sāṅkhya further describes the production of the five faculties of sensual perception (*jñānendriya*) and the five faculties of action (*karmendriya*), co-ordinated by *manas*, the interior sense and inner governor (*antaryāmī*).

94. Though not expressedly mentioned by the authorities of our *paramparā*, *puruṣa*, if considered in relation to a particular cycle of existence, is also designated as the Manu or legislator of that specific cycle (hence, derives its denomination as *manvantara*) which here assumes the role of archetype and legislator of that period and its respective humanity (*mānava*). Such a conception shows some analogies with the Islamic concept of mankind said to descend from Ādam, entrusted with the burden of viceregency (*bār-i amānat*), the memory of which is still preserved in the designation of every human being by the term *ādamī*, descendant of Ādam.

95. Cf. *Bhagavad Gītā*, XV.16-18.

peculiar descriptions of the degrees of irradiations (*tajalliyāt*) and descents (*tanazzulāt*) of the Divine essence, they bear a close resemblance to the interpretations given by the Hindu *jñāna-kāṇḍa*.

The realms of the universe

The next step in the analysis of the cosmological teachings of this order consists of the analysis of the single planes of existence which determine the constitution of the macrocosm and their main characteristics. This will complete the picture of the composite cosmological doctrine current among the Hindu Naqsbhandīs while providing further clues to the master's teachings which, though different in outlay, remain coherent with and insert themselves into the main framework set out by the better known Hindu and Islamic doctrines.

Rāmcandra explains that at the origin of all, the *satpuruṣa* does not participate at the unfolding of the aforesaid *tattvas*, for it consists of pure consciousness (*khāliṣ cetana*).[96] The participartion at this consciousness, different in nature from all other *tattvas*, is possible through the faculty of knowledge (*jñāna*), which is exclusive to Man and is defined as the support (*ādhāra*) of everything. From a macrocosmical point of view, the abode of the *satpuruṣa* is the *satloka* or *brahmaloka*, equally said to be permeated by pure consciousness.[97]

The double mention of the *satloka* (the *satyaloka* of the classical doctrines) and the *brahmaloka* is important for the evaluation of Rāmcandra's teachings since both terms apply in traditional Hindu cosmology to the most sublime among the celestial regions (*devaloka*). Located at the apex of the Mount Meru, the *satloka* extends in a region far beyond the lunar sphere (*candraloka*). It is said to be the dwelling-place of those souls who have attained immortality after their relinquishment from the body (*videha-mukti*) by following the 'path of the gods'

---

96. To be precise, the term 'nature' does not apply to the *satpuruṣa* because He stands really beyond nature.

97. *VS*, p. 25.

(*devayāna*).[98] The term *satloka* appears frequently with the *Kabīr-panthīs* in a similar context. In the *Amar Mūl*, for instance, an important doctrinal work in the Chattīsgarhī branch of the *panth*, the *satloka* is said to be attained to by those who have acquired perfect knowledge of the *satnām*, once reached there, these perfect souls will be nourished by the nectar of immortality (*amṛta*).[99] The notion of *satloka* or *satdeśa* appears later among the Rādhāsoāmīs who describe it as the highest region, consisting of pure spirit.[100] Rāmcandra's description fits, therefore neatly into the general Hindu concept of *satyaloka* considered as the abode of Brahmā, the Creator of the world, Who is identified in the *sant* context with the inferior aspect of the *satpuruṣa*. But once we descend into the realm of relative existence, we enter the reign of *kāla-puruṣa* said to reside in the *kāla-loka* or *kāla-deśa*. There, pure consciousness intermingles with *māyā*, in this context describes as an extremely subtle substance (*mādda-i laṭīf*) which provokes the production of the subtle dominion of the universe.

One further step below there extends the *māyādeśa* composed of gross substance (*mādda-i kathīf*) which constitutes the realm of the corporeal elements (*mahābhūta*) that compose the physical vehicle of the individual souls (*jīva*). To illustrate the nature of these three levels, Ramcandra quotes the following example:

> Look at the flame of a candle! At the top its light is white, similar to that of the pure consciousness in the *satloka*; a little further down its light appears reddish, some way in between the pure white light and a light black — this light resembles the *kāladeśa*. Further descending, close to the wick, the flame produces black

98. Cf. *Chāndogya Upaniṣad*, IV.15:5. This path eventually leading to the identity with the Supreme, is called the 'path of the gods' because it crosses the successive abodes of the gods until reaching the top of the celestial hierarchy, often described as the peak of a mountain on which lies a golden shining city, Brahmapura, the citadel of Brahmā.

99 See, F.E. Keay (1995), pp. 117-18.

100. M.G. Gupta (1994), pp. 152-5.

> smoke — this compares to the *māyādeśa*. The difference between these three consists of the decreasing degree of consciousness and an increasing number of veils covering it. . . .[101]

The *satloka*, defined as imperishable and non-transitory (*ghair-fānī*), represents the immediate principle of the other two. In contrast, the existence in the *kāla-loka* is by definition subject to the conditions of time (*kāla*) and, therefore, transitory (*fānī*), although its relative nearness to the transcendent realm guarantess it a comparatively high degree of reality and temporal extension in comparison to the following one. Due to its distance from the realm of pure consciousness, the *māyāloka* constitutes the most ephemeral realm and in the most affected by the limitative co-ordinates of time and space.

However, it would be erroneous to consider the immortality gained by those who have reached the *satloka* as the ultimate and utmost degree of spiritual ascent, for it is such only if considered in relation to the manifestation of one single world. This is why Rāmcandra affirms in connection with the multiple levels of Rāma the existence of a fourth *loka* which is said to be connected with the 'ascension of the saints' (*santon kā mi'rāj*) who have gone through the purest spiritual experience and are, therefore, granted a place in the everlasting *ikka satyaloka* ('matchless abode of Truth').[102]

Rāmcandra ultimately conceives an additional fifth realm saying that 'although possible to be pronounced by the tongue its comprehension is somewhat difficult'. This fifth plane lies beyond the appellation of *nirguṇa Brahman*.[103] Whatever

---

101. *VS*, pp. 25-6.

102. *VS*, p. 26. The concept of *loka* is clearly intended in a symbolical sense since it here refers to the 'sphere of non-manifestation' indescribable in common terms; the Naqshbandīs refer to it only in negative terms as *lā-makāniyat*, lit. 'not being traceable in space', 'having no dwelling'.

103. Rāmcandra explains in this context that the two terms 'limited' (*maḥdūd*) and 'unlimited' (*ghair-maḥdūd*) still pertain to the plane of relativity (*ṭabaqa-i nisbatī*) beyond which their use becomes →

intervenes between these sublime states and the ordinary world experienced by the common senses is ultimately due to the fancy of *māyā* whose innumerable veils preclude the ordinary individual from a direct vision of Truth. Rāmcandra's account of *māyā* and its veils, reflecting notions of a pan-Indian doctrine common to the Vedānta as well as to Kabīr and his followers,[104] has seemingly adopted some of the Sūfī concepts regarding the veils (*parda*) that separate common man from the direct contemplation (*mushāhada*) of the pure Essence.

According to Rāmcandra, the term *māyā* derives from the Sanskrit *mā*, 'measure' (*māp*, *mātrā*), and *yā*, 'support', 'means' or 'cause' (*waṣīla*), hence, its literal meaning as the 'measure of something'.[105] In cosmology, *māyā* came to coincide with *prakṛti*, whose main characteristic came to be identified with its power of alteration and modification (*tabdīl*). This primordial substance spreads out in space and determines through the manifold possibilities of combination of its inherent qualities the distinctive measure of every single object thereby accounting for the indefinite multiplicity present in the Universe. These qualities, perfectly balanced at the beginning in a state of undifferentiated harmony, are essentially these referred to by Rāmcandra as *triguṇa*, comprising *sat*, *raj* and *tam* (Sanskrit *sattva*, *rajas* and *tamas*).[106]

Sat corresponds to the quality that conforms to Truth and

→ ultimately inadequate. The same applies to the Arabic term 'all-comprehensive' (*muḥīṭ-i kull*, Sanskrit *sarva deśya vyāpaka*), a definition usually applied to the Throne of Allāh and the principle of creation comprehending everything without being comprehended by anything; cf. also *Kabīr-Granthāvalī*, *pada* 157, quoted by R.K. Varma in *Kabīr: Biography and Philosophy*, 1977, p. 90: 'The imperishable *akṣara* is the Supreme *Brahman*, because we find that It supports the end of space'.

104. For the concept of *māyā* in Kabīr, see Hedayetullah, 1977, pp. 221-4 and Varma, 1977, pp. 97-102. For an extensive description among some exponents of the *sant* current including Guru Nānak, see W.H. McLeod, *Guru Nānak and the Sikh Religion* 1968, pp. 185-7.

105. Cf. Latin *metiri*, 'to measure', *mater*, *materia* and *matter*, as indication of the function the substance bears as the measure of the universe.

106. *VS*, p. 29.

the to the pure Being (*satta*). It is characterised by an upward tendency that corresponds to a centripetal attraction towards the principle of manifestation: light (*prakāśa*), beatitude (*ānanda*), knowledge (*jñāna*), etc., are all predominantly characterised by this quality. *Raj* defines the quality that confers colour on things, thereby exalting their individual nature. It denotes the horizontal movement of expansion (*phailāvaṭ*) of the cosmos along one particular plane and as such characterises the active and dynamic aspect of the world. Analytic thought (*khayāl*), engagement in mental activity (*maṣrūfiyat*), ardour (*sar-garmī*), etc., are some of the attitudes dominated by this quality. Finally, *tam* indicates darkness and, thus, represents the opposite of *sat*. It denotes a descending, centrifugal tendency towards the bottom peripheral of the inferior worlds. Dullness, apathy, ignorance, powerlessness and indolence are among the attitudes characterised predominantly by *tam*.

These are the principal attributes of *prakṛti* or *māyā* through which the Divinity in Its creative aspect displays Itself in the Universe.[107] This consideration is extremely important because it confers a second, superior meaning to *māyā* which goes beyond its simple identification with the primordial substance. By the relation with Brahmā as the ultimate principle whence *māyā* and its multiple productions derive, a degree of relative reality is attributed on *māyā* and, by extension, on the created world. It is therefore not entirely correct to define *māyā* as sheer illusion or fantasy which separates us from knowing the Truth. Rather, it is our ignorance (*avidyā*, *jahālat*) that prevents us from recognising its real nature as the creative power of the Principle with whose help It made Itself known, as an effect of the lower quality of *tamas* that creates these veils of separation.

The remarkable acuity of Rāmcandra's vision here goes far beyond the descriptions common in many *sant* texts of *māyā* as a deceitful bewitching woman enchanting both gods and human beings alike and preventing them from knowing Reality. Returning to the beginning of the process of self-revelation of

---

107. *VS*, p. 30.

the Supreme Being that eventually led to the coming into existence of the world, Rāmcandra states:

> The reflection of the *satpuruṣa* . . . on the primordial substance (*ādimāyā*) brought into existence the *kāla-puruṣa* . . . , likewise, the reflection of the *kāla-puruṣa* on the causal *māyā* (*kāraṇa māyā*) generated Brahmā. .[108]

The concept of *māyā*, therefore, extends far beyond the simple notion of a primordial substance in the sense implied by the term *prakṛti*. It rather represents a plane of reflection of the immediately superior principle from which the corresponding inferior degree of determination derives its existence. Ramcandra's perspective therefore in a sense combines the point of view of Rāmānujācārya's viśiṣṭādvaita with that held by the *shuhūdī* doctrine of the Mujaddidīs. In mediaeval Hinduism similar ideas are also brought forward by the advocates of the doctrine referred to as *chāyāvāda* which differs from the purely unitarian view held by the adherents to the kevalādvaita inasmuch as it does not unequivocally reduce the origin of this plane of reflection to an essential part of the Supreme Principle.

Rāmcandra next describes the three levels on which Brahmā, intermingling with *māyā*, manifested Itself in the world. The first of these levels consists of *hiraṇyagarbha,*the golden embryo or germ described in the *Bhāgavata Purāṇa* as containing the seeds of all possibilities of manifestation. This is followed by *avyākṛtaḥ* (lit. the non-manifest, undifferentiated one) and by *virāṭ*, the cosmic intellect and first progeny of Brahmā.[109]In his interpretation of these three terms borrowed from classical Hindu sources, *virāṭ* is associated to Brahmā in the 'state of wakening' (*jāgṛta-avasthā*) during which the exterior forms of the universe are generated through the sensory perception and their elaboration by the mind. It, thus, constitutes the corporeal aspect of existence referred to by the Sūfis as the 'corporeal world' ('*ālam-i ajsām*). *Avyākṛtaḥ*, associated with Brahmā while in the 'state of dreaming' (*svapna-*

108. *VS*, p. 31.

109. *Ibid.*, p. 44.

avasthā), refers to the condition in which the exterior forms are elaborated in an exclusively interior fashion from the ideas and thoughts that are part of the subtle manifestation. Finally, *hiraṇyagarbha*, is associated with the 'state of deep sleep' (*suṣupti-avasthā*) of the Creator, during which His entire workmanship is reabsorbed and condensed in Himself in a seminal state, prior to any formal elaboration.[110]

Together, these three planes comprehend the entire macrocosm and are, therefore, assimilated to the Sūfī concept of the 'greater world' (*'ālam-i kabīr*),[111] which is comprehended by the sphere of possible existence (*dā'ira-i imkān*) and is equally divided into three major realms. It is said to be governed by the universal Intellect which characterises Brahmā (*brahmāṇḍa* man, *'aql-i kullī*) contained inside the cosmic egg whose principal attribute is that of being produced and extended. Through the affirmation of its individual consciousness (*ahaṅkāra*) and the power of imagination (*vāsanā*, *quwwat-i khayāl*) that is one of its faculties, yet another faculty of the Cosmic mind, that of the 'living souls' (*jīva*) was successively originated.[112] This power of imagination, analogous to the concept of 'creative power' (*kriyā śakti*) of the Vedānta, again received its impulse from the primordial desire of the *Brahman*, born out of its *ahaṅkāra*, to expand Itself so as to become known.[113] Hence, It first divided Itself into two correlative parts, defined as masculine (*taẓkir*) and feminine (*tānīth*) and analogous to *puruṣa* and *prakṛti*, whence the multiplicity of the innumerable species populating the world was generated. All of them participate in the hidden nature of the original state (*aṣliyat*) since the essential part of all creatures consists of a reflected image (*'aksī ṣūrat*) of Its inner reality. On the other hand, Brahmā, Himself a projection

110. Cf. *Ṛgveda*, X.121.1, *Māṇḍūkya Upaniṣad,* 3-5, where these three states referring to the *ātmā* are termed as *vaiśvānara*, *taijasa* and *prājña*.

111. See also Bṛj Mohan Lāl Saksenā, *AIB*, part II, pp. 17-20.

112. *VS*, p. 31. The term *vāsanā* is derived from the Sanskrit *vāsanā* meaning both 'covering' and 'abiding'.

113. The resemblance to the often quoted prophetic Tradition is too striking as to be a mere coincidence.

of that Principle, generates their substantial and individual forms (*rūpa*), indicated as both subtle and gross by the terms *avyākr̥taḥ* and *virāṭ*. It is, therefore, possible to affirm with Rāmcandra that 'he is the producer and immediate support of the world who contains everything'.[114]

To further illustrate this point, by Rāmcandra goes to the Veda where the development of the cosmos is described as the result of the self-sacrifice of the primeval Being (*puruṣa-sūkta*):

> In the same way as man offers the oblation (*āhuti*) of the single materials to the sacrificial fire and these, in the guise of smoke, spread all around, He [Brahmā], offering Himself as oblation for His sacrifice (*yajña*), spreads out in the whole universe.[115]

But this description that follows the classical Vedic imagery is immediately followed by an additional consideration, derived from an altogether different background:

> . . . contemplating the result of His sacrifice, [Brahmā], though satisfied with it, no longer experienced His original state of happiness for He felt the lack of something in His creation. Hence, He generated Man from the sum of His attributes in the likeness of the *satpuruṣa*. Watching him, He felt very pleased and from that moment, He entitled him to be the 'most excellent among creatures' (*afḍal-i makhlūq*) and the 'noblest of creation' (*'ashraf al-khilqat*), entrusting His entire creation to him.[116]

Although inserted into the context of the primordial sacrifice as described by the *R̥gveda*, this latter passage clearly refers to the primordial entrustment (*bār-i amānat*) described by the *Koran* whose mention by Shāh Abūl Ḥasan has been quoted earlier. It provides an excellent example of how elements pertaining to the two traditions are inextricably interwoven in

114. *VS*, p. 30.

115. *VS*, p. 32. CF. *R̥gveda,* X.90.

116. *VS*, pp. 32-3.

the doctrinal vision of this Kāyasth authority beyond the formal divergencies subsisting between the perspectives inherent in the two traditions, thus presenting his followers with a unified vision based on their possible points of contact. It is nevertheless important not to lose sight of the different perspectives to which these are liable, especially considering the *Kabīr-panthī* adaptation of the terminology used by the Vedānta which often appears freely mixed with Sūfī terms as used by the Naqshbandīs.

In the two passages quoted above, Brahmā, the Hindu god presiding universal manifestation, is assimilated to the creative aspect of Allāh (*al-Khāliq*). His creation in the formal dominion, identified with the inferior hemisphere of the cosmic egg (*brahmāṇḍa, dā'ira-i imkān*) referred to as *'ālam-i khalq*, is entrusted to mankind as being made in the likeness of the *satpuruṣa* who was earlier said to belong to a sphere far above the planes pertaining to Brahmā, *kāla-puruṣa* or *al-Khāliq*. For Rāmcandra, the *satpuruṣa*, therefore, can possibly designate both the unconditioned and unqualified *pārabrahma* contemplated by the esoteric traditions of both Hinduism and Islam as well as its lower projection as cosmic principle.

But if this is correct, what about the other unnamed plane earlier mentioned as being situated still above the *satyaloka*?. To clarify this ambiguity which runs through the entire preceding description of the cosmological process, it is necessary to juxtapose the Mujaddidī and the *Kabīr-panthī* perspectives. Such a matching between the two doctrinal perspectives and their terminology is furnished by Bṛj Mohan Lāl, the eldest son of Rāmcandra's younger brother Raghubar Dayāl, in his *Ā'īna-i 'ilm-i bāṭin* (The mirror of the esoteric science), which he states is faithfully based on the teachings of Rāmcandra.[117]

According to Bṛj Mohan Lāl, the macrocosm (*brahmāṇḍī man*, *'ālam-i kabīr*) is composed of three planes of existence which collectively correspond to the 'sphere of universal Possibility' (*dā'ira-i imkān*) of thye Mujaddidīs. It is said to

---

117. *AIB*, Akhbar Tarjuman, Hardoi (U.P.), n.d.

contain the germs of this world in a luminous shape analogous to the golden egg (*hiraṇyāṇḍa*) deposed by the goose *haṁsa* on the surface of the primordial waters.

Its upper part consists of spirit (*rūḥ*, *ātmā*) and is characterised by luminosity (*nūrāniyat*), pure consciousness (*cit*) and beatitude (*ānanda*, *sarūr*). These are defined as essential qualities (*auṣāf-i dhātī*) deriving their lofty existence from their reflection on the causal substance (*kāraṇa māyā*). Because of the predominance of the spirit on that subtle substance, this spiritual realm, elsewhere explicitly identified with the *'ālam-i amr* containing the germs of the entire world,[118] remains pervaded by silence and perfect peace in a state of undifferentiated equilibrium (*maḥwiyat*, *laya-avasthā*). Suddenly, through the intervention of a powerful force (*zabardast quwwat*), this motionless harmony is shaken and a ray of light (*nūrānī joṭ*) begins to irradiate from there, illuminating everything around it and giving rise to a new luminous source of existence, referred to as 'pure individual consciousness' (*śuddha ahaṅkāra*, *quwwat-i yazdānī*). Spreading all around, it will constitute the plane of reflection on which the original brilliance of the yet unmanifested seeds (*piṇḍa*, *bīja*) contained in *hiraṇyagarbha* will reflect themselves in the mirror of existentialisation as they acquire their various degrees of differentiated individual existence.

Bṛj Mohan Lāl, thus, identifies this plane with the *barzakh*, known in Sūfī cosmology said to either separating or connecting the two realms of informal and formal existence through a focal point (*markaz*, *nuqṭa*). As we know from the descriptions provided by the Naqshbandī shaikh at Delhi, the *barzakh* is assimilated to the Throne (*al-'arsh al-majīd*), the storehouse of all powers (*quwwaton kā bhaṇḍāra*) which is characterised by unity (*waḥdat*).[119] This unity establishes its abstract unity

118. *AIB*, part I, p.42.

119. Cf. *Koran*, 25:55: 'He it is Who bringeth forth the two seas; one is fresh and drinkable, the other is salty and bitter; and He hath made between the two an isthmus and a closed barrier', and also *Koran*, 55:19-20: 'He bringeth forth the two seas which meet together, between them a barrier they do not overpass'.

→

(*waḥdāniyat*) as the pole of the universe, unifying in its existence (*wujūdat*) its two faces, one turned towards the spiritual existence (*rūḥī wujūd*) of the 'world of order', and the other turned towards the reflected individual existence of the 'world of creation' (*'ālam-i khalq*). This is the reason why both great macrocosmic divisions are said to participate in the prosperity of the 'glory of peerless greatness' (*shān-i nirālī 'aẓīmat*) which attaches to Brahma in his personal aspect of *īśvara* or *al-Khāliq*.[120]

As the *barzakh* is unequivocally defined in all Sūfī doctrines as 'not liable to spatial extension' (*lā-makāniyat*), we recognise in it that very *avyākṛtaḥ* described by Rāmcandra in his tripartition of the cosmos as the intermediate plane. From a different angle, this is also possibly associated to the *kāla-puruṣa*, the all-devouring temporal principle, which limits the duration of the world below.

Terefore, we are now in a position to reassess Rāmcandra's statement that the creation of Brahmā reproduces a perfect copy (*naql*) of the spiritual realm. The reflected existence of the former represents an inverted image of its original, for it is the reflection of the eternal archetypes present in a germinal state in the *'ālam-i mithāl* (which is a part of the *'ālam-i amr*) that determines universal existence by casting the image on the mirror of the *barzakh*. It will be recalled that according to the

---

→ These two oceans separated by a barrier bear a close resemblance with the suprerior and the inferior waters described by the Hindu tradition where they refer respectively to the informal and the formal states of being, reunited in the primordial substance. An interesting analogy which would require an ample study in itself consists in the theological interpretation of the *barzakh* as the intermediate region between this world and the next where the departed souls of the deceased ancestors attend the final dissolution of the world before being judged and accordingly addressed to their further posthumous destination. Such a concept represents also very interesting analogies with the 'lunar realm' (*candra-loka*) that governs the tides, equally described as the abode of souls who have followed the 'path of the ancestors' (*pitṛyāna*) and the place where the forms of the present world are elaborated.

120. *AIB*, pp. 17-19.

Mujaddidī cosmology, what held the highest rank in the spiritual realm occupies the lowest rank in the realm of creation and what was smallest in the realm of spirit will be the biggest in the created world. This is the reason why the innermost reality of the human heart (*ḥaqīqat-i qalb*) corresponds from a macrocos-mic point of view to the *'arsh-i muḥīṭ*, identified by Bṛj Mohan Lāl with the 'citadel of Brahmā' (Brahmapura).

To complete the *shuhūdī* point of view that clearly lies behind these descriptions, Bṛj Mohan Lāl informs us that the primordial unity of the luminous point in conjunction with the Islamic concept of 'Throne' constitutes the dimension held by the doctrine of *waḥdat al wujūd* which contemplates the 'unity of existence' in the transcendent principle resumed in the formula *aham brahmāṇḍa* (sic!).[121] Notwithstanding this ingenious if somewhat imprecise attempt to explain the Mujaddidī position *vis-á-vis* this doctrine in a Hindu context, it nevertheless demonstrates the impact the Naqshbandī teachings have left on their Hindu disciples. This is true for the technical vocabulary which can vary quite unpredictably from author to author, work to work and even passage to passage, between original Sūfī language, Vedānta terminology and terms belonging to the technical vocabulary of the different *panths*. It also applies to some essential points of the genuine Mujaddidī doctrine encountered in the texts of the Delhi-based authorities.

In completing his description of the single planes composing the macrocosm, Bṛj Mohan Lāl turns to the third and lowest realm of the universe, that accounts for the individual existence contained in the *'ālam-i khalq*. This is referred to as *virāṭ-deśa* or *māyā-deśa* and is characterised by gross substance (*sthūla māyā*):

> On a macrocosmic scale, this level characterised by gross substance represents the matrix and storehouse of all those bodies which come into existence in the guise of exterior forms (*ẓahūr pazīr ṣūraten*): they subsist for a limited period of time until they eventually break down

121. *AIB*, part II, p. 19.

> like fragile earthen toys. . . . Their relationship with the gross substance corresponds to that between cause (*kāraṇa*) and effect (*kārya*).[122]

This description stresses the ephemeral nature of the lowest realm of the macrocosm and establishes a relationship between cause and effect, between the immediate principle of this plane and its single derivatives. It remains faithful to the concept of the descending planes of reflection on which an initial relative degree of unity is fragmented into a reflected multiplicity, which is found in later *Kabīr-panthī* doctrines and the Rādhāsoāmīs and represents a further development of a *shuhūdī* or, in Hindu terms, a viśiṣṭādvaita point of view. On the other hand, it is imported to bear in mind that the realm of individual existence symbolised by bodies comprises two further subdivisions, that of subtle existence inhabited by the gods or angels corresponding to the *'ālam-i malakūt*, and that of gross existence properly speaking, composed of the gross elements and known as *'ālam-i mulk*.[123]

These ideas find their parallel in Hindu cosmology according to which the gross elements (*bhūta*) are derived from the subtle principles or *tanmātras* which, although partaking of the individual nature on a subtle plane, constitute the immediate principles or causes of the former in the same way as the senses (*indriya*) have both subtle and gross aspects, either as distinctive faculties or as the corresponding organs.[124] Rāmcandra and his followers do not expressly mention this further subdivision of the formal dominion, thereby contributing to the apparent confusion arising from the double application of the term 'subtle substance' (*sūkṣma māyā*) to the *barzakh* (the *Kabīr-panthī kāla-puruṣa*) as principle of individualisation and plane of reflect-ion between the universal and the individual, the informal and the formal, the non-manifested (*nīstī*, *'adam*) and the manifested (*hastī*, *wujūd*) realms of existence both included

122. *AIB*, p. 19.

123. Cf. ch. II, pp. 191-2.

124. *Sāṅkhya-Kārikā*, *śloka* 3. Cf. also *Mānavadharmaśāstra*, I.14-20.

in the 'cosmic egg'. This is why the immediately lower degree, described as being characterised by the productions of gross substance analogous to *prakṛti*, comprises both subtle and gross manifestation (*bhū* and *bhuvaḥ*) notwithstanding the apparent contradiction in terminology.

Man, described by the Naqshbandīs as 'noblest of all creatures' (*ashraf al-makhlūqāt*) and by the classical Hindu doctrines 'as descendant of Manu' (*mānava*) populating the *mānavaloka*, the 'world of humanity', participates directly in the nature of all three dominions comprised in the formula *bhū*, *bhuvaḥ*, *svaḥ* which compose the universal sphere. He is, hence, described by Rāmcandra as the true reflection of the *satpuruṣa*. The primordial sacrifice of Brahmā sanctions that 'Man was first and man is last' (*insān awwal thā aur insān ākhir hai*),[125] a hint at the most perfect among creatures, the *insān al-kāmil*, who is essentially identical with Rāmcandra's *satpuruṣa*.

The constitution of man and the science of the subtle centres

A precise knowledge of the constitution of the human being covering the nature of and the interrelation between its single components and the superseeding planes of existence on which these are located is fundamental in any spiritual discylene. It constitutes one of the perogatives of every *sādhanā* and prepares the ground of a correct application of the different techniques meant to operate on that aggregate. The resulting process is invariably perceived by all traditions as an interior journey leading the initiate through the stages of his inner selves, the achievement of this goal requires the expertise of a true spiritual master (*murshid bar Ḥaqq*, *satguru*) well acquainted with this science, under whose guidance the disciple can safely cross the succeeding stations of the path (*maqāmāt*).[126]

To illustrate this process, Rāmcandra adopts a simile used by Shāh Walī Allāh Dihlawī which compares the role of the master to the jungle-dweller who, due to his long experience,

125. *VS*, p. 33.

126. *Ibid.*

knows all the hidden tracks and paths leading through the thick forest and who is well acquainted with its various inhabitants and with the dangers one can possibly encounter. The path leading straight towards the goal, explains Rāmcandra, is, the one that requires less hardship and excludes any risk of going astray.[127]

In obvious reference to the Naqshbandī tenet Rāmcandra affirms that this straight path rests nowadays on the 'science of the subtle centres' considered to be an extraordinary gift of the *paramātmā* bestowed by God (*īśvara*) on the great masters of the last age (*ākhir zamāna*).[128] Clearly, the reference here is to the *'ilm-i laṭā'if* handed down by the Mujaddidiyya, and to the corresponding Tāntrik *cakra-vidyā*, first propounded by the *siddha* and *nāth-sampradāya*s and later assimilated and adapted by the mediaeval *sant*s. In Rāmcandra's view, this science represents nowadays the only way for most people to undertake the goal of approaching the most sublime of all human goals. Using a language pertaining to the Sūfī background, Rāmcandra asserts that the task of delivering this science to the world has been entrusted to the 'masters endowed with great authority' (*ahl-i tamkīn*), i.e., to those who by witnessing the Truth have attained to the degree of fixity allowing them to be included among the 'real heirs of the Divine messengers' (*rusūl, avatāra*), called 'those of the fixed abode' (*ahl-i qā'im maqām*).[129]

The reference here is clearly to the 'poles' (*aqṭāb*, pl. of *quṭb*), that is to say those high-ranking saints who in virtue of their extraordinary spiritual qualifications are directly connected with the *axis mundi* that connects this world with the superior regions and heavenly abodes reachings up to the 'region of Truth'. Thanks to their lofty position, these 'chosen ones' participate

---

127. *TP*, p. 34. Cf. also Shāh Walī Allāh: *Altāf al-Quds*, ch. I, p. 3.

128. This 'last age' probably refers to the final part of the present cycle of mankind, the period of major decline of the spiritual values.

129. *TP*, p. 34. The opening motto on the front page of this treatise indicates this importance thus: 'The knowledge of the subtle centres constitutes the superior criterion conceded by the Supreme Being to the modern saints'.

directly at the knowledge communicated through this channel. Only such a qualification can justify their definition as 'heirs of the Divine messengers' (*avatāron ke wārith*)[130] since it enables them to receive and transmit to the rest of humanity the extraordinary 'gift' received from above. For the traditional esoteric authorities, their presence guarantees and sanctions the regularity of the science of the subtle centres and its supra-human origin within the context of both Hinduism and Islam.

We have, already looked at the description given by Rāmcandra in his *Vedānta-Sāgara* regarding the analogy between macrocosm and microcosm from a Hindu Tantra perspective. It is in this analogy that he perceives the possibility to link the two esoteric traditions he has inherited to each other, especially through the 'science of the subtle centres'. Once the analogy between these two has been corroborated by a series of references encountered in both traditions,[131] the author proceeds to describe the human constitution: in his view, the gross body

---

130. The term 'heirs' indicates the Islamic origin of this concept, for Islam does not allow any other human being to claim prophethood after Muḥammad. Hence, all the subsequent 'poles' come from within the broad category of 'friends of God' (*awliyā' Allāh*) irrespective of the degree of their spiritual realisation.

The term *avatāra* hints at the master's own Hindu background which sets out no chronological limit for the advent of Divinely inspired saints. Guided by a direct communication with the source of knowledge, these deliver a new type of spiritual wisdom to their surrounding world, although according to the theory of the *daśāvatāra*, only the tenth Divine descent, conceived as the knight of the white horse, the Kalki-*avatāra*, is left to conclude the present *manvantara*. A similar careful distinction had been made by Mīrzā Maẓhar Jān-i Jānān who came very close to admitting Rāma and Kṛṣṇa as Divinely inspired messengers. In this context it would be interesting to investigate the role played by *al-Khiḍr* in the transmission of the *'ilm al-ladunnī* to a group of high ranking authorities in the spiritual hierarchy of Islam, and the difference that occurs in Hindu doctrines between a 'total descent' (*pūrṇāvatāra*) and a 'partial descent' (*ārdhāvatāra*) of the Divinity.

131. The reference is also to the *Brahma-Sūtra* that states: *yathā piṇḍa tathā brahmāṇḍa* (As the individual germ so the Cosmic Egg'), very similar to the Sūfī maxim: 'The cosmos is like a big Man and man is like a small cosmos'. Cf. also *AIB*, part II, p. 12.

(*sthūla śarīra*, *jism-i kathīf*) of the human individual is analogous to *virāṭ* from a macrocosmic point of view. Similarly, the subtle body (*sūkṣma śarīra*), which bears a particular relation with the mind and inner governor (*antaryāmī*) of the various faculties, is associated with the *avyākṛtaḥ*,[132] while the causal body (*kāraṇa śarīra*) is said to bear a particular relation with the spirit. As such, it is considered antecedent and causal (*kāraṇa*) or primordial (*aṣlī*) with regard to the individual aggregate consisting of the former two bodies. At the macrocosmic level it corresponds to *hiraṇyagarbha*, the golden germ that contains in nuce all possibilities relevant to this present world.[133]

The microcosm, with reference to its inherent potentiality, is generally termed as *piṇḍa* or *piṇḍa śarīra*[134] and participates through these planes in different measures in the three tendencies (*triguṇa*) which qualify the realm of individual existence. If applied to the plane of universal existence in its primordial, luminous aspect, these assume the three-fold Divine aspects of the *trimūrti*, in which Viṣṇu represents *satoguṇa*, Brahmā *rajoguṇa* and Śiva or Maheśa *tamoguṇa*. Further down in the scale of existence, a multitude of gods (*devatā*) act as governors and presiding agents (*adhiṣṭhātā*, *muwakkil*) over the different regions of the Universe, reflected on the microcosmic scale in the various individual human faculties (*indriya*) and their respective organs, and even in the physical elements that equally participate in those qualities in different measures.

---

132. This double aspect of the subtle body enhances its possible assimilation to the *barzakh* or *sandhī* both from a microcosmic and macrocosmic point of view, for it underlines its two faces, either revolved towards creation as the mind that analyses the single parts contained in the creation or as supra-rational intuition that synthesises everything into one unique principle buried at the centre of the spiritual organ that is identified with the heart. Hence, derives the double use of the term *dil* or *qalb* as referring to both, the seat of the mind and of the spirit. Cf. *VS*, pp. 44-5.

133. Cf. *Māṇḍūkya Upaniṣad*, *śruti* 5. For its association with the *suṣupti-avasthā*. Cf. *AY*, pp. 33-4.

134. Here again applies the symbolism of the seed and the cosmic tree that develops from it since it is asserted that what is smallest on one side will be greatest on the other and vice versa.

Rāmcandra lists a series of five inferior subtle centres or *cakras*, situated inside the human body and each presided over by a divinity of the Hindu pantheon. These five centres or subtle organs, their location inside the human organism and their corresponding celestial guardians, are named in gradually ascending order as follows:

gudā-cakra (*maq'ad*)	rectum	Gaṇeśa
liṅgendriya-cakra (*ālat al-tanāsul*)	organ of generation	Brahmā
nābhi-cakra (*nāf*)	navel	Viṣṇu
hṛdaya-cakra (*qalb*)	heart	Śiva
kaṇṭha-cakra (*galā*)	throat	Durgā[135]

The mention of these five subtle centres, their location in the human body in relation to specific physical organs or nervous centres and their association with a particular divinity that presides over their different functions clearly reflect their origin in the Tāntrik environment of the Kabīr-panth to which Rāmcandra was affiliated.[136] Although no explicit mention of the *laṭā'if* known to the Mujaddidī tradition appears anywhere in this context, the authors list just five instead of the usual seven or nine subtle centres commonly described in the *cakra-vidyā* suggest his assimilation to the five subtle organs described by some earlier Sūfi shaikhs in relation to the *'ālam-i khalq*. This idea is further corroborated by Rāmcandra's following statement which hints at the relation between this first series

135. *VS*, p. 36, *JC* (Appendix I), pp. 541-60. For a comparison of these subtle centres with those described, for instance, in Gorakhnāth's *Siddha-Siddhānta Paddhatī*, see A.K. Banerjea, *Philosophy of Gorakhnāth* (with *Gorakhṣa-Vācana-Saṁgraha*).

136. In the Tāntrik doctrines where they appear as the first five out of a total series of six, seven, or nine subtle centres, these are named as: *mūlādhāra*, *svādhiṣṭhāna*, *maṇipūra*, *anāhata* and *kaṇṭha* or *viśuddha*; these are followed by the *tālu-cakra* located at the root of the palate, and the *bhrū-cakra* situated between the two eyebrows in correspondences to the *jñāna-netra* or 'eye of wisdom' associated with the third eye of Lord Śiva.

of subtle centres and the five gross elements (*bhūta*) through their subtle principles (*tanmātra*):

> When the wealth arising out of Brahmā's primordial impulse (*vāsanā*) came into existence, it it appeared in the guise of the subtle sound vibration (*śabda*). From the *śabda* originated the ether and then from the ether, in an established order of succession, all the other elements which, having found their place in the body of Brahmā, thus obtained their particular nature in the macrocosm. . . .[137]

This passage describes the primordial rank attributed to the sound or *śabda* in relation to the subtle manifestation, and its relation to the ether as the primordial determination of the gross dominion. It also recalls the idea that the macrocosm is, in fact, identical with the body of Brahmā itself. Such a conception further enhances the supposed analogy between the macrocosm and the human body in a way altogether similar to the famous Sūfī maxim already quoted. It leads to the conclusion that whatever man wants to know about Brahmā can be discovered through an introspection of the human individual, for both are essentially identical in nature differing only in the degree of their measure (*paimāna* or *mātrā*).[138]

Comparing the process of macrocosmic creation to the delivery of a baby from its mother's womb, Rāmcandra states that the head of Brahmā was the first to see the light of existence following the penetration of the reflection emanating from the *satpuruṣa* into the womb of *māyā*. As a result of this primordial conception, grew *hiraṇyagarbha*, the golden embryo containing the principles of both the subtle and the gross elements. In a microcosmic perspective too, it is, therefore the head which plays host to the quintessence (*jauhar*) of all senses (*ḥawāṣ*) and constituting elements (*tattva*). These comprehend the whole series of faculties of perception (*jñānendriya*), that is to say the senses of hearing (*śrotra*), touch (*tvaca*), sight (*cakṣus*), taste

137. *VS*, p. 36.

138. Cf. *Madhhab aur Taḥqīqat*, p. 112.

(*rasanā*) and smell (*ghrāṇa*).[139] In the process of gradual unfolding, the constituent elements of the individual sphere descended into the realm of manifestation, assuming their outwardly perceptible shape (*pragaṭ ṣūrat*).

First it was the turn of the ether (*ākāśa*) to descend into the gross determination. Establishing its seat within the microcosmic context in the *kaṇṭha-cakra* it is located somewhere in the throat. Reiterating the view of the Mujaddidī shaikhs, Rāmcandra holds that it is in the nature of the way the Divine wishes to display itself in the world that what is of subtle nature has its place above and what is of gross nature has its place below. To illustrate this concept, he quotes the example of the tendency inherent to the three aspects of water as vapour, liquid or solid ice.[140] The difference in the constitution of these three planes of universal Possibility results from the predominance of one of the three primordial qualities (*guṇa*) which permeate this entire world and characterise in their indefinite number of combinations every single degree of existence of every single creature. Rāmcandra calls this Durgā *śakti*, the dynamic display of Divine power that appears to the dazzled observer like an intricate puzzle (*gorakhdhandhā*) in the shape of the marvellous and enchanting play of multiple colours assumed by the Divine mysteries if considered under their creative aspect.

In Haṭha-Yoga doctrines, Durgā is considered mainly in her dynamic aspect of Śakti and consort of the Supreme Lord Śiva. Rāmcandra attributes her the rank of presiding divinity (*adhiṣṭhātā*) of the *ākāśa* residing in the *kaṇṭha-cakra*. Due to her pre-eminent position in comparison to the other four subtle centres she is also referred to as *ādi-śakti*, the primordial power which glares in its primordial brilliance inside the throat of the cosmic Brahmā and is reflected in the human throat. When that ether was stirred by a churning movement (*manthana*), it generated the element air (*vāyu*, *hawā*) which took its seat inside the *hṛdaya-cakra* or *maqām-i dil* located in proximity to the 'waving fan of the lungs', and presiding over the 'dominion of

139. *Mānavadharmaśāstra*, II.89-90.

140. *VS*, p. 38.

the air' (*vāyu maṇḍala*). Its governor is Lord Śiva who along with his consort Durgā represents the primordial duality generated by Brahmā, i.e., *puruṣa* and *prakṛti*. Interestingly this duality is here put in direct relation with the affirmative and negative poles (*ithbāt o nafī*) of universal existence thought by the Sūfīs to be comprised by the first part of the formula of the *shahāda*.[141]

The high rank attributed to Śiva in Tantrism, in regard to both the macrocosm (*brahmāṇḍa*) and the microcosm (*piṇḍa*), is due to his role of destroyer or rather transformer (*saṁhāra*) of the Universe. If interpreted from a gnostic point of view, it comes to represent the dissolution (*laya*, *maḥwiyat*) of the transitory existence of the formal world, implying for the initiate at the same rate the rebirth in a new, more sublime and supra-individual stage of existence (*be-khudī*). However, his subordination to the female goddess Durgā in this description suggests a doctrinal background that took at least partial inspiration from the Śākta environment within Tantrism.

From the union and churning of the two complementary poles in the *hṛdaya-cakra* was generated the principle of the element fire (*agni*, *ātish*) which took its seat inside the human microcosm in the *nābhi-cakra*. Its presiding divinity is Viṣṇu, the protector and cherisher of the Universe who nourishes the entire organism with heat spreading from the heels to the top of the head. From the churning movement produced by the union with his consort Lakṣmī sprang the subtle principle of water (*ap*, *āb*) which, taking its seat inside the *liṅgendriya-cakra*, assumed the characterising aspect of the element water, symbolically represented on the physical plane by the flow of corporeal

---

141. *VS*, p. 40. The polarisation within every single *cakra* into two complementary parts accounts for their tendency to rejoin each other, described in the terminology of Tantra-Yoga as the union between the male divinity and his *śakti*. Rāmcandra describes it in exactly the same manner. Although remaining faithful to his *nirguṇa* perspective which best combines with the integration of an Islamic spiritual discipline into the Hindu context, this is expressed as the mingling of *nafī* and *ithbāt* on the plane of the ether that leads to the production of the element air on an immediately lower degree of manifestation.

liquids from the organs of procreation. Its presiding divinity is Brahmā, the Lord of creation who generated from that very water all living creatures (*jīva-jantu*), moulding them in the fashion of a potter (*kumhāra*) from its mixture with the element earth (*pr̥thvī*, *khāk*) on the revolving wheel in his celestial laboratory.[142]

This extremely simplified description is illustrative of the complex theories which describe the process of cosmic unfolding and its implications for the analogous constitution of macrocosm and microcosm. Following the pattern of the Tāntrik doctrines and their *sant* offshoots, Rāmcandra here clearly intends to point out a common ground between these and the peculiar Mujaddidī doctrine of the subtle centres (*'ilm-i laṭā'if*) which he had inherited from his Sūfī shaikh. Such a reduced though essential illustration must not only be interpreted as a conscious attempt to present a plain and straightforward explanation of the most essential principles, underlying the different cosmolog-ical doctrines, but should also be seen as the identification of existing parallels between the two doctrinal backgrounds.

Such an assimilation, formally suggested by Rāmcandra's frequent use of a parallel terminology drawn from both traditions, is particularly striking in the above descriptions that emphasise the compatibility between the five subtle centres situated in the lower part of the human organism and their correspondence to the single elements which, in varying proportions, represent the fundaments of creation in both cosmologies. The five inferior subtle centres of Tantrism, whose location in the human body extends from the bottom of the trunk to the throat (representing the junction between trunk and head)[143] are, therefore, associated with the five *laṭā'if-i 'ālam-i*

142. *VS*, p. 41.

143. This symbolism goes back to the Purāṇa which describe the cosmic egg and its two halves floating on the primordial waters of the cosmic ocean. On a microcosmic plane, the head or skull as the most elevated part of the body and, thus, closest to heaven represents the celestial spheres and higher planes of Being pertaining to the universal and, therefore, supra-individual states contained in the upper shells of →

khalq which include, apart from the four gross elements air, water, fire and earth (*'anāṣir-i arba'*) also the subtle psychical aggregate or empirical soul (*nafs*), the fifth constituent element of the 'world of creation' which complements the outer aspect (*al-ẓāhir*) of both man and the Universe.[144]

In the Mujaddidī cosmology, the first four of these subtleties compose the physical aggregate of the gross body termed *qālib*. ('model, frame'), to the location of which in relation to subtle organs analogous to the Hindu *cakra*s no importance is attributed. They are conceived as the basic elements which compose the gross realm of the *khalq*, also referred to as the 'world of human sovereignty' (*'ālam-i mulk*). In contrast, the fifth of the series the *laṭīfa-i nafs*, embraces the entire subtle dominion, termed on a macrocosmic scale as the 'world of angelic beings' (*'ālam-i malakūt*). On the microcosmic scale, it includes both the mental or rational sphere (*nafs-i nāṭiqa*) and the lower 'passionate soul' (*nafs-i ammāra*), subject to the pleasures of the senses.[145]

In the parallel Hindu perspective, this subtle realm corresponds to the *antaryāmī* or *sūkṣma-śarīra* which qualifies the nature of the divinites presiding over the five subtle centres. The subtle powers they personify can therefore be possibly associated to the various categories of angels known in the monothei-

---

→ the *brahmāṇḍa* and the trunk represents the lower shells containing the strictly individual aggregate of the human being, while the arms and hands are simply considered as prolongations of the physical organs related to the faculty of prension (*pāni*) the same way as the legs and feet are merely the physical organs that correspond to the faculty of deambulation (*pāda*). These two faculties constitute, along with those of excretion (*pāya*), generation (*upastha*) and speech (*vāc*), the five *karmendriya* that enable man to intervene actively in the outside world.

144. Cf. ch. II, pp. 197-9; *MuM*, p. 76.

145. The Mujaddidī term *nafs-i nāṭiqa* applies to the 'interior governor' of the subtle aggregate and is, thus, slightly inferior to that held by the Vedānta doctrines where it refers to the very centre of being, analogous to *īśvara*. However, Rāmcandra gives it only the rank of *citta* or consciousness as a co-ordinating function of *manas*. Cf. also *Mānavadharmaśāstra*.

stic traditions (Arabic *malā'ika*, Persian *firishta*). From a microcosmic point of view, they represent the mental faculties that govern the individual consciousness (*ahankāra*). The subtle dominion is thus perceived as containing the immediate principles of the gross realm rendered through the description of the generation of the elements (*bhūta*) from the union of the subtle poles or *tanmātra* contained in each *cakra*.

The only exception to this mode of generation is the *ākāśa*, the primordial element and spatial principle considered to be the seat of the *ādi-śakti* located in the throat, which links the upper hemisphere represented by the head of universal Man with the lower hemisphere represented by the trunk. Such a symbolic description suggests a macrocosmic correspondence between the Hindu concept of *brahmāṇḍa* containing the germ of the body of Brahmā conceived as *hiraṇyagarbha* and the Sūfī image of the 'sphere of the universal Possibility' (*dā'ira-i imkān*) containing the germ of the *insān al-kāmil*. It may, therefore, be inferred that the head of Brahmā (or of the *hiraṇyagarbha*) corresponds to the *'ālam-i amr*, of the Naqsbandīs both terms referring to the non-formal states of universal existence which includes the subtle seeds (*bīja*, *piṇḍa*), inner truths (*ḥaqā'iq*) and principles (*uṣūl*) of all possibilities of manifestation prior to their formal elaboration in the *'ālam-i mithāl* or *candraloka* and their descent into the realm of the *khalq* represented by the rest of the body.

From a Sūfī perspective, intermediate role between these two dominions is played by the microcosmic *nafs* and corresponds on the macrocosmic level to the *barzakh* holding the all-encompassing 'Thorns of God' (*'arsh al-muhīt*) that comprehends in its vastest sense the entire series of possibilities contained in both the *'ālam-i malakūt* and the *'ālam-i mulk*. It can, therefore, he assimilated to the *ākāśa* in the Tāntrik perspective held by Rāmcandra in his cosmological exposition. In the microcosmic context too, both *ākāśa* and *nafs* denote the link between the corporal realm of the gross and the subtle body. Such an interpretation is further supported by the affinity of the term *nafs* to another term derived from the same Arabic root, i.e., *nafas*, bearing the meaning of 'breath'. On the other side, the Sanskrit term *prāṇa* indicates the 'vitalising breath',[146] and its five modalities (*vāyu*)[147] during the phases of breathing, which plays an important role in connecting the two realms. The process of respiration is divided into the three major phases of inhalation, retention and exhalation, which determine the assimilation of cosmic elements sustaining the subtle and the gross body alike followed by the expulsion of individual elements into the surrounding environment. On a minor scale this process reproduces the alternating macrocosmic phases of expansion and contraction (*baṣr wa qabḍ*) which, like the two phases of the heartbeat, are symbolically re-enacted in the course of the alchemical process of liquefaction and coagulation that accompanies the 'cleansing of the soul' (*tadhkiya-i nafs*) and the 'purification of the heart' (*taṣfiya-i qalb*). This explains why the discipline of breath-control plays such a fundamental role in both Yoga and many Sūfī *ṭuruq*.[148]

Moreover, we know from the orthodox Mujaddidī teachings that the *ṭarīqa*'s spiritual practice concentrates from the very beginning of the ascending phase (*'urūj*) of the 'journey towards Allāh' on the five subtle centres pertaining to the *'ālam-i amr*, since these are considered as the most subtle spiritual component or 'Divine spark' that descended into the 'abode of the breast' (*maqām-i sīna*) of the human individual. It is only after their reintegration (*fanā*) into their archetypical principles back in the realm of order that the inferior subtle organs pertaining to the dominion of the *khalq* gain importance during

146. Hence the idea of *prāṇāyāma*, the discipline of breath-control, as a Yogic technique meant to subjugate the senses and sensual desires. Similar though more moderate methods are used in numerous Sūfī circles including the Naqshbandiyya where these two phases of restraining and suspending the respiration is known respectively as *ḥabs-i nafas* and *ḥaṣr-i nafas*.

147. In Hindu dictionary this consists of: inhalation (*prāṇa*), inspiration (*apāna*), retention (*vyāna*), espiration (*udāna*) and digestion (*samāna*). Cf. *Chāndogya Upaniṣad*, V.19-23; *Maitrī Upaniṣad*, II.6.

148. The assimilation of the inner path of realisation to an alchemical process is strengthened by Rāmcandra's allusion to the 'touching stone' or 'philosopher's stone' (*kasauṭī*) apt to transmute all metals, especially lead or iron, into gold.

the descending phase (*nuzūl)* of the 'journey from Allāh' back to the contingent world. These two complimentary phases of the spiritual path and the corresponding three degrees of sainthood (*wilāyat*) gradually lead the *murīd* through the ten major stations of his inner journey (*maqāmāt-i 'ashrah*), which in this particular context are set in direct correspondence to the ten subtle organs (*laṭā'if-i 'ashrah*).[149]

Inverting the conventional order followed in other Sūfī *ṭuruq*, this progress is referred to in the Mujaddidī terminology as *sair-i jadhbī* as against the previous one called *sair-i sulūkī* and reiterates from a new perspective the ancient maxim of the order according to which 'the beginning of our path lies there where that of other orders ends and our path ends there where that of others begins'.[150]Although both ways are ultimately equivalent for the attainment of the final goal,[151] it is significant that the way of *jadhba* is recommended as more suitable to the conditions of the present era and is, thus, essential to the Mujaddidī's task of facilitating access to the initiatory path, as is also underlined also by Rāmcandra at the beginning of his *Tattva-Prabodhinī*.

From the time of its first explicit doctrinal formulation by

149. This assimilation is expressedly mentioned in the *HdT*, pp. 8/9. For detailed Mujaddidī description of these ten stations, cf. *MuM*, pp. 50-3; *MaS*, pp. 29-32/48-52. It is important to remember, however, that these indicate only the major stations of the *sulūk* and are, thus, liable to indefinite multiplication into minor realms. Cf. also M. Molé's article 'Traités mineurs de Najm al-Dīn Kubrā', treatise I: *al-uṣūl al-'ashra*' in *Annales Islamologiques de l'Institut d'Études Orientales*, 1965.

150 See Sirhindī, *Mabdā o Ma'ād, manhā* 1, pp. 93-9 and *manhā* 10, pp. 110-14.

151. Sirhindī distinguishes two types of aspirants to the inner path corresponding to the two ways described here: the intellectual type (*ahl-i kashf o ma'rifat*) who receives from the very beginning a detailed knowledge of each single station through the unveiling of an intellectual intuition (*kashf*) through the *sulūk*, and the emotional and devotional type (*arbāb-i jahl wa ḥairat*), suddenly transported and rapidly attracted through the initial stages through *jadhba*. These two are compared to two pilgrims on their way to the Ka'ba who approach their goal differently but nevertheless eventually both reach their destination. Cf. *Mabdā o Ma'ād*, *manhā* 10, p. 112; *MuM*, p. 51.

Shaikh Aḥmad Sirhindī about four centuries ago, this tendency to focus on the accelerated 'way of *jadhba*', which finds its practical expression in the emphasis on the immediate concentration on the spiritual components of the breast, has constantly gained in importance among the leaders of the *ṭarīqa* especially since Mīrzā Maẓhar Jān-i Jānān.[152] It has now become the dominant mode in the order's methodology in all its branches. This is particularly evident in the teachings of the Hindu lineage that developed from it. Its leaders again and again stress the adequacy and ease of the method propounded by their spiritual ancestors which offers a large audience the chance even in the present difficult times of undertaking the spiritual path, and which has found fertile soil in the highly devotional atmosphere of the *Rām-bhakti* that is widely diffused among the Kāyasths of central and eastern Uttar Pradesh.

The detailed elaboration of the subtle centres pertaining to the *khalq*, their origin, their specific properties and functions in the human organism and their evaluation against a Tāntrik background brought forward by Rāmcandra must hence be interpreted in two possible ways. These are closely interconnected between and complemetary to each other:[153] On one side, he integrates the Mujaddidī teachings regarding the *'ilm-i laṭā'if* in its preliminary and inferior aspects not taken in account on the Sūfī side but well elaborated in the corresponding Hindu doctrines of the Tantravāda. On the other, he leaves open the possibility of an alternative and more conventional approach of gradual advancement (*tafṣīlī*) through each of the subtle centres of the lower part of the human organsim which stretch out from the bottom of the back till the throat along the ideal vertical axis represented in the microcosm by the spinal cord (*merū-daṇḍa*).

The reluctance shown by Rāmcandra and his successors to

152. Cf. his interpretation of the role played by the two Hindu *avatāras* Rāmacandra and Kṛṣṇa discussed in chapter 1 in relation to the two major ways of *sulūk* and *jadhba*, and the frequent mention of the shaikh's emotional character.

153 *VS*, pp. 36-41. Cf. also *JC*, Appendix I, pp. 1-20.

reveal anything regarding these *cakras* leads to the assumption that although their function as possible gate of entrance to the inner path is still acknowledged in line of principle, they bear no practical importance in their immediated concerns. They mention by Rāmcandra must be interpreted as a reminisence of the older tradition inherited through his links with branches of the Kabīr- and Nānak-panth and are meant to complete the elaboration of theoretical background. His preference for the elaboration of his *sādhanā* remains focussed on the doctrines and methods received from the Naqshbandī masters who had long shifted to a preference of the *jadhbī* path that tries to exploit the devotional component in human nature rather than being too demanding from a point of view of physical and mental constraints. Nowhere in the authentic recordings of Rāmcandra's and his successors' oral teachings is there any further mention of these inferior *cakras* familiar in the Hindu context of the Kuṇḍalinī- and Haṭha-Yoga, let alone any instruction regarding the methods of how to operate upon them for their reawakening.

On the contrary, a number of hints in Rāmcandra's writings suggest his evaluation of the *'ilm-i sīna* as a superior kind of knowledge bearing a direct relation to some aspects of Rāja-Yoga, the 'royal' discipline and most intellectual among all Yoga doctrines which, in a similar fashion tu the Naqshbandī *ṭarīqa* claims to 'begin where all the other kinds of Yoga end'. Interestingly, its origin is traced back by some of our Hindu authorities to the instructions received by king Janaka of Videha, the legendary father of Lord Rāmacandra's bride Sītā, through his spiritual perceptors Yājñavalkya and Aṣṭāvakra.[154]

The Mujaddidī doctrine, whose practical aspect focusses on a precise knowledge of the subtle centres located in the human breast, represents the kernel of the entire *sādhanā* taught by the Kāyasth-*faqīrs* descending from Shāh Faḍl Aḥmad Khān. Like their Muslim ancestors in the *silsila*, they exalt its value

---

154. Yashpal, *Aṣṭāvakra-Gītāmṛta*, part I, Introduction, pp. 1-6. See also A.K. Coomaraswamy, 'Janaka and Yājñavalkya' in *Indian Historical Quarterly* 13 (1937), pp. 261-78.

as the most sublime and at the same time easiest and most accessible of all initiatory disciplines available to contemporary humanity. Hence, their main concern rests on the outline of different aspects of this science and the methods connected to it. Often, these are elaborated from the standpoint of traditional Hindu theories regarded as analogous to or at least compatible with those aspects too particular to the Islamic perspective to be readily transmitted to an audience increasingly less acquainted with the religious tenets of that tradition.

It is, therefore, important to distinguish between the purely theoretical background (*ta'līm-i 'ilmī*) and the practical aspects (*ta'lim-i 'amli*) of the *ṭarīqa* inherited by Rāmcandra from his Naqsbhandī shaikh. The former was originally based on and derived from a doctrinal background firmly anchored in the Islamic culture and its religious and spiritual tradition, including its images, rhetoric, technical language and other formal characteristics. For this reason, it had to undergo frequent reformulations which, as we have shown, are based to a large extent on the tradition of the Upaniṣad and the doctrines that developed later among the followers of the *nirguṇa-bhakti*. In contrast, the practical aspect comprising methods and specific techniques was largely deemed applicable to Muslims and non-Muslims alike since they are meant to act on the common ground represented by a human constitution subject to universal laws and principles.

After establishing the pivotal role of the *cakra-vidyā* in Rāmcandra's elaborations, we may now turn our attention to some specific notions regarding this science found not only in his own writings but also in several of his successors' works. An important notion encountered repeatedly among the authorities of Rāmcandra's lineage the *pañcakośa* theory expounded in detail in the *Taittirīya Upaniṣad*. It describes a series of five successive sheaths or veils (*kośa*) that cover the most intimate Self (*ātman*) located at the centre of every human being.[155] These veils are commonly represented by five concentric circles layered at an increasing distance around a nucleus constituted by the

155. *Taittirīya Upaniṣad*, III 1-10, I.5.1 and II.8.1.

non-manifested metaphysical Self (*avyākṛtaḥ ākāśa*) which is said to reside in the innermost 'secret chamber of the heart' (*guhā antarhṛdaya ākāśa*)[156] and referred to as *jīvātmā* following its descent into the corporeal frame.

This concept is assimilated by Rāmcandra to the current Sūfī image which depicts the heart as covered by an indefinite number of veils (*ḥijāb*) preventing ordinary human beings from the opportunity of direct witness (*mushāhada*) of the sublime Reality hidden in its innermost space (*'ain al-qalb*). According to this image, the progressive removal or penetration of these veils will eventually allow those capable of reaching the higher stages of the path through the 'purification of the soul' and the 'cleansing of the heart' to get a glimpse of this inner core. Rāmcandra, the author of the *Santmat Darśana* writes:

> To remove these coverings will be the correct way and represents a safe approach towards the final goal. At this [present] stage, innumerable coverings subsist around the Self. The covers which have been woven on our physical body, are in reality the samples of the outer circles of creation. The relation between them is like . . . that of the *brahmāṇḍa* and the *piṇḍa*. But the spiritual authorities . . . have tried to divide them into a series of five covers . . . in order to provide the opportunity to those who want to understand them. . . .[157]

There follows a detailed description of each of these five veils largely based on the description found in the Upaniṣad:

The first and outermost veil consists the *annamaya-kośa*, the covering made of and nourished by food (*anna*). It constitutes

---

156. Note the use of the term *ākāśa* here in reference to the transcendent principle whose seat is conventionally described as the heart considered to be the centre of the microcosm. Represented as a spaceless dot, it lies not only beyond the realm of manifestation but ultimately also beyond the informal realm of the *amr*, thus, identifying itself with the metaphysical Principle referred to in the Upaniṣad as *paramātmā* or Brahmā and analogous to the Sūfī concept of *al-dhāt*, the unqualified Essence of Allāh. Cf. *Chāndogya Upaniṣad*, VIII.3.1.

157. *SD*, p. 56.

the physical body composed of the gross elements (*bhūta*), the most exterior of all modes of manifestation. In Rāmcandra's interpretation, it is this gross body (*sthūla śarīra*) that dominates the soul to the extent of not considering itself apart from it, which is the reason why the human being characterised by ignorance (*avidyā*) attributies an excessive importance to the physical body.

The second cover, called *prāṇamaya-kośa* or the 'sheath made of breath', is constituted by the subtle substance (*prāṇa*) and its five functions, the five *vāyu*, which 'are situated at various places in the body where they perform special functions'.[158]The reflective condition of these five modalities which preside over the five physical organs and their respective faculty, i.e., the five *jñānendriya* and the five *karmendriya*, are also contained in this sheath. Rāmcandra calls them Dhanañjaya (lit. 'wealth acquiring', an epithet of Agni, the Hindu god of fire), Kūrma, (the tortoise and second *avatāra* of the Hindu god Viṣṇu which appears into the Purāṇic episode of the churning of the milk-ocean). Nāga, (the serpentine beings which in Hindu mythology are said to have sprung from the union of the sage Kaśyapa with his wife Kadru,[159] who populate one of the inferior regions of the Pātāla), Devadatta, (lit. the 'Divine gift' *Khudā-dād*) and Krikel.

The third covering is referred to as *manomaya-kośa*. It is characterised by the mental consciousness or the faculty of thought pertaining to the mind (*manas*), the organ which creates, elaborates and reflects the impressions received from the outside world. To explain the impact of this faculty on the human condition, Rāmcandra compares it to a silk worm that produces a thread from its own mouth, wrapping it continuously around itself until it remains protected by its newly created shield while yet remaining entangled by its own product, just like man whose mind continuously creates all sort of bindings for himself.[160] *Manas* presides over the subtle state co-ordinating

158. Cf. p. 337, no. 3.

159. *SD*, p. 58.

160. *Ibid.*

the impulses received from and sent to the ten *indriyas* which are its natural instruments. It is precisely through the interrelation between the mental sphere and the senses that the mind inclines itself towards the outer phenomenal world, creating apparently real yet ultimately illusory bindings for the soul. As the third of the five veils, the mental sphere occupies an intermediate position between the two outer and inner layers. In this mediating position, the mind, if brought under control through a rigorous and continuous discipline, can act as a true viceregent of the '(macro)-cosmic mind' (*brahmāṇḍī man,'aql-i kullī*) and in total harmony with it.

According to Rāmcandra, the 'curtain of the mind' can be removed by two means. The first consists of *śama*, the restraint of the sensual faculties resulting in a growing indifference to the outer objects through concentration, meditation, contemplation of and eventually identification with an abstract inner object.[161] The second is termed *dam* or self-command and resolute discipline, implying, in a Sūfī perspective, the transmutation of the *nafs-i lawāmma* into the *nafs-i muṭma'inna*.[162] The influence of Śrī Ramānujācarya on Rāmcandra, direct or indirect as that may be, becomes here quite evident.[163]

The fourth cover termed *vijñānamaya-kośa* or the 'cover of discriminating knowledge' (*vijñāna*), corresponds to the human intellect, seen as a reflection of the Cosmic Intellect (*buddhi*). Its principal characteristic is that of taking decisions (*viveka, quwwat-i tamīzī*), that is to say to evaluate the pros and contras of an idea and than to reach a decision on the base of a correct assessment.[164] The mind (*manas*) proposes, and the intellect

161. In these terms we recognise the four last members (*aṅga*) of the yogic process described by Patañjalī, here integrated with a Vedāntic intellectual background typical of a Rāja-Yoga perspective.

162. For a description of the positive and negative effects of the *manomaya-kośa* on the rest of the organism, see *AIB*, pp. 9-10.

163. The other faculties listed by Śrī Rāmānujācārya in his four-fold discipline (*sādhanā catuṣṭaya*) leading the *vedāntin* to the correct enquiry into the nature of the *Brahman* are: *viveka* (discrimination), *vairāgya* (non-attachment) and *mumukṣutva* (determination to reach liberation).

164. *VS*, p. 46.

either confirms or rejects the proposal.[165] With its help, man can catch a glimpse of Reality, though only as a brief flash comparable to a Sūfī *ḥāl*. In Sūfī terminology which reflects the religious perspective of Islam, a *ḥāl* refers to a spontaneous spiritual lightning said to be caused by the mercy of the Almighty as a concession to the pious and earnest seeker of Truth. In the Hindu doctrines, the *vijñānamaya-kośa* is said to be composed of the five subtle principles (*tanmātra*) of the five sensual faculties (*khawāṣṣ*, *jñānendriya*) providing at the same time the vital link between these and their principles.[166] However, notwithstanding its elevated degree of subtlety, even this condition can possibly lead to deception, for 'those who penetrate to it begin to obtain extraordinary powers' (*siddhī*, *kharq-i 'adāt*) of every kind, and the initiate could possibly feel so attracted by them that he misses the chance to rise back to the right stage. . . . '[167]

Enraptured by the flashes emanating from the radiance of *buddhi*, the disciple risks to remain allured by this light losing sight of the straight path that leads to the still distant final goal.[168] The shadow or reflection of *buddhi* corresponds to the same *ahaṅkāra* whose first determination in *manas* represents the immediately preceding veil. The danger for those not endowed with the ability to penetrate beyond the *vijñānamaya-kośa* is to remain entangled in its lower reflection in the individual domain, thus falling back into the incessant rotation of the wheel of *saṁsāra* which ensnares the 840,000 species (*lakh caurāsī*) that populate the Universe. This and the two preceding veils constitute the subtle body (*sūkṣma-śarīra*, *jism-i laṭīf*) and are therefore, comprehensively included in the term *nafs*.

Finally the fifth cover, which includes virtually all the possibilities of manifestation, is referred to as *ānandamaya-kośa*, the abode of bliss and joy (*ānanda*). It corresponds to the degree of *īśvara* which entirely transcending the individual

---

165. *SD*, p. 60.
166. *Mānavadharmaśāstra*, 1:17.
167. *SD*, p. 60.

dominion. Here the inner self is alone, contemplating itself free from the bonds of existence. Hence, it is defined as beatitude and characterised by inner peace (*śānti*, *sukūn*). Rāmcandra remarks that it can be considered as the knot (*barzakhī*) that ties up the inanimate, substantial plane (*jar*) with the reviving force of universal conscience (*cetana*) on a very subtle level, so subtle as to subsist only nominally. This fifth cover can be identified with the 'causal body' (*kāraṇa-śarīra*)[169] since it contains the principles or causes of the former two 'bodies'. If considered in relation to the macrocosmic planes (*'ālam-i kabīr*), contemplated by the Mujaddidīs, it corresponds to the *'ālam-i amr* said to contain the non-existence (*'adam*) of the five subtleties whose reflected existence has descended into the physical frame (*qālib*) of the human being pertaining to the *'ālam-i khalq*. From a microcosmic point of view, the *ānandamaya-kośa* anticipates immediately the state of *sat-cit-ānanda*. It preludes to the total identity of the Being as knowing subject (*sat*), the known object (*ānanda*) and the universal conscience (*cit*). The later is pure knowledge linking the two former in a unique entity characteristic of the pure Being that 'knows itself through itself', and as such corresponds exactly to what the Sūfī experiences in the 'abode of bewilderment' (*maqām-i ḥairat*).[170]

---

168. This stands at the base of the warnings issued by many authorities in the esoteric traditions of both Islam and Hinduism, the former mainly in relation to the states of ecstasy linked to the attainment of the degree of 'lower sainthood' (*wilāyat-i ṣughrā*) while the latter links this sort of danger with the gradual awakening of the inferior *cakras* through the ascent of the *kuṇḍalini-śakti* and the connected disclosure of their lotus-petals through horizontal expansion.

169 *SD*, pp. 61-2;*VS*, pp. 58-9. Obviously, the term 'body' is used in this context by analogy with the preceding two realms. This degree lies above the so-called realm of form (*'ālam-i ajsām*), an alternative denomination of the *khalq* used by the Naqshbandīs, being a body by conventional definition limited by its outer form (*ṣūrat* or *rūpa*) which expands into space and whose existence lasts for a certain amount of time.

170. *SD*, p. 26. Cf. Réné Guénon, *Becoming to Man according to the Vedānta*, ch.14, pp. 97-8, no. 2.

This image of the human constitution in terms of the quintuple sheaths of the Self as expounded by the *Taittirīya Upaniṣad*, and integrated by Rāmcandra with many Sūfī concepts, re-proposes the symbolism of the number five peculiar to the *'ilm-i laṭā'if*. Five is the number of the subtle principles that govern each of the two cosmic divisions, five (plus one, since the *laṭīfa-i rūḥ* is qualified by a double prophetic function) is the number of the prophets presiding over the subtle centres on the spititual plane of the *amr*, and five is the number of the corrsponding irradiations (*tajalliyāt*) of the essence of the Divine Reality (*al-Ḥaqq*) which determine the planes of contingency,[171] each corresponding to a degree of sainthood conceived as successive stages on the inner path.

Although few of these features so intimately related to an Islamic context appear anywhere expressedly mentioned by the *silsila*'s Hindu authorities, the similarity between the doctrine described in the Upaniṣad and the Sūfī doctrine of Ibn al-'Arabī in his theory of the quintuple 'planes of existence' (*ḥaḍrāt-i khamsa*) irradiating from the source of the Essence (*al-dhāt*),[172] later absorbed and integrated into the all-comprehensive 'science of the subtle centres' by the Mujaddidī, is too striking to remain unnoticed. The analogy between the two doctrines becomes undeniable if related to the 'science of the quintuple fire' (*pāñcāgni-vidyā*) described by the *Chāndogya Upaniṣad* and mentioned by our Hindu *faqīr*s in connection with the spiritual light (*satprakāśa*) and its irradiations. It is enhanced by the descending perspective used in both cases regarding the Principle that apparently descends step after step into the realm of manifestation clothing Itself into more and more veils. On the other hand, the Mujaddidī concept of the successive stages of sainthood describe an ascending perspective analogous to that

171. Cf. *MnS*, pp. 20/35.

172. For parallels between the *Shaikh al-Akbar* and the *Mujaddid*, see the article by Mir Valiuddin, 'Reconciliation between Ibn 'Arabi's *Wahdat-i Wujud* and the Mujaddid's *Wahdat-i Shuhud*', in *IC* 25 (1951), pp. 43-51. For a broader traditional discussion, cf. Shāh Walī Allāh's *Maktūb-i Madanī in Tafhīmat al-Ilāhiyya*, 2 vols., Shah Wali Allah Academy, Hyderabad (Sind).

assumed by the *Taittirīya Upaniṣad*. Both points of view are harmoniously resumed by the 'science of the subtle centres' whose stress lies, however, on the practical aspect of reintegration depicting the stages traversed by the disciple along the same path taken by the Divine power during the unfolding process of manifestation, but in the opposite direction.[173]

Similarly, there is yet another important concept described in the Upaniṣad and frequently used by Rāmcandra and his successors that must be mentioned here, although it appears less immediately reconcilable with the *'ilm-i laṭā'if* than the preceding one. This classifies the conditions of the microcosmic *jīvātmā* into four major categories in conformity with the theory expounded in the *Māṇḍūkya Upaniṣad* and reiterates the pattern of the three bodies. Proceeding from the bottom upwards, the first of these conditions is referred to as *viśva* or Vaiśvānara (lit. Universal Man) and has its seat in the waking state (*jāgṛta-avasthā*) characterised by the sensory perception and knowledge of the external objects on the gross level experienced by the *sthūla-śarīra*.[174] Accordingly, the type of beatitude (*ānanda*) experienced by man at this stage is, defined as *viṣayānanda*, the beatitude caused through the contact with the multiple objects of the senses (*viṣaya*), considered the lowest and most effimerous sort of joy. It represents the first goal at which any spiritual discipline (*sādhanā*) aims reached by checking and restraining the senses while detaching them from these external objects and turning them inwards in order to transmute the unstable and superficial state of joy (*sukha*) the provoke, always prone to turn into sorrow (*duḥkha*) into a more permanent state of beatitude.[175]Hence, the waking state stands for the entangle-ment of the self in the coarsest degrees of manifestation while at the same time representing the starting point and base for a re-ascent towards the superior states. It is

173. *AY*, pp. 162-3.

174. *VS*, p. 44. Cf. also *SD*, pp. 31-2; *AY*, p. 64 citing *Māṇḍūkya Upaniṣad*, Śruti 3. According to this description, the Vaiśvānara has seven limbs and nineteen mouths, the latter corresponding to the ten *indriyas*, the five *prāṇas*, *manas*, *buddhi*, *ahaṅkāra* and *citta*.

175. *AY*, p. 64.

in this sense that Rāmcandra reiterates the analogy used by the Vedānta between the physical body, the waking state and the *virāṭ* (sometimes also spelt as *virāj*), which is intended as the reflection of the cosmic intelligence on the gross plane where it governs the corporeal state.[176]

Switching over to the Sūfī imagery, the Hindu masters teach that this reflection emanates from the pure light of the Universal Intellect (*'aql-i kullī*) and descends from its topmost position in the cosmos identified with the *'arsh al-muḥīṭ* along a vertical axis into the realm of creation. Eventually it reaches, at the very bottom of the *khalq*, the gross organ of the heart (*qalb-i mudawwarī*, lit. the 'round-shaped heart'),[177] from where it irradiates into the entire human organism. It animates that layer of the human soul revolved towards the outside world, attracted by and exposed to all kinds of sensual desires and distractions which corrupt its integrity and plunge it into the continuous ups and downs of pleasure and suffering permeated by the darkness of *tamas*.[178]

The second condition of the *jīvātmā*, corresponding to the subtle body (*sūkṣma-śarīra* or *jism-i laṭīf*), is called *taijasa*.[179] It

176. *VS*, p. 44. There is a correspondence with the first degree of sainthood in relation to Ādam, like the Vaiśvānara put in relation to the *laṭīfa-i qalb*. In its macrocosmic sense, the term *virāj* corresponds to the 'attribute of creation' (*ṣifat-i takwīn*).

177. Literally 'circular heart', this term underlines the peripherical position of this level as compared to that of the following stages corresponding more properly to the pivotal role the heart plays in the human organism. However, the gradual progression from this outer level towards the inner core renders the idea of a 'purification of the heart' (*taṣfiya-i qalb*) achieved in the course of the post-initiatory process. It is also said to act as the base (*bunyād*) and principle (*aṣl*) of the remaining four subtle organs of the *'ālam-i amr* where it occupies the lowest rank, closest to the *barzakh*. Cf. *MaS*, p. 34.

178. *SD*, p. 40.

179. *VS*, p. 45. Cf. also *Māṇḍūkya Upaniṣad*, *śruti* 4. *Taijasa*, lit. 'radiance', 'splendour', but loosely rendered by Rāmcandra as 'inconstant, unsteady' (*cañcala*) because of the fickle nature of the mental consciousness that continuously produces vortexes of thoughts (*citta-vṛtti*) beyond our control and that has its seat in the state of dreaming (*svapna-avasthā*). The term is used in reference to the luminous →

refers to the inner states of the mind and, in comparison with the former states, is one step closer to the unconditioned *ātman*. While the body lies motionless in sleep, the current of life fuelled through the incessant exchange of information received from and projected towards the outer world is temporarily interrupted and the senses are withdrawn into the inner faculty (*antaḥkaraṇa*).[180]

Characterised by a relatively higher degree of minuteness, its objects consist exclusively in mental images based on the elaboration of subtle forms which derive their existence from the mental impressions (*saṁskāra*) left behind by the impact with the external objects during the waking state. At this level, the mind enjoys a comparatively greater freedom than in the waking state and every imaginable thing or situation can combine and produce itself in a far larger range of possibilities (Rāmcandra quotes the idea of a winged elephant, the capacity of flying, etc.) in order to provoke a sensation of joy and sorrow while maintaining a degree of duality. The beatitude experienced at this level is called *vāsanānanda* or 'beatitude caused by imagination'. Since it still preserves the possibility of replunging into the opposite states of sadness, fear and affliction, its nature is deemed as essentially ephemeral and hence does not conform to the sublime degree of *ānanda*.[181] Moreover, the reliance on form in the ideas which govern it confirms its relation with the individual dominion of manifestation.

→ quality of the igneous element that characterises the gods when intended as presiding over the various subtle faculties enveloped in their potential state and stands for the refraction at this level into multiple shades and colours of the intelligible light (*satprakāśa*).

180. In Patañjali's *Aṣṭāṅga Yoga* doctrine, this withdrawing of the senses is known as *pratyāhāra* and constitutes an important preliminary stage for the attainment of *ekāgratā*, the concentration fixed on one single object which is defined by the Sūfis as *yaksūī*.

181. *AY*, p. 64. Bṛj Mohan Lāl makes an interesting note in this context which is worth quoting:

> . . . yes certainly, the ability to restrain the mind and to follow the *sādhanā* wholeheartedly is not a common thing. [The mind] contains that serpent in form of a vortex of mental impressions pertaining to the ceaseless current of life (*saṁsāra*) which only Lord Kṛṣṇa can tame with the power of his spiritual attention (*tawajjuh*). →

This subtle state is governed by a microcosmic reflection of the golden light emanating from the *hiraṇyagarbha*, situated at the centre of that horizontal plane along which the Universe develops its indefinite number of possibilities. In the human constitution, it is identified by Rāmcandra with the *qalb-i ṣanawbarī*, the pinecone-shaped heart referred to in the often quoted tradition 'you should know that, no doubt, inside the human body there is a piece of flesh — if its condition is sound the whole body is sound, but if it is spoiled the entire body is corrupt' refers.[182] In Rāmcandra's doctrinal vision, this degree corresponds to the reproachable soul (*nafs-i lawāmma*) in the phase of transmutation between the blameable vices and the laudable virtues dominated by the tendencies characterised respectively by *rajas* and *sattva*.[183]

The third condition of the *jīvātmā* is called *prājña* (lit. 'integral knowledge') and corresponds to the state of deep sleep (*suṣupta avasthā*) in which the individual no longer experiences any desire and dreams.[184] Properly speaking, in this condition the 'living Self' is no longer tied to the limiting conditions of human life (*jīva*) in the formal world, since its natural seat is the 'causal body' which is not really distinguished from *ātman* itself. As Rāmcandra remarks:

> When you and I reach this state, our relations with the senses cease altogether to subsist; no sensation exists there and only the minute Self remains.[185]

→ Lord Krishna is our real *satguru* in this world whose sacred spiritual power puts to rights our path by the means of the subtle sound current (*sūrat śabda*) in subduing the power of the *vāsanā*. He reveals a method to be followed during the spiritual practice by which, enlarging upon us the ocean of His compassion and coadiuvated by the means of His *tawajjuh*, he burns and washes away the impressions and vortexes of thought from our consciousness filling our mind with real beatitude, a perception often experienced during the *satsang*. (p. 64)

182. Related by Ibn Māja and quoted by Shāh Abūl Ḥasan in *MaS*, pp. 34-5.

183. *SD*, p. 41.

184. *Māṇḍūkya Upaniṣad, śruti* 5.

185. Cf. *SD*, p. 33; *VS*, p. 45.

In this state of 'mental sleep' (*man kī nīnd*), only the *ātmā* remains present enjoying pure beatitude in Itself.[186] Free from any qualification derived from the contact with the formal world, It is beyond the feeble alteration between joy (*sukha*) and pain (*duḥkha*) and confers upon the mind a condition of absolute peace (*śānti, sukūn*).[187]

On a microcosmic scale it represents the unmanifested (*avyakta*) or non-existent principle (*'adam*) and immediate cause (*kāraṇa*, hence *kāraṇa-śarīra* or 'causal body') of the stage of manifestation (*vyakta*) or existence (*wujūd*), which is situated on the level of pure spirituality. 'All knowledge of the world, such as moral principles or worldly and spiritual issues, has been bestowed on the human being through this stage alone. Divine revelations (*kashf*) are received at this stage [characterised by] annihilation (*fanā*), deep meditation (*murāqaba*) and contemplation (*samādhi*) . . . .'[188] Its centre in the human organism is described as the 'blue lotus-heart' (*qalb-i nilofarī*) corresponding to the pacified soul (*nafs-i muṭma'inna*) in the state of self-effacement (*maḥwiyat, istighrāq, be-khudī*), dominated by *sattva*.[189]

The light that irradiates from that lotus-heart is identified by Rāmcandra with *buddhi* or *'aql-i kullī* on a macrocosmic plane, the super-rational faculty through which the Divine revelation is communicated directly between the transcendent principle of Being (*īśvara*) and the realm of immanence and which crosses and illuminates the entire dominion of the *'ālam-*

---

186. Hence, the identification with the *ānandamaya-kośa* and the connected state of *sat-cit-ānanda*.

187 In order to further exemplify the underlying concept of unity transcending all residuous traces of duality, Rāmcandra quotes a passage from the *Vedānta Upaniṣad*:

'O Maitrayi, where two beings exist, one hears the other, one touches the other, one knows the other and one sees the other. Where only one exists, how will one hear, touch, know and see the other. . .'. Cf. *VS*, pp. 54-5.

188. *SD*, p. 41.

189. The Vedānta identifies it with the inner co-ordinator (*antaryāmī*) mentioned in the *Māṇḍūkya Upaniṣad*, Cf. *AIB*, pp. 23 and 32.

i amr; its original source is the *'arsh-i muḥīṭ*, analogous to *īśvara* in the Yoga doctrines or *sarveśvara* as in the Upaniṣad.[190]

Finally, the fourth stage corresponds to the *turīya* or *caturtha* (lit. 'the fourth').[191] According to Rāmcandra, this fourth stage lies beyond the state of *sat-cit-ānanda* and characterises the pure Being. Only the most perfect saints are aware of it. In Sūfī terminology, it is assimilated to the *'ālam-i lāhūt*, the realm of Divine Ipseity (*ghaib huwiyat*) where the Self is altogether pure from any determination (*lā-ta'ayyun*) whence the fourth stage of the saints is said to begin. In the words of Rāmcandra,

> if one attains or acquires the power of reaching this stage at his own will and whenever he likes during his lifetime, he will experience a sublime and unparalleled pleasure unmatched by any worldly pleasure.[192]

The *Māṇḍūkya Upaniṣad* describes this utmost degree of consciousness in exclusively negative terms. Unlike the preceding state of *prajña* that throughout implies the chance of a return to the lower stages, it is permanent and once attained cannot possibly be lost. But while Rāmcandra agrees with the position held by the Vedānta that the ultimate goal of human life (*paramārtha*, *maqṣad*) effectively consists of the attainment of beatitude (*ānanda*), he interprets this in accordance with his joint Mujaddidī-Vaiṣṇava perspective reflecting a devotional attitude rather than the purely gnostic perspective of Śrī Śaṅka-rācārya in his comments on the major Upaniṣad or, in the Sūfī context, by Ibn al-'Arabī.

Rāmcandra remarks:

> The Śāstras affirm that the aim of humanity lies in bringing to an end all affliction (*duḥkha*) while attaining

---

190. Cf. *Māṇḍūkya Upaniṣad*, *śruti* 6: 'This [*prajña*] is the lord of all, this is the knower of all, this is the inner ordinator; this is the source of all, this is the beginning and end of beings . . .'.

191. *VS*, p. 56. Cf. also *Bṛhadāraṇyaka Upaniṣad,* V.14.3.

192. *SD*, p. 35. Elsewhere, the kind of beatitude characteristic of this stage is descibed as 'Supreme Beatitude' (*paramānanda, ṣarūr-i 'azīm*).

> utmost Beatitude. This proves that the knowledge as intended by the Veda does not represent the aim on its own account but rather that the aim of that very knowledge is only the creation of toil (*rāḥat*) and . . . [the immersion into] Beatitude. . . . The secret lies in *ānanda* while the term *paramānanda* has been used in reference to this subtle thought. *Paramānanda* is identical to the great harmony (*viśāl ham-aghoshī*) which, in a figurative and technical context, has assumed the meaning of 'reverential devotion' (*upāsanā*). This term could no doubt be used in the sense of union (*milāp*) but its figurative and technical meaning is 'labour and toil' ('*amal o shaghl*). So, it has not been used and the term *upāsanā* has been regarded as sufficient. This *paramānanda* corresponds to *upāsanā* at the condition that its original end is accomplished. For this reason, *upāsanā* is pre-eminent and superior to *jñāna*.[193]

This paragraph eloquently exemplifies the agreement possible between the descending perspective of the Mujaddidiya and its stress on the 'merciful' aspect of the Divinity culminating in the state of 'pure servanthood' ('*ubūdiyat-i ṣarfa*). The description is coined on the ideal image of the prophet of Islam here transferred into a Vaiṣṇava context in which the prevailing tendency of selfless service and devotion that combines action (*karma*), knowledge (*jñāna*) and self-surrender in devotional love (*bhakti*) as taught in the *Bhagavad Gītā* integrates itself into the position held by Rāmānujācārya's viśiṣṭādavaita.

If on one hand this reflects the Mujaddidī influence on Rāmcandra's way of interpreting and exposing the *brahma-vidyā*, it is also important to note how well his position agrees with many currents within the mainstream of the *bhakti*-movement to which he was connected. It, therefore, strengthens the idea of an affinity between these two currents in both traditions and provides a remarkable instance of the often

193. *VS*, p. 63.

invoked reciprocal influences between Islamic esoterism and the devotionally oriented *sant*-movement, part of a trend first apparent in mediaeval Hinduism and which in this case goes back in its principles to the eighteenth-century figures of Mīrzā Maẓhar Jān-i Jānān and Tulsī Saḥib Hāthrasī.

Nevertheless, many of Rāmcandra's theoretical exposi-tions confirm the importance of the metaphorical teachings of the Upaniṣad hold in the formulation of his theories. In connection with the stages of Being explained in the *Māṇḍūkya Upaniṣad*, Rāmcandra repeatedly returns to the above-mentioned three levels of the human constitution, i.e., body, soul and spirit (*jism, dil wa rūḥ*) and their correspondence to the states of wakening, dreaming and deep sleep, and hints at the existence of a further, transcending degree as follows:

> . . . since the faculty of comprehension of most people remains limited to these three [stages of Being] and in their utter bewilderment they do not understand even these according to their proper meaning, I have insisted on their description through and through. The ancient *rishis* and *munis* used to declare: '*neti, neti*', that is to say 'neither this nor that'; further beyond, whatsoever can be said consists of mere hints (*ishāra-i maḥẓ*) which only a few exceptional people can comprehend. The ultimate stir and object of the heart's desire aims neither at *īśvara* nor at Brahmā nor at Pārabrahma . . . this is the fourth foot of the saints, . . . for the sake of telling and listening it is called the 'fourth' (*turīya*). . . .[194]

Here, the metaphysical dimension of Rāmcandra's *sādhanā* is seen to accept the impossibility of describing the undefinable in affirmative terms while at the same time rejecting the adequacy of some of the most peculiar Upaniṣad terminology regarding transcendent principles. Nevertheless, he himself repeatedly uses the term *turīya* to designate the unfathomable (*agam*) and invisible (*alakh*) highest Truth the disclosure of which 'cannot be obtained through the means of reason and tongue'. This can

194. *VS*, pp. 64-5.

be easily explained by his adherence to the *nirguṇa* viewpoint of Kabīr-panth and the Nānak-panth. It is, moreover, is perfectly coherent with the *shuhūdī* doctrine of the Mujaddidīs that locates the most intimate essence of Allāh at a level unattainable for the contingent creature, at least in its verbal expression, excluding the possibility of a total identity between Him and them.

Significantly, nowhere in Rāmcandra's works is the classical Sūfī term *al-Ḥaqq* used to describe metaphysical Reality. This accounts for his preference of the *turīya* (of the Upaniṣadic) which maintains the aura of the inscrutable mystery intended by this passage:

> The eye sees everything except itself, the nose smells everything except itself, the ear hears everything except itself, you see everything except yourself, all this is ignorance (*ajñāna*)! To dispel it is necessary to seek assistance of a fictitious mirror (*ā'īna-i maṣnū'ī*). . . . Slowly, slowly, when you will behold your reflection (*'aks*) in the mirror you will acquire certainty and turn silent refraining from any further discussion. . . .[195]

Knowledge is not despised in itself. It is considered as a necessary prerequisite for the removal of the veils of ignorance, but it must not be confounded with the goal itself since for Rāmcandra it still implies the residual persistence of a subtle degree of duality:

> In this world, until you and I are perceived through the exterior glance, we will present the appearance of body-worship (*jism-parastī*); we try to depict the *ātmā*, *brahma*, *rūḥ*, etc., as bodies, although, strictly speaking, they are not. Gross, subtle and casual, all three are names for corporeal degrees: verily, *nāma* and *rūpa*, *nirākāra* and *sākāra*, *nirguṇa* and *saguṇa* still pertain to this stage, *neti*, *neti*.[196]

---

195. *VS*, p. 65.
196. *Ibid.*, p. 66.

The recognition of non-duality as the highest degree of realisation which is maintained in the ancient formula *neti neti* as the only possible description of the 'fourth stage' contrasts with the author's rejection of the terms used in the Vedānta doctrines to design the Supreme Principle. Both the *ātman* and *Brahman* are seen as qualifying only a preliminary stage of that ultimate degree. In the language of the Mujaddidīs, this is described as the 'station of stupor' (*maqām-i ḥairat*) and as the 'forgetfulness (*ghaflat*) of which the inadvertent are negligent', which is linked to the journey of return (*rujū'*) of the six subtleties (*laṭā'if-i satta*) to the physical frame of the body (*qālib*).[197] For the Mujaddidīs, it constitutes the perfection of the human condition in virtue of the reflection of the prophetic perfection attained through the total realisation of the *'ilm-i laṭā'if.*

As Shāh Abūl Ḥasan states at the end of a chapter dealing with the subtle centres:

> Ḥaḍrat Naqshband — may Allāh bless his sepulchre! — has affirmed that he had been blessed with the disclosure of a *ṭarīqa* which can be attained with certainty and whose benefits are numerous. It implies no deprivation or any striving. . . . His successors have further classified and enlightened this noble path . . . to the extent of letting there rise the sun of perfection on the horizon of right guidance. Ḥaḍrat Imām-i Rabbānī Mujaddid Alf-i Thānī Shaikh Aḥmad Sirhindī — may Allāh bless his sepulchre! — has illuminated a world rendering this path of glorious rank (*rāh-i 'azīm al-martabāt*) a royal way of multiple advantages (*shāhrāh-i kathīr al manfa'āt*) and taking it to the furthest limit. . . .[198]

The higher stages of spiritual realisation

The higher stages of spiritual realisation described by Rāmcandra and his successors are too intimately related to the *'ilm-*

---

197. Cf. *MaS*, pp. 26/43. Cf. also *Kena Upaniṣad*, II.1-3.

198. *MaS*, pp. 28-9/47.

i laṭā'if or *cakra-vidyā* to be conceived in isolation of it. It is, therefore, appropriate to consider these two aspects of the *ṭarīqa* or *sādhanā* as complementary sides of a single medal bringing together the theoretical (*'ilmī*) and the practical (*'amlī*) aspects of the esoteric science.

We have already seen that at the beginning of the Mujaddidī path all attention remains focussed on the five subtle organs of the spiritual sphere located in the human breast, while the five lower *laṭā'if* identified with the four gross elements and the lower soul gain importance only in the more advanced stages of the initiatic process. It is, therefore, not surprising that Rāmcandra largely adopted these teachings of his Mujaddidī ancestors. In one of his major works he explains:

> The human body (*jism*) or microcosm (*piṇḍa śarīra*) contains the *hṛdaya-cakra* which, in its turn, contains five mansions (*maqāmāt*) that constitute the reflections in this body of five stations of the macrocosm (*'ālam-i kabīr, brahmāṇḍa*). They are: *laṭīfa-i qalb*, *laṭīfa-i rūḥ*, *laṭīfa-i sirr*, *laṭīfa-i khafī* and *laṭīfa-i akhfā*.[199]

Basing himself partially on notions articulated by Shāh Walī Allāh Dihlawī (*d.* AD 1761) in the introductory chapter of a treatise mainly concerned with a particular elaboration of the Mujaddidī *'ilm-i laṭā'if*,[200] the author explains the differences in the natures of individuals as the result of an innate predominance of one or more subtle organs over the others. Hence, derives for him the necessity of the perfect spiritual guide (*ustād-i kāmil*) who can carefully scrutinise the inner states of his disciple, identify and distinguish the weak and strong components in his breast, and eventually recommend him the appropriate spiritual practice (*abhyāsa*) to follow. For the disciple the main stress is thereby laid on focussing primarily

199. *TP*, pp. 40-1.

200. Cf. Shāh Walīullah of Delhi, *The Sacred Knowledge of the Higher Functions of the Mind*, the English translation of the work *Altāf al-Quds*, by Prof. G.N. Jalbani, ch. I, p. 5. This version unfortunately lacks the explanatory material necessary to the English reader for a better understanding of the complex docterinal issues involved in this treatise.

on those subtle organs whose natural constitution is strong and more developed, while it is the shaikh's task to identify, and successively to strengthen and rectify through his spiritual attention (*tawajjuh*) those spiritual organs which are less developed.

Such a procedure constitutes nowadays an integral part of the teachings current among the authorities in the Mujaddidī lineage and has been adopted by the masters of the Hindu offshoot. It allows the neophyte to concentrate entirely on the immediate goal of awakening and reconducting the latent spiritual principles from their location in the breast back to their original sites in the 'world of order' without involving any major delay, while leaving most efforts and a correct supervision on the shaikh. This shift in competence and responsibility, thus, compares positively with the hitherto conventional method of gradual integration of each single *laṭīfa* one by one,[201] since, we are reminded by the traditional authorities, 'the human lifespan in our present time is short and chances to reach the final stage (*manzil-i ākhirī*) have become extremely difficult, nay rather impossible'.

Moreover, it is possible that the master may identify one particular *laṭīfa* which, if activated through persistent application by the disciple and further assisted by his shaikh's *tawajjuh*, may provoke a sort of chain reaction in the disciple's inner states thereby causing the remaining organs to awaken spontaneously. So, the first innovative steps introduced by Bahā al-Dīn al-Naqshband, to adapt the order's methodology to the changing requirements of difficult historical periods, were followed by the reformulation of the doctrine and the description of the 'science of the subtle centres' by Shaikh Aḥmad Sirhindī. From the eighteeth century onwards yet another sign of that tendency to shift more and more responsibility from the disciple to the spiritual preceptor becomes evident. Further confirming the theory previously advanced, Rāmcandra writes in his hybrid Hindu-Muslim style:

---

201. Cf. *MaS*, pp. 21/38-9 and *HdT*, pp. 10-11. Both stress the importance of the master's *tawajjuh* in accelerating the process.

> Before [Bahā al-Dīn], our spiritual ancestors used to begin their spiritual practice (*abhyāsa*) from the *gudā-cakra*, but he commanded that the following generations should abandon this practice of focussing on these lower (*siflī*), purely human stations (*maqāmāt-i nāsūtī*) and proceed instead to awaken the subtleties of the intermediate state (*maqām-i malakūtī*) pertaining to the *hṛdaya-cakra* according to a precise order of succession, beginning with the *qalb* and advancing gradually upwards; once this process is completed, [the initiate] should proceed to the *nuqṭa-i suwaida* or *prāṇa-bindu*, also called *nafs-i nāṭiqa*. Accordingly, the ancient Naqshbandī masters prior to Shaikh Aḥmad Sirhindī Alf-i Thānī — the mercy of Allāh be upon him! — and those not related to [his lineage] still practise that method. . . .
>
> The authorities after him went on correcting it here and there and to the extent they were acquainted with this science, thought to further clarify, shorten and facilitate its practice . . . [Shaikh Aḥmad] considered the purification of one single among the five spiritual organs of the *hṛdaya*, namely the *laṭīfa-i qalb*, through perfect spiritual attention as sufficient, the remaining organs being included summarily in its fold. He then sanctioned immediate progress to the *nafs-i nāṭiqa* in one step and with the second step directly to the lotus of one-thousand petals (*sahaśra dala-kamala*) and the *trikuṭi*. . . .[202]

Without naming and explaining any of them, Rāmcandra mentions the existence of twenty-one circles or stages (*dawā'ir*, *cakras*) contemplated in the *ṭarīqa* of Shaikh Aḥmad Sirhindī and his followers. His description contains an obvious though somewhat ambiguously formulated hint at the twenty visualisations or contemplations (*murāqabāt*) which are past of the seven major planes of the Mujaddidī *sulūk*, with the addition of one further degree, that of Supreme Identification.[203]

---

202. *TP*, pp. 43-4.

203. Cf. *MaS*, p. 9 (only in Urdu version).

The paragraph quoted above sums up the position assumed during the first phase of the Hindu integration of the Islamic doctrine, while also providing some clue as to the possible sources used in this process. As the integration of entire paragraphs from works by Shāh Walī Allāh Dihlawī had already suggested, the conciliatory position proposed by this outstanding scholar between the predominantly intellectual and metaphysical perspective of Ibn al-'Arabī's *waḥdat al-wujūd* and the devotional and dynamic attitude that lies at the base of Shaikh Aḥmad's doctrines has certainly exercised some influence on Rāmcandra and his successors. The re-elaboration of the *'ilm-i laṭā'if* or transmitted in the Mujaddidiyya and encountered, for instance, in Shāh Walī Allāh's[204] treatise *Altāf al-Quds fī ma'rifat-i laṭā'if al-nafs* (The sacred knowledge of the higher functions of the mind) and the *Al-Tafhīmat al-Ilāhiyya* (The Divine Instructions),[205] show some elements which either directly or indirectly through later, already Hinduised, sources hint at a possible link or source of inspiration between this renowned Mujaddidī authority and the Hindu masters of this lineage. Especially Shāh Walī Allāh Dihlawī's reshaped and expanded model of the superseding and interconnected levels of spiritual organs located inside the human aggregate, which introduces the idea of an additional third series of five *laṭā'if* beyond the subtle organs contained in the *maqām-i sīna* or *hr̥daya-cakra*,[206] are found in a similar fashion in the teachings promoted by Rāmcandra and his successors.

---

204. Very little substantial information regarding the intellectual relationship between these two contemporary leaders at Delhi is available to modern scholarship which could help to show how this process led eventually to the formation of two parallel though contrasting currents in Naqshbandī leadership under their successors. Cf. K.A. Nizami, 'Shāh Walī Allāh of Delhi: His thought and contribution' in *IC* 54, 1980, pp. 141-53.

205. *Al-Tafhīmāt al-Ilāhiyya*, 2 vols., Shāh Walī Allāh Academy, Hyderabad (Sind), 1973.

206. Cf. Sabih Ahmad Kamali, 'The concept of human nature in *Hujjat Allāh al-Bāligha*', in *IC* 36, 1962, pp. 207-24, and Marcia K. Hermansen's 'Shah Wali Allah of Delhi's Arrangement of the Subtle Spiritual Centres (*laṭā'if*)' in *StI*, 1982, pp. 137-50.

On the other hand, although Rāmcandra repeatedly stresses Shaikh Aḥmad Sirhindī's authorship of the revised, accelerated process of focussing on one single of the five organs in the breast (preferably the *laṭifa-i qalb*) before proceeding directly to the subtle organ related to the 'seat of the rational faculty' (*nafs-i nāṭiqa*) and other more sublime organs, he does not name these latter ones along Sūfī lines but terms them as *sahasra-dala-kamala* and *trikuṭī*. The use of these terms as well as the term *prāṇabindu* for the Sūfī *nafs-i nāṭiqa* takes us once more back to the terminology of the Tantravāda and Haṭha-Yoga doctrines where these terms designate three different stations inside the causal body situated in the human skull.

The *prāṇabindu* is put in relation with the minute point (*bindu*) situated at the top of the crescent that stretches act above the *ājñā-cakra* (lit. the subtle centre of the command — *ājñā,* the Sanskrit equivalent to the Arabic term *amr*),[207] a spot on the forefront located between the eyebrows in correspondence of the third eye of Lord Śiva (*śīva-netra*). The *sahasra-dala-kamala* or centre of the 'one thousand petalled lotus' is located somewhere near the centre of the brain and is considered to be the residence of Paraśiva and location of the supreme *bindu* which contains the twenty-fold sound comprising the letters of the Devanāgarī alphabet.[208] Further upwards *trikuṭī* (lit. 'the three peaks') hints at a subtle organ situated somewhere between the *sahasra-dala-kamala* and the *brahmarandhra*, the 'crown of Brahmā' at the apex of the head which is directly connected with the *mukti-dvāra*, the 'gate of liberation' and final link between the individual and the Universe.

Although helpful as primary model, a comparison of this pattern with the classical Haṭha-Yoga doctrines alone is unsuffi-

---

207. Cf. *Ṣaṭacakra-nirūpaṇa*, verses 32-5. In the comment on verse 32 of the English version of this treatise edited by Sir John Woodroffe *alias* Arthur Avalon under the title *The Serpent Power* adds an explanation from the *Gautamaja Tantra*: 'The command of the *guru* is transmitted here [in the *ājñā-cakra*], hence, it is called the spot of the command. . .'. Cf. *The Serpent Power*, p. 302.

208. Being 50 the total number of letters of the Sanskrit alphabet (also referred to as *śabda-mālā*, the sound-garland), 50 x 20 = 1,000.

cient for the understanding of the entire process of conciliation and assimiliation attempted by Rāmcandra. Again, it is through the links of his *paramparā* with the Kabīr-panth and its more recent *nirguṇa* offshoots like of the Rādhāsoāmīs, that provide further clues.

In a much later work compiled by one of the latest disciples to join Rāmcandra's *satsang*, which is purportedly based on some posthumously discovered manuscripts of the late master,[209] we come across a more detailed description of the 'science of the subtle centres'. The descriptions it contains shed further light on the origin and the way this science fits into the frame of Rāmcandra's cosmological and metaphysical considerations. The scheme developed in that work is expressedly said to be based on the teachings of the *Kabīr-panthīs*. It develops around the three major realms of universal existence, viz., gross, subtle and causal, named respectively as *piṇḍa*, *aṇḍa* and *brahmāṇḍa*, and illustrates the succeeding steps of spiritual ascent (*'urūj*, *utthān*). Each of these three major dominions contains six levels making a total of eighteen. These represent the stages of the gradual descent of the *ātman* into the contingent realm of existence, thus, being known as *jīvātmā* or 'living self'. At the same time, they constitute the natural track that can be followed by the individual in the opposite direction when re-ascending the path leading gradually towards liberation from the conditions of existence.[210]

Starting from below, the first series of six levels pertaining to the gross realm (*piṇḍa*) consists of the five subtle centres,

---

209. Har Nārāyaṇ Saksenā *Sākṣātkār kā Rahasya*. This Hindī version of the original Urdu text follows a previous English translation by the same editor published in 1986 under the title *The Secret of Realization*. However, I base myself on the Hindī version since it more faithfully reflects the technical vocabulary and style used by the authorities of this order.

210. *Sākṣātkār kā Rahasya*, pp. 25-7. In agreement with the Tantra doctrines, Har Nārāyaṇ Saksenā affirms that according to these saints, the aim consists raising the living self from the lower *cakras* to the topmost place where it initially entered into the human frame (identified with the seat of *parameśvara*) along the same way it had descended, thus, inverting the order of succession.

already encountered, viz., the *gudā-cakra*, the *indriya-cakra*, the *nābhī-cakra*, *hr̥daya-cakra* and the *kaṇṭha-cakra* situated in the throat, plus an additional sixth, the *ājñā-cakra* located on the forehead. In this list we recognise a reiteration of the classical Tantra Yoga pattern, although the names given to some of *cakras* are slightly different. But while the earlier elaborations in the *Vedānta-Sāgara* remained limited to the account of the lower *cakras* comprising the first five of this series in order to maintain the symbolic analogy with the quintuple series of *laṭā'if* contemplated by the Mujaddidiyya, here the author feels less bound to adhere strictly to the pattern set out by the doctrines of his Islamic ancestors. While maintaining the idea of a quintuple series of subtle organs by inserting them into the context of the *hr̥daya-cakra*[211] and pointing out their relative importance in the process of re-ascent of the fallen self, it shows how far the process of assimilation into an increasingly Hinduised framework based on the *Kabīr-panthī* background had gone during the very lifetime of Rāmcandra.

The *ājñā-cakra*, assimilated by Rāmcandra to the seat of the *nafs-i nāṭiqa* of the Mujaddidīs, is now related to the 'gross mind' (*piṇḍī-man*, *sthūla man*), viz., the physical mind responsible for the co-ordination of the corporeal functions exercised by the respective organs (*indriya*), and, hence, 'contaminated' by the impressions left by the ephemeral objects pertaining to the outer world.[212] Its highest extension is said to be marked by this station, beyond which the reascending current of life (*jīvan-dhārā*) enters the universal realm of the *brahmāṇḍī* man. The link subsisting between the earlier theories of Rāmcandra and the Sūfī doctrine of the Mujaddidīs, even at this level, thus, becomes evident. In what is here defined as

---

211. *SkR*, pp. 21 and 36-7, whose information regarding the five subtle organs is reportedly drawn from Rāmcandra's *Kamāl-i insānī*, a work concerned mainly with methodological aspects.

212. Explicitly mentioning Kabīr as the primary source of these concepts, the author compares this 'contaminated soul' (an obvious reference to the Sūfī *nafs-i ammāra*) to a black wasp (*bhaunrā*) in contrast to the pure, immaculate soul (*nafs-i muṭama'inna*) which is depicted as a white crane (*bag*), also identified with the grey goose (*haṁsa*).

'physical mind' (*piṇḍī man*), we recognise that governing faculty of the formal and individual dominion also described by Rāmcandra as the lower limit of that intermediate meeting point between the two dominions, individual and universal, *khalq* and *amr*. Thus, we learn from the *Sākṣātkār kā rahasya*:

> . . . the five *cakras* below [the *ājñā-cakra*] are gross and physical and the process of cleansing and conquering them constitutes an aspect of Haṭha Yoga. . . . The path of the *sants* is that of love for the *paramātmā* (*prem-mārga*) where insistence (*haṭha*) has no place; these people simply seek the love of God and never insist or indulge in *haṭha* . . . , rather they leave everything to the will of the Supreme. They have therefore ruled out the cleansing of these lower *cakras* . . . their teachings focus on the meditation on the *ājñā-cakra* alone in order to purify it, so that all the lower *cakras* are cleansed . . . automatically.[213]

This passage shows an apparent shift of methodology away from the original Mujaddidī teachings towards a process said to be adopted from the *sants*, viz., the *Kabīr-panthīs* and Rādhāso-āmīs, for it was a major distinctive feature of the Sūfī successors of Shaikh Aḥmad Sirhindī to focus first of all on the *laṭīfa-i qalb*, as earlier explicitly stated by Rāmcandra.

However, the author of this booklet is well aware of the practice used by the Mujaddidī shaikhs, as is illustrated by the following passage:

> Yet some Sūfī saints have introduced [the method of] focussing on the purification of the heart inside the *hṛdaya-cakra* before proceeding to the *ājñā-cakra*. In their perfection, the purification of the subtle heart-organ brings along that of the remaining four subtle organs as well as it facilitates the ascent along the path towards the *ājñā-cakra* and the stations above. Hence, the Sūfī masters have considered it necessary to start

213. *SkR*, pp. 39/36 (English version).

> meditation from the heart . . . and because the invisible powers do not appear by meditating on the heart. . . .[214]

Looking carefully at these two passages, it becomes obvious that the apparent divergence regarding the point of departure and initial stage of spiritual practice can be easily reduced to a simple change in pespective taking into account that in the Islamic tradition only four gross elements are considered in the corporeal realm, to which the Hindu tradition adds a fifth one, the ether (*ākāśa*). Hence, derives that, while the Sūfī masters expressedly define the *laṭīfa-i qalb* as the microcosmic reflection of the *barzakh* or meeting point between the two major dominions of the Universe (*dā'ira-i imkān*) it is only beyond the seat of the ether located in the *kanṭha-cakra* or *viśuddha-cakra* and beyond the *ājñā-cakra* which governs that realm that this degree is possibly contemplated by the *sant* doctrine based on Hindu theories. The whole divergence lies, therefore, again in the double perception of the psychic aggregate or *nafs* and its sometimes confusing assimilation to the *ākāśa* on the lower limit and the seat of *manas* and *citta* on the other hand. It is based on a somewhat oversimplified evaluation of the Mujaddidī doctrine by our Hindu authorities who do not share doctrinally the descending perspective of their Islamic masters to the same extent as they are ready to apply its social implications.

The exact starting point of the ascent to the higher regions 'beyond the stages the *haṭha-yogī* can reach', and to attain which 'it is obligatory to accept [the guidance of] a *satguru*',[215] is described as the third eye of Lord Śiva (*śīva-netra*). Rāmcandra associates it to the *nuqṭa-i suwaida* (lit. 'black spot'), sometimes identified by Sūfīs with the black clot of blood situated in the heart which is the symbolic representation of the primordial corruption of human nature after Adam's fall from paradise. In Tāntrik doctrines, the term *śīva-netra* designates a precise

214. *SkR*, pp. 39/36.

215. *SkR*, pp. 41/37. Here again the discipline is defined as a particular aspect of Rāja-Yoga. So, the hint at the *satguru* can also be interpreted as indicating the birth of the interior master (*āntarik guru*) residing in the intimate chamber of the heart.

location in correspondence to the forehead the subtle activation of which indicates transcendence of the formal dominion and definitive entrance into the realm of the higher stages of Being.[216] The corresponding Sūfī term *nuqṭa-i suwaida* is not found in the current technical vocabulary of the Mujaddidīs. Presumably, it has been adopted from the terminology of the Qāḍiriyya where it is used, for instance, in the works of the Mogul prince Dārā Shukoh when comparing the sacred traditions of Vedānta and *taṣawwuf*. Its description as being 'shaped like a triangle (*trikoṇa*)' reminds us of the description of the heart as a pinecone-shaped triangle whose natural position has been inverted while reflecting its inner reality into the *'ālam-i khalq*.[217] Converging all faculties of sensation (*jñānendriya*) on that subtle spot and assisted by the persistent use of the *satnām* conferred by the *satguru*, the 'third eye' is said to opened eventually, allowing the practitioner to perceive the 'inner light conferring beatitude' (*ānandamayī āntarik prakāśa*) in a possible parallel to the Mujaddidī *sair-i anfusī*, during which the traveller is described as beginning to perceive these lights inwardly.

But in addition to these preliminary elements, our Hindu masters introduce at this stage the concept of *anhad* or *anāhat śabda*, the boundless sound-current said to have originated at the very beginning of time from the supreme source, which in different degrees pervades every single stage of manifestation. This 'soundless sound' is said to be produced 'without striking',[218] and can, therefore, be related to the endless sound-current which constitutes the base for the interior process described by the

---

216. This idea goes along with the descriptions of Śiva the opening of whose frontal third eye reduces the entire phenomenal world into ashes with a single glance, thus, stressing the ephemeral nature of the world of form.

217. Cf. *MnS*, pp. 34/45.

218. Cf. *Haṭha-Yoga-Pradīpikā*, IV.82-6 and *Mahānirvāṇa-Tantra*, V.146. This is clearly related to the ancient Vedic doctrines regarding the mysterious sound *AUṀ* believed to contain *in nuce* the entire Veda. It constitutes, therefore, the base of the science of the sacred sound resumed in the *mantra-vidyā*.

Rādhāsoāmīs as *sūrat-śabd-yoga* said to lead the disciple to the state of *sahaja*. Their interior descipline is therefore, also referred to as *sahaja-yoga*, which shows some interesting analogies with the Mujaddidī technique of *dhikr-i khafī*, the prolonged practice of which is said to lead to the uninterrupted perpetuation of the sound-vibration produced by pronouncing the syllable Allāh, called *sulṭān al-adhkār*. These terms, which are common to several *panth-sampradāyas* concerned with the sound-discipline,[219] occur frequently in the technical explanations of the Hindu masters and indicate their indebtness to these currents in more recent Hinduism as well as their complementary role in Sūfī teachings.

The entire dominion that extends above the *śiva-netra* is referred to as *tārā-maṇḍala*, the 'region of the stars', an allusion to the universal dimension of the *brahmāṇḍī-man* or *'ālam-i amr* to which it refers. The way leading through this celestial region consists of a passage through an extremely subtle channel known as the 'gateway to liberation' (*mukti-dvāra*) and said to be as thin as a needle or one-tenth the size of a mustard seed.[220] The use of these metaphors owes much to the teachings of Tantrism while apparently sharing little with the descriptions given by the Mujaddidī shaikhs. But the underlying concept of a successive series of subtle centres corresponding to hierarchical stages of realisation that need to be crossed by the initiate while progressing on the spiritual path is nevertheless recalled by the idea implied in the description of the seven spheres

219. For similar notions, cf. the doctrines regarding the sound current among the *Nānak-panthīs* described in McLeod (1968).

220. *SkR*, pp. 44/41. In the Upaniṣad, this passage is described as the solar gate (*sūrya-dvāra*) through which those who know the correct answer to the question: 'Who are you?' asked by a non-human (*apauruṣeya*) being, will gain access to the celestial worlds, thus reaching the higher, non-individual stages situated along the 'path of the gods' (*devayāna*). Cf. *Chāndogya Upaniṣad*, IV.15.5-6 and V.10.2; *Bṛhadāraṇyaka Upaniṣad*, V.10.1.

Hence, Rāmcandra affirms that the aspirant's complete surrender to the *satguru* will allow him access to this world since the master, through his love, kindness and favour will assist his protegé to cross that gate by transmuting his inner states.

(*dawā'ir*) the *sālik* on the Mujaddidī path has to travel though on his way towards perfection once he has attained to the centre of the 'sphere of universal existence' (*dā'ira-i imkān*). It recalls the very *barzakh* where the two oceans meet in the *qalb* or, on a macrocosmic scale, on the *kursī* and the *'arsh*, as apparent from the explications given by Shāh Abūl Ḥasan.[221] These seven spheres compare with the seven celestial abodes and dwellings of the gods (*devaloka*) which make up the seven stages the *yogī* is said to cross on the divine path leading towards liberation (*devayāna*), hinted at in the *Bhagavad Gītā*[222] and described in great detail in the Śruti.[223] It also resembles to the concept of the seven or nine planetary spheres mentioned in the *Koran* and developed in the cosmological doctrines of Sūfīsm.[224]

Hence, there derives a possible analogy with the Mujaddidī description regarding the conclusion of the 'journey from the cardinal points' (*sair-i āfāqī*) after the completion of the ascent of the five *laṭā'if* of the breast and the *nafs* related to the brain (*nafs mujāwir-i ḥawāṣṣ ast wa ta'alluq ba dimāgh dārad*) from their physical frame, which leads to the beginning of the 'journey through the stages of the inner self' (*sair-i anfusī*) when 'the *sālik* will perceive numerous colourful lights in the *'ālam-i mithāl* and within his own breast'.[225] In both cases, such a journey towards the higher states of Being is accompanied by the perception of inner lights (*āntarik prakāś, nūrāniyat-i bāṭinī*) which follows a journey from the periphery towards a subtle

---

221. Cf. *Āyat al-kursī* (*Koran*, 2:255): '. . . His Throne doth extend over the heavens and the earth. . . '.

Since the projection of the Throne of God is often identified with the Ka'ba as the symbolic centre of the earth, the *Mujaddid*'s metaphorical image regarding the two modes of reaching the Ka'ba in order to explicate the validity of both *jadhba* and *sulūk* assumes its deeper meaning.

222. VIII. 23-6.

223. Cf. *Chāndogya Upaniṣad*, IV.15.5-6; *Bṛhadāraṇyaka Upaniṣad*, V.10:1-6, VI.2:15; *Kauṣītakī Upaniṣad*, I.3. Cf. also G.G. Filippi, *Post-mortem et libération d'après Śaṅkarācārya* (1982).

224. Cf. Shāh Walī Allāh Dehlawī's *Sata'āt*, 1969, pp. 42-3.

225. Cf. *MnS*, pp. 23-4/39-40.

passage through a centrally located point described as being 'thin as a needle'. The crossing of it is called by the Mujaddidīs the 'opening of the gate' (*fatḥ-i bāb*). It implies a preliminary journey along the horizontal plane of the *khalq* towards a centre enabling the initiate to proceed from there along the vertical axis towards the higher stages of the *amr*.[226]

In the Mujaddidī terminology, the series of these superior stages is identified with the successive degrees of sainthood (*wilāyat*) and prophetic perfections (*kamālāt-i nubuwwat*) and linked to different aspects of the Divinity and Its revelation. Similarly, the Upaniṣad describe the ascent through the celestial spheres as the 'journey of the gods' (*devayāna*) that leads through the abodes (*loka*) of the various gods, i.e., Soma, Varuṇa, Indra, etc., before eventually reaching the *brahmaloka* or *satyaloka*. The teachings of the *sant*s adopted by our Hindu *faqīr*s, which are based on the concepts of Rāja-Yoga tell of a division of the path immediately beyond this point, from where three roads depart (*triveṇī*). The perfect saint chooses the middle path (*madhya-mārga*) leading straight up towards final liberation (*mokṣa*, *mukti*) from the claws of death (*mṛtyu-cakra*).

The next chapter of the treatise is dedicated to the description of the six subtle organs of the cosmic dominion defined as *aṇḍa* which are in ascending order named as: *sahasra-dala-kamala*, *trikuṭi*, *śūnya*, *mahāśūnya*, *bhanwar-gufā* and *satloka* or *sacakhaṇḍa*.[227]

Again, the description of these *cakra*s according to the pattern set out by the *Kabīr-panthī*s of the Dharmadāsī branch, Tulsī Ṣāḥib Hāthrasī and the Rādhāsoāmī masters, does not appear anywhere in Rāmcandra's published works, although (as in the case of the paragraph quoted above) there are sporadic hints at some of these stations in his writings which indicate his acquaintance with this topic. It is likely that these higher

226. The Upaniṣad describe the passage through the hub of a chart's wheel (*cakra*) leading beyond the dominion of mutation, a description that enforces the idea of a fix axis or straight path leading towards and eventually through a central point of conversion.

227. *SkR*, pp. 46-57/43-53.

levels of spiritual wisdom, being unaccessible for the ordinary devotees of his *satsang,* remained reserved to a referred circle of disciples entitled to receive particular oral teachings, a pattern common in both Sūfī and Yoga circles.

Given the strictly Islamic character of the Sunni *ṭarīqa*, here the original Mujaddidī description of the subsequent stages of the *sulūk* proved too inextricably linked with Islamic concepts to provide a possible structural basis for an integration into a Hindu context. It was therefore abandoned and substituted with a striking doctrinal elaboration typical for the *nirguṇa*-current within the *bhakti-sampradāya*s, which by their nature were more compatible with the anti-anthropomorphic perspective of Islam. The description of the six *cakra*s, of this second series, therefore, not surprisingly adheres largely to that provided by the Kabīr-panth and includes hints at the science based on the variations of the subtle sound vibration (*sūrat-śabd-yoga*), a particularly elaborated version of which is found among the Rādhāsoāmīs.

The *sahasra-dala-kamala*, for instance, is the seventh in the series of eighteen *cakra*s and the last and highest in the Haṭha-Yoga doctrines. It is located somewhere in the back part of the skull and is said to be characterised by a profuse and dazzling luminosity irradiating from the one thousand petals of the white lotus it contains. Moreover, this *cakra* is said to be permeated by a series of tunes resembling the sound of bells and conches which attract the living self up to this stage. The reigning divinity of this region is Bhagavān Trilokanāth, also referred to as *Jyoti Nirañjana*, an epithet usually applied to Śiva but in this context more generally referred to the luminous Supreme Being and Lord of heaven, earth and the inferior regions (*naraka*). The creatures that populate these regions are all subject to the law of transmigration (*saṁsāra*), hence, this realm is commonly denominated as kāladeśa.[228] Bhagavān

228. With the necessary precautions, the region of the *sahasra-dal-kamala* can be assimilated to the *candra-loka*, which in the Hindu doctrines constitutes the place where the forms pertaining to this world are elaborated. In many respects, it therefore resembles the *'ālam-i mithāl* which in Sūfī doctrines constitutes the lower limit of the *'ālam-i amr*.

Trilokanāth is said to sustain by the means inherent to his power the three realms of the *piṇḍa* through the mediation of the *ājñā-cakra*.

Such a perspective indicates the possibility that these doctrines have developed from an earlier encounter between Sūfī and Yoga doctrines, for these realms are easily recognised as corresponding to the three main divisions of the *dā'ira-i imkān*, now conceived as the first of the seven principal stages of the Mujaddidī *sulūk*, analogous to the three levels known in classical Hindu doctrines as gross, subtle and causal. All the following stages situated above that sphere are included in the *aṇḍa* and therefore represent the celestial regions situated in the *'ālam-i, amr*, which constitutes the upper hemisphere of the *imkān* beyond the limiting conditions of time (*kāla*) and space (*ākāśa*).[229]

The apparent confusion that arises while comparing the two doctrines is caused by the introduction of this additional level which actually is nothing but a reflection of the previous one. It seems to be caused mainly by the adaptation of the idea of succeeding planes of reflection of decreasing degrees of reality typical for the *shuhūdī* doctrine of the Mujaddidīs and of some Hindu schools within the Vaiṣṇava current, commonly known as *pratibimbavāda* or *chāyāvāda*, and the attempt to reconcile these with the *advaita* point of view dominant in the Upaniṣad and *Brahma-Sūtra*.

The immediately following stage corresponds to the subtle centre called *trikuṭī* or *brahma-cakra*, and is characterised by a lotus of four petals irradiating a pale red light that is said to resemble that of the rising sun. The *mantra* it contains consists of the syllable *oṁ* whose characteristic sound recalls that of the *mṛdaṅgam* accompanied by a low sound of rolling thunder, and

229. The *sahasra-dal-kamala* is not only described as the seat of Kāla, the imprisoner of souls, but also as the highest approach of *cidākāśa*, the cosmos permeated by consciousness.

This divinity closely resembles Yama, the god of death whose dominion extends over all those beings who remain entangled in the multiplicity characteristic of the individual existence.

the elements predominant in its nature consist of water, air and fire.[230] On the authority of Kabīr, this *cakra* is described as containing in its fold a minute well the shaft of which points in a downward direction, pouring out drops of sweet nectar (*amṛta*) which quench the thirst of the vagrants who have arrived there.

Any possible doubt about the implicit sense of the symbolism employed in this context, too self-evident to require further explanation, is removed by Rāmcandra's statement that those who have attained to this lofty station are saved from the 'ocean of contingent existence' (*bhāv-sāgar*) while granting the treasure of universal knowledge to the *sādhu* who by reaching there will not be found to return but will continue to progress 'like the rising sun'.[231] Similar to the language employed by the Mujaddidīs, here too we come across the symbolism of an opening gate used to describe the seeker's access to the stage of *trikuṭī*. The latter is compared to an inaccessible fortress (*durga*) to reach which the initiate has to cross nine gates plus an additional tenth (*daśam dvāra*) which is usually locked and that grants access to the *brahmāṇḍa* or the realm of Pārabrahma.[232]

The key that gives access to this secret of immortality lies initially with the *satguru* alone who concedes its vision (*darśana*) only to those few selected ones eligible to receive his grace (*kṛpā*). This grace is described as being granted in a *kashfī* way, by a sort of intuition linked to *buddhi* that is produced entirely by the master's intervention on the disciple's inner states without involving the latter's active participation. Only later will the *abhyāsī* learn to reach this stage through his own efforts. This latter technique is referred to as the *kasbī* method.

---

230. *SkR*, pp. 47-52/44-8. The reference here is obviously no longer to the corporeal elements, but to their subtle principles (*tanmātra*), as confirmed in very similar terms by Shāh Abūl Ḥasan.

231. *SkR*, pp. 50/46-7.

232. The nine gates correspond to the two eyes, two ears, two nostrils, the mouth, the organ of reproduction and the rectum. This description is strikingly similar to Agni as Vaiśvānara described in the *Māṇḍūkya Upaniṣad*, which states that the soul of the deceased leaves the body through any of these nine gates, in contrast to the saint's soul which leaves the physical aggregate through this tenth *daśamdvāra*.

As so often, the concepts thus expressed are too similar to the teachings of the Mujaddidī shaikhs to be explained away as merely coincidental. This is further proved by the abrupt switch between the Persianate vocabulary used for explaining concepts evidently pertaining to a Tantra and *sant* background and shows the extent to which elements originally belonging to two different and independent traditions are here inextricably interwoven in an interesting but coherent blend.

The opening of the tenth gate, analogous to the opening of the *brahmarandhra*, situated in the conventional Yoga doctrines at the apex of the head, grants the initiate access to the intelligible light of *buddhi* thereby connecting him with the path through the celestial regions. It, hence, represents a striking similarity with the *fatḥ-i bāb* described by the Mujaddidīs as occurring in relation to the eight entrance gates which provide access to the sublime region of paradise (*bihisht-i barīn*) and the residence of the 'sublime assembly of contentment and of the apex of acceptance' (*ḥazīrah-yi riḍā wa auj-i qabūl*) once the ascent of the five *laṭīfa*s to the 'world of order' has been completed.[233] On this subject, Shāh Abūl Ḥasan Dihlawī remarks:

> . . . since . . . those who have reached the reintegration of all five subtle organs into their principles gradually along the path shown by the five prophets of right determination . . . are closer to the 'abode beyond space and time' (*lā-makāniyat*). Their degree of excellence is higher [as compared to those who have reached there through just four or less *laṭā'if*]. The individual determination of each human being and the peculiarity of the different tempers occurs as result of a present bestowed by God (*amr-i mauhībatī*) [the Urdu translation uses the term *wahbī* frequently encountered with the Hindu masters]. The attainment of such a high station does not depend

233. Referring to a Tradition according to which Abū Bakr al-Ṣiddīq will be among the few chosen ones on whom Allāh will bestow His grace (*raḥmat*), so that he may be called into Paradise through all the eight gates, i.e., Abū Bakr reunites all the virtues corresponding to each of the eight gates in himself. Cf. *MnS*, pp. 21/37.

> on individual skill and effort (*kasb*) of the disciple but rather on the exceeding attraction (*kashish-i zā'id-i pīr-i kāmil*) of the perfect spiritual master. . . .[234]

The intervention of the extraordinary power attributed to the *satguru* or *pīr-i kāmil* results here in some subtle way as being associated to the mediation of a supra-human attraction that lifts the passive disciple in a state of total surrender all at a sudden to this very elevated degree of spiritual insight. This force of attraction (*kashish, ākarṣaṇa*) recalls the Sūfī concept of *jadhba*. It finds a close parallel in the Hindu tradition in the figure of the *avadhūta* mentioned frequently in the Tantra-Śāstra and later by the *Kabīr-panthīs*, where it is closely related to the idea of the interior guide (*āntarik gurū*) said to reside in the cavern of the heart. It is mentioned also by the Hindu Naqshbandīs, who describe it as the spiritual child that lives in the womb of the heart and that must be nourished in order to grow and develop its latent potentialities.

Just above the *trikuṭī*, in some Sūfī circles referred to as *muthallathī* (triangular-shaped) which comprises the degree of the *'ālam-i jabarūtī* including the heavenly spheres, there is another minor station known as 'white emptiness' (*śveta-śūnya*) or 'ocean of nectar' (*amṛta-sāgara*), sometimes also referred to as *mānasarovara* ('lotus pond of spiritual bliss'). Following the descriptions provided by Hindu mythology, this is the abode of the white swans or royal geese (*rāja-haṁsa*) who feed pearls. These swans symbolically correspond to the attainment of an extremely sublime spiritual degree. They have the capability to drink milk, absorbing its essential ingredient and releasing the water it contains. Their intrinsic significance is explained by Har Nārāyaṇ Saksenā as follows:

> When *abhyāsī* reaches the degree of *haṁsa* or

---

234. *MnS*, pp. 21/36. All agree that the path crossed by those who have chosen the way of spiritual realisation in life reiterates the journey accomplished by the soul of the deceased, at least if the degree of perfection is sufficiently elevated to determine its course to the higher station of *krama-mukti*, *videha-mukti* and *jīvan-mukti*, beyond the solar gate.

> *paramahaṁsa*, he develops the quality of discrimination (*viveka*) by the means of which he accepts only what pertains to Truth (*yathārtha*) while discarding all the rest. . . .
>
> When the self of the disciple reaches the sublime stage, it joins the company of those who have already reached there before and is fed with nectar thus attaining to immortality. . . . He now knows about the Supreme and seeks impatiently union with It.[235]

This description shows that this stage alludes to the condition of those who have attained to *krama-mukti*, or liberation by stages. It comprehends those potentially proceeding towards the attainment of *videha-mukti*, or total liberation after the relinquishment of the physical body, when the Self proceeds directly to the summit of the heavenly hierarchy represented by the *brahmaloka* without stopping at any of the celestial mansions situated along the *devayāna*. There they will remain 'in the company of those who have already reached there' till the end of the present cycle (*pralaya*, *qiyāmat*).

The remaining four *cakras* and their corresponding celestial regions, viz., *śūnya*, *mahāśūnya*, *bhanwar gufā* and *sacakhaṇḍa*, must, therefore, be intended as intermediary degrees on the journey of the *yogī* or *mutaṣawwuf,* by now unrelentlessly progressing towards the attainment of the final aim.

The immediately following station of *śūnya* is described as a lotus of six petals the characteristic sound of which is said to resemble that of the *sāraṅga*. This *cakra* is said to radiate a colourless light (*be-raṅgī prakāśa*) and is associated to the Sūfī *'ālam-i lāhūt*, the 'world of the Divinity', which is also termed 'void' (*khalā*) in a literal Arabic rendering of the Sanskrit term *śūnya*. Certainly not part of the technical vocabulary used by the Naqshbandīs, the significance of this term in the present context is clarified by the author's mention of its better-known

235. *SkR*, pp. 52/48. For a definition of *haṁsa* and *paramahaṁsa*, cf. *KmI*, p. 4, which associates these two types of saints with a category of sainthood contemplated by the Mujaddidīs.

equivalent *'adam* or 'non-existence' as complementary to *wujūd* or 'existence' and their Persian synonyms *nīstī* and *hastī*. Both terms are essential in the *shuhūdī* doctrine since they denote the principle and its immediate cosmic derivative. Strictly speaking, their complementarity is applicable only to two terms situated on the same level, but according to Shaikh Aḥmad Sirhindī it is out of the pure Being of Allāh and His names and attributes reflected into the world that the 'opposed non-existence' (*'adam-i mutaqābila*) gain a relative degree of finite existence, which nevertheless depend on the irradiations of the Divine qualities. After transcending the indefinite multiplicity of His attributes contained in the reflected forms (*ṣūrat*) that appear in the immanent realm of the contingent world, the *sālik* now experiences the last residue of duality subsisting after his acquired treasure of knowledge has revealed him the ultimate transitoriness (*fanāiyat*) of the world and himself.

The perfection of this state of *fanā* is reached, however, only at the successive stage called *mahāśūnya* or 'great vacuity'. Described as a lotus of eight petals, it is characterised by the absolute darkness (*andhakāra*, *ẓulmat*) of non-existence or, according to the Hindu perspective, of non-manifestation (*avyakta*), comparable to the condition of primordial chaos prior to the descent of the 'command'. This station is said to include two islands, situated respectively on the left and right side of the lotus: *sahaja*, having ten petals, and *acinta* with twelve. Although this region, ruled by the immaculate *māyā* (*śuddha māyā*), possesses no light on its own, it is illuminated by the pure souls inhabiting in it. There are said to irradiate the light of the twelve suns, in reference to the twelve *āditya* corresponding to the twelve solar mansions through which the sun rotates every year around the central axis of the poles. Enjoying this sublime stage, they entreat and bequest the bypassing souls on their upward journey. Their role, thus, resembles that of the *karman-devatā* who inhabit the superior regions above the moon who have gained their position as gods through the effects of their positive actions (*karma*) accomplished in a previous cycle of existence. Reaching a high degree of spiritual realisation, their journey has led them to this abode of indescribable beauty, but having ultimately failed in their aim to reach the Supreme Goal of liberation in life (*jīvan-mukti*), they remain 'imprisoned' in this lofty though still imperfect domain. Only the *satguru* can provide the aspirant with the guidance necessary to progress further by merging the individual entity of his protegés into the pure Sound of the *śabda*. However, the attainment of this sublime state presupposes the total extinction of the disciple in his master (*fanā fī'l-shaikh*) and the consequent assumption of the lead by the inner *guru* inside the heart. This stage corresponds to the previously described state of *prajñā*.[236]

The following *cakra* and its corresponding state, called *bhanwar gufā* ('whirling cave'), constitutes the final gateway to the *satyaloka* or *maqām-i Ḥaqq*. Here, the *satguru*s are said to reunite for their celestial assembly (*darbār*, *majlis-i 'ālā*). *sacakhaṇḍa*, the 'land of Truth', is permeated by a sweet fragrance and the melodies of the *vīṇā*. It is the abode of ultimate perfection and virtual identity with the invisible (*alakha*), unapproachable (*agama*) and undescribable (*akaha*) *paramātmā* at the very top of the Mount Merū, which is identified with Brahmapurī, the citadel of Brahmā in classical Hinduism, and the all-embracing Throne of God (*'arsh-i-muḥīṭ*) in Sūfism.

According to the *Kabīr-panthī*s, this is the region inhabited by the *satpuruṣa*, the true and unique Lord of all creatures. There, the selves who have attained to *krama-mukti* reside in the service of their Lord, awaiting the end of the cosmic cycle for their final deliverance. Recognisable as the supreme abode depicted by Muslim saints as man's highest fulfilment and identified by the Mujaddidīs with the state of 'pure servanthood' (*'ubūdiyat-i ṣarfa*), this is the last and most perfect state possibly conceivable leaving the purely transcendent essence of Allāh (*al-dhāt*) beyond the reach of the contingent creature. In keeping with the *shuhūdī* perspective, according to which prophets occupy a rank superior to that of saints and which declares the imitation of the saint's mission described in the formula 'solitude amidst the crowd' (*khilwat dar anjumān*) this is the ideal way

---

236. For a comprehensive explanation, see Shāh Abūl Ḥasan's *Waḥdat al-Wujūd aur Waḥdat al-shuhūd kā tafṣīlī bayān* (1984).

of behaviour for a perfect saint. The Hindu author of the treatise remarks:

> The souls who alight from this place to the *mṛtyu-loka* [viz., our human world subject to death] with the purpose of assisting the beings there to attain liberation themselves, are the true saints. They themselves are liberated ones and are moreover capable of leading others to liberation. Such *guru*s extend their mercy (*dayā*) and compassion (*kṛpā*) to their disciples thereby raising them in their special favour to this lofty stage and granting them a glimpse of the Supreme — this is called the 'way of Divine favour' (*wahbī-mārga*).[237]

What lies beyond this degree of realisation is divided in the doctrinal concept of the *Kabīr-panthīs*, Rādhāsoāmīs and ultimately our Hindu masters linked to the Mujaddidiyya Maẓhariyya, into the final series of six further degrees. It regards the purely metaphysical, all-transcendent realm of identity with the Immutable Principle (*al-Ḥaqq*, *Allāh Ta'ālā* or *Parabrahma*), describable only in negative terms as the realm of non-duality at which the symbolic denomination of the first three levels as *alakha*, *agama* and *akaha* hints. There no divisions are possible except by analogy with the description of previous levels. It represents the ultimate aim of all those who have attained total liberation, either during the present life (*jīvan-mukti*) or immediately after the death of the physical envelope (*videha-mukti*).

There, the long journey of the *yogī* reaches its conclusion and he finally enjoys pure Beatitude (*paramānanda*) in the stage of the unconditioned *turīya*.[238] Rāmcandra reminds us of the widely diffused Sūfī concept according to which the aspirant adept has to complete each of the single stages to its full perfection before eventually proceeding onwards: '. . . every

---

237. *SkR*, pp. 57/53. Here, the similarity between the Naqshbandī ideal of a perfect saint and the Mahāyāna Buddhist concept of *bodhisattva* is particularly striking.

238. *VS*, p. 47.

single spiritual station and degree along the path is divided by the respective levels of *jāgṛta*, *svapna*, *suṣupti* and *turīya*',[239] just as every major sphere or level of the path is subdivided into a series of minor sub-degrees. This largely accounts for the divergence in the number and denomination of the stations (*manāzil*, *maqāmāt*, *manāhij*) listed by different authorities. Such variation depends largely on the inclusion or omission of particular stations and thus does not represent an unresolveable contradiction in the doctrinal pattern.

It has emerged from the description of the subtle centres from the *ājñā-cakra* upwards that the dominant features of each subtle centre are often intimately related to each other in their symbolic implication and denote the development of one major degree into multiple smaller progressions. The total number of eighteen *cakras* should, therefore, cause no confusion or doubt about a possible compatibility of the different doctrines involved in the case of our present study. What appears far more interesting is the adoption of a three-fold level of subtle centres. This arises from the doubling of one essentially unique stage in the metaphysical realm, due to the adaption of the Mujaddidī point of view to a *nirguṇa sant* doctrine that traces its origin back to the ancient Vedānta and its mediaeval elaborations.

The techniques of spiritual realisation

The previous chapters have shown that on a speculative (*'ilmī*) plane the transition of a Sūfī *ṭarīqa* into a Hindu environment demanded a number of formal adaptations, reformulations and attempts at assimilation, a task which in the present case was facilitated by a number of outer and inner circumstances favourable to such a development. It now remains to determine whether and to which extent a similarly intricate development was required for the corresponding operative (*'amlī*) aspect of the *sādhanā* promulgated by Rāmcandra consisting of a range of techniques that aim at transmiting the subtle states of the initiate.

Although the technical vocabulary (*istilāḥāt*) used in the

239. *TP*, p. 44.

methodological context of each initiatory discipline naturally reflects the fundamental principles of the tradition in which it is embedded, it is legitimate to assume that the subtle human constitution on which these operative disciplines (*abhyāsa*) intervene constitutes a common ground untouched by any link to a specific religion and potentially suitable for any sort of cultivation. Such an assertion stands at the base of Rāmcandra's vision that wants leave open to each initiate the possibility to partake of his spiritual discipline without the need to renounce the performance of the exoteric rituals and social customs of each individual's inherited religious tradition.

It, therefore, comes as no surprise that notwithstanding some formal alterations, the core of the Mujaddidī methodology based on the fundamental concepts of the all-comprehensive *'ilm-i laṭā'if* appears essentially unchanged in the teachings of this Hindu master. In view of the frequent change of perspective witnessed in the theoretical outline of the 'science of the subtle centres' between the Mujaddidī *'ilm-i laṭā'if* and the *sant* elaboration of the Tāntrik *cakra-vidyā*, involving the use of a highly symbolic language on both sides, the question arises as to how far the use of a methodology safely embedded in its original religious environment can remain applicable if transferred to another context. This problem becomes even more pertinent in the case of a *ṭarīqa* which appears so intimately linked with the religious tenets set out by the *sharī'at* as the Mujaddidiyya, not usually accredited with the flexibility needed for the establishment of such an intercultural link.

An oversimplification in the analysis of this process of cultural transition or, perhaps more appropriately, of gradual cultural absorption, along narrowly erected ideological categories would certainly fall short of providing an exhaustive solution to this question and, thus, risk not rendering sufficient justice to the complex factors involved. Even if the subject of the present case study might be dismissed as bearing only minor importance in the mainstream history of a great Indian Sūfī order or for the spiritual history of the sub-continent in general, it nevertheless provides in our eyes a fascinating glimpse of India's extraordinary capacity to lay bare and absorb the essential substratum that underlies every truly regular tradition beyond the supplanting of formal elements that distinguish the immanent expression of the transcendent Truth among different people in successive historical periods.

The operational part of the discipline based on doctrinal fundamentals (*siddhānta*) consists of the use of a series of precisely focussed methods (*abhyāsa*). This practical aspect of the *sādhanā* represents the most immediate concern of the Hindu authorities of the Mujaddidiyya and reflects their anxiety to achieve concrete and lasting results in the spiritual advancement of their followers.[240]

The Kāyasth background of this Hindu lineage did not point directly towards an emphasis on sophisticated intellectual elaborations and theoretical discussions from a purely gnostic perspective (*jñāna-mārga*), more typical of a Brāhmaṇical environment. It suggested rather the development of a more practically oriented discipline based on a subtle but concrete activity (*karma*) and devotional self-surrender (*upāsanā*), in which the historical circumstances during the later half of the nineteenth and early twentieth centuries and their impact on the Kāyasth community may have played some part by amplifying the pragmatic tendencies so characteristic for the modern period in general.

The rapid increase in the number of disciples during the

---

240. Often during my field-research I was confronted with a great reluctance to supply any tangible information regarding the speculative background of their *sādhanā* and their unwillingness to commit themselves to any theoretical excursion in the context of their daily public *satsang*. Although this hermetic attitude towards outsiders also extends to initiates of lower degrees, it stood in contrast to the master's general readiness to allow me free access to the written sources diffused in the more restricted circle of intimate disciples, which often contained highly valuable material regarding the esoteric science of the order and the doctrinal expositions elaborated by the past generations of its leadership. It also differed widely from the lively debates and discussions common between master and disciples in many of the Sūfī *khānaqāh*s I visited, where a fairly balanced combination of speculative and operative instructions governed the daily rhythm of the inmates.

formative period of the branch (*c*. 1920-55), which was partially a result of the accelerated 'democratisation' of the order 'open to all caste and creeds' propagated by Rāmcandra on the directions of his shaikh and further enhanced by the charismatic appeal of its leaders during that time, led to a truly heterogeneous range of affiliates. Most of them were hailing from a lower middle-class background with a relatively limited acquaintance with either Sūfī or Hindu esoteric teachings. This resulted in a successive redefinition in the way of instruction, imparted according to the individual disposition and capacity of each single member of the *satsang*. Notwithstanding the declared aim of being open indiscriminately to all seekers of truth, it led to the re-emergence of the natural division between those commoners who passively derived some benefit from the presence of the lineage's leaders during the public *satsang*, and the more restricted number of those intimate initiates qualified to work under the guidance of the *satguru* for progressing in the *sādhanā*.

These factors must be taken into account while assessing the teachings of Rāmcandra and his successors. The apparent discrepancy between the simple style of their daily public *satsang* and the rather sophisticated doctrinal explanations encountered in the treatises published under their name provides some useful indication in this direction. Remarkably the written sources containing Rāmcandra's teachings do not show the homogeneous character, both in regard to content and style, that would facilitate a coherent analysis of the underlying elements of his 'path'. It suggests the diversity of sources at the origin of his spiritual and operational synthesis. From an attentive analysis of his works it emerges that, far from claiming any originality, Rāmcandra's teachings represent an attempt to combine the oral directions received from his spiritual preceptors with additional notions gathered from various written sources more or less closely related to his own spiritual affiliations so as to confer a more universalistic appeal to his call for self-realisation. Rāmcandra's own Hindu background, combining the piety of a traditional Vaiṣṇava household imbued with Rāma-*bhakti* with his membership of an unspecified branch of the Kabīr-panth and possibly the Nānak-panth, inclined him and his successors to preserve many doctrinal notions, ritual attitudes and prescriptive norms of behaviour, e.g., a strictly vegetarian diet and the stress laid on strict sobriety refraining from the consumption of wine or of any other intoxicating substance.[241] In view of these considerations, the science of the subtle centres constitutes a fertile ground for possible assimilations between the esoteric doctrines of Islam and Hinduism. The related methodology represents therefore yet another field in which the use of a different symbolism and ritual perceptions could be overcome opening the way for an encounter between these two traditions.

The work most specifically concerned with the methodological aspects of the *sādhanā* significantly bears the Persian title *Kamāl-i Insānī* ('The human Perfection').[242] More than any other of his works, it bears the distinctive mark of the Sūfī *ṭarīqa* Rāmcandra inherited from his shaikh. The descriptions it contains are permeated with technical terms currently used by the Mujaddidīs and very little effort is made to provide a rendering more suitable for non-Muslim readers. The bulk of the treatise consists of Rāmcandra's comments, personal considerations and clarifications of a treatise most probably compiled by Shāh Faḍl Aḥmad Khān. It is, therefore, useful in tracing the first steps of the process of transition between the two generations.

In the first paragraph of his opening chapter, Rāmcandra

---

241. An outline of the preliminary duties and rules of behaviour recommended to the members of his *satsang* is provided in Rāmcandra's small booklet entitled *Satsangion ke kartavya* ('The duties of the members of the *sansang*'), Fathegarh, n.d.

242. The Hindī title of the first printed edition reads *Mānava jīvan kī uncca śikhā* (The lofty peak of human perception). The edition used here is the second one, dated 1973 and published from the small press run by Rāmcandra's grandson at Fatehgarh, Adhyatma Dhara Prakashan, in 1,000 copies. This follows a first edition published in the early 1960s which was in turn preceded by the publication of parts of the integral text in the journal circulated by Rāmcandra in the late 1920s under the title Farrukhsiyar.

reiterates the goal of the order's spiritual discipline reassumed in the very title of the work:

> Human perfection consists of the 'extinction in the Divine' (*fanā fī Allāh, īśvara men laya ho jānā*) and culminates in the 'permanence in the Divine' (*baqā bi Allāh*)... To reach the end of this path is called *fanāiyat*, characterised by co-existence (*ma'iyat, sālokyatā*) and proximity (*qurbat, sāmīpyatā*); its upmost perfection lies in [the degrees of] conformity (*baqā, sārūpyatā*) and finally identification (*baqā bi'l-baqā, sāyujyatā*). . . .[243]

Unconstrained by the Islamic dogma of Allāh's absolute transcendence which imposed upon the Sūfis the need for a careful balance in their descriptions of the higher states of spiritual realisation, the Hindu master feels free to explain the ultimate degree of perfection envisaged by the classical term *baqā bi'l-baqā* as 'identity' with the Divine Principle, corresponding to the final stage reached by the *yogī* at the end of his intiatory process (*sāyujyatā*).

Later passages make it clear that the states described above in Naqshbandī terms and provided with their Sanskrit renderings, are comprehended in the author's vision under the general term of Yoga whose final degree is named *sāyujyatā*, derived from the same Sanskrit root *yuj* and meaning 'unification'. For Rāmcandra the first stage of Yoga is reached at the end of the 'journey towards Allāh' (*sair ilā Allāh*) with the attainment of the state of *fanā* or *laya avasthā*. For him it refers to the realisation of *īśvara*, the principle of universal existence contained in the *dā'ira-i imkān*, also denominated *saguṇa Brahman*. If considered from a Hindu perspective, however, the paramount perfection of the human state can only be intended as the stage of final liberation (*mukti*) obtained through the identification with the Supreme *Brahman* devoid of any positive quality (*nirguṇa*), equivalent to the Sūfī concept of 'permanence in permanence' (*baqā bi'l-baqā*) in the 'Supreme Reality' (*Ḥaqq Ta'ālā*).

---

243. *KmI*, p. 1. The Sanskrit term *yoga* later appears as a rendering of the Arabic term *waṣl*.

When considered from the perspective of a path of realisation leading the initiate gradually to the experience of union, these two objectives correspond to the aims envisaged by Haṭha-Yoga and Rāja-Yoga respectively, the latter only corresponding exactly to what according to Rāmcandra constitutes the *brahma-vidyā*, i.e., the metaphysical realm, and considered as the most sublime Knowledge (*para-vidyā*).[244] To achieve this most sublime of all human goals, the Hindu masters have presented their distinctive form of *sādhanā* consisting of elements that reflect in an interesting fashion a combination of features traceable in both traditions.

In one of the written sources attributed to Rāmcandra's nephew Bṛj Mohan Lāl, the following definition of the way is proposed:

> The path (*mārga*) that leads to the attainment of beatitude is derived from tasting the rain of the nectar of immortality. We call it 'Ānanda-Yoga', which constitutes the subtle part of Rāja-Yoga. It represents the fruit of the object of human pursuits kept in view by the saints. Out of compassion, they have brought forth this very easy and simple way for the prosperity of the entire human species. . . . Ānanda-Yoga constitutes the path of bounty and grace (*faiḍ o faḍl, kṛpā aur prasād*) which has included since the very beginning the grace and assistance of the Divinely inspired guide (*gurudeva*); that is, he continues to assist [his disciple] with his interior spiritual force of attraction (*tawajjuh, ākarṣaṇa śakti*) to return from his unsteady course of conduct to his original state (*aṣlī ādhāra*) and to get absorbed in beatitude. Since the state of consciousness of the true

244. *KmI*, pp. 1-2. In the introduction to the work containing the teachings of Bṛj Mohan Lāl's, compiled by his eldest son and present head of the main *satsang* at Kanpur, Oṁkār Nāth Saksenā, and published in 1958 under the title *Ānanda-Yoga*, these two successive and in some way complementary stages are reassumed under the main categories of *jadhba* and *sulūk*. Cf. *AY*, p. 22. For the implications of the term *brahma-vidyā*, used as a synonym of *'ilm-i sīna* (the 'science hidden in the breast') and *'ilm-i 'irfān* (science of the Knowledge), see *AIB*, Part I, p. 2.

> master remains constantly immersed in knowledge (*jñāna*), spiritual beatitude and peace (*sukūn*, *śānti*), the penetration of his glance full of subtle grace and of the spiritual current into the inner states of the disciple cause in the latter's heart the rise of his spiritual beatitude and peace. This sanctions the beginning of the spiritual path.[245]

This passage underlines the crucial role assumed by the spiritual preceptor in relation to the neophyte, especially during the initial phase of the *sādhanā*, consisting of the former's subtle intervention on the latter's as yet uncultivated inner soil. The grace and spiritual munificence (*faiḍ*) involved during this process contribute to the establishment of a subtle link between *guru* and *śiṣya* (or *pīr* and *murīd*), nourished by the spiritual attention (*tawajjuh*) of the master while focussing on his disciple. Eventually, it creates an intimate and indissoluble connection between the two rendering thereby effective the pact sanctioned by the preceding initiaton (*bai'at*). Moreover, it allows the novice to derive the benefit of instantaneous subtle purification and inner rectification leading him to the state of beatitude promoted by the spiritual attraction perceived in his heart. This pulls him spontaneously towards the source of all grace and effluence with which he will finally establish an intimate relation (*nisbat*). In the case of a Sūfī *ṭarīqa*, this source consists first of all of the spiritual preceptor and the uninerrupted chain of eminent authorities of the *silsila,* than in the archetypal model of human perfection represented by the prophet Muḥammad, the fountainhead of every regular spiritual lineage, and finally in Allāh, going through the entire series of venerable saints that constitute the chain of spiritual transmission.[246]

The establishment of such a powerful connection, although known also in other Sūfī orders, holds particular importance in the teachings of the Naqshbandiyya, where it is known under the term of *rābiṭa*. Under some aspects, it comes close to the

245. *AY*, pp. 28-9.

246. For a Hindu interpretation of the concept of *silsila* and *nisbat*, see *Madhhab aur Taḥqīqat*, pp. 38-40.

Hindu concept of *sahaja* (lit., ease, naturalness, spontaneousness) found in Kabīr and other *sant*s since the mediaeval period, which was most likely adopted from the teachings of Gorakṣa Nāth's Nāth-*sampradāya*.[247] In the *nirguṇa* perspective of the popularly revered Rāma-*upāsaka*s, the term came to denote the state of spontaneous absorption into and virtual identification with the Divine principle prior to the undertaking of any path of realisation, here for the sake of analogy denominated as Rāma.[248]

We recognise in this surprisingly intellectual perspective a reminiscence of the gnostic point of view held by the Vedānta. There is an interesting parallel with the binary Naqshbandī terminology of *jadhba* and *sulūk*. Traces of it can be detected also in the above-quoted description of one of the order's Hindu authorities, albeit in a less explicit way. In this context, it is particularly noteworthy that similar to Śrī Rāmānujācārya, Rāmānanda and Kabīr, these Kāyasth masters describe knowledge (*jñāna*) as a preliminary stage for the attainment of beatitude (*ānanda*). They characterise it as the highest degree of spiritual realisation and assimilate it to the state of bewilderment (*ḥairat*) and supreme forgetfulness (*ghaflat*) which is considered by the Mujaddidīs as the only possible description of the loftiest station (*ikmāl-i maqāmāt*) of the spiritual path. The negative implicati-ons rendered by these terms remind us of the terminology used by the Vedānta in the Upaniṣad in regard to the uneffable reality of non-duality.[249] There are, however, several degrees of beati-tude. Only the most sublime state of *paramānanda* applies truly to such a comparison, while on a more general scale *ānanda* as used by the authorities of this joint Mujaddidī-Kabīr-panthī tradition, denotes the utmost perfection reached at every single stage of realisation (*maqām*).[250]

---

247. Cf. *Kabīr-Granthāvalī*, *pada* 179, *Dādudayāl kī bānī*, vol. I, Allahabad, 1941, p. 28, and *Rāīdāsjī kī bānī*, Allahabad, 1948, p. 21.

248. For this and other considerations, see G.G. Filippi, 'Des composants culturels dans le Granthāvalī de Kabīr', in *Indologica Taurinensia* VI ,1978, pp. 137-41.

249. Cf. *MnS*, pp. 26/43.

250. Cf. *VS*, p. 64.

In the course of a lengthy description aimed at defining the state of sainthood (*wilāyat*) in the introductory pages of the *Kamāl-i Insānī*, Rāmcandra associates the *walī* drawn by the force of spontaneously arising attraction (*jadhba*) to the lower realms of sainthood with the Hindu *haṁsa* and *paramahaṁsa*. These latter two are included in the broader category of *ṣāḥib-i talwīn* (lit., the people of unstable nature), i.e., those individuals who are suddenly enraptured by a state of upward attraction during which they experience in a sort of inebbriation (*nashā*) the beatitude of selflessness (*be-khudī*). Unaware of their body and unable to direct the experiences of their inner states by their own intention, they are said shiver in a sort of ongoing alteration of contraction (*qabḍ*) and expansion (*vastu*) until, after an indefinite span of time, they return to their previous state (all these events lying beyond their own control).

Such a description reminds of the characteristics attributed to the *majdhūb*, here associated with the Hindu concept of *avadhūta*,[251] who is seen in contrast to the fixity of the *aṣḥāb-i tamkīn* (lit. 'those possessing a stable abode', *sthitaprajña*), who are outwardly characterised by sobriety and by a high degree of awareness (*hosh*), and who never tumble on their path of progression but maintain perfect control over every single step.[252]

Here the Naqshbandī origin appears undeniable, and the reason advanced for associating the degrees of *haṁsa* and *paramahaṁsa* with the first category of saints, unable to proceed beyond the stage of 'minor sainthood', is quite interesting. The *haṁsa* is perceived as being still exposed to the alternating phases of ascent and descent (*utāra-carhāv*), a definition analogous to the above-mentioned phases of contraction and

251. This connection with the concept of *avadhūta* is highly interesting in view of the particular relation this type of initiate bears with Dattātreya, the Hindu divinity linked to a particular kind of initiation in many respects similar to *al-Khiḍr* in the esoteric tradition of Islam and of the Naqshbandiyya, which apparently played an important role among the mediaeval *sants*.

252. *KmI*, pp. 3-4; *TP*, p. 34.

expansion, and is, therefore, unable to acquire a degree of lasting realisation that transcends any residual trace of duality. The *paramahaṁsa* in contrast penetrates into the highest realm of sainthood (*santgati*) where he remains permanently for the rest of his life.[253] While *jadhba* and *sulūk* had primarily been described as two successive degrees or attitudes assumed by the 'spiritual traveller', the Hindu masters, basing themselves on notions derived from the Naqshbandī doctrine, add some further details to this definition.

To complete this picture, quote the following paragraph from the text attributed to Rāmcandra, which in view of its content and style, has almost certainly been adopted from a written source going back to Shāh Faḍl Aḥmad Khān. It reflects very well the underlying attitude of this lineage:

> Everyone has a preference for a [particular] method that suits one's natural inclination. My personal preference lays emphasis on the *sālik*'s need to turn his full resolution on getting disengaged from the obligatory statutes of the [Islamic] Law (*farā'iḍ*), the religious tenets (*sunnat-i mu'qīda*) and all the additional ritual ways of conduct (*sunnat-i zubā'ida*), and to concentrate all his attention on the formula of Divine Unity (*kalima-i tawḥīd*) remaining firm in the stage of *dhikr*, *fikr* and intimacy with God (*uns*) while resorting for some days to supererogatory acts of worship (*nawāfil*), the recitation of the Holy Book (*talāwat-i Koran*), praising God (*tasbīḥ*), spiritually charged worship (*waẓīfa*) and the abundance of individual prayers (*du'ā-i kathrāt*). . . . One should withdraw from the attachment to virtuous actions and try hard, day and night, to annihilate one's own imaginary existence (*hastī-i mauhūm*) . . . than there is hope that the attraction of the everlasting bounty (*jadhba*, *'ināyat-i azlī*) may drive that person away from his individual limits towards the state of *fanā-i fanā* and from there eventually to the extreme

253. Cf. *AIB*, p. 26.

> limit of *baqā-i baqā* where he will witness the Essence of God. . . .[254]

This statement leaves little doubt about the shift in attitude that had taken place in this sub-branch of the Mujaddidiyya Maẓhariyya even before it reached among the Kāyasth Hindus and which prepared the ground for a definitive departure from the original religious and ritual context in which the *ṭarīqa* had been hitherto deeply anchored. Only such a radical change in perspective, away from the apparently inextricable connection between ritual code of behaviour sanctioned by the *sharī'at* and the underlying transcendent principles which confer upon them their deeper meaning which was so skilfully achieved in the doctrinal outlay of Shaikh Aḥmad Sirhindī, the Mujaddidī, could have made the passage of this previously orthodox and orthopractice Sunni order into a Hindu environment possible. It, thus, provides the partial answer to the question if and how the Sūfī authorities were themselves involved in this process of re-interpreting the *ṭarīqa* distinguishing between spiritual practice and a corpus of ritual acts and legal tenets conceived as ultimately accidental and of only secondary relevance for spiritual advancement.

Such a trend began to appear with the directions given by Sayyid Abūl Ḥasan al-Naṣīrābādī to his successor Aḥmad 'Alī Khān following the instructions he had received in an admonitory dream, and was strongly emphasised by Shāh Faḍl Aḥmad Khān, the spiritual preceptor of Rāmcandra Saksenā. Under the influence of Svāmī Brahmānanda, the authority affiliated to the Kabīr-panth, the latter began to question the essential role played by the exoteric ritual code while maintaining intact the corpus of rites and methods linked to the spiritual discipline. In this attitude we recognise the unmistakable mark of the *bhagats* and *sants* like Kabīr and other *nirguṇa bhaktas* who preached a universal message relieving their followers of the stringent need for strict ritual observance. Shāh Faḍl Aḥmad Khān deals as follows with this crucial question:

254. *KmI*, p. 6.

> Regarding the path, the Sūfīs used to impart their teachings in consonance with the religious tenets of those who followed Islam; they instructed their disciples in how to focus entirely on the supreme goal primarily by observing rigorously the prescribed religious duties, like the daily ritual prayer (*namāz*), and all those things and acts which have been enjoined by the messenger of Islam; then again, all those things and acts which have been recommended by the messenger of Allāh — peace be upon him! — . . . and then only the initiate was allowed to focus on the various aspects of the spiritual discipline. . . .
>
> [Instead], one should give preference to those acts which have been ascertained as being useful for this purpose and avoid any shortcomings at this regard; this is the conventional practice of all communities and the Sūfīs of all orders agree upon this. Hence, the earnest seeker of truth (*ṭālib*) should give preference to those practices which shall lead him to the attainment of the state of *be-khudī*. In this matter, there is nothing exceeding [the practice of] *dhikr* and *fikr*.[255]

In this passage, a partial reiteration of the paragraph quoted above, the shaikh's position appears more cautious. He himself was indeed a Muslim and a renowned local Sūfī authority, whatever his convictions and attitudes regarding the spiritual discipline may have been with regard to his Hindu disciple. As a matter of fact, most of his followers and desciples were Sunni Muslims who were instructed in the *ṭarīqa* according to the conventional Mujaddidī pattern. One has therefore to remain cautious in the interpretation of his statements, available mainly through the mediated version of his Hindu disciple, for the attitude he assumed while instructing the latter has certainly differed from that imparted to the former. Rather than an outright rejection of the validity of the religious tenets, it appears that he regarded these simply as not essential for

255. *KmI*, pp. 7-8.

conferring efficacy to the spiritual discipline, at least to a certain degree.

At the same time, Shāh Faḍl Aḥmad Khān stresses his preference for those activities which are prone to guarantee access to the higher degrees of realisation, resumed under the terms *fanā*, *be-khudī* and *baqā al-baqā*. Especially with regard to the attainment of the immediate goal, the attainment of the degree of *be-khudī* which among the Mujaddidīs sanctions entry into the sphere of minor sainthood, he mentions a range of methods included in the broad categories of *dhikr* and *fikr*, that is to say the invocative and the contemplative aspects of the operational discipline. As conveyed by the transposition of our Hindu author, these include *japa* and *manana*, a fairly adequate translation of these two technical categories in Sūfīsm into the yoga-viśiṣṭādvaita context. The former pertains to the science of subtle invocation based on the knowledge of rhythm and sound vibrations used to awaken the subtle organs in the human constitution, more or less equivalent to the Hindu *mantra-vidyā*. The latter relates to the mental sphere (the Arabic term *fikr* embraces a wide range of activities based on the mental faculty) aimed at achieving control of the mind and the fixation of the thought-current that surfaces from the vortex of consciousness (*citta-vṛtti*), and denotes the whole complex of techniques apt to achieve progress in checking the feeble mind until reaching the capacity of contemplating and thereby penetrating the inner reality of an object.[256]

Following these important premises, the rest of the work, entitled *Kamāl-i insānī* provides a general introduction to the methodology of the Sūfī ancestors. It consists of the presentation of a wide range of techniques gathered from various sources. Apart from the first-hand instructions received from Shāh Faḍl Aḥmad Khān they contain notions originally ascribed to leading

---

256. The significance of this lies in the technical sense these terms have assumed in their respective traditions. As the use of the terms *japa* and *manana* suggests, the Hindu masters adopt a vocabulary intimately connected to the technical language used in the various Tantra-Yoga doctrines following the classification operated by Patañjali in his *Yoga-Sūtra*.

authorities of other orders and of different epochs, including Abū 'Abd al-Rahman al-Sulāmī (333/942-412/1021), the Chistī Shaikh Sayyid Mīr Muḥammad al-Ḥusainī Gīsūdarāz (*d.* 1422) and the renowned authority of the Firdawsī order, Shaikh Sharaf al-Dīn Yāḥyā al-Manerī (*d.* 782/1382).

The largest section is concerned with the *dhikr* or *japa* and follows broadly the conventional Sūfī pattern that divides the *dhikr* into the two principal categories of vocal invocation performed with the tongue (*dhikr-i zabānī*) and the hidden or silent invocation performed exclusively on an inner, mental plane (*dhikr-i khafī, mānasik japa*). On the authority of Abū 'Abd al-Raḥmān al-Sulāmī, Rāmcandra outlines the specific context to which these invocations are applicable. Focussing mainly on the silent *dhikr* which is predominantly used by the Mujaddidīs, he introduces among them the *dhikr-i sirr*. This peculiar invocation is closely linked with the subtle centre bearing the same name. Its regular repetition, if focussed on the particular spot in the human breast said to be the seat of this subtle organ, is said to create an impenetrable shield around the mind protecting it from being invaded by distracting thoughts (*khaṭra*). It, thus, represents an important tool in achieving the ability to focus the thought while maintaining a high level of awareness, known by the Naqsbandhīs as the rise of the 'perpetual presence' evoked by the fixation of the mind on the one true Object (*ḥuḍūr-i dā'īmī*).

Yet another variety of subtle invocation consists of the *dhikr-i rūḥ*, described as effacing every remaining trace of the *sādhaka*'s individual attributes to the extent of leaving him engaged in the invocation of this *dhikr* while being completely deprived of his self-consciousness, so that nothing remains interposed between him and the only Object (*lakṣya*), Allāh or *paramātmā*. It brought to utmost perfection, the performance of this invocation is said to lead to such an intimate compenetration between the invoking subject and the invoked object that the performer's mind perceives the very Object as the Subject invoking.

But what appears most striking is that this description,

developed entirely along an Islamic perspective, concludes with a verse from Kabīr which sums up the entire preceding description. It adds, moreover, that integrating element of a parallel tradition so spontaneously perceived by the authorities of this order:

> *jāp mithāi ajapā mithāi, anhad bhī mithāi* ।
> *surati samānī śabd main, tāhi kāl na khāi* ।।

> Efface the oral invocation, efface the inner invocation,
> efface the infinite sound.
>
> Contain the sound current in the one sound vibration,
> so that time may lose its grip upon you.[257]

Here, the author takes for granted the association between the 'science of the *dhikr*' and the ancient Hindu *mantra-vidyā*. Perpetuated from the epoch of the *R̥gveda* till the present day, the latter assumed the specific aspect of the 'science of the sound vibration' (*śabda-yoga*) in the Tāntrik doctrines and among many *sant*s, especially in the Kabīr-panth and the Dādū-panth. Particularly interesting is the connection established here between the two main categories of *dhikr*, the vocal and the silent invocation, with the concept of *japājapa*, current among the mediaeval Rāma-*upāsaka*s but already known in previous epochs under the name *vajra-japa*. To declared purpose of this technique is to disperse the numerous veils *māyā* has spun around the mind of the profane by focussing and meditating on the name and essence of God alone. Elsewhere, we learn that the 'name of the essence' (*bīja-mantra*, *satnām*) used and further transmitted by Rāmcandra and his successors, consists of either the *ism-i dhāt* inherited from their Muslim ancestors, recommending the formula consisting of the syllables *Allāh* or *Hū*, or alternatively of the invocation of the *satnām* that makes use of the repeated invocation of the name *rām-rām* or of the *akṣaras* — syllable *oṁ-oṁ*, both current among the followers of Kabīr and essentially playing the same role.[258]

---

257. *KmI*, p. 10.

258. Savitri Shukla, 1963, p. 281. Cf. *KmI*, p. 14 and *AY*, pp. 57-8.

As the quotation of the verse cited above indicates, Rāmcandra's *sādhanā* maintains the Kabirian perspective of the unqualified by pointing out the ultimate transcendence of the qualified state as the supreme goal envisaged by this technique encapsulated in the primordial syllable *oṁ* that can be used as a substitute for the *rāma-nāma* at the more advanced stages of the path.

The application of the subtle sound vibration (*sūrat-śabda*) reproduced by the repeated invocation of these sacred syllables does not remain limited to a specific *cakra* or *laṭīfa*, but can be extended to the entire series of subtle centres following the progress made by the initiate. It is a peculiar feature of this contemporary discipline that the type of invocation or syllable used in the varying degrees of the initiatic process does not undergo any change, but rather the effect it produces while employed in the awakening of the specific organ upon which it is directed. This determines, moreover, the name given to the particular *dhikr*.

The most immediate result achieved by the initiate who has reached a certain perfection and interiorisation of the *dhikr-i qalb* or *mānasik japa* consists of the prolonged perception of the sound vibration characteristic for that particular subtle organ, which endures, even after the active performance of its invocation is interrupted, not only in the subtle organ most directly concerned but in various parts of the body. It is, moreover, said to extent to the sound produced by many exterior objects, like the tinkling of temple-bells, the sound of a whirling grinding-stone, the whizzing sound of the wind or the rustling of the leaves of a tree moved by a light breeze. This particular sound will initially reproduce the sound vibration evoked by the syllable chosen by the disciple according to his personal preference. But once it is thoroughly impressed on the *laṭīfa-i rūḥ* the different sounds produced by outer objects are said to be perceived as all pertaining to the *paramātmā* alone, that is to say the apparent subsistence of multiplicity will be transmuted by the perception of their underlying unity.

Elaborating on the difference between these two degrees of

invocation, our author returns to the original Naqshbandī terminology that describes the effects provoked by the *dhikr-i qalb* as balanced between the 'presence of the Truth' (*ḥuḍūr-i Ḥaqq*), or increased awareness of the purely transcendent realm, and the 'presence of creation' (*ḥuḍūr-i khalq*), corresponding to an increased awareness of the immanent realm. However, the *dhikr-i rūḥ*, tends predominantly towards an increase of transcendent awareness dominated by the quality of *sat*. Brought to ultimate perfection with the *dhikr-i sirr*, the *abhyāsī* is left with nothing but the lasting awareness of the transcendent Principle (*īśvara*) in which the mind remains permanently immersed in itself (*ḥuḍūr-i dā'imī, dhyāna*).

Progressing further, the *sādhaka* attains to the *dhikr-i khafī*, intended here not merely in its general sense as 'hidden invocation' but in its technical context as being focussed on the *laṭīfa-i khafī*. It also has a specific context indicating a stage in the spiritual progress in which the separate existence of the *dhikr* invoked and the *śabda*, now intended as the subtle, non-human (*apauruṣeya*) seed or essence said to reside in the treasurehouse of the heart-chamber, mingle with each other while getting absorbed in the subtle sound-current (*sūrat*). According to the Haṭha-Yoga and *panth*-doctrines, this current consists of a soundless sound (*anahada dhvani*) that pervades the entire universe irradiating from a source located at the exact centre of the universe.[259]

Notwithstanding the difference in nature that characterises the mode of *japa* and the effects it provokes on the inner states of the *abhyāsī*, which ranges between smooth and abrupt leaving some people deprived of its benefits for their entire life-span, the perfection reached at this sublime degree leads to the disappearance of the sense of duality (*duvidhā*) subsisting between the *dhākir* who invokes and the *dhikr* invoked. At that stage, the disciple is said to lose even the perception of the beatitude that had previously begun to pervade his inner self and is led directly to the final two degrees obtainable through the practice of the *japa*. These are the *dhikr-i akhfā* and the

259. *KmI*, p. 17.

dhikr-i khafī-akhfā, which confer a progressively deeper penetrating sense of unity that gradually effaces all remaining traces of dualistic perception connected with the separate existence (*ana*, *aham*) of the spiritual traveller. Rāmcandra specifies that the use of the *dhikr-i khafī* is specific to the *kaṇṭha-cakra*, while the *dhikr-i khafī-akhfā* pertains to the *nuqṭa-i suwaida* or *ājñā-cakra*.

Consonant with the method taught by Shāh Faḍl Aḥmad Khān in the Naqshbandī tradition, Rāmcandra too insists on the stringent necessity to pursue in the performance of the silent invocation from the very moment of entering the spiritual discipline until reaching the most advanced spiritual states. He leaves aside the ancient Mujaddidī conventions that tend to exalt the efficacy of the *dhikr* while performing the night and early morning prayers, in particular once the initiate has entered into the 'sphere of supreme sainthood' and that of the 'prophetic perfections'. It puts once more in evidence the shift effected by the transmission into an environment not bound by the religious duties of the *sharī'at*. This results in an entirely inner discipline which, thus, fills the gap left and assumes, in the specific case of the *dhikr*, an even more important role in obtaining the one essential goal envisaged over and over again. In the words of Shāh Faḍl Aḥmad Khān this is expressed thus:

> . . . in my opinion the *dhikr-i khafī* alone should be performed so as to keep the heart clean from any . . . heterogeneous images and focus one's spiritual attention on the Supreme goal alone. One should strengthen the determination to maintain the heart present in the unification of the mind (*yaksū'ī, ekāgratā*) trying to attain to a deeply intimate relation with the Truth (*sat*) by extinguishing oneself into It, than try to extinguish oneself in that application . . . this is the closest and most certain mean of reaching the original abode (*aṣl-pada*). . . .[260]

There follows a long list of twenty points that outline the formal

260. *KmI*, p. 19.

conditions required for a correct and successful performance of the *dhikr-japa*, to be followed before, during and after its recommended daily performance. These resemble too closely the accompanying regulations set out in the original Islamic context to require any detailed description here, e.g., the maintenance of the state of ritual purity (*ṭahāra, śauca*), the wearing clean clothes, a pure and pleasently scented environment, etc. Interestingly, these preliminary conditions include the fundamental issue of fixing the image of the *satguru* in the heart (*taṣawwur al-shaikh*) laid down as an indispensable condition for promoting the 'divinely inspired and infallible master' (*gurudeva*) to the rank of *iṣṭadevatā,* i.e., the divinity chosen for personal worship to whom one must surrender. Its description certainly constitutes an expression of the greater freedom enjoyed by Hindus in formulating the essential *pīr-murīdī* relationship in unrestricted terms of selfless devotion (*upāsanā*) even if the immediate object belongs outwardly to the immanent sphere.

These descriptions are particularly striking in the explicit recommendation to refrain from the ancient practice of suspending the breath (*ḥabs-i nafas*, *prāṇāyāma*). They are so explicitly derived from the Naqshbandī shaikhs that we can safely assume a substantial adherence to the principles sanctioned by the masters of this *ṭarīqa*, which were found sufficiently compatible to leave them unaltered. An explicit mention is made in this context of the Rādhāsoāmī authorities who, according to Rāmcandra, prescribe to their disciples the habit also current among the Mujaddidīs of covering with one's fingers the two nostrils, the cavity of the ears and both eyes. The aim of this practice is to reduce the sensual perception from the outside world through these organs while being engaged in the performance of the *japa*. It is a practice not shared by Rāmcandra but which could well provide vague indication of a Sūfī matrix at the base also of the Rādhāsoāmī teachings.

The observation of certain rules meant to sanction a precise rhythm of breath that accompanies the invocation is, however, not outrightly rejected, but even recommended in exceptional cases if undertaken under the expert guidance of an authoritative master who regards them as suitable to the disciple's inner nature. Two degrees or categories of practitioners are distinguished in this context both unheard of among the Mujaddidī authorities at Delhi. The first comprises those individuals less expert in refraining the breath, defined as 'travellers' (*musāfir*) since they have not yet attained to a lasting control over the discipline, who are said to be affected by a powerful wave of heat especially in the heart-region.[261] The second embraces those more advanced in the performance of this technique, defined as 'constant' (*muqīm*), who no longer perceive neither cold nor heat and who have thereby attained to the perfection of the *ajapā-japa*, remaining immersed in the perpetual presence of the Sovereign (*al-Mālik*).[262]

Beginners are, moreover, advised not to remain frightened by the sensible increase in blood circulation which provokes an increase in the temperature of the body, but to persist in the performance of the *dhikr* and strictly observe the instructions they receive, for this corresponds to a transitory period of purification that only in very exceptional circumstances brings along major risks for the inner equilibrium and health of the disciple. The possible risks involved by an indiscriminate use of the techniques connected with *ḥiḍr-i nafas* are very similar to those described by the *ācārya*s of many contemporary *yoga-sampradāya*s among whom a similar tendency away from the extremely rigid disciplines regarding the restraint of the breath can be equally recognised as no longer adequate in recent times. Caution in increasing too rapidly the rhythm of every period of conscious respiration and of raising the number of silent invocations pronounced in its course are discouraged as they invoke the risk of creating an inner unbalance and lasting mental damage. Including such apparently crude recommenda-

261. This heat is said to dissolve the layers of fat around the heart thereby contributing to its purification. Apart from its literal meaning, such a perception obviously includes also a more subtle interpretation, although the production of physical heat is certainly one of the immediately perceptible effects of these techniques, often stressed by the *ācārya*s of different *yoga-sādhanā*s.

262 *KmI*, p. 24.

tions as expelling the breath exclusively through the nostrils in order to avoid damaging the teeth, such advice is currently found in the treatises of numerous Hindu masters. They reflect a general tendency towards a simplification of the discipline considered as within the reach of the average modern disciple.

Notwithstanding the master's opinion that generally discourages this practice as not strictly necessary for the average disciple, the detailed account provided by Rāmcandra regarding breath-control exceeds by far that provided by the orthodox Mujaddidīs and betrays the great importance attributed originally to this science in the general context of the *japa*. As confirmed by my personal observations while assisting at the *satsang* of his successors at Kanpur and elsewhere, however, simple and kept at a low rate, breath-control still constitutes a fundamental ingredient of the spiritual discipline practised today.

The description of the *dhikr-japa* is completed by a detailed list of a range of secondary applications to which this technique is liable, including the two, four and even six-stroke variety of the *dhikr-i nafī wa ithbāt*, the performance of which imitates in every detail the guidelines provided by the Sūfī authorities. Although it does not occupy among Hindus the same prominent rank which it holds among the Muslims initiates, this includes a series of dietary prescriptions that should accompany the performance of this *dhikr*, like recommending the consumption of milk and fruit only, clear indication of an influence originally pertaining to a Yoga discipline. For the sake of completeness, the text provides also the description of a number of minor invocations aimed at obtaining results in more contingent fields often considered as dangerous, such as obtaining telepathic capacities, communication with the spirits of the deceased, the fulfilment of worldly desires, etc., some of which can be distinguished as authentically Naqshbandī while others refer to practices current among other Sūfī orders, such as the Shaṭṭāriyya and the Qādiriyya.[263]

The transmission of the *dhikr* is normally conceived as an

263. *KmI*, pp. 46-59.

essential of the pact sanctioned between master and disciple, which allows the neophyte effective entrance into the spiritual discipline. Rāmcandra describes the method of his shaikh regarding his Hindu disciples in particular but to some extent also including his Muslim protegés in a rather unconventional way:

> . . . the method adopted by our *murshid* was that normally to Hindus and in some particular cases also to his Muslim disciples initiation was not conferred immediately, and for a certain period the *dhikr* was neither effectively transmitted nor even hinted at by subtle allusion. Only after ascertaning the disciple's firm desire to receive initiation after his acquaintance with the method of the *ṭarīqa* accompanied by his firm intent to apply himself thoroughly to the inner discipline, did the Shāh proceed to the performance of this ritual. . . . Sometimes, this [intermediate] period could last for months or even years. . . .[264]

This statement assumes great importance considering the prominent position held by the *dhikr* as compared to that of the *murāqaba* and other meditation techniques to which it is said to be ultimately preferable. It represents the most concrete tool for the initiate to participate actively through his own efforts in his spiritual progress, while its absence implies the restriction to an entirely passive attitude for those disciples whose initial duty consists exclusively of attending their master's *satsang*, defined in this context as a spiritual school (*ādhyātmika pāṭhaśālā, rūḥānī madrasa*).[265] There emerges in unequivocal terms the particularity of the cross-cultural *sādhanā* adopted by our Hindu authorities. The absence of the *dhikr* leaves the potential initiate exposed to the grace of his *satguru* who, through the transmission his *tawajjuh*, prepares the ground in

---

264. *KmI*, p. 40.

265. *AY*, p. 224. In this passage, the author makes a subtle distinction between the merely exterior *satsang* and the inner *satsang* which constitutes part of the so-called 'introverted discipline' (*antarmukhī sādhanā*) centred on and fixed entirely in the innermost heart.

the heart for a future post-initiatory involvement of the disciple. In this role, the master is said to resemble the peasant who must carefully plough the soil before planting the seed that promises him an abundant harvest. Such a revised attitude, interpreted in base of the dichotomy between *jadhba* and *sulūk* that compose the Naqshbandī path, finds some analogies in the Hindu disciplines included in the ancient Rāja-Yoga disciplines renewed in later periods in the sahaja-yoga disciplines promoted by the *nirguṇa sant*s. It underlines impressively the extreme consequences derived from the tendency of increasing simplification begun, in the specific context of the Islamic *ṭarīqa*, with the innovatory methods taught to Khwāja 'Abd al-Khāliq and Bahā al-Dīn al-Naqshband by al-Khiḍr.

Once the preliminary period of trial has lapsed, the subtle invocation of a sacred syllable constitutes thus the primary means at disposition of the Hindu initiates exactly like their Muslim brethren from the very moment they are granted access to the *sādhanā* through the initiatory pact. Only after the inner states of the seeker are variegated by the subtle influence produced by its vibration the *sādhaka* is said to be ready to receive instructions in the performance of the methods of *fikr* and *murāqaba*. However, the performance of the *dhikr* is never altogether abandoned. It is rather gradually sublimated into a more and more seminal state while progress is made in concentration, meditation, contemplation and finally identification, the principal steps of the mental discipline resumed under the term *fikr*, which are concerned primarily with the refinement of the faculty of thought.

It is noteworthy that the descriptions regarding the performance of the *dhikr* refer exclusively to the subtle organs contemplated by the *'ilm-i laṭā'if* of the Mujaddidīs while no explicit reference ever appears in relation to the successive series of *cakra*s described elsewhere on a Tāntrik background. These, we assume, belong to the successive stage of the *sulūk*. This attitude is explained by the fact that our Hindu masters regard the entire *'ilm-i sīna*, concerned with the ascent of the five subtle organs of the *'ālam-i amr*, as comprising the intermediate sphere resumed in the *hr̥daya-cakra*. They, therefore, regard the conscious spiritual energy sent forth by the heart in relation to the degree of *jadhba*, which describe the journey from the heart to the *ājñā-cakra* situated inside the skull, as the initial field of application for these techniques.

The focus shifts at this stage from the heart, which is related intimately to the manifestation of the Divine attraction (*jadhba*), to the second phase consisting of the control and sublimation of the psycho-mental component of the human nature, i.e., the mind and the senses, which is comprised under the term *sulūk*. Bṛj Mohan Lāl explains as follows:

> Our spiritual masters have given precedence to the *jadhba* over the *sulūk*, that is to say they have anticipated the way and discipline related to the Divine attraction integrating it, according to necessity, with elements pertaining to the way of *sulūk*. The different techniques employed for the control and purification of *man*, *buddhi*, *citta*, *ahaṅkāra* and the senses are referred to as *sulūk*, in correspondence to what the Muslims call 'purification of the soul' (*tadhkiya-i nafs*, *hṛdaya kī nirmalatā*). Since this important modification implies the arrival of the *jijñāsu* and devotee permeated by love at the *iṣṭapāda* with the assistance of the spiritual attraction transmitted through the heart, and since it is moreover necessary to purify the interior agent (*antaḥkaraṇa*), the compassion and the grace (*dayā aur kṛpā*) of the *satguru* are essential till the very beginning.[266]

There derives that the immediate aim of the initiate consists of the attainment of the condition of *fanā* or *laya-avasthā*. It is reached mainly through the interior power (*āntarik śakti*) and spiritual love (*ādhyātmik prem*) of the master, further assisted by the disciple's active involvement in the practice of the *japa*. Eventually, it leads to a withdrawal of the mind and the senses it governs from the objects of the outside world that eventually results in a contraction of these inner faculties into the intimate

266. *AV*, pp. 229-30.

spiritual chamber of the heart, regarded as the seat of the interior Divinity. This helps the disciple to overcome or (to remain faithful to the terminology used in this context) to realise the dissolution of the limiting conditions of his individual existence (*upādhi*) and return to a sort of embryonic state of involution. Once this stage, that goes along with the permanent recollection of *īśvara*, is reached the journey begins from the *ājñā-cakra* upwards along the polar axis (*dhruva-pāda*) towards the superior states of being.[267]

The various degrees crossed during that stage of vertical ascent consist of the well-known Sūfī *maqāmāt* that correspond to Rāmcandra's descriptions of the *cakra*s or *loka*s contained in the *aṇḍa* and *brahmāṇḍa* dealt with in the preceding chapter. The last of these 'stations' is defined as the 'station of bewilderment' (*maqām-i ḥairat*) in which the *abhyāsī* is said to have lost the perception of the triple time while remaining still in one place 'like an idol-stature', detached from the ephemeral ups and downs of the world and the impact its objects have normally on the mind and liberated from any doubt in front of the radiance of the *paramātmā*.[268] The saint who has reached this sublime station appears outwardly involved in worldly affairs just like any ordinary man, but inwardly he has reached the degree of realisation of the *avadhūta* remaining untouched by happiness and grief alike while unable to explain the reason for his state.

We notice that in this description the author apparently maintains the Mujaddidī idea of witnessing the supreme Truth rather than an identification with It. He limits himself to replace the Islamic term *Allāh Ta'ālā* with that of *paramātmā*, a fact that shows the still relatively considerable adherence to many of his shaikh's Sufi teachings, although these already begin to reflect his own Hindu heritage.

These descriptions develop along the lines of the Mujaddidī doctrine, but maintain throughout the Hindu perspective

---

267. *AV*, p. 139.
268. *KmI*, p. 26.

regarding the quality of this stage of realisation. Rāmcandra here distinguishes two types of 'bewilderment', the 'contemptible bewilderment' (*ḥairat-i madhmūm*), typical for the state of stupor when something goes beyond the comprehension of our mental capacity, which is considered negative and is found among the common folk (*al-'awāmm*), and the 'commendable bewilderment' (*ḥairat-i mamdūḥ*), which is considered positive and is limited to the elite among the saints, as a sign of reaching the stage when the limits of knowledge are transcended.

Such a perspective fits well into Rāmcandra's joint Mujaddidī-Vaiṣṇava perspective and reflects the natural affinity between the point of view held by the viśiṣṭādvaita on one side and the *waḥdat al-shuhūd* on the other. Far from rejecting the validity of knowledge (*jñāna*, *ma'rifat*) as a means of access to the higher degrees of spiritual identity, both propound a relatively dynamic concept of the ultimate Truth. They, thus, retain a certain degree of difference in union which sanctions the superiority of completely selfless devotion to and meditation on the Supreme Object of worship and service to the world over the purely contemplative attitude assumed by the kevalādvaita and the *waḥdat al-wujūd*.

4

The Emergence of Regional Hindu Sub-branches

A Kāyasth Path to Liberation?

The death of Rāmcandra Saksenā in 1931, followed by that of his younger brother Raghubar Dayāl in 1947 marked the end of the first generation of Hindu authorities affiliated jointly to the Mujaddidiyya Maẓhariyya and the Kabīr-panth. Thereafter, the responsibility to face the numerous challenges arising from the generational passage was left to their disciples and designated successors. The main line of succession focussed around the authoritative figure of Bṛj Mohan Lāl, the eldest son of Raghubar Dayāl and his chief *khalīfa* at Kanpur and Lucknow, and apparently proved stable enough to provide his *satsang* with a cohesive energy for the next decade. But it was among the early members of Rāmcandra's *satsang* at Fatehgarh that the seeds of schism were sown ready to emerge after their master's death. In contrast to the pattern followed by their predecessor, most of these newly emerged leaders did not maintain a close relationship with the contemporary Muslim authorities of the *silsila* but began to claim independent authority on their own. Their effort to institutionalise their *satsang* by expanding it into a widely recognised spiritual mission with different headquarters across India and abroad has often been accompan-ied by the increasing tendency to omit any explicit mention of the *sādhanā*'s Islamic origin, and to lay instead greater emphasis on the enduring strength of India's indigenous spiritual traditions.

From the written sources left by Rāmcandra we know that he was well aware of and extremely concerned about the latent danger of the *sādhanā*'s fragmentation among his chief disciples after his departure from this world. In one of his writings, he complains:

> . . . Sincerely, until the present day this humble one has not been able to comply fully with the methods and determination needed to fulfil the task entrusted to him, but certainly my heart acknowledges them. Unfortunately, among my friends and dear ones and all those who have accompanied me on this path there is not a single person endowed with the required determination and qualification to accept and acknowledge the importance of the tenets of this new path. . . . I consider it as my own utter failing that until now I have never presented them with any textual support [regarding the path], delivering all my teachings orally according to the circumstances. I do not know who among my intimate disciples has accepted and understood them and to what extent they have done so. . . .[1]

Conscious of the absence of a worthy successor in the intimate circle of his desciples, Rāmcandra did not apparently appoint a chief *khalīfa*, but handed over responsibility for the surveillance and organisation of his *satsang* partly to his younger brother at Kanpur, partly to his only surviving son Jag Mohan Nārāyaṇ at Fatehgarh.[2] Among other close disciples who had joined Rāmcandra's company during the early stages of his mastership, four appear of particular importance for the ongoing

---

1. *JC*, p. 434.

2. This is clearly stated in Rāmcandra's testament (*wasiyat-nāma*), written in October 1930 and handed over to his son a few days before his death (cf. *JC*, pp. 432-5). A copy of this manuscript containing the master's last will adorns nowadays wall of the room where the daily *satsang* of Oṁkār Nāth takes place in a part of the fragmented Raghubar Bhavan at Kanpur, as if to legitimise outwardly his claim to successorship.

history of the lineage. Each of them has perpetuated the tradition inherited from their *gurudeva* in a particular way, and provided it with the institutional fundamentals which have turned these newly emerged *satsang*s or 'missions' into widely acclaimed spiritual centres attracting people of all ages and from different social backgrounds.

A common characteristic one can observe among these sub-lineages is the process of accentuated Hinduisation of both the doctrinal background and the methodology of the Sufi *ṭarīqa* accompanied by the gradual omission of any mention of the Islamic origin of the spiritual treasure from which it has drawn so many aspects of its teachings. This tendency of gradual absorption into an indigenous background has been a typical phenomenon of Indian culture since ancient times and shows the extreme vitality of the subcontinent's spiritual heritage which, although undergoing numerous formal adaptations, has survived in multiple facets largely unperturbed in its essential features by the influences of modernity. The present study, therefore, concludes with a brief glance at the four branches of the Hindu Naqshbandiyya which have developed from the four disciples of Rāmcandra just mentioned. An attempt is thereby made to describe the lines along which each of these developed, trying to single out distinctive elements and the underlying common ideological framework that have accompanied the rise of these independent branches of esoteric instruction.

Mathura: Personal cult or pathway towards liberation?

One of Rāmcandra's oldest and closest disciples was Dr. Caturbhuj Sahāy who first met his master as early as 1910, reportedly on the banks of the Ganges at Fatehgarh while he was in the company of Svāmī Brahmānanda. Caturbhuj Sahāy was born on 3 November 1883 at Chamkarī village in the Etah district of western Uttar Pradesh in a pious Kāyasth household. His father held the rank of superintendent of village accountants (*qānūn-go*) in the colonial administration of the British Raj. However, following the death of his parents that left him an orphan at the early age of fourteen, he was brought up by his maternal grandparents at Fatehgarh.[3] After a standard education in Arabic, Persian and English, he later pursued his higher studies in Hindī and Sanskrit before enrolling and graduating as a medical student at Agra Medical College. Initially a fervent member of the Ārya Samāj, he was reportedly soon disappointed by the self-centred policy of its leaders. Turning his back on the Hindu reform movement he fully dedicated himself to exercise his profession as medical doctor in Fatehgarh, where he eventually joined the emerging *satsang* of Rāmcandra.[4]

In 1914, Caturbhuj Sahāy received *dīkṣā* into the lineage and after serving his master for several years, he eventually received the full licence (*ācārya padavī*) from him in 1921 and returned to his native town of Etah, where, in the late 1920s, he began to organise his own *satsang*. On the occasion of *Mahāśivarātrī* 1930, following the example set by his *guru*, he celebrated the first *bhaṇḍārā* there in the auspicious presence of Rāmcandra. Several years later, in 1951, he moved from Etah to Mathura in order to be closer to his numerous followers living in the Braj region that stretches out along the Yamunā river.

The message conveyed through his teachings largely reached the public through the monthly review *Sādhanā* which continues to be published from the Sadhana Press at Mathura down to the present day (1996), and through a series of works dealing with different aspects of the spiritual discipline promoted by the author. On 23 September 1957, Caturbhuj Sahāy died at the age of 74 at his home at Mathura leaving behind his wife, three sons and two daughters. His successors appointed to continue and consolidate his mission from the *āśrama* at Mathura, include his eldest son Bṛjendra Kumār Sahāy (*d.*1987), and Paṇḍit Mihīlāl (1901-83), a learned brāhmaṇa from Tundla, a small country town near Agra.[5] At

3. *LVV*, p.172
4. *Sādhanā aur anubhav*, Ramashram Satsang, Mathurā, 1993, vol. I, p. 6.
5. For a brief biographical note on these two figures, see *LVV*, pp. 262-3, 264-7.

present, the *satsang* and the annual *bhaṇḍārā* at Mathura are organised by his second son Hemendra Kumār Sahāy.

The teachings

The spiritual discipline (*sādhanā*) and associated doctrinal background (*siddhānta*) expounded by Caturbhuj Sahāy are to a large extent explained with reference to the classical texts of the Hindu tradition. The principal sources used for this purpose are represented by the *prasthāna-traya* which constitute the bulk of scriptural authority of the Vedānta and consist of the major Upaniṣad, the *Brahma-Sūtra* including the comment (*bhāṣya*) of its two principal interpreters, Śrī Śaṅkarācārya and Śrī Rāmānujācārya, and finally the *Bhagavad Gītā*. He explains:

> From the doctrinal point of view, the *santmat* and the school of *advaitavāda* coincide with each other. Their difference lies in the practical aspect of the *sādhanā*. The *santmat* is based on the balanced equilibrium of the three components of *karma*, *upāsanā* and *jñāna*. *Santmat* does not reject any activity (*karma*) related to the discipline of Yoga, ritual sacrifice, acetic exercises and the method of *jap*, but integrates them with *upāsanā* and *jñāna*. . . . The Vedānta prescribes the performance of all those actions which conform to each individual's nature (*svābhāvika karma*) and the devotion of the Unqualified (*nirguṇa*), and considers the devotion of identity (*abheda bhakti*) as utmost, while refraining from any other ritual activity.[6]

The methodology proposed by Chaturbhuj Sahāy inserts itself into the technical context of a Yoga-*sampradāya*. In its central aspects it reverts around the last five stages of the eight-membered (*aṣṭāṅga*) module formulated by Patañjali in his *Yoga-Sūtras* and is integrated here and there with those notions derived from the teachings of the Mujaddidī authorities which were considered compatible with those of the *sant*s and their Tāntrik forerunners.

---

6. *SkA*, vol. I, p. 72.

Compared with Rāmcandra's apparently simple, often naïve descriptions which are based more on a genuine intuition than on thorough textual erudition, the expositions of Caturbhuj Sahāy show a much greater fluency in style and betray a closer acquaintance with the classical Hindu concepts which is derived from a systematic study of the traditional sciences. Consequently, in most cases Caturbhuj Sahāy replaces the Koranic and Persianate vocabulary used by the Mujaddidīs with that current in the Sanskrit culture, leaving the former unaltered only in explicit references to the methods taught by his master. His most exhaustive opus, comprising seven volumes, is entitled *Sādhanā ke anubhava* ('The authority of the discipline') and reflects in its style and content the sound erudition of an educated Hindu. Only here and there do we come across single chapters and sporadic references to the Sūfī doctrines and methods, particularly in relation to the technical aspects focussing on the 'science of the sound' and the *dhikr*.[7] As with Rāmcandra, the theoretical and purely doctrinal background regarding cosmological and metaphysical issues has supplanted the Islamic component resorting to those Hindu concepts regarded by the author as the most suitable for his audience. Well acqua-inted with the sacred language of Hinduism, Caturbhuj Sahāy's theoretical excursions are often interspersed with lengthy Sanskrit quotations from the sacred texts. However, occasionally a number of Persian and Urdu verses attributed to different Sūfī authorities are integrated in support of these elaborations, thus, aligning him with the pattern of exposition traced by his immediate spiritual ancestor albeit on a minor scale.

In the tradition of his lineage, the *sādhanā* conceived by Caturbhuj Sahāy lays great emphasis on the devotional element based on the disciple's love and unconditioned surrender (*upāsanā*) to the master. Ultimately, the perfection of this inner attitude is said to lead to the union with *īśvara* and, at a later stage, to identification with the *nirguṇa Brahman*. While acknowledging the validity of the triple aspects of knowledge (*jñāna*), selfless devotion (*upāsanā*) and action in conformity to

7. *SkA*, p. 37.

the cosmic order (*dharma*) as expounded in the *Bhagavad Gītā*, the superior aspect of this *sādhanā* is defined by the author as the 'Yoga of love' (*prem-yoga*) and the 'Yoga of surrender' (*samarpaṇa-yoga*), and is conceived as lying essentially beyond this conventional tri-partition.[8]

Through a brief excursion into the process of manifestation (*sṛṣṭi kā pravāha*) that draws inspiration from the *pañcāgnividyā* and *pañcakośa* theory described in the Upaniṣad, Caturbhuj Sahāy remains concerned with the description of the path which, if covered in the opposite direction upwards, is said to lead those desirous for knowledge (*jijñāsu*) back to the original source of immortality and beatitude. Though assuming a prevalently gnostic and devotional perspective in the outlay of his *sādhanā*, this does not by any means imply that the other traditional branches of Yoga, viz., Haṭha-Yoga, Kuṇḍalinī-Yoga, Laya-Yoga, etc., are not deemed as effective and useful for the progress of the *sādhaka*. These are rather seen as preliminary stages concerned with the first four sheaths or veils (*āvaraṇa* or *kośa*) described by the *Māṇḍūkya Upaniṣad*, viz., *annamaya-kośa*, *prāṇamaya-kośa*, *manomaya-kośa* and *vijñānamaya-kośa*, all said to pertain to the sphere of the *jīvātmā* and corresponding respectively to the three kinds of karma-yoga, bhakti-yoga and jñāna-yoga. In an altogether similar fashion to the Ānanda-Yoga propounded by Bṛj Mohan Lāl Saksenā, the ultimate discipline proposed by the prem-yoga, claims to be concerned primarily with the supra-individual sphere constituted by the *ānandamaya-kośa* thereby providing the chance to overcome with relative ease this last intermediate stage before reaching the central core constituted by the *paramātmā*. In view of the great difficulties implied in the first and third type of realisation for the majority of human beings, the author recommends the *upāsanā-mārga* as the easiest of the traditional paths.[9]

Since this purpose is achieved through the assistance of the spiritual master who constitutes the immediate point of reference and sole object worthy of love and devotion for the

---

8. *SkA*, p. 10.
9. *Ibidem*, p. 32.

disciple, the *guru-śiṣya* relationship occupies with Caturbhuj Sahāy a rank of utmost importance on a par with the *pīr-murīdī* relationship that developed among the Sūfis.

> *na ham hain, na īśvara hai, keval guru hai;*
> *guru īśvara hai, īśvara guru hai.*
>
> Neither 'I' nor God, only the master alone exists;
> he and God are ultimately identical.[10]

This relationship develops on three successive levels in accordance with the inner approach of discipleship (*śiṣyatva*) towards the master. On the first level, the disciple preceives the master in his purely human form while in the awareness that he is not an ordinary human being but endowed with numerous powers and Divine knowledge. At the intermediate level, the master is considered in the likeness of Divinity and finally, at the third stage, the adept experiences the exitinction into and identification with the essence of the object of worship (*sākṣātkāra*) during which it appears to him that it is the Divine blessing (*divya kalyāṇa*) alone which has enlarged this human shape to his *gurudeva*. Such an interpretation leds directly to the theory of the *avatāraṇa* fundamental to the *sant*-doctrines which provides a fertile ground for the assimilation of concepts encountered both in classical Hiduism and in the prophetology of the Semitic religions hinted at by Mīrzā Maẓhar and further developed by the Hindu masters of our lineage. It explains the increasing importance attributed to the human master in these two esoteric traditions over the past centuries as he is perceived as a living symbol of the realm of the transcendent that represents the latest stage in the development of the spiritual discipline where the shaikh or *satguru* assumes the role of natural heir of the ancient messengers and prophets or, in a Hindu perspective, Divine descends (*avatāra*). In this connection Caturbhuj Sahāy affirms:

> In past epochs, the *paramātmā* has enforced the *dharma* by assuming the shape of Rāmacandra and Kṛṣṇa, thus

10. *SkA*, p. 33.

> manifesting the unseen in the human sphere. Nowadys, It provides us assistance in crossing the ocean of pain and torment assuming the shape of the *guru*. He is identical to It. The only difference lies in the fact that It is devoid of form (*nirākāra*) while he is endowed with form (*sākāra*) . . . .[11]

Only after the disciple has acquired the awareness of this fundamental truth is he considered ready for official initiation into the order the formal execution of which is still described according to the Mujaddidī way.[12] It is, therefore, not surprising that Caturbhuj Sahāy reiterates in terms very similar to those encountered among Sūfī shaikhs the importance for the aspirant disciple of determining his choice carefully and without haste, in order to avoid the risk of falling prey to the many self-styled *gurus* who populate every corner of the world. Even after finding the right person, said to be recognised by the infusion of a spontaneous feeling of peace in the heart, the aspirant is advised to refrain from asking immediately to be accepted as disciple, but to wait and observe the master's habits and attitudes for a while. As in the words of Kabīr,

> *guru miliyā tab jāniye āpa miṭāi santāp*
>
> When the *guru* comes to you, you will know and get rid of the suffering of the self.[13]

---

11. *SkA*, p. 18.
12. In the chapter on initiation, the author nevertheless distinguishes three kinds of *dīkṣā*: *mantra-dīkṣā*, conferring the ability to handle the outer means of realisation, like the invocation (*japa*), techniques of ascetics (*tapa*), the performance of devotional hymns (*kīrtana*), etc., the second type, referred to as 'spiritual initiation' (*adhyātma-dīkṣā*), corresponds to the interiorisation of the discipline performed exclusively at a subtle level and, hence, unperceptible to the outside world which implies an inward surrender to the master. The third and most elevated type of initiation, termed *ācārya-dīkṣā*, is reserved to a very limited number of initiates said to be chosen to receive the Divine order of spreading a particular message to the people; for details, cf. *SkA*, vol. I, chapter 2, pp. 19-27.
13. *SkA*, vol. I, p.13.

Differing from Rāmcandra and his Sūfī ancestors, Catubhuj Sahāy considers the control, purification and pacification of the mind (*fikr*), summarised in the Sūfī concept of *tadhkiya-i nafs*, in connection with the ascending phase of the spiritual journey (*ūrdhva-gamana*) to be the most immediate priority in his *sādhanā*. In its corrupted, uncultivated state, the mind is considered as the main adversary to the spiritual ascent since it is due to its intrinsic powers that it allures, seduces, tempts and thereby ties the most intimate part of the human being (*jīvātmā*) to the lower relams of the gross world.

> . . . the first enounter that we have to face is that with our mind. The mind is similar to the honey-bee that . . . dislikes remaining in its live but desires to run outside covetous to taste the sweet juice of the buds in the form of sensual pleasures . . . at one time it is seen sitting on one flower, in another moment it reaches the next leaving the first and then catches hold of the third and so on.[14]

These distracting impulses are presided over by the inner mental governor (*antaryāmī*) consisting of a particular type of consciousness which prevents every attempt to escape the enchanting game (*līlā*) and entangling net spun by the subtle internal current to be successful. In the perspective of the monotheistic religions, these powers are personified in the conceptual figure of the anti-divinity personified as *shaiṭān* or *satan* whereas the Indian doctrines describe it as *māyā* and, with the later *sants*, as *kāla-puruṣa*. As such *māyā* is analogous to the dark, *tāmasik* aspect of the qualified Brahman.

The opposed forces, characterised by *sattva*, which are apt to uplift the human being towards the subtle realms of the spiritual world, are referred to as 'powers of mercy' (*dayālu śakti*). Though the medium of the *satguru*, these celestial influences are said to exercise their corrective power on the inner states of the neophyte. This current of grace alone (*kṛpā-dhārā*) is considered sufficient to prepare the disciple for the initial

14. *Our Yoga Sadhana*, Ramashram Satsang, Mathura, n.d., p. 28.

stage of the discipline constitued by the first stages of the *upāsanā-mārga* which, according to Caturbhuj Sahāy, consist of the three degrees described by Patañjalī as *dhāraṇā*, *dhyāna* and *pratyāhāra*.

Caturbhuj Sahāy describes the difference between this path characterised by elements of utmost devotion and the conventional Yoga disciplines as consisting mainly of the fact that while the latter expect their followers to be capable of strenuous and continuous efforts to achieve the final goal of reacquiring the proximity and finally union with their Lord, the path of devotion is based on the assumption that in reality the Lord resides in the most intimate region of the heart (*hṛdaya-deśa*), therefore, rendering obsolete any far-fetched research, for example, through the gradual penetration of the entire series of subtle centres located in different parts of the body. Such a position reminds us not only of the language used by the Upaniṣad in regard to the symbolism of the heart[15] but recalls also the frequent reference made among Sūfis to the Koranic verse: 'We are closer to you than your jugular vein'. Unconcerned with the extraordinary powers (*siddhi*) obtained through the disclosure of the divinities presiding over each of the *cakras*, the *sādhaka* who follows this path is promised to reach his Beloved straightaway recognising Him in a first moment in the guise of the exterior *guru* and later, as he investigates His truth with his interior eyes, in the hidden cavern of his heart.

With the assistance of the spiritual preceptor, the disciple's aim at this stage consists of detaching himself from the sense of egoism (*ahaṅkāra*), technically achieved through the transmission of the *guru*'s flow of grace (*tawajjuh*) focussed on the disciple's *hṛdaya-cakra*, that results in the state of effacement of his perception as a separate individaul entity (*be-khudī*) and eventually culminates in the identification with the immediate point of reference (*fanā fī'l shaikh*). The familiar Sūfī terminology still used by Rāmacandra with regard to the methodology termed alternatively as *fikr* or *manana* is here

15. Cf. *Chāndogya Upaniṣad*, VIII.3.

entirely replaced by the Yoga terminology concerned with the more advanced stages of meditation, that is to say *dhāraṇā*, *dhyāna*, *pratyāhāra* and finally *samādhi*. Based on the sensory introversion and the mental concentration on the heart alone, these stages are described on the base of the elucidations made by the author of the *Yoga-Sūtra* as gradually leading to the fixation of the thought on the sole goal desired (*dhāraṇā*) before culminating in the full comprehension and identification with the object of mediation during the stages of *dhyāna* and *nirvikalpa samādhi*.[16]

Following Vyāsa's comment on the *Yoga-Sūtra*, the author introduces the five conceptual planes of consciousness inherent to the mind (*citta-bhūmi*) as instable (*kṣipta*), obscure (*murha*), stable-unstable (*vikṣipta*), fixed on a unique point (*ekāgra*) and completely restrained (*nirodha*).[17] While the first three are common to all human beings and result in the incessant production of waves of consciousness of obscure origin and beyond control (*vāsanā*), the last two states are peculiar to those engaged in the spiritual discipline. All five are put in relation to the three essential qualities that permeate the emanations of the primordial substance (*prakṛti*).

The primary task of the practitioner therefore consists of a sublimation of these restless and fickle mental states dominated by the two inferior *guṇas*, viz., *tamas* and *rajas*, into those last two planes dominated by peace and beatitude. This goal is achieved through the unification of the thought current (*ekāgratā*), which is characteristic of the predominance of *sattva-guṇa*. It is analogous to the perpetual presence (*ḥuḍūr-ī āgāhī*) described by the Mujaddidī authorities. Only at the very end of every spiritual discipline, when the mind of the *sādhaka* is completely freed of any activity (*nirodha*), has the *sādhanā* properly speaking come to an end. The interior process will now take place entirely on the plane of knowledge. Once even this state is overcome, it will be possible to re-establish the original state of harmony inherent in the *triguṇa* prior to the process of

16. *SkA*, vol. III, pp. 142-3.
17. *Ibid.*, p. 37; *Yoga-Bhāṣya* by Vyāsa, I.1.

manifestation (*triguṇātīta*), leading back to the unconditioned state or *kaivalyāvasthā* that guarantees final liberation (*mokṣa*).

The other fundamental means at disposal of the disciple who follows the *upāsanā-mārga* consist of the technique of the repeated invocation of the Divine name known as *nāma-japa*. In the first volume of his work, Caturbhuj Sahāy dedicates an entire chapter to this particular method and the different aspects it involves. Explicit reference to the methodology and terminology used by the Naqsbhandī shaikh occupies hardly two out of twenty-three pages that make up this chapter. Notwithstanding the evident attempt to play down the importance of the Islamic *ṭarīqa* at the base of the major part of the technical explanations provided in the course of this chapter, his elucidations nevertheless still betray their Mujaddidī origin to those familiar with the descriptions provided by the shaikh.

As with the original teachings of both the Mujaddidiyya and most *sant-sampradāyas*, the two major categories of invocation comprise the vocal one performed with the lips and the tongue and the silent, inaudible invocation performed exclusively on an inner, mental plane. However, the coresponding Sūfī concept *dhikr-i khafī* is introduced only at a very late stage and is a rather marginal way, while the main focus remains centred on the *ajapā-japa* method current among various Hindu traditions, from the *so'ham* and the *aham brahmāsmi* used by the *vedāntins* to the *rāma-nāma* used by many mediaeval north-Indian *panths*. In a curious contradiction to this tendency, in the midst of an entirely Hindu based exposition of the *mantra-vidyā*, Caturbhuj Sahāy distinguishes the two main groups of invocation regarded as suitable for the purpose of illuminating the heart and awakening the subtle centres as *dhātī* and *ṣifātī*, without, however, making the slightest mention regarding the origin and etymology of the two terms. The first one related to the 'name of the essence' (*ism-i dhāt*), is said to consist of the sacred syllable *auṁ* as referring to the unqualified Principle of the Veda that refracts itself in innumerable attributes (*ṣifāt guṇa*) and forms (*rūpa*) while descending into the world. In principle, the qualified sounds (*śabda*) derived from it can amount to an indefinite number.

Faithful to the vision adopted in this lineage, Caturbhuj Sahāy deliberately refrains from suggesting any particular name as preferable to another leaving the choice open to every single devotee according to the personal divinity (*iṣṭadevatā*) adopted for his worship:

> Be the name invoked *dhātī* or *ṣifātī*, if it is performed with the right intention (*śraddhā*) and fastened properly to the mind, both will be surely effective. By whatsoever name we invoke with sincere and determined intention the Lord (*bhagavān*), no sectarian difference should arise out of this. For the sake of a wholehearted devotion alone they are all equally qualified. . . .[18]

The only thing that matters for the performance of the *jāpa* is that it regards the field of pure devotion as concerned with the innermost part of the heart and thus directed towards the very core of one's individual existence that connects one with the superior states of Being. As such it constitutes the most efficacious tool for penetrating the intimate realm of the heart necessary for the awakening of the interior, non-human *guru*, to whom devotee ultimately surrenders himself. As Lord Kṛṣṇa says in the *Bhagavad Gītā*:

> *yajñānam japa yajño'smi*
>
> Among all sacrifices I am the one performed through invocation.

In a fashion similar to the descriptions given by various Sūfi authorities but encountered also among Hindus, the reader is then provided with the description of four different kinds of subtle invocations, the invocation of one, two, three and four syllables (*ekamukhī*, *dvimukhī*, *trimukhī* and *caturmukhī japa*), referred to by some Sūfis as 'strokes' (*ḍarb*). The one-syllable invocation, considered as the most preferable and easiest to perform, consists of the mental invocation of the syllable *auṁ*. The two-syllable *jāpa* which reproduces a rhythmical alteration

---

18. *SkA*, vol. I, p. 48.

of the two phases of breathing, viz., inspiration and expiration, consists for the *vedāntin* of the syllables so, corresponding to the phase of inhalation, and *haṁ*, pronounced during the phase of exhalation. However, the utility of this *jāpa* nowadays is strongly doubted and therefore rejected as of little use in a contemporary *sādhanā*.

More importance is attributed to the three-stroke *jāpa*, consisting according to the method adopted by Caturbhuj Sahāy of the formula *auṁ tat sat*. The description of its performance neatly imitates the method current among the Mujaddidīs with regard to the *dhikr-i nafī wa ithbāt*. It entails the pronunciation of the syllable *auṁ* pulling it from the navel up to the top of the head, followed by that of the syllable *tat* while inclining the head backward slightly in direction of the left shoulder and than impressing with all force the final syllable *sat* on the subtle heart-organ, located at exactly the same position as that of the *laṭīfa-i qalb* described by the followers of Shaikh Aḥmad Sirhindī.[19] This entire process must be accomplished during one complete phase of respiration and has to be kept in rhythm with it. Its correct and prolonged performance is said to result in the illumination of the heart-chamber by the subtle light of consciousness that irradiates from the current of *kuṇḍalinī-śakti*, pulled up along the channel of the *suṣumnā* by the subtle sound-vibration produced through the inner invocation of the syllable *auṁ*. Through the numerous subtle arteries (*nāḍī*) that extend from that central organ, this subtle energy charged with the *jāpa* irradiates to the entire body until every single organ and member is permeated by the primordial vibration contained in the *akṣara*-syllable. Such a description comes too close to that given by the Naqshbandī authorities of the utmost degree of perfection reached by the technique of *dhikr* and referred to as *sulṭān al-adhkār* to be a coincidence It can be interpreted in all likelihood as consisting simply of a formal substitution of the formula used for that purpose.[20]

---

19. *SKkA*, vol. I, pp. 52-3.

20. Cf. *Durr al-Ma'ārif*, note taken on Friday 17 Rajab AH 1231, p. 236; *MuM*, pp. 31-4.

Last but not least, mention is made of the four-faced invocation (*caumukhī jāpa*). This consists of the fourfold repetition of the name *Rām*, each corresponding to an expansion into one among the four cardinal points. Its performance, recommended while being posted in the *svastikāsana* and keeping the eyes shut, requires full concentration on the outer aspect of the spiritual guide while imagining that the *paramātmā* permeates one all around and inside. The silent invocation of the *rām-nām* is then directed first towards the right shoulder followed immediately by one on the left shoulder extending over the phase of inspiration. During the phase of exhalation, the *jāpa* should be directed first upwards to the head, then finally downwards on to the heart. Although here too the master leaves the choice of the name invoked to the preference of the individual practitioner, the *rām-nām* is described as the most efficacious for this type of performance, in a perpetuation of the tradition current among the *Kabīr-panthī*s.[21]

The Sūfī origin of these methods regarding the subtle invocation appears undeniable and is reflected also in the descriptions of the outer conditions to be observed. Their performance is said to be equally efficient while following the discipline of *upāsanā-yoga* and serves the sole purpose of achieving the fixation of the mind on the Goal and later, through the stage of *dhyāna*, the encounter (*sākṣātkāra*) with it. The efficacy of the method is determined by the rhythmic application of the sacred syllable charged with spiritual energy on the different centres of the subtle body independent of the religious context to which the practitioner belongs. With specific reference to Rāmcandra, Caturbhuj Sahāy affirms:

> Our Srī Mahārājjī used to instruct me that while practising the *jāpa* I should first of all preserve the memory of my *guru*, and than, through the power of imagination acquired by the discipline, pull the Divine radiance of *paramātmā* in front of me trying to consider myself like a drop in Its endless ocean, and finally with

21. *SkA*, vol. I, p. 56.

the help of the *satnām* imagine to immerse my *jīvātmā* in the radiant current of Its light. . . .[22]

In conclusion, in a rare mention of the predecessors in the *paramparā*, Caturbhuj Sahāy reveals that the method regarded as the most useful by his spiritual perceptor is that of the four-syllable *jāpa* which he himself had practised for years on the advice of his master Shaikh Faḍl Aḥmad Khān. Preferably, its performance should be accompanied by a series of contingent dietary prescriptions evidently based on the *niyama* restrictions in the Yoga disciplines. These are meant to alleviate the danger of being affected by the wave of heat produced on the subtle level by the repeated invocation of the *satnām* that irradiates into the gross body from where it can possibly provoke a psychological unbalance and mental disturbances. The sophisticated techniques of breath-control and breath-suspension that in the past used to accompany both the Sūfī practices related to the *dhikr* and the respective techniques used by the Haṭha-Yoga are largely abandoned among the masters of this lineage in favour of an increased focus on meditation in line with their more intellectual approach characteristic for the Rāja-Yoga disciplines.

In conclusion of this brief excursion into the teachings of this spiritual authority of the second generation of Hindu Naqsbhandīs it is possible to affirm that notwithstanding the progressive transposition of the *sādhanā* into a background based on various aspects of the *brahma-vidyā*, this does not imply a departure from the principles set out by his predecessor Rāmcandra on the base of the Sūfī teachings received from his Naqsbhandī shaikh, it rather illustrates once more the existence of numerous points of contacts between the esoteric disciplines set to meet in the particular context of this study and thereby demonstrates impressively the intellectual liveliness of this contemporary *sant-paramparā* beyond the delicate moment of transition in the lifetime of Śrī Rāmcandra.

With regard to the adaptations operated by Catubhuj Sahāy

22. *SkA*, vol. I, p. 58.

in regard to the *'ilm-i dhikr*, these remain essentially limited to the formal substitutions regarding the Islamic formula of invocation with those current among various Hindu traditions. The following affirmation that concludes the sober and distanced description of the Sūfī invocational techniques provided by Caturbhuj Sahāy is a sufficient indication of the reason behind such an attitude:

> . . . *jāpa*, *kīrtana*, *prāṇāyāma*, *upavāsa*, the awakening of the subtle centres, all these ritual practices can be safely defined as a mixture of elements pertaining to both the Yoga and Bhakti disciplines. They have all been derived from [the sacred traditions] of Hindustān and include their methods which too are extremely similar to those of the Hindus: however, having reflected on the contingent circumstances and their peculiar context, [the Muslim] learned authorities have adapted them to their particular requirements so as to increase the efficacy of their method.[23]

Shahjahanpur: A universal movement

Another major branch that developed in the course of the second generation of the Hindu lineage wihin the Mujaddidiyya goes back to Madhe Mohan Lāl *alias* Rāmcandra Shāhjahānpurī, a close disciple of Rāmcandra's who later assumed the same name as his illustrious spiritual preceptor. Born on 30 April 1899 at Shahjahanpur in an affluent Kāyasth *zamīndārī* family, his father Badrī Prasād, a locally renowned lawyer and special magistrate, was able to offer his eldest son a higher education in law. This was immediately followed in 1925 by his employment at the local Civil Court where he kept working till his early retirement in 1955.[24]

Rāmcandra Shāhjahānpurī reportedly met his master for the first time at Fatehgarh in 1922. After having been accepted as his disciple, he remained for many years in close contact

---

23. *SkA*, vol. I, p. 65.

24. *LVV*, p. 218.

with his spiritual perceptor mainly through an intense exchange of letters in which he used to enclose notes made in a diary describing his inner experiences and spiritual progress. After the death of his *satguru* in 1931, he claims to have received hidden instructions and teachings from him and the spiritual ancestors of the Mujaddidī *silsila* according to the *nisbat-i 'uwaysī* pattern until 1955. The spiritual discipline allegedly revealed to him through this intimate channel of supernatural communication is described in numerous works whose nucleus consists for the autobiographical *Ātma-kathā* published in three volumes.[25]

In 1945, under the Uttar Pradesh Society Act, he founded the 'Sri Rāmcandra Mission' at Shahjahanpur, allegedly in memory of his master, with the declared aim of spreading the universal message he had received from him. Reportedly on the instructions of his hidden guide, Rāmcandra Shāhjahānpūri set out to imitate the example set half a century earlier by Svāmī Vivekānanda and began to travel extensively around India to promote his newly established mission, especially in the south. He also undertook a series of journeys to North America, South Africa and some European countries where he attracted a number of Western disciples. His last journey abroad took place in 1982 when he went to Paris to assist the members of his *satsang* there. On his return to India, however, he fell seriously ill and after a brief admission at the Vivekananda Hospital in Lucknow followed by a prolonged stay at the All India Hospital of Delhi, he eventually died on 19 April 1983 and received the last rites in his native town. There, around the imposing *samādhi-sthāna* erected in his honour, a huge and well organised *āśrama* complex-*cum*-mediation centre had been developed under his directions meant to accommodate the numerous national and international followers of his newly proposed spiritual discipline that came to be known under the name of *sahaja mārga*.

---

25. This work was first published in English in 1947 under the title *The Autobiography of Rama Chandra* edited in three volumes, followed by its Hindī version three years later. The source cited in the context of the present study is based on that English version.

The teachings

Although the *sādhanā* proposed by Rāmcandra Shāhjahān-purī remains in its principals faithful to the *ṭarīqa* of his master, the teachings of this self-styled missionary leader collected in the abundant number of works attributed to him, show more than the texts of any of the rival branches the desire to distinguish itself through the introduction of a number of individual modifications and reformulations. The lines along which these develop reflect a distinctively scientific approach towards the topic indicative not only of the author's educational background, but they appear to have arisen out of the urgent need to communicate the conceptions peculiar to traditional esoterism to a large international audience strongly influenced by modernity. For this purpose, unique among the authorities affiliated to this lineage, his works have been translated into most of India's major regional languages as well as into English.

Thus, the inclination towards a self-affirmation as spiritual leader remains palpably present throughout his works. It strangely contrasts with the sometimes exaggerated tributes and homage paid to 'our great master' and 'the spiritual genius' Rāmcandra Fatehgarhī, to whom the introduction of this method of spiritual training is said to be entirely due.[26] The way he describes the purpose of the mission established by him reflects the general attitude assumed by its founder throughout.

> Shri Ram Chandra Mission was established at Shahjahanpur (U.P.) on 31st March 1945 in memory of this great personality [Śrī Rāmcandrajī], by me as his successor, through his grace; and slowly it is attracting the seekers of Truth from everywhere. I am happy that the Master's grace is working in this respect and people are attracted to benefit from his grace.[27]

Under the new name of *sahaja-mārga*, Rāmcandra Shāhjahānpurī has formulated a spiritual discipline assertedly based on his own personal experience 'irrespective of what Śrī

26. *Sahaja Mārga Philosophy*, Shri Rām Chandra Mission 1969, p. 4.
27. *Ibid.*, p. 5.

Śaṅkarācārya, Śrī Rāmānujācārya and others might have said about their own'. Its principal aim consists of providing means of spiritual self-realisation and the awakening of the 'sleeping masses to Divine consciousness'. One of the most important outer features of this *sādhanā* is said to consist of the possibility to follow it in conjunction with the normal worldly life of the common man, that is to say in the *gṛhastha-aśrama* while keeping in mind both factes of life, the worldly and the Divine.[28]

To achieve successfully the primary objective consisting of the state of detachment from worldly bonds (*vairāgya*) and considered in the Vedāntic context of the 'fourfold discipline' (*catuṣṭaya sādhanā*) that follows the gnostic stage of discrimination (*viveka*),[29] it is claimed that the ancient mechanical methods involving forced austerity and penances (*tapas*) must be set aside and replaced by more simple and natural means. For this purpose, the *sahaja mārga* is defined along the lines of Rāja-Yoga, enriched with 'certain amendments and modifications to purge out superfluous elements from that system'.[30] Following the overall pattern of the lineage, the practical aspect of the *sādhanā* is based mainly on the master's support meant to assist the *sādhaka* in awakening his latent inner forces and to direct the flow of the Divine current (*daivik dhārā*) through his spiritual power transmitted by the yogic process of *prāṇāhuti* or transmission of vital energy to his herat, obviously intended as the Hindu equivalent of the Sūfī concept of *tawajjuh*. Thus, once more one of the most distinctive features of this discipline remains the shifting of the active task from the disciple to the master who alone bears the responsibility for starting his protegé's inner path of realisation.

The repeated stress on Rāja-Yoga encountered here as among all authorities of the order underlines the importance of the purely interior, that is to say mental and intellectual, practice pursued in this *sādhanā*. It focusses on the meditative aspect of the discipline rather than attributing any major

---

28. *Sahaja Mārga Philosophy*, p. 46.
29. *Satya kā udaya*, Shāhjahānpur, 1993, p. 98.
30. *Sahaja Mārga Philosophy*, p. 52.

significance to outer rules and regulations since these are regarded as separative and, therefore, inappropriate for the universalistic approach envisaged by the propagators of the cultural joint-venture represented by all these lineages. Certainly, in some measure this attitude arises out of the need to propose a methodology that owes many of its ingredients to an Islamic *ṭarīqa* which, in order to remain applicable to a largely non-Muslim following, had to cast aside the specifically Islamic elements which could not easily be shared by those unfamiliar with this background, focussing instead on the inner aspects of the discipline that claims to transcend formal religious divisions. The *nirguṇa*-current represented within Hinduism by the mediaeval *sant*s, whose approach towards the Divine realities was supposedly based on the metaphysical doctrines of the Vedānta, and the Tantravāda, furnished the ideal framework for such a renewed attempt of cultural symbiosis. Its actuality in modern times shows the existence of a continuous thread of thought that links the medieval *sant*s with the heirs of Shāh Faḍl Aḥmad Khān and his Hindu disciple Rāmcandra Saksenā. Following the pattern of gradual replacement of the doctrinal background developed around cosmological and metaphysical theories set out by the first generation of Hindu Naqshbandīs, it, comes therefore, as no surprise if all successive attempts to absorb the methodology of the Mujaddidiyya into a Hindu context insert themselves quite naturally into the intellectual terrain of Rāja-Yoga, for that the 'royal discipline' owes much of its conceptual approach to the Vedānta in its largely intellectual approach towards the goal of union with the Divine and liberation (*mokṣa*) from the tedious cycle of birth and death sanctioned by the *saṁsāra*. Thus, in an attempt to shape a coherent and homogeneous body of teachings, the technical terminology employed in the formulation of Vedānta and *sant* doctrines are extended to the exposition of the methodological aspect of the *sādhanā*.

According to Rāmcandra Shāhjahānpurī, the *sādhanā* consists primarily of the heart-meditation, pursued with the aim of attaining to that ultimate state or central point (*kendra-bindu*) considered to be the seat of the *ādiguru* that constitutes the primordial cause (*ādi kāraṇa*) of creation in which everything will be reabsorbed after the dissolution of the universe (*mahāpralaya*). Meditation (*dhyāna*) and the gathering of thought on one single point (*ekāgratā*) is recommended in order to achieve the return to an embryonic and seminal condition by reversing the process of creation (*sṛṣṭi*) reverting to the primordial state of dissolution (*laya*, *fanā*). The constant practice of this method is said to allow the *abhyāsī* to penetrate through the indefinite number of subtle layers that have developed through the incessant series of mental impressions (*saṁskāra*) in the course of each cycle of existence around the uncontaminable nucleus of the *ātmā* residing in the heart. Aided by the steady supervision and assistance of the *satguru*, this practice will lead the initiate back to the source of the primordial stirring thought (*upādāna, kṣobha*) that brought the present world into existence.[31] It will eventually guarantee the attainment of *sākṣātkāra* (lit. what causes to be visible before one's eyes), considered to be the final degree on the path of realisation. This term, frequently encountered among the Hindu authorities affiliated to the Mujaddidiyya, is taken from the technical vocabulary of Śrī Rāmānujācārya and compares very closely to the Mujaddidī concept of *muṣāhada* or 'direct vision'. It thereby combines, at least in its technical formulation, the *shuhūdī* point of view inherited from the *paramparā*'s Muslim ancestors with that held by the viśiṣṭādvaita, which maintains even on the highest stage of realisation the ultimately unbridgeable difference between the immanent subject that contemplates and the absolutely transcendent Object contemplated.

Ranking as seventh among the eight members described by Patañjalī's *aṣṭāṅga-yoga*, *dhyāna* constitutes the starting point of the discipline taught in this branch while, in consonance with the Naqshbandī path, all preceding degrees are considered to fall automatically into the lap of the earnest practitioner, thus, saving him a lot of time and effort. Through this interior process, it is believed that the rightly guided initiate is direccted by the four landmarks of the Vedānta doctrine, termed

31. *Efficacy of Rāja Yoga in the light of Sahaja Mārga,* 1950, p. 2.

discrimination and right cognition of the Truth beyond the numerous forms assumed by the veil of *māyā* (*viveka*), the detachment of the senses from and inner indifference towards everything except that one permanent and unchanging reality (*vairāgya*), the various degrees of concentrating and meditating on the sole desired Object (*śama*, *dama*, *uprati*, *titikṣā*, *śraddhā* and *samādhāna*), and finally the desire of a direct partaking at the supreme Truth (*mumukṣa*). This last step is traditionally descri-bed as the crowning of the ancient process obtained after successfully going through the three preliminary degrees of enquiry. However, the modern method (*paddhatī*) described by Rāmcandra Shāhjahānpurī differs from this perspective. It does not consider the succeeding degrees of the eight-membered Yoga as separate from each other but includes the right positioning meant to confer stability to the body (*āsana*), the control of conscious breathing (*prāṇāyāma*) the concentration on a single object (*dhāraṇā*), deep meditation (*dhyāna*) and the condition of perfectly equiliberated enstasy (*samādhi*) in the practice of innermost meditation (*antargata dhyāna*) in its fold.[32]

The highest degree of realisation consists, however, in conformity with Patañjali, in the state of *samādhi* and *ekāgratā* which is divided into three stages. The first, termed 'differentiated self-revelation' (*samprajñāta samādhi*) corresponds to a state of self-effacement in which all senses and sentiments (*bhāva*) are dissolved in a sort of deep sleep that leaves no awareness of any object in the individual consciousness. This state is analogous to that described in Sūfī doctrine as *fanā*. The second stage referred to as 'non-differentiated self-revelation' (*asamprajñāta samādhi*) is described by this master as a 'state of consciousness in unconsciousness' in which the initiate though completely focussed on one single point (*ekāgra-citta*), reacquires a partial awareness of his surroundings. This second type of *samādhi* is described as similar to the awareness a person deeply immersed in the reflection on a particular problem maintains of the surrounding environment while walking along a busy road, thus preventing him from suffering

32. *Satya kā udaya*, p. 105.

a bad accident. The third and most advanced degree of *ekāgratā* is termed *sahaja samādhi* and represents an innovative addition to the traditional teachings. At this stage the initiate remains fully aware of his actions and the mind is yet again focussed on the surrounding environment while remaining firmly present in the real object of Truth. Its lower consciousness returns to the outer world while its higher consciousness remains with the Divine. Apparently, its perceptions (*pratyakṣa*) are involved in the affairs of the ephemeral world, but in reality it is detached from it all, remaining permanently in a state of sublime *samrādha*.

This description shows evident affinities with the Mujaddidī concept of 'supreme negligence' (*ghaflat*), characteristic of the saints considered as 'real heirs of the prophets' who, in a vision superior to the 'saints living in seclusion', dedicate their attention to the rectification of their fellow human beings themselves staying on a degree that allows them to act in this world while remaining permanently connected with the superior abodes of the Divine. Such a saint is said to have penetrated to the very centre of the 'knowledge of the quintuple fire oblation' (*pañcāgnividyā*) described by the ancient wisdom of the Śruti.

> To those who have attained to such a degree of knowledge is unfolded in a natural manner the innate wisdom (*sahaja jñāna*) of the distinctive knowledge of the elementary world (*bhautika vijñāna*), which . . . they can employ according to their desire.[33]

Those who are granted the privilege of attaining to such a lofty station are comparable to the ancient seers of the golden age, the *ṛṣi*s, whose field of activity compares on a smaller scale to that of the gods and whose degree (*pada*) is referred to as *Vasu*. These *ṛṣi*s, originally seven in number like the stars of the great bear (*saptarṣi*), show numerous similarities to those elevated beings who, in the hierarchy of Islamic spirituality, are described

33. *Satya kā udaya*, p. 107. This concepts resembles very closely to the description given by the Mujaddidīs of the 'journey through the things of the world' (*sair dar ashiyā*), corresponding to the highest stage reached by the 'perfect heir of the prophet'.

as the poles of the seven climates (*ṭabaqāt*) responsible for maintaining the cosmic order in each of these regions. Above these lies the polar abode of the *dhruva* inhabited by those who, classified as *munis*, are said to possess the knowledge of the entire *brahmāṇḍa-maṇḍala*. Their field of activity is even more extensive and their duty consists of maintaining the purity of the atmosphere (*vātāvaraṇa*) from all impure influences liable to bring disorder into this world. This state is said to be attainable through the illumination of the innermost space or 'hylem shadow' (*sic*!) of the heart.

Further up in the spiritual hierarchy, Rāmcandra Shāhjahānpurī places the 'Lord of the pole' (*dhruvādhipati*) and director of the poles' activities. This state is reached after acquiring control over the navel-point (*nābhi-bindu*). Acting again under the authority of and in harmony with the universal nature (*prakṛti*), their sphere of activity comprehends the entire universe (*viśva*) including the safeguard of its spatial extension.

One of the most sublime places in this hierarchy is held by the *pārṣada* whose intervention into the cosmic order is said to be rendered necessary only under very particular circumstances, including devastating wars such as Lord Rāmacandra's victory over Rāvaṇa and the battle of Kurukṣetra[34] or other important events in the development of the cosmic manifestation. The *pārṣada* co-ordinates the actions of all these subordinate governors, limiting himself to a silent presence beyond the sphere of action. The perfection of this sublime stage is related within the microcosmic context to the *sahasra-dala-kamala-bindu* situated at the very top of the skull.

On top of the entire spiritual hierarchy Rāmcandra Shāhjahānpurī places the *mahāpārṣada*, a rank very rarely conceded to anyone. He is said to intervene only in those extremely uncommon cases in which violent changes are due to occur in the destiny of the world. As he who detains the supreme power, the centre of its energy lies within the microcosm slightly at the right of the occipital bone at the very top of the head.[35]

34. *Satya kā udaya*, p. 112.

35. *Rāja-yoga kā divya darśana*, p. 32, diagram No. 5.

The description of these spiritual degrees, again claimed to be derived from the secret doctrine of Rāja-Yoga, represents a very interesting addition to the notions already disclosed by Rāmcandra and constitute a curious parallel to the spiritual hierarchy known to Islamic esoterism, while is said to overview the destiny of the Universe.[36] It constitutes one of the most stimulating contributions made by this authority towards the understanding of the spiritual position held by the masters of this spiritual lineage and evidences the depth of the traditional roots at the base of a *sādhanā* which claims to supplant the old arrangements with a new one granted by the Divine power (*īśvarīya śakti*) to the present humanity in the wake of a period of destruction which will show itself in the light of striking events that are soon to come. The central theories of the path presented by this somewhat eccentric personality, thus, integrate themselves into the mainstream attitude and positions of the lineage inherited from his illustrious predecessor, although the desire for creating an individual imprint on the world vision to which his path proposes itself to respond shine through in the emphasis laid on the redemptory significance he attributes to the mission at Shahjahanpur established by him. In this sense, however, the notions regarding the final dissolution of the universe (*mahāpralaya*) and its relation to the movement of the polar star (*dhruva tārā*) lead us to the belief that notwithstanding the personal ambitions of some of these authorities, they still represent an extremely stimulating spiritual lineage concerned with some of the most delicate aspects of the sacred knowledge, that is to say the knowledge regarding the modalities that govern the cosmic cycle.

Sikandarabad: santmat or taṣawwuf?

The headquarters of this branch in proximity to the capital Delhi was established by Dr. Kṛṣṇa Lāl Bhaṭnāgar, yet another member of the Kāyasth community who became one of the most intimate disciples of the Saksenā saints at Fatehgarh and

36. For a detailed account of the single degrees comprised in the spiritual hierarchy of Islam, their role and function, see M.E. Blochet's work *Études sur l'ésoterisme musulmane* (1979).

Kanpur. Born on 9 October 1894 in the small town of Sikandarabad in the Bulandshahr district of western Uttar Pradesh as the eldest son of a public officer of the Public Works Department, Bhagawat Dayāl Bhaṭnāgar, he belonged to a wealthy family holding regular ties with the Rādhāsoāmī *satsang*. His paternal grandfather, Vr̥ṣabhānu, had been initiated by the second Rādhāsoāmī master, Rāy Sāhib Śāligrām, a pact later renewed also with Śrī Sāwan Singhjī, establisher of the order's Punjābī branch at Beās. Following this tradition, his parents had both made their vow of allegiance to these masters, and this contributed to the devotional atmosphere of *Kr̥ṣṇa-bhakti* in which the young Kāyasth was to grow up.

Due to his father's posting at Fatehgarh, Kr̥ṣṇa Lāl spent most of his youth in that town attending the local schools for his primary education. His first encounter with Rāmacandra reportedly occurred in 1914 in the local Exchequer Office (*khazānā*) where his future *gurudeva* was employed as an officer. Some nights later, the master repeatedly appeared to him in a dream invoking the names of Allāh, Rāma and Kr̥ṣṇa and calling the young student to his feet. Although initially reluctant to grant immediate initiation to his newly arrived devotee, on the insistence of the latter this was eventually conceded in that same year, followed in 1915 by the license to organise his own *satsang*.

In 1916, Kr̥ṣṇa Lāl was married to one Candra Devī with whom he was to have three sons and two daughters. After a few unsuccessful attempts to earn his livelihood running a small shop and working as a clerk in a local school, in 1919 he enrolled at the Agra Medical College from where he successfully graduated three years later. During that period he was granted full license (*ijāzat-i tā'amma, pūrṇa ācārya padvī*) and appointed as *khalīfa-i khaṣṣa* with the mission to spread the lineage's message.

After being employed for a short while in government service Kr̥ṣṇa Lāl resigned from that position and began to run a small clinic in his ancestral hometown of Sikandarabad, where he was to remain for the rest of his life participating in the town's worldly and social life as well as attracting many of his fellow-citizens to the spiritual path propagated from his *satsang*. In his role of medical adviser he continued to serve his master Rāmcandra and, after the death of the latter, he took care of his younger brother Raghubar Dayāl *alias Cācājī*. Constantly engaged in the task entrusted to him by his spiritual predecessors, he founded numerous centres of spiritual teaching around northern India, including Baksar in Bihar, Gorakhpur in eastern Uttar Pradesh, Bareilly, Ghaziabad, Kasganj and Roorkee in western Uttar Pradesh and Alwar and Jaipur in Rajasthan, In 1951, he met Sardār Kartār Singh Dhīṅgrā (*b*. 1912) appointed shortly before the master's death as one of his successors who guides till the present day a small *satsang* at his residence in the Paharganj area close to the New Delhi railway station.[37]

From 1958 onwards, while staying at Gorakhpur, Kr̥ṣṇa Lāl established an intimate relationship with Dr. Akṣay Kumār Banerjī, than principal of the local Mahārāṇā Pratāp Degree College and the author of a series of authoritative books on Hinduism and Tantrism. He instructed the Kāyasth master in the knowledge of the Veda and the Mīmāṁsā while accepting him as his spiritual guide.[38] Among other main successors and heirs appointed by Dr. Kr̥ṣṇa Lāl were his son Dr. Hari Kr̥ṣṇa Bhaṭnāgar (1923-87), who took over the responsibility for his father's *satsang* at Sikandarabad,[39] Dr. Sewatī Prasād Sahāwarī

---

37. For a short biographical introduction to this authority whose *satsang* I was able to attend for sometime during my sojourn at Delhi, see *LVV*, pp. 272-3.

38. See *Discourses on Hindu Spiritual Culture*, 3 vols., Ramashram Satsang Publication, 1971, 1974 and 1980, and *The Philosophy of Gorakhnath* (with *Gorakṣa-Vācana-Saṁgraha*), 1988.

39. For a biographical survey of him, see *LVV*, pp. 268-71. At present, the local *satsang* and the annual *bhaṇḍārā* are organised by his eldest son Dr. Narendra Bhāratī, who also runs the small family-run clinic first established by his grandfather. To him I am indebted for furnishing me much information about his grandfather's activities and teachings during my stay there from 14-16 February 1996.

(1899-1989) at Kasganj (district Etah), Dr. Śyām Lāl Saksenā (1902-87) at Ghaziabad[40] and Dr. Brijendra Kumār Saksenā (*b*. 1938) at present Professor of Physics and Engineering at Roorkee University (district Saharanpur).[41]

Apart from a limited amount of writings concerned with his teachings, Kṛṣṇa Lāl began to publish from 1953 a monthly review under the title *Rāmsandeśa* ('The message of Rāma') containing a range of articles written by himself and by some of his intimate disciples, which was meant to serve as a public organ for the diffusion of the message propagated by the masters. In line with the prevailing custom, he began to celebrate an annual *bhaṇḍārā* meeting held during the *Daśaharā* festivities at his residence at Sikandarabad in order to provide an occasion for the members of the spiritual family to gather and meet each other for an exchange of ideas, integrated by a series of speeches delivered by the leading authorities and a series of common meditation sessions.

In 1968, Kṛṣṇa Lāl's health began to deteriorate and his public appearances were greatly reduced until, on 18 May 1970 (12 *Rabī al-awwal* AH 1390), he passed away at his home in Sikandarabad.[42] There, a commemorative chamber is still used for the daily meditations and devotional singing sessions of his local followers.

The teachings

What appears most striking in the teachings of Dr. Kṛṣṇa Lāl Bhaṭnāgar is that, unlike the other authorities so far examined, the process of Hinduisation brought forward from both a

40. For some biographical notes, see *LVV*, pp. 239-40.

41. *Ibid.*, pp. 274-7

42. Interestingly, the biographies of this leader stress the coincidence of this date with the date of death of the prophet Muḥammad. This may lead to the assumption that to some extent the memory of the link with a Sūfī tradition is kept very much alive among the Hindu followers of this *sādhanā* and reverts some importance beyond the explicit statements made by the other leading authorities in this generation.

conceptional and a terminological point of view in the second generation of this lineage occupies with him a far less important role. Many of the technical terms employed by this authority either maintain their original Sūfī connotation reminiscent of the Islamic *ṭarīqa*, or alternatively propose a choice of both Sanskrit terms and their Arabic or Persian correspondent. This pattern reflects outwardly the different attitude assumed this Kāyasth master who repeatedly hints at his spiritual connection (*nisbat*) as going back to the messenger of Islam and fountainhead of the spiritual lineage he had inherited from his *satguru*.

Recognising the close relationship between Islamic *taṣawwuf* and Hindu *santmat*, Kr̥ṣṇa Lāl and some of his close disciples have tried to identify some of the doctrinal elements common to both *brahma-vidyā* and the *'ilm-i Ilāhī*, proposing a vision of the *sādhanā* that is declaredly based on the integration of both traditions. This integrated version finds its expression in the formulation of the seven steps (*manzilāt, sopān*) of realisation also referred to as *haft khawān* or *sapta darśana*. These seven steps or degrees are identified as the following:

(1) the desire of knowing the Truth (*ṭalab, jijñāsā*)
(2) devotional love (*'ishq, upāsanā*)
(3) knowledge (*ma'rifat, jñāna*)
(4) the perception of Divine unity (*tawḥīd, ekabhāva*)
(5) indifference (*istighnā, uparām*)
(6) annihilation of the ego (*fanā, laya*)
(7) permanence (*baqā, pūrṇajīvan*)[43]

The first degree, termed *ṭalab* or *jijñāsā*, is described as similar to the innate desire of the new-born baby to suckle milk from his mother's breast in order to be nourished, and crying if prevented from reaching this goal. Provoked by this call, his mother, in a gesture of pure love (*'ishq*), offers him her breast by which the child recognises her out of innumerable women as

43. Dr. Krishna Svarup, *Faqīron kī sāt manzilen* (*santon kā saptadarśana*), Ramashram Satsang Prakashan, Sikandarabad, 1959, p. 11.

his mother. This is knowledge (*ma'rifat*). Sucking eagerly the milk from the mother's nipple, both the mother that nourishes and the baby that is nourished, are so strongly attracted to each other as to become like one, inseparable from each other. This state of naturally belonging to each other without reflecting upon it is termed as *tawḥīd*.[44]

Clearly, the baby of this metaphysical image corresponds to the neophyte and the mother to the spiritual master without whose assistance it remains an extremely arduous, if not impossible task to achieve any spiritual growth. Again, the master's vital role in guaranteeing the disciple's progress in the *sādhanā*, is depicted, as a prerogative that is shared not only by the representatives of Islamic esoterism but also by those of Hindu spirituality where it found its expression in the adaptation of the devotionally oriented *sants* of mediaeval India whose legacy our present-time masters assert to represent. Hence, the reference to Kabīr's message expressed in the following verses that hint at the stage described in the Sūfī doctrines as 'self-extinction in the master' (*fanā fī'l-shaikh*):

> *jab main thā tab guru nahīn, ab guru hain main nāya* ।
> *prem galī ati sāṅkarī, yā men do na samāya* ।।
>
> When only I existed, there was no master, now only the master exists and I am no more ।
> United through the narrow path of love like a small chain, oh none of us two did subsist ।।

The second degree of realisation, reached after the search for the true master is met with success, consists of passionate and selfless love for the world and its Creator (*'ishq*, *upāsanā*). If arising out of the knowledge that every action of God is accomplished independently and unselfishly, it ultimately leads to the selfless service (*niṣkāma sevā*) of every single creature.[45] The source of this infinite current of love consists at first of the figure of the spiritual guide to whom the disciple must learn to

44. *Faqīron kī sāt manzilen*, pp. 20-1.

45. *Ibidem*, pp. 38-9.

surrender. But on a more advanced level, once he has penetrated the veils that cover the true light of his heart, it will be the interior master through Whom the initiate, assuming the role of heir of the great Divine descents (*avatāra*) of the past, will be pervaded by selfless love for the surrounding creatures. He will spare no effort to let them participate at the Truth through the path which shines through them and illuminates their immediate environment.

Such a description makes once more clear how the Kāyasth authorities of this lineage integrate the Hindu perspective of the Divine *avataraṇa* smoothly with the position assumed by the Naqshbandiyya Mujaddidiyya which considers its great authorities as real heirs of the last Divine messenger. In the same way these contemporary Hindu *sant*s consider themselves as the heirs of Lord Rāma or Lord Kr̥ṣṇa who, followed by either the Buddha, Muhammad or the Christ, have concluded the cycle of godly envoys sent down to earth in order to re-establish the Cosmic *dharma* shaken from time to time by the state of disorder created by an imbalance between the major tendencies inherent in Divine manifestation.

The third stage listed by Kr̥ṣṇa Lāl corresponds to knowledge (*'irfān*, *jñāna*), metaphorically considered as the fruit growing on the spiritual tree whose root corresponds to the desire to know and whose trunk is put in relation with the application to a means to acquire this wisdom. Associated with the Sūfī trilogy of *sharī'at*, *ṭarīqat* and *ḥaqīqat*, or with the alleged Hindu equivalent described in the *Bhagavad Gītā* as *karma*, *upāsanā* and *jñāna*, knowledge is said to bear a close relation with the intellect (*'aql* or *buddhi*) and ranks, therefore, highest among these three degrees. Its most sublime level regards of the knowledge of the Essence (*'ilm-i dhāt*) that provides the answer to the fundamental question 'Who are You?' or 'Who am I?' But, it is stressed in reality, knowledge is nothing but the result of the previously achieved direct vision of the primordial origin residing in the most intimate part of the heart, beyond the states described in the Upaniṣad as 'state of awakeness' (*jāgr̥ta-sthāna*) and 'state of dream' (*svapna-sthāna*) and beyond the Sūfī tripartition of the Universe into *jabarūt*, *malakūt* and *nāsūt*. Interestingly, this tripartition, already mentioned by Rāmcandra, does not constitute part of the standard Mujaddidī terminology but rather belongs to the terminology used in Qādirī cosmology and among those orders generally associated with holding a *wujūdī* point of view. This appears even more noteworthy as the position held by the Kāyasth authorities of this order, although recognising the high rank of knowledge, does not regard it as the highest one obtainable. Following Śrī Rāmānujācārya, and their predecessors in the *sant* environment they, normally, subordinate it to the stage of pure selfless devotion (*upāsanā*). In contrast, Kṛṣṇa Lāl describes knowledge as leading to certitude (*yaqīn*) intended as the certainty of the Oneness of Reality (*tawḥīd* or *ekatā*) which constitutes the immediately following, fourth of the seven stages of realisation, allegedly regarded as highest by the *wujūdī*s.

In his description of the stage of *tawḥīd*, Kṛṣṇa Lāl asserts that the differences of perspective held by the adherents to the doctrines of dvaitādvaita, viśiṣṭādvaita and kevalādvaita are all equally far from grasping the truth and that the dialectic divergencies in their respective points of view are ultimately illusory. But rather than criticising the specific perspective held by each of these schools the author's position underlines once more the aversion felt by the masters of this lineage to any sort of purely speculative approach typical for the *vedāntin*. This underlying assumption is equally present in the doctrinal expositions of Shaikh Aḥmad Sirhindī and his Sūfī heirs, thus, preparing the ground for their position resumed by the Mujaddidīs in the formula *hamā az ost*. In the words of Kṛṣṇa Lāl:

> . . . pure unity (*tawḥīd*) does not and can never exist. The affirmation of the One always presupposes the persistence of duality. Until the notion of the lover (*'āshiq*), that is to say the subject that affirms Unity, and its [complementary] in the shape of the beloved (*ma'shūq*), subsists, this residual duality will impede the [experience of] pure identity. . . this term reflects a purely theoretical notion that has nothing to do with real Unity . . . Truth (*Ḥaqq*) is Truth, non-Truth (*na-*

> *Ḥaqq*) is non-Truth — Divine Unity lies beyond these two. . . .[46]

This simple statement describes in a very succinct manner the position that underlies Kr̥ṣṇa Lāl's doctrinal version, and the unconstrained way in which the technical vocabulary pertaining to both the Mujaddidī and the *sants* teachings is mixed together in an apparently loose manner betrays to an extraordinary extent the synthetic vision characteristic of the entire lineage. In the specific context of various degrees implied in the notion of *tawḥīd*, for instance, the author lists four categories current in Sūfīs teachings:

(a) *tawḥīd-i sharʿī*, described as equivalent to the Hindu concept of *karma-kāṇḍa*, based essentially on the dogmatic acceptance of God's unicity (*waḥdat*) and recognising His transcendence reality.

(b) *tauḥīd-i ṭarīqatī*, described as equivalent to the Hindu concept of *upāsanā-kāṇḍa*, and further subdivided into two categories, namely *tauḥīd-i ʿafʿālī*, regarding the active aspect of the Divine that intervenes in nature, and *tauḥīd-i ṣifatī*, that is to say the awareness that all creatures are characterised by the reflections of the divine attributes.

(c) *tawḥīd-i dhātī*, i.e., to consider everything as pertaining to the essence of God.

(d) *tawḥīd-i ḥaqīqatī*, i.e., the individual's total identification with the Divine.

This list, which clearly betrays its origin in the Mujaddidī concept of the multiple reflections of the Divine, is then associated to the Hindu concepts of (a) *sālokya*, i.e., to penetrate into the Divine realm; (b) *sāmīpya*, i.e., proximity to God; (c) *sārūpya*, i.e., to participate consciously at the numerous Divine aspects; and (d) *sāyujya*, i.e., to penetrate into and reach identification with God's essence.

These are identified as four successive degrees of liberation

46. *Faqīron kī sāt manzileṅ*, p. 60.

(*mukti*) gradually leading the initiate from a perspective of duality towards the experience of Identity. They can be, therefore, associated with what in the language of the *Kabīr-Panthī*s and Rādhāsoāmī saints is described as the degree of *sun* or *śūnya*, already mentioned in the precedent chapter in the context of Rāmcandra's concepts of the higher stages of being. Interspersed with several sometimes extensive quotations of verses ascribed to Kabīr (but more certainly to be attributed to later members of the Dharmadāsī branch of the *panth*), the author attributes the possibility to gain access to them as the result of the growing intensity in the *guru-śiṣya* relationship which sees the spiritual master as the immediate object of the initiate's longing and only fix point of reference for attaining to the primary level of *tawḥīd* which culminates in the state of 'self- effacement in the master' (*fanā fi'l-shaikh*).

Once this primary goal is achieved, the spiritual traveller has reached the fifth of the seven stations, termed according to the vocabulary used by Islamic esoterism as *istighnā* (lit. 'non-dependence') and rendered in a terminology pertaining to Patañjali's classical Yoga doctrine as *nirvikalpa-samādhi*. It is said to bear a direct connection with the previous stage and is defined as a deepening of that one, hence also identified with the state of *savikalpa-samādhi*. The initiate who has attained to this degree has effectively reached the identification with the Object sought for (*dhyeya*) and can, therefore, truly be termed as *yogī* or Sūfī.

In the technical vocabulary of the *santmat* this stage is referred to as *mahāsun* or 'great emptiness'. Those who have attained to it are given the title of *haṁsa* or even *paramahaṁsa*, since, it is asserted, only at this level the entire meaning of what the Sūfīs intend with *tark-i duniyā*, the detachment from any worldly tie, analogous to the Hindu concept of *tyāga*, is entirely achieved and the initiate, although apparently related to the world and its objects, is in reality totally independent of it (this being the literal meaning of the Arabic term *istighnā*). To further clarify the idea the underlying this notion, the author cites a beautiful Persian couplet that emphasises the *nirguṇa* perspective held by him and his predecessors:

sar birahnā nīstam dāram kullāh-i chār tark ।
tark-i duniyā, tark-i 'uqbā, tark-i maulā, tark-i tark ।।

My head is not naked but covered with a fourfold cap, relinquishment from the world, from the hereafter, from the Lord and from the very concept of relinquishment.[47]

A purely interior attitude is assumed by those who have explored the full depth of detachment in their hearts. It is easy to understand that the ideal *tyāgī*, in the view of our masters, does not comply with the conventional archetype of the Vedic ascetic living a life of hardship and penance in seclusion in a remote place somewhere in the Himālayas or the Vindhya mountains. He is rather identified with the simple and honest householder (*gr̥hasthī*) who combines the common responsibilities of social life with an inner detachment from all worldly deeds resulting from his proximity to the Divine inside himself. This state of inner beatitude is referred to as *sahaja samādhi* since it is said to be reached without any need of undergoing painful exercises of renouncement and self-castigation as the natural result of an inner awareness reached exclusively through the surrender to the master's benevolent flow of spiritual energy.

The next level on the seven-fold path is that termed as 'extinction' or 'annihilation' (*fanā* or *laya*) and said to bear a direct relation with the subtle centre located in the brain, referred to by contemporary *sant*s as *bhanwara gufā* or the 'whirling cave'. According to Kr̥ṣṇa Lāl, rather than merely pertaining to the state of non-existence or non-subsistence of the individual (*nīstī*) as commonly assumed, it indicates a spiritual state in correspondence to the condition of deep sleep (*suṣupti*) in which the heart has returned to its primordial condition prior to its illusory implication in and limitation by the outer objects. This state is said to correspond to *sat-cit-ānanda* to which some *sants* refer also as *unmanī avasthā*. Its negative description as 'non-being' or 'non-existence' characterises its ineffable nature beyond description.

47. *Faqīron kī sāt manzilen*, p. 75.

Finally, the seventh and utmost degree contemplated in the perspective of this *sādhanā* is called 'permanence' (*baqā*), somewhat oddly rendered by the term *pūrṇa-jīvana*, (the 'living Principle') in reference of the *ātman*, since, in contrast with the previous stage related to what is in fact of a fundamentally ephemeral nature (only thus it is possible to refer to it as something subject to extinction), this stage pertains to a stable and permanent Reality, not subject to any alteration of time and space, neither to birth nor to death, everlasting (*bāqī*), beyond duality, beyond multiplicity, lying beyond the abodes of the gods. It is said that while It bears no names, all names are comprehended by It. It transcends the alpha and omega of the entire Universe where only Truth (*al-Ḥaqq*, *satya*) subsists. Forever hidden to the eyesight, this is the Supreme Principle; he who fully realises It becomes one with It and knows that he has never been separated from It. Birth, youth, adulthood and old age, all this reveals its fanciful truth in a Divine display of the everlasting game of creation, on the unfolding of its possibilities and their reabsorption, both on a macrocosmic and microcosmic plane, which is unreachable even by knowledge. This is the realm of the *ātmā*, the *turīya* of the Upaniṣad whose inner reflection lies at the utmost limit of the *satyaloka* or the *dayāla-deśa* of the Rādhāsoāmīs.

Delhi: Continuity in diversity

The last authority to be discussed in the context of this lineage is known as Yaś Pāl. Born on 5 December 1918 at Bulandshahr to Sohan Lāl, a head-clerk (*munṣarim*) at the district's Judge's Court, he spent the early years of his life in that town near Delhi before moving to Allahabad for his higher education. After successfully completing his studies there, he joined the P&T Department as a telegraphist and retired from the position of director in the department of telecommunications in December 1976.[48]

Unlike the other authorities discussed, he was not a direct disciple of Rāmcandra Fatehgarhī but belongs to a yet later

48. *LVV*, p. 298.

generation of authorities grown under the leadership of Rāmcandra's nephew Bṛj Mohal Lāl. Reportedly, Yaś Pal was first introduced to his future spiritual guide by his paternal uncle in 1942, but it was not until four years later while posted at Calcutta, after a traumatic first-hand experience of the outbreak of communal violence there in August 1946 during the events of the 'Direct Action Day', that he was reportedly driven towards spiritual life that could 'rise humanity above its beastly nature'. Later, he was posted at Delhi and, on the suggestion of his younger brother Satya Pāl, began to attend Kṛṣṇa Lāl's *satsang* at Sikandarabad. There, in October 1948 during the annual *Daśaharā* meeting, he was officially introduced to his master and in July 1949 he was granted initiation by Bṛj Mohan Lāl (*dādājī*),[49] until in June 1951, after 'merging completely with his *gurudeva*', he was granted permission (*ijāzat*) to establish his own spiritual circle.

After the sudden death of Bṛj Mohan Lāl in January 1955, while posted at Jabalpur (Madhya Pradesh), Yaś Pāl was at loss and decided to abandon every responsibility in the *sādhanā*, However, soon afterwards, assertedly following a dream in which his master appeared to him delivering a series of instructions, he regained confidence and decided to resume his role as spiritual leader. Two years later, he organised his master's *bhaṇḍāra* at Bombay, and sometime later he started to run an organised *satsang* programme at Delhi culminating with an annual meeting, held since 1958 on the day of *Rāmanavamī*.

Considering himself ever since as the undisputed leader and heir of the entire lineage, in 1969 he laid the foundation for the 'Akhil Bharatiya Santmat Satsang' which was officially registered in August of the same year. With a number of smaller centres spreadout all over India, but also in Canada, the U.S.A., the Philippines and the U.A.E., the headquarters of this mission are situated at the master's residence in New Delhi while the annual *bhaṇḍārā* is organised at the Anangpur *āśrama* in

49. *Highlights of Param Pujya Bhai Sahib's life*, Akhil Bharatiya Santmat Satsang, Delhi, 1992, p. 6.

Faridabad district of Haryana, which is spacious enough to accommodate and feed the great number of devotees gathering on that occasion. There, he has established the 'Shri Brij Mohan School', recognised up to the eighth standard, where young children are instructed according to the master's humanitarian ideals.

As considered necessary for a charismatic leader of an institution that claims to promulgate an integral spiritual discipline, Yaś Pāl too claims authorship of a vast range of written works supposedly based on the teachings received from his 'revered *dādājī*', which contain the most important doctrinal guidelines and practical instructions for his followers spread over vast areas of the country. Among these we find *Ānanda-Yoga*, published in two volumes and available in both Hindī and English based on the instructions of Bṛj Mohan Lāl the quarterly periodical *Sant-Sudhā*, containing various articles in both languages and numerous other booklets including a lengthy comment on the *Bhagavad Gītā*.

The *sādhanā* promoted by Yaś Pāl in the name of his *guru* Bṛj Mohan Lāl maintains the denomination attributed to it by the son of Raghubar Dayāl, viz., Ānanda-Yoga, the 'Yoga of beatitude'. Like all the other disciplines in this lineage regarded as the subtle essence of Rāja-Yoga, Ānanda-Yoga claims to suit the needs of our days by eliminating most of the physical exercises hitherto current in most disciplines while maintaining the intellectual perspective held by the Vedānta. It leaves to the master the task of cleansing the disciple's inner states (*antaḥkaraṇa*) from the impurities created by the mental impressions (*saṁskāra*) with the aim of taking him to the inner experience of a lasting state of beatitude.

Said to be derived from the *brahma-vidyā* taught by Maharṣi Aṣṭāvakra to the enlightened king of the solar dynasty (*sūrya-vaṁśa*) Janaka 'Videha' of Maithilī, father of Lord Rāmacandra's bride Sītā, in the pre-historical period of the *dvāpara-yuga,*[50]

50. This idea is further elaborated in Kṛṣṇa Lāl's *Aṣṭāvakra-Gītāmṛta*, first published in two small volumes from the Akhil Bharatiya Santmat Satsang at New Delhi in 1979, which deals extensively →

the science and method taught in this mission is not considered a new invention but rather a reintroduction and revival of that ancient knowledge dedicated to the people of India. Most interestingly, the merit of this task is attributed to Khwāja Bāqī Billāh, the spiritual guide of Shaikh Aḥmad Sirhindī who introduced the Naqshbandiyya to the Indian subcontinent in the sixteenth century AD from Afghanistan and Central Asia, thus, establishing a vital link between the ancient Hindu wisdom, Islamic esoterism and the contemporary lineage of ours.

Based on the ideal of leading modern mankind, perceived as increasingly weakened by the impact and comforts of its twentieth-century lifestyle, towards the attainment of the most sublime spiritual states in consonance with the performance of their worldly duties, it proposes itself to bring about the merging of the individual soul (*jīvātmā*) with the immobile abode (*dhruvapāda*) of the *satpuruṣa* through the vitalisation of the spiritual plexuses or *cakras*.

The frequent textual references quoted in support of the elaborations made in his works apart from the usual *sākhīs* attributed to Kabīr, are taken largely from the *Bhagavad Gītā*, reflecting the background of the author's own religious tradition oriented along the lines of the prevailing devotional current of the nearby land of Braj, the *Kṛṣṇa-bhakti*. His *sādhanā* referred to alternatively as *sahaja-mārga*, the 'easy path', is said to consist of a balance between the three paths described by Lord Kṛṣṇa in his sermon to Arjuna as the key to a successful spiritual realisation, i.e., *karma*, *jñāna* and *upāsanā*. It is said to lead ultimately to the attainment of the state of *sahaja samādhi* as the perfection of sincere and selfless devotion to the master, the spiritual ancestors and finally God.[51]

This discipline, for which an intense yearning and whole-hearted devotion are the only necessary prerequisites, is based on the grace (*kṛpā*) and kindness of the Lord (*īśvara*), that

---

→ with and comments upon some selected verses of the *Aṣṭāvakra-Gītā*.

51. *AnY*, vol. I, p. 96.

crystallises itself in the guise of the real master attracting the chosen ones towards Himself. Acting through the material support of his physical shape, the teacher's spiritual current (*ādhyātmik dhārā*) is said to possess such a power of penetration that even the slightest glance conveys into the heart of the aspirant a feeling of immense joy, calmness and serenity (*bhakti-bhāva*). This transfusion of power is known among the Hindu masters of this lineage as *śaktipat*.[52]

The three fundamental ingredients of the discipline's operational aspect consist of *satsang*, the company and service of a truly qualified saint, a concept that re-echoes the Sūfī idea of *suḥbat*, besides *satnām*, the practice of invoking internally the sacred name comparable to the Sūfī method of *dhikr*, and *satguru*, the affiliation and total surrender to the master, called by the Sūfīs shaikh or *pīr-i kāmil*. These three, referred to as the 'trinity of the path', constitute the entire edifice of the *sant* teachings, referred to as *santmat*, and are complementary to each other.

Since the ancient techniques of Laya-Yoga and Kuṇḍalinī-Yoga that keep in view the awakening of the spiritual centres from the *mūlādhāra* upwards along the spinal cord, require a strict discipline based on abstinence and contentment (*brahma-carya*) the prerequisites of which are rarely found among the human beings of the present age and rather irreconcilable with the life of a householder (*gr̥hastha*), this discipline focusses entirely on the concentration and meditation on the *hr̥daya-cakra*, seat of the germ from which will germinate the spiritual child under the influence of the master's current of *prāṇa*. Nourished and invigorated by the spiritual energy, thus, received, the *sādhaka*'s *prāṇa* is lifted spontaneously from the lower regions centred around the seat of the latent power (*kuṇḍalinī*) in the *mūlādhāra* up to the subtle heart-organ, known by the Mujaddidīs as *laṭīfa-i qalb*, thereby provoking the rise of a state of spiritual rapture (*avadhūta* or *jadhba*).

Only after the completion of this preliminary step, the

52. *AnY*, vol. II, ch.2, pp. 13-18. The related methodology is described in ch. 8, pp. 84-9.

initiate is ready to face the challenge of putting his feet on the *sulūk* which is described unequivocally by Yaś Pāl as the gradual penetration behind the quintuple sheaths listed by the Upaniṣad. The description of each of these five sheaths, however, follows too closely the one given by Rāmcandra to offer any new clues for the evaluation of this method.[53]

Once reached at this stage, the *sādhaka*, now guided by the inner master, will be able to concentrate his mind on that single point (*ekāgratā*) at the centre of his heart from which not only the spiritual light irradiates but in whose continuous palpitation there also reverberates the name of the Supreme (*japājapa* or *dhikr-i qalb*) previously focussed on that very spot by the mind's rhythmic invocation of the sacred syllable (*mantra*, *dhikr-i khafī*). This technique, commonly known as *sūrat-śabda yoga* so important among the Rādhāsoāmīs, which leads to the expansion of the subtle sound vibration (*āntarik śabda* or *udgītha*)[54] from the region of the heart to the entire breast (in exact correspondence to the *maqām-i sīna* that comprehends the five *laṭā-'if* contemplated by the Mujaddidīs) lifts the subtle sound vibration upwards towards the *ājñā-cakra* located somewhere on the forehead between the eyebrows (in correspondence to the *laṭīfa-i nafs*, known by the followers of Shaikh Aḥmad Sirhindī). The diagram that illustrates the location of the central knots in the human breast reproduces exactly that given by the Mujaddidīs, although Yaś Pāl does not nominate any of of these 'centres'. Far greater importance

53. *Madhhab aur Taḥqīqat*, 1989, pp. 129-34.

54. The latter term *udgītha*, as also mentioned at by the author (*AnY*, vol. I, p. 70), refers to *Chāndogya Upaniṣad*, I.1-V.5 elucidating the deeper significance of the sacred syllable *AUṀ* which introduces every single hymn of the Veda. Acoustically symbolising the Supreme Priniciple, this text recommends its use as the object of meditation of the *nirākāra* or formless Divinity, for it is directed towards the metaphysical essence of everything including in its fold all the multiple aspects of manifestation. There, hence, results the highly intellectual perspective that lies behind the often repetitive expositions of the masters of this lineage, which draws its ultimate inspiration from the very source of all sacred knowledge in the Hindu tradition, the Vedānta.

is ultimately attributed by him to the *ājñā-cakra* or *laṭīfa-i nafs* as the passage between the intermediate, individual dominion of the *piṇḍa-deśa* and the universal realm of the *brahmāṇḍaman*.

A particular feature that distinguishes Yaś Pāl's exposition from that of other authorities in the same lineage consists of the definition of his doctrinal perspective as *iti-mārga* or 'path of addition', said to go back to the teachings of Maharṣi Aṣṭāvakra. These are seen in contrast to the *neti-mārga* or 'path of denial and renunciation' hitherto most currently held by the *vedāntin* or *yogī*, that is outwardly manifested through the choice of the state of *saṁnyāsa*. Although the latter is recognised as the shortest way for obtaining the desired results as it absolves the *sādhaka* from all other objectives but the one, leaving him all energies for the pursuit of the spiritual quest, preference is ultimately given to the *iti-mārga* which, in contrast, adds to the daily responsibilities incumbent on the householder the quest for the *jīvanmukti-avasthā* or 'state of liberation from any bondage while alive'. For the achievement of this objective, two things are regarded as essential: the perpetual remembrance of the Lord (*smaraṇa*), comparable to the condition of *ḥuḍūr-i āgāhī* or perpetual presence envisaged by the Naqshbandī through the *dhikr* and referred to by the *sant*s as *japa*; the second, directly derived from the former, consists of the performance *niṣkāma karma* or selfless action which leaves no residual impressions on the practitioner's subtle state that would condition the projection of his *jīva* into a future existence. To illustrate this point, the author quotes the well-known verses pronounced by Kr̥ṣṇa to Arjuna shortly before the start of the epic battle of Kurukṣetra:

> *tyaktvā karmaphalāsaṅgam nityatr̥pto nirāśrayaḥ* ।
> *karmanyabhipravr̥ttopi naiva kiñcitkaroti saḥ* ।।

> Having abandoned attachment for the fruits of action, ever content, dependent on none, though engaged in actions, nothing at all does he do.
>
> — *Bhagavad Gītā*, IV.20

and also

> *gatsaṅgasya muktasya jñānāvasthita cetasaḥ* ।
> *yajñāyācarataḥ karma samagram pravilīyate* ।।
>
> Of the man whose attachment is gone, who is liberated, whose mind is established in knowledge, who acts for the sake of sacrifice, his whole action melts away.
>
> — *Bhagavad Gītā*, IV.23

Once again one can observe how the original Sūfī methodology is integrated neatly into a Hindu doctrinal perspective without creating any friction between the respective points of view since the role of the heirs of the prophets as intended by Sahikh Aḥmad and his followers, and that of the modern *sant*s who similarly consider themselves as heirs of the divine *avatāra* Rāma and Kṛṣṇa ultimately share the same objective of proposing a spiritual realisation that combines both the attainment of the highest abode for the practitioner while maintaining his responsibility to render selfless service to his fellow human being in communicating him the message of a path open to a large number of individuals even in the final period of the *kali-yuga*.

As it has emerged from these descriptions, the heirs of the tradition begun by Rāmcandra Saksenā and his master Shāh Faḍl Aḥmad Khān continue, each in their own peculiar way, to perpetuate a *sādhanā* that reunites elements based on a mixed Hindu-Muslim background. Faithful to the principles set out by their illustrious predecessors, they all start their elaborations from the common ground prepared by him. Although we can clearly recognise in their expositions a gradual shift towards a more indigenised conceptual background and vocabulary, the Islamic substratum of the Mujaddidī tradition can hardly remain hidden to the attentive observer and illustrates the flexibility of adopting different sacred teachings to a common purpose. This tendency can be partially accounted for by the master's sounder theoretical acquaintance with the classical Hindu texts borne out of their expressed desire to exalt the 'glorious spiritual heritage of Hindu India'. Such an attitude reflects to some extent the changed attitude and the new role assumed by the educated Hindu middle-class since the beginning of the century and in particular after Independence. This is particularly marked in the Kāyasth community which, in a sense, summarises the general pattern of Hinduisation that accompaneid the growing feeling of nationalism in India. It reflects the redefinition of the community's social role over the last one-hundred years away from their loyalty to and collaboration with the Islamic rulers towards their full integration into and identification with contemporary India proud of its deep millennarian culture, claiming their place in modern society. As such, these authorities act as natural vehicles of that peculiar Indian tendency to absorb the impulses and stimuli received from outside and to synthesise them in a fashion which, though reshaping its outer form, leaves largely intact their underlying essence. All four examples, while laying emphasis on slightly different elements in their teachings, reiterate, thus, in great lines the doctrinal outlay proposed by their spiritual guide and can, therefore, rightly be considered in their own way as perpetuators of the modern *sant* tradition.

Conclusion

THE Hindu offshoot of the Mujaddidiyya Maẓhariyya which about a century ago began to spread from Fatehgarh and Kanpur across the Ganges plain and adjacent areas is still alive although on a reduced scale. Its period of major glory and force of attraction went from around 1920, when its first and foremost leader Rāmcandra Saksenā began to promote actively the *sādhanā*, he had inherited from his shaikh and which he further elaborated, to 1955 when Rāmcandra's grandson Bṛj Mohan Lāl Saksenā died at Lucknow. Since then, a gradual process of fragmentation has allowed the contemporary representatives of this branch to spread the discipline and its connected message to various parts of India and abroad, while at the same time losing much of its inner force and cohesion. This development notwithstanding, some of its leaders in both the spiritual and the genetic genealogies have carried on the gradual cultural assimilation of the original Islamic *ṭarīqa* into a new Hindu environment in a fashion similar to that which can be observed in other modern *sant* traditions, such as the Rādhāsoāmī *satsang*s at Agra and Beas.

In general terms it is possible to affirm that, while the theoretical and doctrinal background of the original Mujaddidī teachings has been largely replaced by those current among the various *sant-panth*s (in particular the Dharmadāsī branch of the Kabīr-panth at Chattīsgarh to which Rāmcandra was affiliated and by Rādhāsoāmī teachings), yet the methods and techniques which make up the practical aspect of the discipline have been left substantially inalterated and therefore remain essentially indential to those used by the Mujaddidīs. Very much a part of the modern twentieth-century *sant* tradition with its accompanying component of social reform, Rāmcandra and his successors significantly belong like most of their renowned predecessors to the Vaiṣṇava tradition which is focussed around this divinity's popular descents (*avatāras*) Rāma and Kṛṣṇa. Taking into due account the natural formal differences intercurring between the two traditions, these take the central place held by Muḥammad among the Mujaddidīs in both his historical and purely spiritual dimension. Beginning with Mīrzā Maẓhar Jān-i Jānān, some of the leading authorities of the order have cautiously hinted at the underlying parallels subsisting between the Hindu *avatarana* doctrine and the Semitic concept of a series of prophets an law-giving messengers intervening in crucial moments of human history with the task of restoring order among those people who had forgotten their Divine origin. Hence, the major affinity between the prophetical vision of the Mujaddidīs and the Vaiṣṇava environment among Hindus in general and *sants* in particular.

From the point of view of self-realisation, the perspective held throughout the doctrinal elaborations of the Hindu Naqshbandīs is that of the Vedānta, the most purley metaphysical part of the Hindu doctrine which as *brahma-vidyā*, goes well along with the gnostic aspect of the Sūfī *'ilm-i Ilāhī*. Here again it appears more than a pure accident that the position assumed by the Mujaddidī *sants* to a large extent reflects the viewpoint held by Śrī Rāmānujācārya's Vaiṣṇava viśiṣṭādvaita which agrees much better than Śrī Śaṅkārācārya's Saiva kevalādvaita with the Sūfī doctrine developed by Shaikh Ahmad Sirhindī known as *waḥdat al-shuhūd*. It would be highly interesting to undertake a thorough comparison of the two mentioned Vedānta doctrines, one consonant with a Vaiṣṇava perspective and the other corresponding to a Śaiva perspective, with the two Sūfī doctrines, i.e Sirhindī's *waḥdat al-shuhūd* and Ibn al 'Arabī's *waḥdat al-wujūd*.

However, the 'science of the subtle centre' or *'ilm-i laṭā'if*, peculiar to the Naqshbandīs and in many respects similar to the Hindu *cakra-vidyā* common to most Tāntrik doctrines, constitutes a common ground on which Rāmcandra and his successors have built a bridge to link the two traditions in both their theoretical and practical aspects. Only at a later stage is the Mujaddidī methodology assimilated more clearly to the techniques used by the Yoga-*darśana* which is defined as Rāja-Yoga in view of its peculiar stress on a purely interiorised discipline consonant with the tendency prevailing also among their Muslim predecessors.

It may, therefore, be conclude that in spite of notable formal differences arising out of the different perspectives held by Islam and Hinduism in general and by the Mujaddidīs and *Kabīr-panthīs* particular, the example of the lineage of contemporary *sants* analysed in the present study shows that the apparently most irreconcilable positions held from an exoteric point of view and the different social and ethical circumstances, are nevertheless insufficient to prevent the development of a common spiritual terrain on which an encounter between these two great traditions offers the chance for a real synthesis from above, in the twentieth century just as it did in the fifteenth century at the time of Kabīr.

Glossary of Technical Terms

abhyāsa	the 'spiritual discipline', with emphasis on its active, technical aspect consisting of numerous exercises and inner practices.
abhyāsī	the 'practitioner', i.e., the initiate who is engaged in the various spiritual practices that are part of the *sādhanā*.
'aks	'reflection', that is to say the image of a higher principle cast on one or more of the lower degrees of reality.
akṣara	the unperishable, primordial sound vibration consisting of the syllable *oṁ*.
'ālam	lit. 'world, dominion'; in the technical context of the cosmological doctrine of the Naqshbandīs, it denotes one of a series of specific, hierarchical superseding degrees of existence.
'ālam-i amr	the 'world of order', so-called because it came into being instantly on the single command (*amr*) of Allāh: *Kun*! (Be!) (cf. *Koran* 36:82); it refers to the unmanifested world, situated beyond the 'Throne of Allāh' and the *barzakh*.
'ālam-i arwāḥ	the 'world of spirits', part of the *'ālam-i amr*; it is said to contain the spirits of all living beings prior to their descent into the realm of creation.
'ālam-i kabīr	lit. 'the great world', hence denoting in

	Naqshbandī cosmology the macrocosm or universe, divided into two hemispheres along the equatorial axis consisting of the *barzakh*.
'ālam-i khalq	the 'world of creation'; it constitutes the lower hemisphere of the *'ālam-i kabīr* or macrocosm, the upper hemisphere being constituted by the *'ālam-i amr*.
'ālam-i malakūt	the 'world of the angels and spirits'; it refers to the subtle dominion within the greater realm of the *'ālam-i khalq*, immediately above the *'ālam-i mulk* and is divided from it by the line of the horizon (*āsmān-i duniyā*).
'ālam-i mithāl	the 'world of the archetypes', part of the *'ālam-i amr*; it contains the celestial archetypes of all those entities that are to be manifested in the course of universal existence.
'ālam-i mulk	the 'world of dominion'; the term denotes the dominion of the physical world perceptible to the common senses, the gross aspect of creation.
'ālam-i ṣaghīr	the 'microcosm', that is to say the human being conceived as a reflection of the universe on a minor scale, sanctioned by God's appointment of Man as his viceregent (*khalīfa*) in the realm of creation.
'aql	the 'intellect'; can denote both the universal intellect (*'aql al-kullī*) and the individual, human intellect.
'arsh al-muḥīṭ	the 'all-encompassing Divine throne', the central spot of the universe whence the entire creation came into being by expansion around it, the focal point of the Divine command following the

descent of the order that sanctions the passage from non-being to being.

avyakta — lit. 'unmanifested', referring to the realm of non-manifestation; in the cosmological doctrines of the Hindu Naqshbandīs, the term denotes the intermediate degree of the cosmos that constitutes the limit between the seminal or archetypical manifestation and the realm of form; as such, it is put in relation with the *barzakh*.

a'yān al-thābita — the 'Divine prototypes', denoting the images arising in the Divine Intellect prior to their taking shape in the realm of creation.

bai'at — lit., 'the pact of allegiance', between the shaikh and the disciple that sanctions the formal initiation into a Sūfī *ṭarīqa*.

baqā — 'permanence'; denotes the state beyond that of the extinction of the individual attributes when the initiate fully adheres to the Divine attributes of his Creator.

barzakh — generally, the term refers to something that intervenes or lies between two entities or dominions, at the same time separating and linking the two; in Naqshbandī cosmology, it denotes the interval and link between the two hemispheres that constitute the universal 'sphere of Possibility', the 'world of order' (*'ālam-i āmr*) and the 'world of creation' (*'ālam-i khalq*); cf. *Koran* 18:53, where the term is put in relation with the meeting-point of the two oceans (*majma' al-baḥrain*).

bāṭin — 'the inner'; one of the names of Allāh,

	denotes the hidden, esoteric aspect of His being, pertaining essentially to the metaphysical realm.
bāz gasht	'retreat'; the sixth of the eleven spiritual principal which refers to the technique of the *dhikr*; it denotes the interval in the repeated rhytmical invocation of the *dhikr* to be observed by the initiate; during this pause, the *sālik* is advised to invoke and reflect upon a specific formula of request to God to concede His love and knowledge upon him.
bhūta	the 'gross element'; these are traditionally numbered as five: earth (*pr̥thvī*), water (*ap*), fire (*tejas*), air (*vāyu*) and ether (*ākāśa*); the resemblance with the five subtleties of the 'world of order' is evident.
dā'irah	lit. 'sphere, circle'; the term denotes one major state or degree of being, containing in its fold an indefinite series of further sub-degrees.
dhāt	the pure essence of Allāh without considering any of His attributes.
dhikr	lit. 'recollection, remembrance'; in the technical sense, it denotes a method common to all Sūfī orders representing a powerful means of impressing the subtle vibration produced by pronouncing rhythmically the sacred syllables, usually names of God, on the subtle states of the initiate.
dhikr-i khafī	the 'hidden invocation', performed exclusively on the inner, mental plane, not audible to the surrounding world.
faiḍ	'grace' (pl. *fuyūḍ*); denotes the effusion of spiritual blessings granted by Allāh

to the earnest seeker of Truth as a sign of His mercy.

fanā — lit. 'extinction, dissolution'; an important step on the esoteric path that denotes the overcoming of the most immediate individual limitations in the gradual process of universalisation; the perfection of this process is often referred to as *fanā al-fanā*; an equivalent to *laya* in Yoga doctrines.

fikr — lit., 'thought'; refers to the mental activity in the wider sense; in the technical context of the *ṭarīqa*, the term represents the series of techniques that are concerned with the discipline of the mind, bringing about an increasing capacity of focussing, concentrating, meditating and contemplating a series of Divine aspects until penetrating the inner truth contained in them; as such, complementary to the *dhikr* and the various aspects to this method.

ghaflat — lit. 'forgetfulness', 'negligence'; this term can have two connotations: in its inferior sense it refers to the condition of ignorance that characterises the uninitiated common folk unaware of the transcendent principles and inner truth of things, similar to the Sanskrit *avidyā*; in its superior sense, the Naqshbandīs intend with this term the stuphor arising out of the awareness reached in the higher stages of realisation, that man and God are two separate entities.

ghaib — 'hidden', the invisible world beyond the realm of creation perceptible to the common senses.

gṛhasthī-avasthā — the condition of 'householder'; the second of the four phases that characterise according to the ancient Hindu tradition human life; in the context of the present study, it denotes the way of life led by the Hindu Naqshbandīs of active participation in social life in all its aspects reflecting the ideal sanctioned by the Naqshbandī tenet of *khilwat dar anjuman*; contrasts strongly with the ascetic ideal that recommends the withdrawal from the world and its activities in order to reflect outwardly the inner renounce as part of the discipline.

ḥadīth — a 'Tradition', a saying attributed to the prophet Muḥammad, distinguished from the *Koran*, which represents the word of God revealed to His prophet through the archangel Gabriel.

ḥāl — a spiritual 'state', attained to spontaneously and in most cases beyond the full control of the initiate; hence, it is still liable to vanish as sudden as it has appeared.

ḥalqa — 'circle, an assembly'; the circle of intimate disciples gathering around a shaikh.

ḥaqīqat — 'truth, reality'; in the context of the esoteric doctrine, the term denotes the different degrees of insight into the essential principles and their extensions in the realm of immanence; in the highest sense, it refers to the very goal of every esoteric doctrine, the comprehension of the Divine in the aspect of *al-Ḥaqq*, supreme Truth.

hiraṇyagarbha — the 'golden germ', containing the potentialities of the entire manifestation in its fold, the possibilities of manifestation in their seminal state, analogous to the 'world of order' in Naqshbandī cosmology, corresponds to the head of Brahmā in the context of the primordial sacrifice or *puruṣa-sūkta* as mentioned in the *R̥gveda*.

hosh dar dam — 'awareness while breathing'; the first of the eleven principles that characterise the Naqshbandī path since Bahā al Dīn al-Bukhārī al-Naqshbandī; refers to the necessity to maintain a high level of awareness in every moment of life, during every single breath — hence, similar in its implications to the Yoga concept of *prāṇāyāma*, although later Naqshbandī practice does not call any longer for the need of restraining or even temporarily suspending the breath in the couse of some spiritual exercises.

ijāzat — 'licence', 'permission'; it refers to the licence conferred by the shaikh to his disciple to initiate and instruct independently new aspirants to enter the *ṭarīqa*.

'ilm — knowledge, science; the Arabic equivalent to the Sanskrit *vidyā*.

'ilm al-ladunnī — the 'Divinely inspired science', of non-human origin and, therefore, pertaining essentially to the transcendent realm, said to be revealed on those exceptionally qualified human beings whose role is to intervene; in most cases, related to and transmitted through the mysterious guide of the transcendent, *al-Khiḍr*.

'ilm-i ḥuḍurī 'intuitive knowledge'; refers to the spiritual knowledge acquired while proceeding on the path of esoteric realisation, regarding the inner Truth pertaining essentially to the transcendent realm, the knowledge of the spiritual principles that govern the realm of immanence.

'ilm-i ḥuṣulī 'discoursive knowledge'; the knowledge acquired on the rational plane though the apprehension of mental notions, hence the knowledge of the erudite and the learned scholars.

'ilm-i lāhī the 'Divine science', esoteric knowledge, pertaining to the Divine mysteries, the equivalent to the Hindu *brahma-vidyā*.

jadhba 'spontaneous attraction', 'spiritual rapture'; refers to the state which takes the initiate suddenly and abruptly from one condition to a higher state of awareness that enables him to enter into contact with the realm of transcendence, said to be produced as a result of earnest devotion and wholehearted surrender either to the shaikh, to the ancestors in the spiritual lineage, or directly to the Lord.

jam'iyat 'composure of the heart or mind', analogous to the state of *ekāgratā* in the Yoga discipline.

jñāna 'knowledge', 'wisdom'; the intuitive knowledge of the Sacred acquired through an inner comprehension of the doctrine.

jñānendriya the 'faculties of knowledge', corresponding to the five faculties of the senses through the mind of the individual receives the multitude of sensual impressions from the outside world: these faculties consist of: the sense of hearing (*śrotra*), the sense of touch (*tvaca*), the sense of sight (*cakṣus*), the sense of taste (*rasana*) and the sense of smell (*ghrāna*).

karāmat — extraordinary deeds ascribed to a saint in virtue of his spiritual achievements that enable him to intervene, in an apparently miraculous manner, on various degrees of nature and its elements.

karmendriya — the 'faculties of action' through which the individual intervenes in the surrounding world; these are five, listed as: the faculty of prension (*pāṇi*), the faculty of deambulation (*pāda*), the faculty of excretion (*pāya*), the faculty of generation (*upastha*) and the faculty of speech (*vāc*).

kashf — 'opening', 'disclosure'; refers to the sudden revelation of a supernatural truth, based on spiritual intuition.

khānaqāh — 'hospice'; the seat and residence of a Sūfī shaikh including residential quarters for his disciples, a common space where the spiritual instructions take place and, usually, a mosque with the annexed facilities.

kharq-i 'adat — a miracle or extraordinary deed, apparently against the natural course of things, synonym of *karāmat*.

khilwat dar anjuman — 'solitude amidst the crowd'; the fourth of the eleven principles of the Naqshbandī path that defines the attitude assumed by the Sūfīs linked to this *ṭarīqa*, which sanctions their involvement in the outer affairs of the world while inwardly remaining detached from it.

laṭīfa lit., 'subtle' (pl.: *laṭā'if*) ; in the technical context of the Mujaddīdiyya it denotes the subtle centres or spiritual organs located inside the human body, on which the disciple is taught to focus as essential part of his spiritual practice; analogous to the *cakra* in Yoga disciplines. The five subtleties of the *'ālam-i khalq* are listed as: earth (*khāk*), water (*āb*), fire (*ātish*), air (*hawā*) and breath (*nafas*); the five subtleties pertaining to the *'ālam-i amr*, located inside the human body in the heart region, are: heart (*qalb*), spirit (*rūḥ*), secret (*sirr*), mystery (*khafī*) and utmost mystery (*akhfā*).

ma'iyat 'co-presence'; the degree reached by the initiate during the stage of 'major sainthood', when he conceives himself as acting in perfect harmony with the Divine will, in the continuous awareness of being in the company of his Lord.

maqām 'station'; refers to a major degree of spiritual advancement acquired on a permanent basis; by convention, these are listed as ten, but can be multiple in number.

murāqabat lit., 'visualisation'; in the Naqshbandī context, it denotes a series of meditation exercises, the object of which varies according to the degree of advancement through the 'spheres' or stages of the esoteric path; the perfection of this technique implies the contemplation of the object sought and, finally, its full comprehension through identification with the truth inherent to it; the total number of visualisations is eighteen.

nafs — the 'soul', the psychological aggregate pertaining to the subtle state of the individual; it stretches out between the subtle centre situated at the bottom of the back, roughly in coincidence with the *mūlādhāra-cakra* known in Haṭha-Yoga doctrines, and the *laṭīfa-i naf*s, situated somewhere on the forehead, in coincidence with the *ājñā-cakra*.

nafs-i ammāra — the 'uncultivated soul' of the common human individual, subject to the lower human instincts and unreceptive to any unveilings from the hidden world.

nafs-i lawamma — the 'blameworthy soul',that is to say the subtle part of the individual aggregate that is critically scrutinised by the initiate for its deficiencies and weaknesses while proceeding in the process of introspection during his spiritual career.

nafs-i muṭama'inna — the 'pacified soul', that is to say the purified inner states of the disciple void of its former corruption and in peace with itself while experiencing the closeness to its Creator; indicates the final degrees of the initiatic process defined by Muslim saints as 'cleansing of the soul'.

nafs-i nāṭiqa — the 'rational soul' referring to the faculty of reason that is part of the subtle dominion.

naẓar bar qadam — 'keeping one's eyes on one's steps'; the second of the eleven spiritual principles that sanctions the necessity for the initiate to keep a vigilant eye on every single step forwards in the interior discipline in order to protect himself from the manifold dangerous distractions encountered on the way.

nigāh dāsht — refers to the necessity to safeguard carefully the degree of lasting awareness acquired during the practice of *dhikr*, creating a shield of protection around one's inner states.

nuzūl — 'descent'; this term denotes the advanced stage of the Naqshbandī path, referred to as 'journey from Allāh' (*sair 'an Allāh*), leading the initiate back from the sublime Divine abode down into the degree of contingent reality represented by the created world; also referred to as *rujū'* ('return').

prakṛti — the 'primordial substance' in the Sāṅkhya doctrine; also the feminine principle, as such complementary to *puruṣa*; the matrix of universal manifestation from which everything possessing name and form has sprung; in the context of the present study, often identified with *māyā*, the mind-alluring image of universal manifestation in its multiple facets.

prāṇa — the 'vitalising breath' that animates everything; its five modalities are listed by the Upaniṣad as: inhalation (*prāṇa*), inspiration (*apāna*), retention (*vyāna*), expiration (*udāna*) and digestion (*samāna*), which indicate their function in the absorption of elements from the macrocosm into the microcosm and the expulsion of individual elements from the microcosm into the macrocosm; closely related to the *nafs* of the Naqshbandīs which in a similar manner is conceived as being nourished by the breath (*nafas*), hence the importance of *prāṇāyāma* and *ḥabs-i nafas* in the respective doctrines.

puruṣa — lit. the 'masculine principle' and essence; by extension universal Man and, in a less personal perspective, the underlying principle or prototype of a degree of existence; hence, in the cosmology of the Naqshbandī *sants*, the term can denote the supreme, unqualified principle as *satpuruṣa*, the principle of the dominion of creation as *kāla-puruṣa* and *puruṣa* as the universal mankind that is the central creature in the present cycle.

qalb — the heart, considered as the centre of the microcosm and said to represent the nexus with the transcendent world; hence, the most important subtle organ and starting point in the Mujaddidī teachings from where the 'way of *jadhba*' is said to originate.

qurbiyat — 'proximity'; in the language of the Naqshbandīs, the closeness to God reached by the initiate in the advanced stages of the path; in its superior interpretation equivalent to the identification with the Divine principle described by the *wujūdī* doctrine.

rābiṭa — 'connection', 'tie'; refers to the subtle connection between *pīr* and *murīd* that guarantees the active participation of the shaikh in the inner progress and supervision of his pupil, mainly achieved through the transmission of spiritual energy (*tawajjuh*) by the *murshid*, focussed on the subtle organs of the heart region.

safar dar waṭan — 'travelling in one's homeland'; the third of the eleven Naqshbandī principles that denotes the inner 'journey' leading the disciple from the purely human attributes upwards to the attainment of the virtues connected with the angelic attributes, and from there to the lofty station of the Divine attributes; this 'journey' consists of an entirely inner process leading through the various stages of the microcosm and requires a high degree of responsibility from the disciple.

sair — 'walk', 'excursion'; the journey the initiate undertakes whils progressing on the spiritual path.

sair-i āfāqi — the ' journey along the cardinal points'; denotes the first part of the process of awakening the subtle organs during which the initiate contemplates the Divine truths in the spatial realm of the cosmos that extends along the co-ordinates of the cardinal points.

sair-i anfusī — the 'journey along the inner selves'; refers to the second stage of reintegration of the subtle organs when the spiritual seeker contemplates the Divine truths along the vertical axis of his inner states departing from the focal point of the interior 'heart-chamber'.

sair-i naẓarī — the 'visual way'; refers to the final stage of the Naqshbandī path which, strictly speaking, does not lead the initiate through any further degrees of progression towards the Divine, but rather implies an intensification of the vision of It.

sair-i qadamī — the 'walkable way', consisting of the various stages or *maqāmāt* through which the *sālik* advances in the process of interior realisation, metaphorically indicated as foot-steps on the inner path.

satnām — the 'true name', indicating the essential sound vibration reproduced while invoking mentally a specific formula containing the *bīja* or seed of that subtle sound; can also refer to the degree of utmost realisation among in some *sant* doctrines which are based on the science of the sound.

sharī'at — lit., the 'broad way' following which every Muslim is secured salvation in the hereafter; it refers to the exoteric, religious Law sanctioned by the *Koran* and the *āḥādīth* that comprehends the guidelines to every aspect of social, legal, religious and ritual behaviour incumbent upon the members of the *umma*.

ṣifat — 'attribute', usually used in the context of the innumerable attributes of Allāh that qualify the Divinity (pl. *ṣifāt*) and thus distinguished from Its pure, unqualified aspect of *al-Dhāt*; the Naqshbandīs distinguish the following major categories of attributes.

ṣifat-i salbiyya — 'the transcendent attribute', pertaining to the transcendent aspect of the Divinity, hence part of Its essential aspects (*ṣifāt-i dhātiyya*).

ṣifat-i thabūtiyya — 'the affirmative attribute'; this category of Divine attributes comprehends all those that affirm positively the existence of Allāh and His creation; it is described as one step higher up in the heirarchy of the Divine attributes as compared to the 'existential attribute'.

ṣifati-i iḍāfiyya — 'the additional attribute'; it refers to the Divine attribute that brings things into existence (*ṣifat-i takwīn*); the existential cause.

silsila — 'chain'; the chain of spiritual authorities of a *ṭarīqa*, which, if uninterrupted, guarantees the link of the present-time shaikh with the ancestors of the order (*buzurgān-i ṭarīqa*) and, eventually, with the fountainhead of all spiritual blessings, the prophet Muḥammad; analogous to the Hindu concept of *paramparā*.

ṣuḥbat — lit. 'company'; in the Sūfī context, it denotes the company of the spiritual master enjoyed by his disciples, whose presence alone is seen as the source of spiritual benefits; similar to the Hindu concept of *satsang*.

sulūk — the way or path that is crossed by the initiate or spiritual traveller (*sālik*) while progressing through a series of gradually ascending steps or degrees.

sūrat-śabda — the subtle sound current that pervades the entire universe; among many *sant*s, it constitutes the base of their entire discipline which develops around the invocation of different names or syllables containing in seminal form an increasingly sublime degree of subtle sound vibrations and culminating in the return to the essence contained in the primordial sound, symbolically represented by the syllable *oṁ* (*sūrat-śabda-yoga*).

ta'ayyun — 'determination', 'individualisation'; denotes the various degrees of dependance that limits every contingent being (*al-mumkin*) to its Divine principle; the latter is referred to as *lā ta'yyun*, undetermined.

tadhkiya-i nafs — 'purification of the soul'; the process that leads to the attainment of the 'pacified soul' (*nafs-i muṭama'inna*) by substituting the lower, beastly individual attributes with the laudable attributes of the angels and, finally, the essential attributes of the Divinity; part of the descending path.

tajallī — 'irradiation'; the way through which everything that exists in the universe participates at the Divine nature; the expansion of the Supreme into the realm of contingence as a result of Its primordial desire to be known; divided along two major categories: *tajalliyāt-i dhātiya*, the essential irradiation pertaining to the higher degrees of the non-maifested world, and the *tajalliyat-i iḍāfiya*, pertaining to the inferior degrees manifested in the realm of creation.

tanmātra — the subtle principles of the gross elements described in the Sāṅkhya doctrine that lists them in correspondence to the sensible qualities as: audible (*śabda*), tangible (*sparśa*), visible (*rūpa*), tasteable (*rasa*) and smelling (*gandha*); these are in a way analogous to the five subtleties said to pertain to the 'world of order' in the Naqshbandī doctrine.

tanzīh — the realm of the transcendent, complementary to *tasbīḥ*, referring to the immanent realm.

ṭarīqa — lit. 'path'; the term describes the initiatic path leading the human being from its peripherical position to the comprehension of the Divine mysteries, hence the Sūfī path, that comprises both the knowledge of the doctrine and the methodology to ascend to the higher sphere of being; roughly equivalent to the Hindu concept of *sampradāya*.

tasbīh — the immanent realm pertaining to creation, complementary to the transcendent realm (*tanzīh*) of the Divine.

taṣfiya-i qalb — 'cleansing of the heart'; an integral step of every Sūfī *ṭarīqa*; in the Naqshbandiyya, it refers to the initial stage of the path consisting of the awakening of the five subtle organs (*laṭā'if-i khamsa*) located in the heart region (*maqām-i dil*) and their re-unification with the principles in the 'world of order'; part of the ascending path.

tawajjuh — the 'spiritual attention' of the shaikh that represents the means of transmission of the spiritual energy from his inner states to those of his disciple, thereby screening his inner states and assisting him in his inner growth.

tawḥīd — the all-transcending Unity of the Divine, the term denotes the supreme metaphysical principle in the *wujūdī* tradition of *taṣawwuf*.

'ubūdiyat — the state of 'supreme servanthood'; in Mujaddidī terminology, this denotes the highest degree of realisation corresponding to the sublime awareness that man is essentially the servant of the all-transcendent God and that in the conscious acceptence of this role lies the highest degree of human perfection.

'urūj — 'ascent'; this term is used in the Mujaddidī doctrine in reference to that part of the spiritual part conceived as an ascent towards the spheres of sainthood that are part of the 'journey towards God' (*sair ilā Allāh*) and the 'journey in God' (*sair fī Allāh*).

vāsanā — lit., 'vortex'; indicates the incessant flow of thoughts in the uncultivated human mind distracting it from the concentration on and fixation of one particular object; in Sūfī teachings, these are known as *khaṭrāt*.

wajd — 'rapture', arising of an intense feeling of love and devotional self-surrender.

wājib al-wujūd — the 'Necessary Being', an epithet of God intended as the only essential being as compared to the possibilities (*mumkināt*) of his creation, whose existence is essentially contingent and dependent on Him for everything.

waqūf-i 'adadī — 'numerical awareness'; refers to the technique of breath control while being engaged in the practice of the *dhikr-i nafī o ithbāt*, for which a series of uneven numbers is strongly recommended.

waqūf-i qalbī — 'awareness of the heart'; the last of the eleven principles, can possibly indicate the increasing degrees of awareness maintained while being engaged in the practice of *dhikr*.

waqūf-i zabānī — 'awareness of the tongue'; a particular aspect of the technique of breath-control indicating the necessity to increase gradually one's awareness of the inner, spiritual states in connection with a partial restraint of the breath and its different phases.

waswasa — 'evil inspiration'; the term refers to any mental distraction arising out of the; in the religious perspective of Islam, this mental suggestion is said to be whispered by *shaiṭān* in order to distract the earnest seeker from focussing on the real goal, viz., Allāh.

wilāyat — 'sainthood'; the degree of universalisation attained to after transcending the narrow limitations of the individual existence; in the context of the Naqshbandī *ṭarīqa*, this degree is reached after completing the journey through the sphere of universal Possibility.

wilāyat-i kubrā — 'major sainthood'; the second degree of sainthood, corresponding to the completion of the 'journey towards Allāh' (*sair ilā Allāh*) that sanctions the beginning of the 'journey in Allāh' (*sair fī Allāh*).

wilāyat-i ṣughrā — 'minor sainthood'; the first degree of sainthood reached after the five *laṭā'if* located in the human breast are awakened and have re-ascended to their original realm in the 'world of order'.

wilāyat-i 'uliyā — 'supreme sainthood', reached according to the Mujaddidīs when the *sālik* has begun his descending journey from Allāh back towards the immanent realm of creation (*sair dar ashiyā'*), endowed with a high degree of awareness of the Divine mysteries that guide him in his mission of intervening for the correction of the world and its people.

yād dāsht — 'accomplished remembrance'; the eight of the eleven principles denotes the perfection of the state of *yād kard*.

yād kard — 'remembrance' the fifth of the eleven Naqshbandī principles, implying the necessity to increase the level of subtle awareness while being engaged in the practice of invoking silently the *dhikr*; in fact, it is the very *dhikr* that acts as a tool for imprinting the remembrance of Allāh on the subtle organ of the heart thus contributing to the mind's capacity to focus increasingly on the very aim of the discipline represented by the name invoked.

ẓāhir — 'the apparent'; one of the names of Allāh, denotes the exoteric aspect of His creation and as such complementary to the inner, esoteric aspect of His essence (*al-bāṭin*).

zill — 'shadow', intended by the Naqshbandīs as the reflection of a higher degree of reality on a lower degree of existence, similar to the concept of '*aks*.

Appendix I

Noble Genealogy (*shajra-i sharīf*) of the Mujaddidiyya Maẓhariyya Na'īmiyya Faḍliyya

1. Ḥaḍrat Shaikh Aḥmad Sirhindī (*d.* 28 Ṣafar 1034/30 Nov. 1624 Sirhind)
2. Ḥaḍrat Shaikh Ma'sūm Sirhindī (*d.* 9 Rabī'al-awwal 1079/7 Aug. 1668 Sirhind)
3. Ḥaḍrat Shaikh Sa'īf al-Dīn Sirhindī (*d.* 19 Jumāda al-awwal 1095/24 Apr. 1684 Sirhind)
4. Ḥaḍrat Shaikh Nūr Muḥammad Badāyūnī (*d.* 11 Dhī'l-Qa'da 1135/2 Aug. 1723 Delhi)
5. Ḥaḍrat Ḥabībullāh Mīrza Maẓhar Jān-i Jānān (*d.* 10 Muḥarram 1195/6 Jan. 1781 Delhi)
6. Ḥaḍrat Mawlānā Na'īmullāh Bahrāichī (*d.* 5 Ṣafar 1218/27 May 1803 Bahrāich)
7. Ḥaḍrat Shāh Murādullāh Thānesarī (*d.* 21 Dhī'l-Qa'da 1248/11 Apr. 1833 Lucknow)
8. Ḥaḍrat Sayyid Abūl Ḥasan Naṣīrābādī (*d.* 1 Sha'bān 1272/7 Apr. 1856 Nasīrābād)
9. Ḥaḍrat Mawlānā Khalīfat al-Raḥman Aḥmad 'Alī Khān (*d.* 9 Rabī'al-awwal 1307/3 Nov. 1889 Kāimgañj)
10. Ḥaḍrat Faḍl Aḥmad Khān Rā'īpurī (*d.* 22 Sh'bān 1325/1 Oct. 1907 Rāipur Khāss)
11. Mahātmā Śrī Rāmacandra Saksenā Mahārāj (*d.* 14 August 1931 Fatehgarh)

12. Mahātmā Caturbhuj Sahāy (*d.* 23 September 1957 Mathurā)

12. Mahātmā Dr. Kṛṣṇa Lāl Bhaṭnāgar (*d.* 18 May 1970 Sikandarābād)

12. Mahātmā Rāmacandra Shāhjahānpurī (*d.* 19 April 1983 Shāhjahānpur)

12. Mahātmā Śrī Raghubar Dayāl Saksenā (*d.* 7 June 1947 Kānpur)

13. Mahātmā Yaśa Pāljī Mahārāj (*b.* 5 December 1918 Delhi)

13. Mahātmā Śrī Bṛj Mohan Lāl Saksenā (*d.* 18 January 1955 Bombay)

14. Mahātmā Śrī Oṁkārnāth Saksenā (*b.* 1933 Lucknow)

Appendix II

A SCHEMATIC outline of the subtle centres' (*laṭā'if, cakra*) location in the human organisation according to the authorities of the Mujaddiddiyya Maẓhariyya:[1]

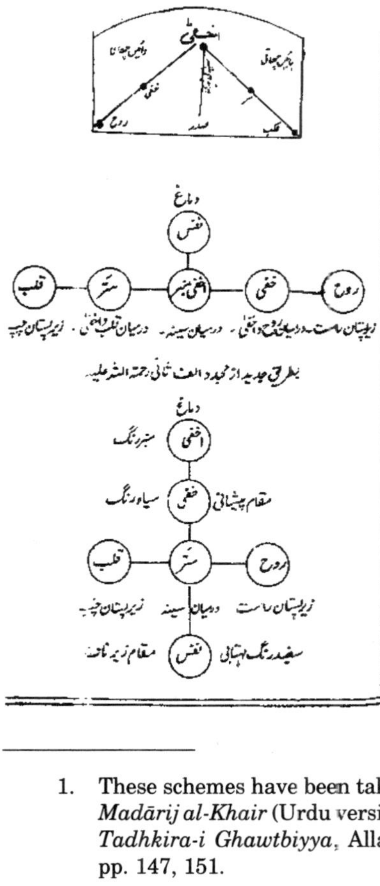

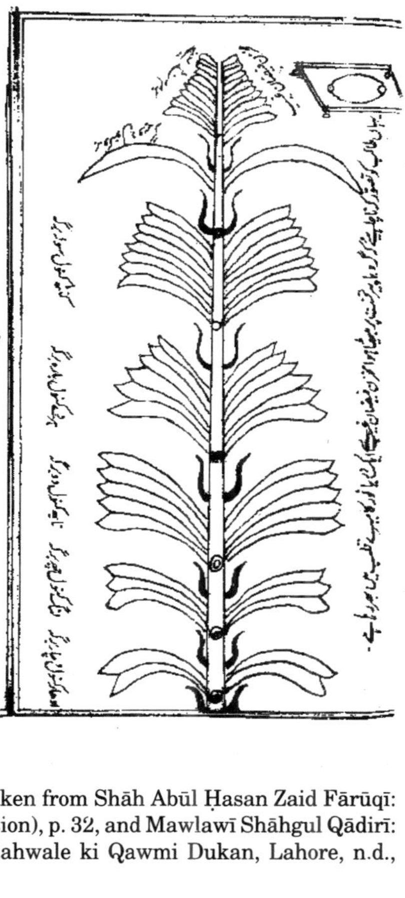

1. These schemes have been taken from Shāh Abūl Ḥasan Zaid Fārūqī: *Madārij al-Khair* (Urdu version), p. 32, and Mawlawī Shāhgul Qādirī: *Tadhkira-i Ghawtbiyya*, Allahwale ki Qawmi Dukan, Lahore, n.d., pp. 147, 151.

Bibliography

Hindi works

Basuk, B.B., *Lakṣya Vedhī Vaṁśāvalī ke santon kā saṁkṣipt jīvan paricaya* (an abridged biography of the saints of the Naqshbandī *silsila*), Saini Printing Press, Mathura, 1992 (fourth edn.).

Bhargav, Raj Kumari, *Santmat: prārambhik jñāna*, Saral Auto Press, Lucknow, n.d.

Chaturvedi, Parashuram, *Uttarī Bhārat kī Sant Paramparā*, Bharati Bhandar Leader Press, Allahabad, 1964.

Dvivedi, K.N., *Kabīr aur Kabīr-Panth*, Hindi Sahitya Sammelan, Allahabad, 1965.

Kaviraj, Gopinath, *Kavirāj-Pratibhā*: a collection of select articles of Mahāmahopādhyāya Gopīnāth Kavirāj on *Dharma, Darśana* and *Sādhanā*, ed. by Prof. Lakshmi Narayan Tiwari, University Silver Jubilee Series No. 6, Sampurnanand Sanskrit University, Varanasi, 1987.

Khare, Bal Kumar, *Mahān Sūfī Sant Ḥaḍrat Maulānā Shāh Faḍl Aḥmad Khān Rāypurī*, Sarvodaya Sahitya Prakashan, Varanasi, 1981.

———, *Sūfī Santmat kā Naqshbandiyya silsila*, 2 vols., Sarvodaya Sahitya Prakashan, Varanasi, 1984.

Krishnalal, Dr., *Jīvan-Caritra:* a biography of Paramsant Mahātmā Rāmacandrajī Mahārāj Fatehgarh Nivāsī, Ashram Publications, Sikandarabad (U.P.), 1973.

———, *Guru-Śiṣya Saṁvād*, Indian Printing Press, Roorkle (U.P.), n.d.

———, *Paramārthi Patra* (letter collection), Ramashram Satsang, Sikandarabad, n.d.

Krishnasvarupji, Dr., *Faqīron kī sāt manzilen*, ed. Dr. Krishnalalji, Acharya Ramashram Satsang, Sikandarabad, n.d.

———, *Sant Bānī Saṁgraha* (part 1), Pandit Hiralal Vaidhya Prakashak, Rawti (M.P.), Samvat 2013/1972.

Narayan, Shiv Pratap, *Yādon ke ujāle*, Sant Karyalaya, Kanpur, 1983.

Ram Chandra, *Satya kā udaya*, 4th edn., Prakashan Vibhag Sri Ram Chandra Mission, Shahjahanpur (U.P.), 1993.

———, *Ānand kī or*, 2nd edn., Prakashan Vibhag Sri Ram Chandra Mission, Shahjahanpur, 1981.

Ramchandra, Mahatma Sri, *Akṣar Satya*, (a Hindi translation from the original Urdu letters of Samarthguru Śrī Rāmcandrajī by Laxmi Shankar), Sri Ram Chandra Mission, Shahjahanpur, 1982.

———, *Kamāl-i Insānī*, Adhyatma Dhara Prakashan, Fatehgarh, 1973 (2nd edn.).

———, *Rāmāyana kī rūḥānī tashrīḥ*, Sadhan Press, Fatehgarh, 1963.

———, *Rām-Sandeśa*, Sri Akhilesh Kumar Sansthapak, Adhyatma Dhara Prakashan, Fatehgarh, 1974.

———, *Sādhanā Catuṣṭaya*, Ramashram Satsang, Sikandarabad, n.d.

———, *Santmat Darśana*, Naqsh-Mum Ramchandra Mission, Fatehgarh, 1986.

———, *Santmat Praveśikā*, Ramashram Satsang, Sikandarabad, n.d.

———, *Satsangiyon ke kartavya*, Vinay Kumar evam Samir Kumar, Sahaj Marg Printers, Shahjahanpur, 1995.

———, *Tattva-Prabodhinī,* Sri Ramchandra Publication League, Fatehgarh, 1971.

———, *Vedānta-Sāgara*, Akhilesh Kumar Prakashan, Fatehgarh, 1964.

Sahāy, Dr. Caturbhuj, *Sādhanā ke anubhav* (part 1-7), Sadhana Prakashan, Mathura (U.P.), n.d.

Saksenā, Bṛj Mohan Lāl, *Jīvan-Caritra*: *a biographical account of Sri Ramchandraji and Sri Raghubar Dayalji*, Sant Prakashan, Kanpur, 1993 (third edn.).

———, *Ānanda-Yoga*, Sant Prakashan, Kanpur, 1953-5.

Saksenā, Har Nārāyaṇ, *Yāden*, Ramashram Satsang Sansthan, Fatehgarh, 1993.

———, *Sakṣātkāra kā rahasya*, Saksena Brothers, Jaipur, 1994.

Saksenā, Raghubar Dayāljī, *Ātmā-Kathā*, Ram Raghubar Ashram, Kanpur, n.d.

———, *Pūyūś-Vānī*, ed. Sri Shiv Narayan Das Gandhi, (discourses of Śrī Cācājī Mahārāj), D.P.C. Varma Prakashan, Kanpur, n.d.

———, *Pār hone kā saral upāya*, Ram Raghubar Ashram, Kanpur, n.d.

———, *Śrī Raghubar Sandeśa* (letter collection of Pūjya Śrī Cācājī Mahārāj) ed. by B.K. Khare, Sriman Surendra Nath Saksena Publishers, Kanpur, 1990.

Sanyal, Usha, *Devotional Islam & Politics in British India: Ahmad Riza Khan Barelwi and his movement, 1870-1920*, Oxford University Press, 1996, Delhi.

Sharma, Prem Bahadur, *Bhogāv — atīt se vartamān*, Nisha Prakashan, Mainpuri (U.P.), 1989.

Singhania, Bal Krishna, *Parampūjya Satguru; Śrī Oṁkār Nāth Ṣāḥib ke pravacanon ke ādhār par*, Adabi Moti Prakashan, Kanpur, n.d.

Srivastava, Raj Bahadur, *Naqshband Sitāren*, Kidwai Nagar, Kanpur, n.d.

Tripathi, Hari Vamsha Lal, *Arghvānī*, Sri Hari Adhyatmik Sansthan, Lucknow, n.d.

———, *Ānand kī khoj*, Sri Hari Adhyatmik Sansthan, Lucknow, n.d.

———, *Pyārā Satguru*, Sri Hari Adhyatmik Sansthan, Lucknow, n.d.

———, *Jīvan-Caritra, a hagiographical account of Paramsant Mahatma Raghubar Dayalji Maharaj*, Lucknow, n.d.

Umar Muhammad, *Sūfī Sant Mīrzā Maẓhar Jān-i Jānān: a biography*, Bharat Prakashan Mandir, Aligarh, n.d.

Varma, Dr. Prakash Chandra, *Śrī Raghubar Caritāmṛita*, Avasthi Printing Press, Kanpur, n.d.

Yashpal, *Ādhyātmik Dhārā*, December 1969-July 1973, monthly review, Fatehgarh.

———, *Aṣṭavākra-Gītāmṛita,* part 1, Akhil Bhratiya Santmat, Delhi, 1987 (third edn.).

———, *Gīta-Sudhā*, Akhil Bharatiya Santmat, Delhi, 1995 (3rd edn.).

———, *Madhhab aur taḥqīqat*, Akhil Bharatiya Santmat, Delhi, 1989.

———, *Sant Patrikā*, Sant Prakashan, Kanpur, n.d.

———, *Śrī Kṛṣṇa Sandeśa*, ed. by Brijendra Kumar: the teachings of Paramsant Sri Krishna Lalji Maharaj part 3, Ramashram Satsang, Sikandarabad, n.d.

Urdu works

'Abd al-Rahman Jami, *Nafaḥāt al-Uns* (Urdu translation from the original Persian by Hazrat Shams Barelvi), Danish Publishing Company, New Delhi, 1994.

Abul Hasan Zaid Faruqi, Shah, *Hindustānī qadīm madhāhib*, in collaboration with Maulana Sayyid Akhlaq Husain, Shah Abul Khair Academy, Delhi, 1986.

———, *Ḥaḍrat Mujaddid aur unke nā-qadīn*, Shah Abul Khair Academy, Delhi, 1397/1977.

———, *Manāḥij al-Sair wa Madārij al-Khair*, (Urdu version translated from the original Persian by Maulana Muhammad Na'im Khan Khayali Bahrāichī under the abbreviated title *Madārij al-Khair*, Shah Abul Khair Academy, Delhi, 1404/1983), ed. Haji 'Abd al-Ghaffar Pasran Tajiran, Qandahar, 1377/1957.

———, *Maqāmāt-i Khair* (Urdu version), Shah Abul Khair Academy, Delhi, 1409/1989 (reprint).

Abu Sa'id Faruqi, Maulana Shah, *Hidāyat al-Ṭālibīn wa marqat al-sālikīn* (including the *Risāla-i ma'ārif wa 'ulūm-i Mujaddidiyya*), edited and translated into Urdu from the original Persian by Prof. Dr. Ghulam Mustafa Khan, Ala Kutubkhana, Nazimabad Karachi, 1377/1958.

Amim, Thana al-Haqq, *Mīr wa Saudā kā daur*, Silsila-i Matbu'at Adara-i Tahqiq wa Tasnif, Karachi, 1965.

Faruqi, Bashir, *Gulzār-i Murād, Tadhkira-i Ḥaḍrat Murād Allāh Thaneśarī,* Irada-i Farigh-i Urdu, Lucknow, 1988.

Fazl Ahmad Khan, Maulana Shaikh, *Ḍamīma-i ḥālāt-i māshaikh-i Naqshbandiyya Mujaddidiyya*, Matba Ahmadi Waqa'i, Aligarh, 1943.

Ghulam 'Ali Dihlawi, Shah, *Maqāmāt-i Maẓharī*: life, work and teachings of a prominent Sūfī and poet: Mīrzā Maẓhar Jān-i Jānān (*d.*1195/1780), compiled by Shah Ghulam 'Ali Dihlawi, translated and annotated with a comprehensive introduction by Muhammad Iqbal Mujaddidī, Urdu Science Board, Lahore, 1983.

Gul Hasan Qadiri, Maulawi Shah, *Tadhkira-i Ghawhiyya*, (biography of Ḥaḍrat Maulānā Ghauth Bī 'Alī Shāh Qalandar), Allāhwale kī qaumī dukān, Kashmiri Bazar, Lahore, n.d.

Hafiz Ghulam Habib, Maulana, *Majālis-i Ḥabīb; musamme beh Irshād al-murshid*, ed. Maulana Ahmad 'Ali Panjgori, Jām'at al-ī' Ulīm al-Islāmiyya, Educational Press, Karachi, 1404/1987.

Khaliq Anjum, *Mīrzā Jān-i Jānān ke khuṭūṭ*, an Urdu translation of Mīrzā Maẓhar's Persian letters and some other prose texts by Khaliq Anjum, 2nd edn, Maktuba-i Burhan, Delhi, 1989.

Khan, Muhammad Najm al-Ghani Rampuri, *Tā'rīkh-i Awadh*, (History of Oudh), The Indian Press, Allahabad, 1909-13.

Nasim Ahmad Faridi, Maulana, *Qāfila-i ahl-i dil*, the image of Shah Ghulam 'Ali Naqshbandi in the light of his *malfūẓāt* and *maktūbāt*, Furqan Book Depot, Lucknow, 1981.

Na'im Allah Bahrāichī, Maulana, *Ma'mūlāt-i Maẓhariyya*, part 1, Urdu translation by Mahmud 'Abd al-Sattar Bholepuri, ed. by Hafiz Muhammad Ajmal, Nishat Offset Press, Tanda (dist. Faizabad), 1413/1992.

Nu'mani, Muhammad 'Ali Manzur, *Tadhkira-i Imām-i Rabbānī*, Furqan Book Depot, Lucknow, 1977.

Quraishi,' Abd al-Razzaq, *Mīrzā Maẓhar Jānjānān aur unkā kalām*, Matba Ma'arif Dar al-Masnafin, Azamgarh, 1979 (2nd edn.).

Rauf Ahmad, Hazrat Shah, *Durr al-Ma'ārif* (*malfūẓāt* of Shah 'Abd Allah Ghulam 'Ali), trans. from the original Persian into Urdu by Muhammad Fazl al-Rahman, Inayata Foundation, Rawalpindi, 1413/1992.

Saksenā, Bṛj Mohan Lāl, *Āīna-i 'Ilm al-bāṭin*, Bulanjar Akhbar Tarjuman, Hardoi (U.P.), n.d.

Shaikh Ahmad Sirhindī, *Mabdā o Ma'ād*; Urdu translation from the original

Persian version by Hazrat Maulana Sayyid Zawwar Husain Shah Naqshbandī Mujaddidī, Irada-i Mujaddidiyya, Nizamabad/Karachi, 1398/1968.

Shaikh Badr al-Din Sirhindī, *Ḥaḍrāt al-Quds*, translated into Urdu from the original Persian version by Dr. Ghulam Mustafa Khan, Danish Publishing Company, New Delhi, 1991.

Works in European languages

Abu Raihan al-Biruni, *Alberuni's India*, English translation of al-Biruni's *Taḥqīq mā lil Hind* by Edward C. Sachau, 2 Vols. (bound in one), Munshiram Manoharlal, New Delhi, 1992. (orig. published by Kegan Paul, Trench, Trubner & Co. Ltd., London, 1910).

Affifi, A.E., *The Mystical Philosophy of Muhyid Din-Ibnul Arabi*, Cambridge University Press, Sh. Muhammad Ashraf, Lahore, 1964 (reprint).

Ansari, Abd ul-Haqq, *Sufism and Shari'ah; a study of Shaikh Ahmad Sirhindi's effort to reform Sufism,* The Islamic Foundation, Leicester, 1986.

Avalon, Arthur, *Shat-Chakra Nirupana and Pāduka Panchaka* (*The Serpent Power*), Madras, 1954.

Aziz, Ahmad, *Studies in Islamic Culture in the Indian environment*, Oxford University Press, Oxford, 1964.

———, *Modernism in India and Pakistan 1857-1964*, Oxford University Press, Oxford, 1967.

Babb, Lawrence A., *Redemptive encounters: Three Modern Styles in Hindu Tradition,* University of California Press, Berkeley/Los Angeles, 1984.

Baljon, J.M.S., *Religion and Thought of Shah Wali Allah Dihlawi (1703-62)*, E.J. Brill, Leiden, 1986.

Banerjea, A.K., Discourses on Hindu Spiritual Culture (3 vols.); Ram Ashrama Satsang Publication, Sikandarabad (U.P.) 1971 and 1980.

———, *The Philosophy of Gorakhnath,* (with *Gorakṣā-Vacana-Saṁgraha*), Motilal Banarsidass, New Delhi, 1988 (reprint).

Barnett, Richard B., *North India between Empires: Awadh, The Mughals and the British, 1720-1801*, Berkeley, 1980.

Barthwal, P.D., *Traditions of Indian Mysticism based upon Nirguna School of Hindi Poetry*, Heritage Publishers, New Delhi, 1978 (reprint, 1st edn. 1936)

Bhagavad Gītā, The (with the commentary of Śrī Śaṅkarācārya), Samata Books, Madras, 1977 (1st edn. 1897).

Bhatt, S.R., *Studies in Rāmānuja Vedānta*, Heritage Publishers, New Delhi, 1975.

Bhattacharya, N.N. (ed.), *Medieval Bhakti Movements in India*, Sri Chaitanya Quincentenary Volume, Munshiram Manoharlal Publishers, New Delhi, 1989.

Blochet, M.E., *Études sur l'esotérisme musulman*, Tradition Islamique-7, Édition Oriental, Paris, 1979.

Buehler, Arthur F., *Sufi Heirs of the Prophet: the Indian Naqshbandiyya and the Rise of the Mediating Sufi Shaykh*, University of South Carolina Press, 1997.

Chakravarti, V.R. Srisaila, *The Philosophy of Śrī Rāmānuja (Viśiṣṭādvaita)*, Bharati Vijaya Press, Madras, 1974.

Chand, Tara, *Influence of Islam on Indian Culture*, The Indian Press, Allahabad, 1976 (reprint).

Clothey, Fred W., *Images of Man: Religion and Historical Process in South Asia*, New Era Publications, Madras, 1982.

Cole, J.R.I., *Roots of North Indian Shi'ism in Iran and Iraq; religion and state in Awadh, 1722-1859,* University of California Press, Berkeley/Los Angeles, 1987.

Crooke, William, *The Tribes and Castes of the North-Western Provinces and Oudh,* 4 vols., Office of the Superintendent of Government Printing, Calcutta, 1896.

Dara Shukoh, *Majma' al-Baḥrain or The Mingling of the Two Oceans*, edited in the original Persian with English translation, notes and variants by M. Mahfuz ul-Haqq (M.A.), Biblioteca Indica No. 246, Asiatic Society of Bengal, Calcutta, 1929.

Daniélou, Alain, *Yoga: The Method of Re-Integration*, Christopher Johnson, London, 1949.

Eliade, Mircea, *Techniques du Yoga*, La Montagne Sainte-Geneviève, Gallimard, Paris, 1948.

Elst, Koenraad, Ram Janmbhumi vs. Babri Masjid: a case study in Hindu-Muslim conflict, *Voice of India*, Delhi, 1980.

Ernst, C.W., *Eternal Garden: Mysticism, History and Politics at a South Asian Sufi Centre*, State University of New York Press, Albany, 1992.

Farquhar, J.N., *Modern Religious Movements in India*, The MacMillan Company, New York, 1915.

Faruqi, Burhanuddin Ahmad, *The Mujaddid's Conception of Tauhid*, Idara Adabiyat-i Delhi, Delhi, 1977 (reprint).

Filippi, G.G., *Mṛtyu: The Concept of Death in Indian traditions*, Reconstructing Indian History and Culture Series No.11, D.K. Printworlds (P) Ltd., New Delhi, 1996.

———, *Post-mortem et libèration d'après Śankarācārya*, Cahièrs de l'Unicorne, Archè, Milano, 1982.

French, Hal W. and Sharma, Arvind, *Religious Ferment in Modern India*, B.R. Chawla, Heritage Publishers, New Delhi, 1981.

Friedmann, Y., *Shaikh Aḥmad Sirhindī an Outline of his Thought and a Study of his Image in the Eyes of Posterity*, McGill University (McGill Queen's

University Press), Canberra, 1971.

Fusfeld, W.E., 'The Shaping of Sufi Leadership in Delhi: the Naqshbandiya Mujaddidiya, 1750-1920', PhD Dissertation, University of Pennsylvania, 1981.

V. Glasenapp, H., *Religiöse Reformbewegungen im heutigen Indien, aus*: Morgenland: Darstellungen aus Geschichte und Kultur des Ostens, Heft 17, Verlag der J.C Hinrichschen Buchhandlung, Leipzig, 1928.

Gold, Daniel, *The Lord as Guru: Hindi Sants in North Indian Tradition*, Oxford University Press, New York, 1987.

Goldziher, Ignaz, *A Short History of Classical Arabical Literature*, (transl. from German by Desomogyi), Georg Olms Verlagsbuchhandlung, Hildesheim, 1966.

Gommans, Jos J.L., *The Rise of the Indo-Afghan Empire*, c. 1710-1780, Brill, Leiden, 1995.

Guénon, Réné, *Introduction to the Study of the Hindu Doctrines* (tr.by Marco Pallis), Munshiram Manoharlal, New Delhi, 1993 (reprint, 1st English edn. 1945).

———, *Man and his Becoming according to the Vedanta*, (tr. from the original French by R.C. Nicholson), Luzac & Co., London, 1945.

Gupta, M.G., *Modern Indian Mysticism: a commentary on Western response to Radhasoami Faith*, MG Publishers, Agra, 1994.

Haig, Lt. Col. Sir Wolseley, *Comparative Tables of Islamic and Christian Dates*, Kitab Bhawan, Delhi, 1981.

Harsh, Narain, *The Ayodhya Temple-Mosque Dispute: focus on Islamic sources*, Penman Publishers, Delhi, 1993.

Hasrat, Vikramjit, *Dara Shukoh: Life and works*, Munshiram Manoharlal, New Delhi, 1982.

Hedayetullah, Muhammad, *Kabir: The Apostle of Hindu-Muslim Unity*, Motilal Banarsidass, New Delhi, 1977.

Horten, Dr. M., *Indische Strömungen in der islamischen Mystik II*, in 'Materialien zur Kunde des Buddhismus', Heidelberg, 1928.

Iqbal, Muhammad, *The Reconstruction of Religious Thought in Islam*, [orig. edn. 1934; first published as *Six Lectures on the Reconstruction, 1930*].

Irvine, William, *The Later Mughals*, ed. Jadunath Sarkar, New Delhi, 1972.

Jalbani, G.N., *Teachings of Shah Walyullah*, Sh. Muhammad Ashraf, Lahore, 1967.

Johnson, J., *The Path of the Masters: The science of Surat Shabda Yoga*, Sawan Service League, Beas (Punjab), 1939.

Juergensmeyer, M., *Radhasoami Reality: The Logic of a Modern Faith*, Princeton University Press, Princeton, 1991.

Keay, F.E., *Kabir and his Followers*, Mittal Publications, New Delhi, 1995 (1st edn. 1931).

Kopf, David, *The Brahmo Samaj and the Shaping of the Modern Indian Mind*, Princeton University Press, Princeton, 1979.

Lawrence, Bruce B., *Shahrastani on the Indian Religions*, Religion and Society 4, Mouton, 1976.

Leonard, Karen I., *Social History of an Indian Caste: the Kayasths of Hyderabad*, Sangam Books, Madras, 1977.

Lewisohn, L. (ed.), *The Legacy of Mediaeval Persian Sufism*, Khaniqahi Nimatullahi Publications, London, 1992.

Liebeskind, Claudia, 'Sufism, Sufi Leadership and 'Modernization' in South Asia since *c*. 1800', Ph.D. Dissertation, Royal Holloway, University of London, 1995.

Lorenzen, David N. (ed.), *Bhakti Religion in North India: Communal identity and political action* ; in SUNY Series in Religious Studies, State University of New York Press, Albany, 1995.

Maclean, D.M., *Religion and Society in Arab Sind*, E.J. Brill, Leiden, 1989.

Mahipati, *Bhaktavijaya*, translated by E. Abott and N. Godbole as *Stories of Indian Saints*, Delhi, Motilal Banarsidass,1988.

Majumdar, R.C., *The History and Culture of the Indian People*, vol. 6: *The Delhi Sultanate*, 4th edn., Bharatiya Vidya Bhavan, Bombay, 1990.

Mathur, Agam Prasad, *Radhasoami Faith: A historical study*, Vikas Publishing House, Delhi, 1974.

McLeod, W.H., *Guru Nānak and the Sikh Religion*, Oxford University Press, New Delhi, 1968.

Meier, F., *Zwei Abhandlungen über die Naqšbandiyya*, Beiruter Texte und Studien, Band 58, Istanbul, 1994 (in Kommission bei Franz Steiner Verlag, Stuttgart/Wiesbaden).

Metcalf, Barbara, *Islamic Revival in British India: Deoband 1860-1900*, Princeton University Press, Princeton, 1982.

Monier-Williams, Sir, *A Sanskrit-English Dictionary (etymologically and philologically arranged)*, reprint, Marwah Publications, New Delhi, 1986.

Mujeeb, Muhammad, *Indian Muslims*, George & Unwin Ltd., London, 1967.

Nizami, K.A., *Akbar and Religion*, IAD Oriental Series No. 33, Idara-i Adabiyat-i Delhi, Delhi, 1989.

———, *Some Aspects of Religion and Politics in India during the thirteenth century*, Asia Publishing House, New Delhi, 1961.

———, *The Life and Times of Farid ud-Din Ganj-i Shakar*, Idara-i Adabiyat-i Delhi, Delhi, 1973 (1st reprint).

Platts, J.T., *A Dictionary of Urdu, Classical Hindi and English*, 2nd Indian edn., Munshiram Manoharlal, New Delhi, 1988.

Qanungo, K.R., *Dara Shukoh*, S.C. Sarkar & Sons Ltd., Calcutta, 1952 (2nd edn.).

Quraishi, Ishtiaq Husain, *The Muslim Community of the Indo-Pakistan Subcontinent (610-1947)*, Renaissance Publishing House, Delhi, 1985, (reprint).

al-Qur'ān al-Karīm, *The Holy Qur'ān*: English translation of the meanings and Commentary, al-Madinah al-Munawarah, 1413 A.H.

Ram Chandra, *Sahaj Marg*, Sri Ramchandra Mission Publication Department, Shahjahanpur (U.P.), 1982 (3d edn.).

———, *The Autobiography of Ram Chandra*, vol. I (1899-1932), Sri Ramachandra Publication Department, 1993 (3rd edn.).

Rizvi, S.A.A., *A History of Sufism in India*, 2 vols., Munshiram Manoharlal Publishers, New Delhi, 1983 (reprinted 1992).

———, *Muslim Revivalist Movements in Northern India in the Sixteenth and Seventeenth Centuries*, Munshiram Manoharlal Publishers, New Delhi, 1995 (reprint; 1st edn. 1965).

———, *Shāh 'Abd ul-'Azīz: Puritanism, Sectarian Polemics and Jihad*, Ma'rifat Publishing House, Canberra, 1982.

———, *Shāh Walī Allāh and his Times: A study of eighteenth-century Islam, Politics and Society*, Ma'rifat Publishing House, Canberra, 1980.

Roy, Asim, *The Islamic Syncretistic Tradition in Bengal*, Princeton University Press, Princeton, 1983.

Roy Chaudhari, M.L., *The Din-I-Ilahi or The Religion of Akbar*, Oriental Reprint, Munshiram Manoharlal, New Delhi, 1941 (3rd edn. 1985).

Russell, R. and Khurshidu'l-Islam, *Three Mughal poets: Mir, Sauda, Mir Hasan*, George Allen & Unwin Ltd., London, 1968.

Śaṅkara, *Muṇḍakopaniṣadbhāṣya*, commentaire sur la Muṇḍaka-Upaniṣad (introduction, traduction et notes par Paul Martin-Dubost), Michel Allard-Editions Orientales, Paris, 1978.

Scott, David, *Kabir's Mythology*, Bharatiya Vidya Prakashan, Delhi, 1985.

Sen, Kshiti Mohan, *Medieval Mysticism of India*, Luzac & Co., London, 1931.

Shackle, C. and Snell, R., *Hindi and Urdu since 1800: A common reader*, London, 1990.

Sharma, S.R., *The Religious Policy of the Mughal Emperors*, Asia Publishing House, London, 1962 (1st edn. 1940)

Shayegan, Daryush, *Hindouisme et Soufisme: les rélations de l'Hindouisme et du Soufisme d'après le Majma al bahrain de Dara Shukoh*, Éditions de la Différence, Paris, 1979.

Schimmel, Annemarie, *Mystical Dimensions of Islam*, University of North Carolina Press, Chapel Hill, 1975.

———, *Islam on the Indian Subcontinent*, E.J. Brill, Leiden/Köln, 1980.

Shomer, K. and McLeod, W.H., *The Sants: A study in a devotional tradition of India*, Berkeley Religious Studies Series, Motilal Banarsidass, Delhi, 1987.

Srivastava, K.L., *The position of Hindus under the Delhi Sultanate (1206-1526)*, Munshiram Manoharlal, New Delhi, 1980.

ter Haar, J.G.J., *Follower and Heir of the Prophet: Shaikh Ahmad Sirhindi (1564-1624) as Mystic*, Het Oosters Instituut, Leiden, 1992.

Thursby, G.R., *Hindu-Muslim Relations in British India*, E.J. Brill, Leiden, 1975.

Trimingham, J.S., *Sufi Orders in Islam*, Oxford University Press, Oxford, 1971.

Troll, Ch.W., *Muslim Shrines in India: their character, history and significance*, Oxford University Press, New Delhi, 1989.

Tulpule, S.G., *The Divine Name in the Indian Tradition (a comparative study)*, Indus Publishing Company, New Delhi, 1991.

Umar, Muhammad, *Islam in Northern India during the eighteenth century*, Munshiram Manoharlal, New Delhi, 1993.

Valiuddin, Mir, *Contemplative Disciplines in Sufism*, East-West Publications. London-The Hague, 1980.

Varma, R.K., *Kabir: Biography and Philosophy*, Prints India, New Delhi, 1977.

Vaudeville, Ch., *Bhakti traditions from the regions of India*, ed. Diana L. Eck and Françoise Mallison, 1991.

———, *Kabir*, 2 vols., Oxford University Press, Oxford, 1974.

———, *A weaver named Kabir: selected verses with a detailed biographical and historical introduction*, Oxford University Press, New Delhi, 1993.

Waliullah of Delhi, Shah, *The Sacred Knowledge of the Higher Functions of the Mind (Altaf al-Quds)*, tr. Prof. G.N. Jalbani, The Octagon Press, London, 1982.

Zaid Faruqi, Shah Abul Hasan, *Hazrat Mujaddid and his critics*, (translated into English by Mir Zahid Ali Kamil), Progressive Books, Lahore, 1982.

Articles

Algar, Hamid, 'The Naqshbandi Order: a preliminary survey of its history and significance', in *Studia Islamica 44* (1976), pp. 123-52.

———, 'Some notes on the Naqshbandi Tariqat in Bosnia', in *Die Welt des Islam 13* (1971), pp. 168-203.

Aziz, Ahmad, 'Religious and Political Ideas of Shaikh Ahmad Sirhindi', in *Rivista degli Studi Orientali XXXVI* (1961), pp. 259-70.

Bausani, Alessandro, 'Note su Shah Waliullah di Delhi', in *Annali dell'Istituto Orientale di Napoli* (1960), pp. 93-147.

Chand, Tara, 'Dara Shikoh and the Upanisads', in *Islamic Culture 17* (1943), pp. 397-413.

Dani, Prof.A.H., 'Al-Biruni's India — a re evaluation', in *Al-Biruni Commemorative Volume,* Hamdard Academy, Karachi, 1979, pp. 182-9.

Digby, Simon,' 'Abd al-Quddus Gangohi (AD 1456-1537): The Personality And Attitudes of a Medieval Indian Sufi', *Medieval India — A miscellany,* vol. III, Aligarh, 1975, pp. 1-66.

———, 'Anecdotes of a provincial Sufi of the Delhi Sultanate, Khwaja Gurg of Kara', in *The British Institute of Persian Studies* (reprint), 1994, pp. 237-67.

Elboudrari, H., 'Entre le symbolisme et l'histoire: Khadir im-mémorial', in *Studia Islamica 76* (1992), pp. 25-39.

Filippi, G.G., 'The polar function of the Tasawwuf', in *Contemporary Relevance of Sufism*, Indian Council for Cultural Relations, ed. Syeda Saiyidain Hameed, 1993, pp. 117-26.

———, 'Gli attributi divini secondo la bhakti hindu e l'Islam', in *Verifiche*, Trento, 1974, pp.135-45.

———, 'Les composants culturels dans le Granthāvalī de Kabīr', in *Indologica Taurinensia* VI (1978), pp. 137-41.

Friedmann, Y., 'Medieval Muslim views on Indian religions', in *JOAS 95* (1975), pp. 214-21.

———, 'The Naqshbandis and Aurangzeb: a reconsideration', in *Varia Turcica: Naqshbandis*, Istanbul-Paris, 1990, pp. 209-20.

———, 'The temple of Multan. A note on early Muslim attitudes to idolatry', in *Israel Oriental Series 2* (1971), pp. 176-82.

Gaborieau, Marc, 'Les protestations d'un soufi indien contemporain', in *Varia Turcica: Naqshbandis*, Istanbul-Paris, 1990, pp. 237-67.

Habib, Madeleine, 'Some notes on the Naqshbandi order', in *Muslim World 59* (1969), pp. 40-9.

Hasrat, Bikramjit, 'Three little-known works of Dara Shukoh', in *Islamic Culture 25* (1951), pp. 52-72.

Hermansen, Marcia K., 'Shah Wali Allah of Delhi's arrangement of the subtle spiritual centres (*lata'if*)', in *Studies in Islam*, July 1982, pp. 137-50.

———, 'Shāh Walī Allāh's Theory of the Subtle Centres (latā'if): A Sufi Model of Personhood and Self-Transformation', *Journal of Near Eastern Studies 47/1* (1988), pp. 1-25.

Husaini, A.S., 'Uways al-Qarani and the Uwaysi Sufis', in *Muslim World 57* (1967), pp. 103-14.

Irfan, Omar, 'Khidr in the Islamic tradition', in *Muslim World 83*(1993), pp. 279-91.

Khan, Maulawi 'Abdu'l Wali, 'Hinduism according to Muslim Sufis', in *Journal of the Royal Asiatic Society 19* (1923), pp. 237-52.

Khan, M.I., 'The attitude of the Delhi Sultans towards non-Muslims: some observations', in *Islamic Culture 69* (1995), pp. 41-56.

Khan, M.S., 'Al-Biruni on Indian Metaphysics', in *Islamic Culture 55* (1981), pp. 161-8.

Lawrence, B.B., 'Shahrastani on Indian idol-worship', in *Studia Islamica 38* (1973), pp. 61-73.

Mishra, L.P. , 'Di certi termini ricorrenti nella letteratura mistica dell'Hindi medioevale', in *Annali di Ca' Foscari X, 3* (1971), pp. 39-49.

Molé, Marijan, 'Autour de Daré Mansour: l'apprentissage mystique de Baha al-Din Naqshband', in *Revue des Études Islamiques 27* (1959), pp. 35-66.

Mushirul Haq, 'Muslim understanding of Hindu religion', in *Islam and the Modern Age 4* (1973), pp. 71-7.

Nadvi, S., 'Religious relations between Arabia and India', in *Islamic Culture 8* (1934), pp. 120-39 (part I) and pp. 200-11 (part II).

Nasr, Seyed Hossein, 'Islam and the encounter of religions', in *Islamic Quarterly X* (1966), pp. 47-68.

———, 'The Sufi Master as Exemplified in Persian Sufi Literature', in *Studies in Comparative Religion* (1973), pp. 140-9.

Nizami, K.A., 'Naqshbandi influence on Mughal rulers and politics', in *Islamic Culture 38* (1965), pp. 41-53.

Qamber, Akhtar, 'The mirror symbol in the teachings and writings of some Sufi masters', in *Islamic Culture 62* (1988), pp. 57-73.

Rehatsek, E., 'Early Moslem Accounts of the Hindu Religion', in *Journal of the Bombay Branch of the Royal Asiatic Society*, 1878, pp. 20-9.

Schimmel, Annemarie, 'The Sufi ideas of Shaikh Ahmad Sirhindi', in *Die Welt des Islam 14* (1973), pp. 199-203.

Sharma, Arvind, 'Al-Biruni on the Hindu notion of Samsara', in *Islamic Culture 51* (1977), pp. 165-69.

Thukral, Uma, 'The Avatar Doctrine in the Kabir Panth', in *The Sants: A study in a devotional tradition of India* (ed. Shomer, K. and McLeod, W.H.), pp. 221-30.

Umar, Muhammad, 'Mirza Mazhar Jan-i Janan: a religious reformer of the eighteenth century', in *Studies in Islam 6* (1969), pp. 118-54.

Valiuddin, Mir, 'Reconciliation between Ibn 'Arabi's wahdat ul-wujud and the Mujaddid's wahdat ul-shuhud', in *Islamic Culture 25* (1951), pp. 43-51.

Ventura, Alberto, 'Natura e funzione dei pensieri secondo l'esoterismo islamico', in *Annali dell'Istituto Orientale di Napoli 46* (1986), pp. 391-402.

Place Index

Index of Names of Individuals

Technical Terminology Index (Islamic)

Technical Terminology Index (Hindu)